THE ENCYCLOPEDIA OF LEADERSHIP

A PRACTICAL GUIDE TO POPULAR LEADERSHIP THEORIES AND TECHNIQUES

Murray Hiebert
Bruce Klatt

McGraw-Hill

New York   San Francisco   Washington, D.C.   Auckland   Bogotá
Caracas   Lisbon   London   Madrid   Mexico City   Milan
Montreal   New Delhi   San Juan   Singapore
Sydney   Tokyo   Toronto

McGraw-Hill

A Division of The McGraw·Hill Companies

How to Contact the Publisher

To order multiple copies of this book at a discount, please contact the McGraw-Hill Special Sales Department at 800-842-3075, or 212-904-5427 (2 Penn Plaza, New York, NY 10121-2298).

To ask a question about the book, contact the author, or report a mistake in the text, please write to Richard Narramore, Senior Editor, at richard_narramore@mcgraw-hill.com.

 This book is printed on recycled, acid-free paper containing a minimum of 50% recycled, de-inked fiber.

To our parents:
Edie and Hank Klatt
Helen and the late Paul Hiebert

CONTENTS IN BRIEF

How to Use and Benefit from this Book   xxiii
Leadership Tool Finder: Here's My Problem,
What Tool Do I Need?   xxvi
Tool Finder: A Map of Leadership Gurus to Tools   xxviii
Acknowledgments   xxxi

SECTION 1: FOUNDATIONAL CONCEPTS

➠ 1.1   Leadership in the Twenty-First Century   2
➠ 1.2   Contrasting Management and Leadership   5
➠ 1.3   How Effective Leaders Act: An Overview   8
➠ 1.4   Principles to Guide Your Use of Leadership Techniques   11
➠ 1.5   The Basic Habits and Practices of Successful Leaders   15
➠ 1.6   Leadership: The Boards of Play   18
➠ 1.7   The Leadership Results Equation   21
➠ 1.8   Recursive Leadership: The Logic of Leadership   25
➠ 1.9   Paradigms: Understanding the Thinking behind Your Thinking   29
➠ 1.10 The GAS Model: Designing Practical Organizational Processes   33
➠ 1.11 Integrity: Gut-Level Ethics   36

SECTION 2: TOOLS FOR BIG-PICTURE THINKING

➠ 2.1   Introduction to Systems Thinking for Leaders   40
➠ 2.2   The 7S Model: Aligning for Success   45
➠ 2.3   Directional Statements: Three Levels of Clarity   48
➠ 2.4   Visioning and Vision Statements   51

➡ 2.5   Values and Leadership   55
➡ 2.6   Clarifying Purpose: Harnessing People Power in Organizations   59
➡ 2.7   Writing Clear Goal Statements   62
➡ 2.8   Measuring Success: The Balanced Scorecard   65

SECTION 3: TOOLS FOR STRATEGIC THINKING

➡ 3.1   The Leader As Strategist   69
➡ 3.2   The Sigmoid Curve: Anticipating and Preparing for Change
        Despite Current Success   73
➡ 3.3   SWOT: Strengths, Weaknesses, Opportunities, and Threats   76
➡ 3.4   The Fundamentals of Business-Unit Strategy   79
➡ 3.5   Strategic Resourcing: Defining High-Value Work
        for Service Groups   82
➡ 3.6   Strategic Relationships: Analyzing Your Client Base   86
➡ 3.7   RAIR Logic: Aligning Customers, Strategy, Culture,
        and Leadership   89
➡ 3.8   Partnering for Success: Joint Ventures and Strategic Alliances   92
➡ 3.9   Marketing a Professional Service Group   96

SECTION 4: TOOLS FOR DESIGNING PRODUCTIVE PROCESSES AND ORGANIZATIONS

➡ 4.1   Designing Productive Organizations   101
➡ 4.2   Hierarchy: Leadership Levels in an Organization   105
➡ 4.3   Business Process Reengineering   108
➡ 4.4   Employee Involvement: A Range of Possibilities   112
➡ 4.5   Organizational Culture: Sail or Anchor?   117
➡ 4.6   Open-Book Leadership: Developing Entrepreneurial Thinking   121
➡ 4.7   Job Satisfaction: Involving Workgroups in Designing Jobs   126
➡ 4.8   Revitalizing the Board of Directors in a Nonprofit
        Organization   129
➡ 4.9   Using Professional Expertise: A Modern Leadership Skill   132
➡ 4.10 Surveying Employees: Leading the Survey Process   135

SECTION 5: TOOLS FOR LEADING CHANGE

➡ 5.1   Leading Change: A Change Equation   140
➡ 5.2   Leading Major Change in Your Organization   142
➡ 5.3   Assessing Readiness for Change   145
➡ 5.4   Leading Change: Small Wins or Breakthroughs?   147

➡ 5.5   Change Window: A Balanced Approach to Winning
         Support for Change   150
➡ 5.6   Aligning Systems: Building Systems Compatibility into
         Change Plans   153
➡ 5.7   Stakeholder Groups: Understanding and Mapping
         Stakeholder Systems   156
➡ 5.8   Human Transitions: Helping People Work through
         Major Change   160
➡ 5.9   Surfacing and Dealing with Resistance   163
➡ 5.10   Appreciative Inquiry: Building Change on Success   166

SECTION 6: TOOLS FOR CRITICAL THINKING AND INNOVATION

➡ 6.1   The BS Detector Kit: Recognizing Errors of Logic   170
➡ 6.2   Assumption Analysis: Testing Decisions by Examining
         Their Underlying Biases   173
➡ 6.3   Sorting Out Complex Situations   176
➡ 6.4   Dealing Verbally with Complexity   179
➡ 6.5   Force-Field Analysis: Organizing and Understanding
         Complexity   183
➡ 6.6   Optimizing Your Thinking—A Hat 6-Pack   186
➡ 6.7   Creativity and Innovation: The Leader's Role   189
➡ 6.8   Mind Mapping: A Breakthrough Tool   193
➡ 6.9   Brainstorming: Generating Ideas Quickly   196

SECTION 7: TOOLS FOR PROBLEM SOLVING, DECISION MAKING, AND QUALITY

➡ 7.1   Reframing: Working the *Real* Problem   200
➡ 7.2   A General Problem-Solving Model for Leaders   204
➡ 7.3   Problem Solving: A Systematic Approach to Finding Cause 207
➡ 7.4   Polarities: Dealing with Intractable Problems   212
➡ 7.5   Decision Making: Making Decisions Logical and Defensible 215
➡ 7.6   Potential Problem Analysis: Dealing with Risk to a Plan 219
➡ 7.7   Total Quality Leadership Overview   223
➡ 7.8   Affinity Diagrams: Organizing Mountains of Data   227

SECTION 8: TOOLS FOR COMMUNICATION

➡ 8.1   Powerful Leadership Conversations   232
➡ 8.2   Direct Leader-to-Employee Communication Still Works Best 236
➡ 8.3   The Leader's Role in Organizational Communication   239

➠ 8.4   Levels of Communicating: Debate, Dialogue, and Discussion   242

➠ 8.5   Metacommunicating: Talking about Talking   245

➠ 8.6   Communication 101: Dealing Effectively with Feelings at Work   248

➠ 8.7   Actively Listening for Content, Feeling, and Meaning   251

➠ 8.8   Listening Techniques: Tactics to Improve Your Listening   254

➠ 8.9   Cross-Cultural Communication   257

➠ 8.10 Media Relations for Leaders   260

Section 9: Tools for Leading and Influencing Others

➠ 9.1   Leadership Versatility: Matching Your Role to the Situation   264

➠ 9.2   Matching Your Leadership Style to the Situation   267

➠ 9.3   Leadership Strategies for Delegating Work   271

➠ 9.4   Increasing Your Impact: Understanding Control, Influence, and Interest   274

➠ 9.5   Principled Negotiation: Creating Long-Term, Win–Win Agreements   277

➠ 9.6   Making Great Presentations   281

➠ 9.7   Selling Wheel: Getting Your Recommendations Accepted   284

➠ 9.8   Selling Large Projects: A Much-Valued Leadership Skill   287

➠ 9.9   Power: A Fundamental Element of Leadership Success   291

➠ 9.10 Support Networks: The Secret of All Successful Leaders   294

Section 10: Tools for Leading Teams and Groups

➠ 10.1   High-Performing Teams: Organizing to Achieve Results   298

➠ 10.2   Improving Team IQ   301

➠ 10.3   Team Competencies: Thinking, Relating, and Acting   305

➠ 10.4   Inclusion, Control, and Affection: Developing Commitment and Teamwork   308

➠ 10.5   Dealing with Disturbances in Workgroups and Teams   311

➠ 10.6   Assessing Your Group Leadership Skills   314

➠ 10.7   Getting Participation   317

➠ 10.8   Ground Rules: Helping Groups to Achieve Business Results   320

➠ 10.9   Making Information Visible   323

➠ 10.10 Closure: Helping Groups Make Decisions and Plans Efficiently   326

➠ 10.11 Priority Setting in a Workgroup or Team   329

➠ 10.12 RASCI: A Planning Tool for Workgroups and Teams   332

Section 11: Tools for Leading Meetings

➡ 11.1 Process Cycle: Planning Effective Meetings and Events   336

➡ 11.2 Meetings: Purpose and Function in Workgroups
        and Teams   339

➡ 11.3 Meeting Checklist: From Planning to Follow-Up   342

➡ 11.4 Meeting Roles   347

➡ 11.5 The Chairperson's Role: Duties and Accountabilities   350

➡ 11.6 The Meeting Agenda: Why, What, and How   353

➡ 11.7 The Chairperson's Opening Remarks   356

➡ 11.8 The Meeting Minutes: Why, What, and How   359

Section 12: Tools for Leading Relationships

➡ 12.1 The Relationship Bank: Maintaining Working
        Relationships   363

➡ 12.2 Building Trust into Working Relationships   366

➡ 12.3 Triangulation: The Surest Way to Damage
        a Relationship   369

➡ 12.4 Giving and Receiving Feedback: The Dos and Don'ts   372

➡ 12.5 Preparing Yourself to Give Negative Feedback   375

➡ 12.6 The 5Cs: Escalating Confrontation Judiciously   378

➡ 12.7 Conflict: Five Levels for Dealing with Conflict   381

➡ 12.8 Dealing with Difficult People: A Timeless Leadership
        Challenge   384

➡ 12.9 The Essentials of Customer Service   387

Section 13: Tools for Leading Performance

➡ 13.1 Coaching and Supporting the Success of Others   391

➡ 13.2 Coaching High-Performers: An Overlooked Element of Success 395

➡ 13.3 Accountability Agreements: Defining Accountability within
        Organizations   399

➡ 13.4 Management by Objectives   402

➡ 13.5 Urgency and Importance: The Essential Elements of
        Managing Your Time   406

➡ 13.6 Attribution Theory: Assessing Performance
        and Behavior   409

➡ 13.7 Documenting Employee Performance and Behavior   412

➡ 13.8 Job Competencies: Measuring and Predicting
        Performance   415

⮕ 13.9   Human Capital: Truly the Most Valuable Asset   418

⮕ 13.10 The Four Stages® Model: Understanding Career Strategies   421

⮕ 13.11 Professional Leadership: Delivering Expertise   424

SECTION 14: TOOLS FOR LEARNING

⮕ 14.1   Scarcity and Abundance: The Importance of Attitude   428

⮕ 14.2   Single-Loop and Double-Loop Learning: When to Stay the Course and When to Reevaluate   431

⮕ 14.3   Needs Analysis: Measuring Return on Training Investments   434

⮕ 14.4   Adult Learning: Principles for Helping Adults Learn   438

⮕ 14.5   Teaching a Job: An Essential Skill for Frontline Leaders   441

⮕ 14.6   Leaders and Learning Styles   444

⮕ 14.7   Personal Preferences: Capitalizing on Individual Differences   447

SECTION 15: TOOLS FOR TAKING CARE OF YOURSELF

⮕ 15.1   Balance: Take Care of Yourself!   451

⮕ 15.2   LEQ: The Leadership Emotional Quotient   455

⮕ 15.3   The JoHari Window: What You Don't Know Can Hurt You   459

⮕ 15.4   Understanding Our Assumptions and Biases   462

⮕ 15.5   Habits: The Good and Bad News That Leaders Need to Know   467

⮕ 15.6   Managing Your Defensive Reactions   470

⮕ 15.7   Managing the Stress Associated with Being a Leader   472

Index   476

ANNOTATED CONTENTS

SECTION 1—FOUNDATIONAL CONCEPTS

1.1 Leadership in the twenty-first century   2
➡Assesses where you are now as a leader, where you would like to be, and actions needed to get you there.

1.2 Contrasting management and leadership   5
➡Helps leaders with an important distinction between management and leadership.

1.3 How effective leaders act: An overview   8
➡Moves leaders above their day-to-day leadership activities to take a bird's-eye view of the fundamentals and their leadership styles, strengths, and development needs.

1.4 Principles to guide your use of leadership techniques   11
➡Summarizes important principles for leaders and how to use them as a springboard for developing beliefs, thinking, and action as a powerful leader.

1.5 The basic habits and practices of successful leaders   15
➡Helps leaders take specific leadership actions; inspired by Stephen Covey's *Seven Habits.*

1.6 Leadership: The boards of play   18
➡Shows how leaders who can "play" at higher "board levels" necessarily have more power and influence than those at the lower levels.

1.7 The leadership results equation   21
➡Helps leaders understand leadership attributes and how to make optimum use of these attributes to achieve four areas of results.

1.8 Recursive leadership: The logic of leadership   25
➡Extends, in a novel way, a mathematical and computing science term, *recursion,* to explore some modeling aspects of effective leadership.

1.9 Paradigms: Understanding the thinking behind your thinking   29
➡Helps leaders understand, reflect on, and prepare for paradigm changes within a workgroup, organization, or industry.

1.10   The GAS model: Designing practical organizational processes   33

➡Helps leaders optimally design or redesign leadership processes, by making trade-offs to ensure processes are practical and usable.

1.11   Integrity: Gut-level ethics   36

➡Takes the cerebral concept of ethics and places it where leaders can understand and act on it—at gut level.

Section 2—Tools for Big-Picture Thinking

2.1   Introduction to systems thinking for leaders   40

➡Introduces leaders to the elements of systems thinking—looking for patterns and relationships, then understanding and optimizing all systems.

2.2   The 7S model: Aligning for success   45

➡Encourages leaders to think systemically, particularly when planning large systems or systemwide change within an organization.

2.3   Directional statements: Three levels of clarity   48

➡Helps leaders make sense of a Babel of directional terms—mission, purpose, strategy, values, beliefs, goals, objectives, vision, and so on.

2.4   Visioning and vision statements   51

➡Assists leaders with an important skill—visioning. The vision of this tool is to inspire you to create, with others, an inspiring vision!

2.5   Values and leadership   55

➡Provides guidance for clarifying and living one's values, the bedrock of an organization's culture.

2.6   Clarifying purpose: Harnessing people power in organizations   59

➡Helps leaders to define purpose and meaning, a skill that distinguishes leadership from management.

2.7   Writing clear goal statements   62

➡Provides the concepts and tools needed to define and write clear result statements.

2.8   Measuring success: The balanced scorecard   65

➡This modern tool helps leaders establish measurements beyond the traditional financial and production numbers.

Section 3—Tools for Strategic Thinking

3.1   The leader as strategist   69

➡Summarizes and compares the most prominent perspectives on strategy of the past 20 years.

3.2   The sigmoid curve: Anticipating and preparing for change despite current success   73

➡Challenges, in a novel way, the maxim, "If it ain't broke, don't fix it," by asking leaders to think about new directions while things are still going well.

3.3   SWOT: Strengths, weaknesses, opportunities, and threats   76

➡As a springboard for strategy clarification, asks leaders to examine the current state of the organization, both inside and out.

3.4   The fundamentals of business-unit strategy   79

➡Focuses on how to compete within a market defined by the larger corporation.

3.5   Strategic resourcing: Defining high-value work for service groups   82
➡Helps internal service groups compete for work within their own organizations against the very best external service providers.

3.6   Strategic relationships: Analyzing your client base   86
➡Provides a framework for leaders to examine their client and customer bases to ensure they are offering the highest value-added services and products to the right people.

3.7   RAIR logic: Aligning customers, strategy, culture, and leadership   89
➡Provides a way of checking to ensure alignment among an organization's leadership style, culture, business strategy, and customer needs and markets.

3.8   Partnering for Success: Joint Ventures and Strategic Alliances   92
➡Assists leaders with an alliancing model that sorts out and tracks an alliance development process.

3.9   Marketing a professional service group   96
➡Helps leaders prepare a marketing plan for an internal professional services group working within an organization.

SECTION 4—TOOLS FOR DESIGNING PRODUCTIVE PROCESSES AND ORGANIZATIONS

4.1   Designing productive organizations   101
➡Provides leaders with a model for the overall design of an organization, division, or workgroup.

4.2   Hierarchy: Leadership levels in an organization   105
➡Provides a novel and practical model to help leaders determine the number of levels of leadership and the spans of control of leaders.

4.3   Business process reengineering   108
➡Highlights core processes leaders need to consider if they intend to undertake business process reengineering.

4.4   Employee involvement: A range of possibilities   112
➡Helps leaders determine how and when to involve others.

4.5   Organizational culture: Sail or anchor?   117
➡Outlines the basics of organizational culture, its importance and how leaders can work with it.

4.6   Open-book leadership: Developing entrepreneurial thinking   121
➡Contains guidelines for adopting open-book management—the sharing of information that would help employees adopt a more entrepreneurial and business-thinking orientation.

4.7   Job satisfaction: Involving workgroups in designing jobs   126
➡Helps leaders engage employees in assessing the challenge, opportunity, and meaning they get from their work.

4.8   Revitalizing the Board of Directors in a nonprofit organization   129
➡Outlines a systematic approach to Board of Directors design, and emphasizes the central role of the Board in developing and overseeing policy.

4.9   Using professional expertise: A modern leadership skill   132
➡Helps leaders obtain and use knowledge workers' professional advice more effectively.

4.10   Surveying employees: Leading the survey process   135
➡Assists leaders with the overall employee survey process, from planning and involving stakeholders to responding to and acting on survey results.

SECTION 5—TOOLS FOR LEADING CHANGE

5.1   Leading change: A change equation   140

➥Pulls together a number of elements of successful change, complete with a checklist of suggested actions.

5.2   Leading major change in your organization   142

➥Blueprints how to lead change in a large part of an organization.

5.3   Assessing readiness for change   145

➥Helps leaders understand how ready they and their organizations are for change; identifies the major barriers early enough so you can do something about them.

5.4   Leading change: Small wins or breakthroughs?   147

➥Helps leaders decide whether the change should be incremental—based on a series of small wins; or breakthrough—a discontinuous break with the past.

5.5   Change window: A balanced approach to winning support for change   150

➥Helps leaders visualize a balanced approach to change, recognizing the pull to the familiar against the push to move on.

5.6   Aligning systems: Building systems compatibility into change plans   153

➥Recognizes that, designed in isolation from the larger system into which it needs to fit, change is almost certainly doomed to fail; helps leaders to understand and work the system.

5.7   Stakeholder groups: Understanding and mapping stakeholder systems   156

➥Helps leaders visualize who needs to be involved in sustainable change and in what way.

5.8   Human transitions: Helping people work through major change   160

➥Deals with a challenging piece of the change puzzle: Ultimately, successful change means *people* successfully changing.

5.9   Surfacing and dealing with resistance   163

➥Recognizes that change inevitably causes resistance. This tool will help leaders understand, surface, and deal with resistance.

5.10   Appreciative inquiry: Building change on success   166

➥This is a tool for building success on success. Change starting from a positive base differs from traditional change, which usually arises out of a negative—a problem.

SECTION 6—TOOLS FOR CRITICAL THINKING AND INNOVATION

6.1   The BS detector kit: Recognizing errors of logic   170

➥Outlines typical errors of logic committed by both leaders and others.

6.2   Assumption analysis: Testing decisions by examining their underlying biases   173

➥Helps leaders surface and challenge their own and other people's assumptions, as a way of ensuring quality of decisions in complex and dynamic business environments.

6.3   Sorting out complex situations   176

➡Deals with the multicausal nature of complex situations; their need to be broken into their constituent parts and then prioritized; and subsequently, how to plan action for highest-priority areas.

6.4   Dealing verbally with complexity   179

➡Provides an on-the-spot, effective questioning strategy for verbally sorting out complex situations with others.

6.5   Force-field analysis: Organizing and understanding complexity   183

➡Helps leaders to analyze and act on problems that are difficult to measure, by comparing the driving and restraining forces of leadership problems.

6.6   Optimizing your thinking—A hat 6-pack   186

➡Unscrambles thinking, surfaces hidden assumptions, keeps discussion from drifting, generates a wide range of innovative possibilities, and leads to better decisions and plans.

6.7   Creativity and innovation: The leader's role   189

➡Provides overviews of some typical creativity tools, including their use and implementation

6.8   Mind mapping: A breakthrough tool   193

➡Promotes creative problem solving by helping participants to visualize data, see interrelationships among data elements, and look at new solutions.

6.9   Brainstorming: Generating ideas quickly   196

➡Describes a commonly used group process and innovation tool, usually used to generate a lot of ideas quickly.

SECTION 7—TOOLS FOR PROBLEM SOLVING, DECISION MAKING, AND QUALITY

7.1   Reframing: Working the *real* problem   200

➡Helps leaders put problems into a new frame to ensure that the time people spend solving problems is well invested, and that their efforts are highly leveraged.

7.2   A general problem-solving model for leaders   204

➡Outlines a general problem-solving process that provides leaders with a way to deal with problems, decisions, or concerns.

7.3   Problem solving: A systematic approach to finding cause   207

➡Describes a systematic process for getting at the most probable cause of a problem *before* taking expensive and often misdirected action.

7.4   Polarities: Dealing with intractable problems   212

➡Provides a model for handling any situation in which two people or groups defend two ends of a spectrum in a mutually exclusive way.

7.5   Decision making: Making decisions logical and defensible   215

➡Describes a general-purpose decision-making tool that helps meets two criteria: (i) it's logically defensible and (ii) it's supported by key stakeholders.

7.6   Potential problem analysis: Dealing with risk to a plan   219

➡Shows how to protect any plan in a systemic way.

7.7   Total quality leadership overview   223

➡Provides an overview of some key quality tools and principles.

7.8   Affinity diagrams: Organizing mountains of data   227

➡Helps groups organize a large number of ideas into logical groupings, ready for action.

Section 8—Tools for Communication

8.1   Powerful leadership conversations   232

➡Helps leaders "read" face-to-face conversations, diagnose typical conversation difficulties, and also coach others.

8.2   Direct leader-to-employee communication still works best   236

➡Helps leaders communicate openly and directly with employees, contributing to the success of the organization.

8.3   The leader's role in organizational communication   239

➡Provides specific advice for leaders who communicate with large, geographically dispersed groups of employees.

8.4   Levels of communicating: Debate, dialogue, and discussion   242

➡Shows how dialogue and discussion can move a group to develop new options for action and achieve consensus.

8.5   Metacommunicating: Talking about talking   245

➡Gets leaders beyond "more of the same" communication that isn't working, and invites both parties to "talk about how you are talking."

8.6   Communication 101: Dealing effectively with feelings at work   248

➡Provides a range of approaches on how to deal with difficult feelings in a group.

8.7   Actively listening for content, feeling, and meaning   251

➡Starts with the basic mechanics of listening, and builds up to the highest forms of listening. Includes a listening assessment.

8.8   Listening techniques: Tactics to improve your listening   254

➡Lists specific situations and gives concrete suggestions on the techniques of listening.

8.9   Cross-cultural communication   257

➡Helps recognize some subtle cultural cues, providing suggestions for dealing with cross-cultural differences within organizations.

8.10   Media relations for leaders   260

➡Provides basic tips on how to work effectively with the media, at both planning and tactical levels.

Section 9—Tools for Leading and Influencing Others

9.1   Leadership versatility: Matching your role to the situation   264

➡Shows the range of behaviors leaders use to suit a leadership situation at hand.

9.2   Matching your leadership style to the situation   267

➡Provides a specific diagnostic for matching a leadership situation, and the people involved, with the best leadership style.

9.3   Leadership strategies for delegating work   271

➡Combines the work of a number of experts to help leaders delegate tasks in a variety of organizational situations.

9.4   Increasing your impact: Understanding control, influence, and interest   274

➥Assesses the personal influence of leaders, from what they should control to what they should let go.

9.5   Principled negotiation: Creating long-term, win–win agreements   277

➥Outlines the "Harvard" negotiating strategy, which sets up win–win agreements that achieve intended results, when followed through.

9.6   Making great presentations   281

➥Provides a model and worksheet for an effective presentation.

9.7   Selling wheel: Getting your recommendations accepted   284

➥Provides a model for a specific kind of presentation, in which leaders wish to persuade others of an idea, recommendation, or project.

9.8   Selling large projects: A much-valued leadership skill   287

➥Outlines the well-researched distinctions for selling a large project or proposal.

9.9   Power: A fundamental element of leadership success   291

➥Widens a leader's perception and sources of power, using a well-known model.

9.10   Support networks: The secret of all successful leaders   294

➥Shares a widely known secret—that leaders need the support of many kinds of people to achieve their business, professional, and personal objectives.

SECTION 10—TOOLS FOR LEADING TEAMS AND GROUPS

10.1   High-Performing Teams: Organizing to achieve results   298

➥Clarifies the different ways of organizing to optimize people's effort and contribution.

10.2   Improving team IQ   301

➥Provides leaders with guidelines that engage the collective mind of the team—the team IQ—so that the whole is greater than the sum of the parts.

10.3   Team competencies: Thinking, relating, and acting   305

➥Outlines the skills a team needs in three fundamental competency areas in order to operate effectively.

10.4   Inclusion, control, and affection: Developing commitment and teamwork   308

➥Answers the question, "What inspires people to become other-centered, as opposed to self-centered, within workgroups and organizations?"

10.5   Dealing with disturbances in workgroups and teams   311

➥Contains a powerful, yet simple, set of ideas for leaders and teams, designed to prevent problems and to correct problems when they occur.

10.6   Assessing your group leadership skills   314

➥Helps leaders stand back and, by means of a questionnaire, assess their effectiveness as leaders.

10.7   Getting participation   317

➥Helps with a checklist of ideas to plan the optimal amount of participation and determine how to secure it.

10.8   Ground rules: Helping groups to achieve business results   320

➥Describes how to establish clear and empowering ground rules; helps leaders achieve results through workgroups and teams.

10.9 Making information visible 323

➥Offers how-tos for making information visible, so meetings will quickly become more effective.

10.10 Closure: Helping groups make decisions and plans efficiently 326

➥Helps leaders improve the efficiency of group meetings by ensuring that clear decisions and plans are understood, and people are committed to taking appropriate action.

10.11 Priority setting in a workgroup or team 329

➥Focuses the workgroup's energy and commitment by setting priorities on the critical few high-impact items.

10.12 RASCI: A planning tool for workgroups and teams 332

➥Helps leaders organize and manage complex projects, involving a range of stakeholders, by using a RASCI chart.

SECTION 11—TOOLS FOR LEADING MEETINGS

11.1 Process cycle: Planning effective meetings and events 336

➥Helps leaders plan and communicate events of any duration—meeting, seminar, conference, employee session, or workshop.

11.2 Meetings: Purpose and function in workgroups and teams 339

➥Describes the range of purposes and functions that workgroup or team meetings serve when they are managed and led well.

11.3 Meeting checklist: From planning to follow up 342

➥Provides a quick-reference checklist to guide a workgroup or team meeting.

11.4 Meeting roles 347

➥Provides a list of meeting roles for a workgroup or team, and describes the benefits of role clarity.

11.5 The chairperson's role: Duties and accountabilities 350

➥Outlines the accountabilities of the chairperson—the person who has the most influence on meeting success.

11.6 The meeting agenda: Why, what, and how 353

➥Provides useful tips and an application framework for effective meeting agendas; helps ensure that meaningful results are achieved.

11.7 The chairperson's opening remarks 356

➥Outlines a brief introduction for the beginning of a meeting that sets the direction and tone for an effective meeting.

11.8 The meeting minutes: Why, what, and how 359

➥Provides guidelines for writing meeting minutes that encourage action and follow-through.

SECTION 12—TOOLS FOR LEADING RELATIONSHIPS

12.1 The relationship bank: Maintaining working relationships 363

➥Uses the metaphor of a relationship bank: With nothing on deposit, a withdrawal puts the relationship into the red (i.e., a negative balance).

12.2 Building trust into working relationships 366

➥Provides essential how-tos for developing trust within organizations.

12.3   Triangulation: The surest way to damage a relationship   369
➡Describes destructive triangulation—talking with a third person to complain or to put down another person.

12.4   Giving and receiving feedback: The dos and don'ts   372
➡Describes the challenging skill of giving and receiving feedbackm including the dos and don'ts.

12.5   Preparing yourself to give negative feedback   375
➡Prepares leaders for giving difficult feedback to others.

12.6   The 5 Cs: Escalating confrontation judiciously   378
➡Helps leaders resolve people or performance problems, whether they involve inappropriate action or failing to take action.

12.7   Conflict: Five levels for dealing with conflict   381
➡Lifts a load from leaders' shoulders by providing them with a wider range of options than simply demanding complete resolution or living in anger.

12.8   Dealing with difficult people: A timeless leadership challenge   384
➡Helps leaders understand difficult people, whether employees, bosses, or customers; suggests ways of dealing with them.

12.9   The essentials of customer service   387
➡Acquaints leaders with some essentials of customer service, and provides suggestions on customer service delivery.

Section 13—Tools for Leading Performance

13.1   Coaching and supporting the success of others   391
➡Describes the conditions necessary for a successful coaching relationship and explains the seven elements of the coaching process.

13.2   Coaching High-Performers: An Overlooked Element of Success   395
➡Clarifies the difference between problem-based coaching and high-performance coaching, and provides steps to develop a style for coaching high-performers.

13.3   Accountability Agreements: Defining accountability within organizations   399
➡Helps leaders transform often unspoken and misunderstood jobs, roles, and employment contracts into explicit expectations, personal promises, and business results.

13.4   Management by objectives   402
➡Adapted to present-day realities, helps leaders set goals, then plan and manage toward achieving those goals.

13.5   Urgency and importance: The essential elements of managing your time   406
➡Assists leaders to accept responsibility for their own development and to stay on top of important and urgent work, while also accomplishing meaningful results in the long term.

13.6   Attribution theory: Assessing performance and behavior   409
➡Challenges leaders to evaluate the performance of people, especially when the behavior is difficult to evaluate objectively.

13.7   Documenting employee performance and behavior   412
➡Makes easier what is often a chore: keeping specific, accurate, current records on significant employee performance and on-the-job behavior.

13.8   Job Competencies: Measuring and predicting performance   415
➡Helps leaders to find and use objective measures for recruiting, training, and rewarding employees.

13.9   Human capital: Truly the most valuable asset   418
➡Focuses attention on human capital, the most important but hardest-to-measure asset.

13.10   The Four Stages® Model: Understanding career strategies   421
➡Provides a powerful tool for guiding career planning and improving the leadership potential of others.

13.11   Professional leadership: Delivering expertise   424
➡Provides professional leaders with a simple, five-step model to better deliver expertise in a timely, appropriate way, so they are perceived as valued members of their organizations.

SECTION 14—TOOLS FOR LEARNING

14.1   Scarcity and abundance: The importance of attitude   428
➡Highlights how leaders' underlying attitudes have profound and far-reaching effects within their workgroups and organizations.

14.2   Single-loop and double-loop learning: When to stay the course and when to reevaluate   431
➡Describes how to distinguish when to hold the course and when to readjust goals—a highly sophisticated leadership skill.

14.3   Needs analysis: Measuring return on training investments   434
➡Outlines how crucial involvement is in translating participants' learned ideas and skills into organizational results.

14.4   Adult learning: Principles for helping adults learn   438
➡Distinguishes between traditional teaching and adult learning, whereby leaders build upon adult experiences, creating relevance for the learning and making learning concrete.

14.5   Teaching a job: An essential skill for frontline leaders   441
➡Provides a time-honored, step-by-step methodology for on-the-job training.

14.6   Leaders and learning styles   444
➡Helps leaders understand their learning preferences and those of others, and how they can turn these differences—often sources of conflict—to sources of enrichment for strength, team diversity, and improved business results.

14.7   Personal preferences: Capitalizing on individual differences   447
➡Helps leaders develop a better understanding of themselves and their own preferences, as well as those of other people, leading to more effective leadership interactions.

SECTION 15—TOOLS FOR TAKING CARE OF YOURSELF

15.1   Balance: Take care of yourself!   451
➡Helps leaders navigate through a maze of external influences, toward finding, establishing, and maintaining balance in their own lives, then helping others to do the same.

15.2   LEQ: The leadership emotional quotient   455

➡Provides an overview of a leadership competence area known variously as emotional intelligence (EI), emotional quotient (EQ), emotional literacy, emotional smarts, or emotional competence.

15.3   The JoHari window: What you don't know can hurt you   459

➡Helps leaders think about how they relate with others, and about their need to know themselves and to be open to feedback from others.

15.4   Understanding our assumptions and biases   462

➡Enables leaders to inquire into, challenge, and check their assumptions, conclusions, and beliefs.

15.5   Habits: The good and bad news that leaders need to know   467

➡Helps leaders understand their familiar and comfortable habits and learn how to change a habit.

15.6   Managing your defensive reactions   470

➡Explains how defense mechanisms reduce anxiety; that some defenses are healthy; and that others can severely limit a leader's potential for success.

15.7   Managing the stress associated with being a leader   472

➡Focuses on personal stress and how to deal with it. A diagnostic checklist is provided to help leaders understand personal stress and the stress levels within a workgroup.

How to Use and Benefit from this Book

Who is this book for?

This book is for leaders, consultants, and trainers in all industries and organizations, at all levels of experience.

If you are...	Here is how this book will help you:
➡ a **new leader:** manager, team leader, supervisor, project leader, ready to get going but nervous about your new role	✓ With a quick introduction to key leadership tools, it offers an overview of the leadership field, along with action-oriented tools that you can use immediately. ✓ Leave this book on your desk to provide just-in-time help when you need it.
➡ a **veteran leader** with numerous workshops, conferences, and books crammed into your over-extended gray matter	✓ By reminding you how much you already know, this book will help you put your knowledge to work. ✓ Use it like a dictionary. When you wonder, "What were the characteristics of a clear goal?" You can find your answer quickly using one of the methods described.
➡ a **consultant**	✓ In this fast-moving world, if you cannot explain a leadership tool clearly and within a few minutes, you will lose your client's attention. ✓ This book is an unparalleled source of ideas and applications.
➡ a **trainer** or leadership development advisor	✓ With over 130 core leadership models and skills briefly and clearly described, including practical application suggestions, you have a concise training resource for new leaders and refresher course for veterans. ✓ For much-needed follow-through, this book can be left on participants' desks for quick on-the-job reference.

If you are…	Here is how this book will help you:
→ an **educator**	✓ For introductory leadership courses, this book, organized into coherent sections for study modules, provides overviews of all the major topics in the field. ✓ This book is one students will carry from the desks of academia to the desks of industry.
→ a leadership **coach** or mentor	✓ So, you've been asked to coach. This book provides the basis for over 130 coaching meetings! ✓ For each coaching meeting, pick a pertinent leadership tool, read and discuss the brief description together, then plan an application using the ideas in the book.

HOW TO FIND WHAT YOU NEED (WHEN YOU NEED IT)

Our goal is to provide just-in-time assistance for typical leadership concerns.

Information Source	Location:
A traditional table of contents	page v
An annotated table of contents with a brief description of each leadership tool	page xi
A traditional keyword index	page 476
A listing of typical leadership concerns matched to book resources: *"Here's my problem. What tool do I need?"*	page xxvi
Leadership Gurus matched to the topics they inspired	page xxviii

Leadership tools have been gathered into 15 sections. Within each section, leadership tools have been arranged from general to specific. You may wish to browse an entire section to find precisely what you need, or just browse the expanded table of contents.

WHY THIS BOOK?

Cycle times are shorter. "Work smarter, not harder!" "Cut the organizational fat." Change is changing more rapidly. Moore's Law has microprocessors doubling in performance every 18 months. The information age seems to be verging on the chaos age. Even slogans are getting shorter!

Our response: "We've done your homework!" We've summarized over 130 of the most useful leadership tools, and we present them here in an easy-to-use format. We have highlighted core ideas of leadership—both classic and modern—and made it easy for you to apply them. Like a dictionary, this is a reference you can leave at hand, ready to use, with models and ideas for most of your leadership needs and questions.

WHAT WE'VE DONE FOR YOU

We've included tools that we use regularly in our leadership roles, those we consider to be the most useful and enduring tools of the leadership trade. We've condensed them, so you can locate and use the exact tool for your unique situation in just a few minutes. You'll be able to put the right tool to work immediately, whether at your next meeting or with the next person who comes into your office.

How we've done this

Each tool has:

➠ An "Inspired by" line names the leadership experts who inspired the tool.

➠ A brief description of the leadership tool is presented, in checklists, tables, or diagrams whenever possible.

➠ A How to Use This Leadership Tool section will help you apply the idea. Application worksheets are available for download from the Internet in Microsoft Word format at www.books.mcgraw-hill.com/training/dowload.

➠ Internal references [e.g., ☛2.7 Goal Statements] are liberally available throughout the book. These direct you to further assistance on a particular topic.

➠ A Related Leadership Tools section tells you where to find more information related to a topic, just in case the tool doesn't quite hit the mark.

➠ A For Further Assistance section refers you to original sources, should you wish to obtain more information or read the original work.

How we selected these tools

We used the following criteria to select the leadership tools that are included in this book. These tools:

✓ Are practical and useful immediately. ✓ Are regularly used and valued by our clients.
✓ Can be summarized briefly. ✓ Share a leadership philosophy.
✓ Are reasonably well known by leaders. ✓ Have endured and stood the test of time.

LEADERSHIP TOOL FINDER: HERE'S MY PROBLEM, WHAT TOOL DO I NEED?

If your need is:	Look for these resources:
? selling a recommendation to others	☛ 9.6 Presentations ☛ 9.7 Selling Wheel ☛ 9.8 Selling Large Projects
? preparing a strategy	☛ 3.1 Strategy ☛ 3.2 Sigmoid Curve ☛ 3.3 Environmental Scan
? dealing with resistance	☛ 5.9 Resistance ☛ 15.2 Emotional Intelligence
? leading change	☛ 5.1 Change Equation ☛ 5.2 Major Change
? reducing the stress of change	☛ 5.1 Change Equation ☛ 5.8 Human Transitions
? sorting out complex situations	☛ 6.3 Complex Situations ☛ 6.5 Force-Field Analysis ☛ 6.8 Mind Mapping
? clarifying your leadership role	☛ 1.6 Boards of Play ☛ 9.1 Leadership Versatility ☛ 13.10 Careers
? improving your listening skills	☛ 8.1 Conversations ☛ 8.4 Dialogue and Discussion ☛ 8.7 Active Listening
? dealing with multiple stakeholders	☛ 2.1 Systems Thinking ☛ 5.7 Stakeholder Groups
? knowing where to put your time and effort	☛ 13.5 Time Management ☛ 15.1 Balance
? enhancing your career as a leader	☛ 1.6 Boards of Play ☛ 13.10 Careers
? getting at the real problem	☛ 7.1 Problem Framing ☛ 7.3 Finding Cause ☛ 8.5 Metacommunicating
? making a good decision	☛ 7.2 Problem Solving ☛ 7.5 Decision Making
? reaching closure	☛ 10.10 Closure
? leading a group meeting	☛ 10.6 Group Leader Skills ☛ 11.1 Process Cycle ☛ 11.3 Meeting Checklist
? (re)designing a work group	☛ 4.4 Employee Involvement ☛ 10.1 High-Performing Teams ☛ 10.3 Team Competencies
? giving or receiving feedback	☛ 12.4 Feedback ☛ 12.5 Negative Feedback
? coming up with a creative approach	☛ 6.6 Six-Hat Thinking ☛ 6.7 Creativity and Innovation

If your need is:	Look for these resources:
? setting goals or objectives	☛2.7 Goal Statements ☛13.4 MBO
? setting up a team	☛10.1 High-Performing Teams ☛10.3 Team Competencies
? managing conflict	☛8.1 Conversations ☛8.5 Metacommunicating ☛12.6 Confrontation ☛12.7 Dealing with Conflict
? designing a learning event	☛14.3 Needs Analysis ☛14.4 Adult Learning ☛14.6 Learning Styles
? coaching others	☛13.1 Coaching ☛13.10 Careers
? getting participation	☛8.4 Dialogue and Discussion ☛10.7 Getting Participation
? facilitating groups	☛8.3 Organizational Communication ☛10.6 Group Leader Skills ☛10.8 Ground Rules ☛11.1 Process Cycle
? negotiating an agreement	☛8.5 Metacommunicating ☛9.5 Negotiation
? improving work processes	☛4.3 Reengineering
? relieving stress	☛15.1 Balance ☛15.7 Stress
? working in another culture	☛4.5 Culture ☛8.9 Cross-Cultural Communication
? dealing with difficult people	☛5.9 Resistance ☛8.5 Metacommunicating ☛12.8 Difficult People
? surfacing and challenging assumptions	☛1.9 Paradigms ☛6.2 Assumption Analysis ☛7.1 Problem Framing
? When and how to involve others	☛4.4 Employee Involvement ☛9.2 Situational Leadership
? expanding your influence	☛9.4 Leader Impact
? developing relationships with others	☛8.1 Conversations ☛12.1 The Relationship Bank ☛12.2 Trust ☛13.1 Coaching
? understanding differences	☛8.9 Cross-Cultural Communication ☛14.6 Learning Styles ☛14.7 Personal Preferences
? understanding yourself	☛14.7 Personal Preferences ☛15.2 Emotional Intelligence ☛15.3 JoHari Window ☛15.5 Habits

The Leadership Gurus	Inspired These Tools
Argyris and Schon	☞14.2 Rethinking Your Thinking
Beckhard and Harris	☞10.12 Team Planning
Bellman, Geoffrey	☞1.3 Leadership ☞1.4 Leader Principles ☞1.8 Recursive Leadership ☞13.2 High-Performers
Bennis, Warren	☞1.3 Leadership
Block, Peter	☞5.9 Resistance
Boyett, Joseph and Jimmie	☞1.2 Manage or Lead? ☞2.8 Balanced Scorecard ☞3.1 Strategy
Bridges, William	☞5.8 Human Transition
Carver, John	☞4.8 Revitalizing the Board
Champy and Hammar	☞4.3 Reengineering
Cleese and Skynner	☞15.6 Defenses
Covey, Stephen	☞1.5 Seven Habits ☞9.4 Leader Impact ☞12.1 The Relationship Bank ☞13.5 Time Management
Crainer, Stuart	☞1.2 Manage or Lead? ☞2.2 7S Model
Dalton and Thompson	☞13.10 Careers
De Bono, Edward	☞6.6 Six-Hat Thinking
Drucker, Peter	☞1.2 Manage or Lead? ☞4.9 Professional Expertise
Dyer, William	☞10.6 Group Leader Skills ☞10.11 Priority Setting
Emery, Fred	☞4.4 Employee Involvement
Fisher, Roger	☞9.5 Negotiation
Galbraith, Jay	☞4.1 Organizational Design
Goleman, Daniel	☞15.2 Emotional Intelligence
Grove, Andy	☞1.2 Manage or Lead? ☞11.3 Meeting Checklist
Handy, Charles	☞3.2 Sigmoid Curve
Harrison, Roger	☞14.1 Scarcity and Abundance
Hersey and Blanchard	☞9.1 Leadership Versatility ☞9.2 Situational Leadership ☞9.3 Delegation ☞9.9 Power
Jacques, Eliot	☞4.2 Hierarchy
Jay, Antony	☞11.2 Meeting Purpose ☞11.3 Meeting Checklist ☞11.5 Chair Accountabilities

The Leadership Gurus	Inspired These Tools
Johnson, Barry	☛7.4 Polarities
Jones, John	☛4.1 Organizational Design
Kaplan, Robert	☛2.8 Balanced Scorecard
Katzenbach and Smith	☛10.1 HiPo Teams
Kepner and Tregoe	☛6.3 Complex Situations ☛7.3 Finding Cause ☛7.5 Decision Making ☛7.6 Potential Problems
Kilmann, Ralph	☛6.2 Assumption Analysis
Knowles, Malcom	☛14.4 Adult Learning
Kolb, David	☛14.6 Learning Styles
Kotter, John	☛1.2 Manage or Lead? ☛5.2 Major Change
Kuhn, Thomas	☛1.9 Paradigms
Lawlor, Edward	☛4.4 Employee Involvement
Lerner, Harriet	☛12.3 Triangulation ☛13.6 Attribution Theory
Lewin, Kurt	☛6.5 Force-Field Analysis
Milstein, M.M.	☛11.2 Meeting Purpose ☛11.3 Meeting Checklist ☛11.5 Chair Accountabilities
Mintzberg, Henry	☛3.1 Strategy ☛9.9 Power
Novokowsky, Bernie	☛1.6 Boards of Play ☛4.1 Organizational Design ☛6.8 Mind Mapping ☛9.9 Power ☛12.7 Dealing with Conflict
Peters, Tom	☛2.2 7S Model
Pitman and Bushe	☛5.10 Appreciative Inquiry
Purkey, William	☛12.6 Confrontation
Rackman, Neil	☛9.8 Selling Large Projects
Reich, Robert	☛4.9 Professional Expertise ☛13.9 Human Capital
Rogers, Carl	☛8.7 Active Listening
Russo and Shoemaker	☛7.1 Problem Framing
Sagan, Carl	☛6.1 Logic Errors
Scholtes, Peter	☛2.1 Systems Thinking ☛7.7 Quality Tools
Schultz, Will	☛10.4 Team Commitment
Senge, Peter	☛2.1 Systems Thinking ☛8.4 Dialogue and Discussion
Smallwood, Norm	☛1.7 Results-Based Leaders
Tannen, Deborah	☛8.5 Metacommunicating

The Leadership Gurus	Inspired These Tools
Ulrich, David	☞1.4 Leader Principles ☞1.7 Results-Based Leaders ☞2.8 Balanced Scorecard ☞3.3 Environmental Scan ☞13.9 Human Capital
Ury, William	☞9.5 Negotiation
Weick, Karl	☞1.10 The GAS model
Weisbord, Marvin	☞1.9 Paradigms ☞4.5 Culture ☞5.5 Change Window ☞6.5 Force-Field Analysis
Wilkins, Alan	☞2.3 Directional Statements ☞4.5 Culture
Zenger, Jack	☞1.4 Leader Principles ☞1.7 Results-Based Leaders ☞2.8 Balanced Scorecard ☞13.9 Human Capital

ACKNOWLEDGMENTS

A book is never the work of the authors alone. In particular, a book of this nature leans heavily on the ideas of the people acknowledged at the beginning of each leadership tool. We thank these inspirational people for blazing a trail the rest of us can follow.

This book would be incomprehensible without the timely and brilliant editing of Eilis Hiebert. With loving care, and without bruising the delicate egos of the writers, Eilis converted tortured sentences into readable text.

Some friends and colleagues contributed material to the book: Clem Blakeslee, Mel Blitzer, George Campbell, Layton Fisher, Wilf Hiebert, Diane MacDonald, and Ursula Wohlfarth.

A number of other friends provided constructive feedback and encouragement, particularly in the sensitive early stages of development: Joan Batycki, Mel Blitzer, George Campbell, Wes Carter, Wilf Hiebert, Peter Justo, Diane MacDonald, Ben Macht, Bernie Novokowsky, Brenda Spilker, Jim Webber, Ursula Wohlfarth, and Ken Zdunich. Thank you all. Cathy Klatt and Leighton Wilks were very helpful with manuscript preparation.

Richard Narramore of McGraw-Hill cheerfully coached us throughout: from the idea of the book, to its sponsoring, through many doubts and questions, and through dozens of drafts. Thank you, Richard.

Finally, many people encouraged us in the broad sense of providing ideas, support, and counsel at critical times. These people inspired us with their "you can do it" attitude. Thus, in addition to those listed above, we express our appreciation to our spouses, Cathy Klatt and Eilis Hiebert; our sons, Bryan and Jeff Klatt, Paul and Quinn Hiebert; and to the Milis family, Bernie and MJ Novokowsky, Norm Smallwood, Clem and Mary Blakeslee Geoff Bellman, the late Bernice Mattinson, David Irvine, and Shaun Murphy.

FOUNDATIONAL CONCEPTS

In an age of quick fixes, fads, and techniques, leaders need a strong understanding of the basics of leadership techniques. As Stephen Covey puts it in *Principle-Centered Leadership,* "Without understanding the principles of a given task, people become incapacitated when the situation changes and different practices are required to be successful." Especially in a book like this, focused on brief descriptions of leadership tools, you need to understand the foundations so you don't build a "house of fads." The tools in this section provide some underpinnings for a successful leadership role.

1.1 Leadership in the Twenty-First Century

Inspired by John Kotter, Peter Drucker, Bill Gates, Ikujuro Nonaka, Hirotaka Takeuchi, Alvin Toffler, and others.

Bill Gates suggests that, "if the 1980s were about quality, and the 1990s were about reengineering, then the 2000s will be about velocity, about how quickly business itself will be transacted." This tool will help you look into a crystal ball and forecast your leadership future!

Late Twentieth Century		Early Twenty-First Century
Organizational Culture ✘ Focused on internal processes ✘ Hierarchical, centralized, boundaries ✘ Inwardly focused ✘ Slow to change, long cycle times, risk-adverse ✘ Follow procedures	⟹	*Organizational Culture* ✔ Focused on results and customers ✔ Flat, distributed, no functional stovepipes ✔ Focused on customers, environment ✔ Quick to adapt, encourages appropriate risks ✔ Innovative, entrepreneurial
People ✘ Executives, management, professionals, etc. ✘ Top-down thinking, the General Manager ✘ Individuals working in a coordinated way ✘ Job descriptions and roles ✘ Production workers ✘ Long-term careers, loyalty	⟹	*People* ✔ Leaders at all levels; everyone solves problems ✔ Everyone strategic, thinking, leading, and doing ✔ Teams with joint accountability for results ✔ Project descriptions, roles, and accountabilities ✔ Knowledge workers ✔ Project-based employment
Systems ✘ Bureaucratic ✘ Few performance systems ✘ Lots of middle tiers ✘ Policies, procedures ✘ Control-based, production-based ✘ Large inventories, long lead times	⟹	*Systems* ✔ Think of the whole system; think systemically ✔ Multiple performance systems and measures ✔ Multiple interdependencies ✔ Values, principles, targets, accountabilities ✔ Value-based, quality-based ✔ Just-in-time inventories, delivery, learning
Information ✘ Less time-dependent; controlled ✘ Paper-based processes and tools ✘ Political; information used for personal power ✘ Face-to-face teams only ✘ Business at the speed of talk and paper	⟹	*Information* ✔ Real-time, multiple, and widely shared ✔ Digital-based processes and tools ✔ Open and candid, widespread information sharing ✔ Use of digital tools creates virtual teams ✔ Business at the speed of thought and light
Leadership Style ✘ Individual work and rewards ✘ Management knows best ✘ Doing things right ✘ Content ✘ Risk avoidance ✘ Telling and selling	⟹	*Leadership Style* ✔ Teamwork and team rewards ✔ Everyone is a leader ✔ Doing the right things ✔ Context (hypertext) and processes ✔ Taking appropriate risks ✔ Coaching and delegating

Job Design		Job Design
✘ Single-task jobs	➠	✔ Whole job
✘ Management defines problems and solutions		✔ Everyone is a problem solver
✘ Most isolated from customer		✔ Everyone serving customers or clients
✘ Work in the office, and within your function		✔ Cross-functional project teams
✘ Paper, pen, pencil, and telephone		✔ Computer monitors and input devices
✘ Sparse feedback systems		✔ Multiple performance systems and measures

HOW TO USE THIS LEADERSHIP TOOL

"You know you have built an excellent digital nervous system when information flows through your organization as quickly and naturally as thought in a human being and when you can use technology to marshal and coordinate teams of people as quickly as you can focus an individual on an issue."

—Bill Gates, *BUSINESS @ THE SPEED OF THOUGHT*

No leader is immune to the information revolution and the subsequent demands from organizations and employees.

WEB WORKSHEET

Summarize your leadership style along each of the dimensions in this table. Note where you are now as a leader, where you would like to be, and actions needed to get you there.

Leadership area	Current leadership behavior	Desired leadership behavior	Action plans for makimg the change
Organizational culture			[☛ 4.5 Culture]
People			[☛ 4.4 Employee Involvement]
Systems			[☛ 2.1 Systems Thinking]

Information			[☛ 2.2 7S Model]
Leadership style			[☛ 9.1 Leadership Versatility]
Job design			[☛ 4.1 Organizational Design]

Related leadership tools

1.2 Manage or Lead?	1.5 Seven Habits	2.2 7S Model
1.4 Leader Principles	2.1 Systems Thinking	4.1 Organizational Design

For further assistance

Drucker, Peter. "The Coming of the New Organization." *Harvard Business Review.* January–February 1988, 45–53.

Drucker, Peter. "The Next Workplace Revolution." *Globe and Mail.* September 1989.

Gates, Bill. *Business @ the Speed of Thought: Succeeding in the Digital Economy.* Warner Books, 1999.

Kotter, John. *Leading Change.* Harvard Business School Press, 1996.

Nonaka, Ikujiro, and Hirotaka Takeuchi. *The Knowledge-Creating Company: How Japanese Companies Create the Dynamics of Innovation.* Oxford University Press, 1995.

Toffler, Alvin. *Power Shift.* Bantam Books, 1991.

1.2 CONTRASTING MANAGEMENT AND LEADERSHIP

Inspired by numerous sources, including Joseph and Jimmie Boyett, Stuart Crainer,
Peter Drucker, Andy Grove, John Kotter, and others.

The distinction between management and leadership is not either-or; rather, it's a balance. While powerful leaders are more than just excellent managers, an essential aspect of their credibility stems from their management expertise. As you read this table, keep in mind that the distinction between management and leadership is not a dichotomy, but rather a blend or balance. Both are needed in today's knowledge-based organizations.

Manager	Leader
• success based on predictability	➡ success based on innovation and adaptation
• goals	➡ vision and values
• plans	➡ energy
• defines vision and purpose statements	➡ lives vision and purpose
• defines value statements	➡ models values
• does things right	➡ does the right things
• top-down strategy	➡ leadership at all levels; everyone strategic
• measurement of activities	➡ measurement of results
• short-term results emphasized	➡ long-term results, big picture emphasized
• linear, rational, analytical	➡ systems, aligning the whole, intuitive
• "head stuff" (e.g., behavior, compliance)	➡ "heart stuff" (e.g., morale, commitment)
• controls	➡ inspires, creates new ways, coaches, mentors
• one best style (plan, organize, delegate, control)	➡ multiple, situational leadership roles and styles
• techniques	➡ principles
• focus on content	➡ sets context, pays attention to process
• quality control	➡ everyone responsible for quality
• inward-looking	➡ customer-focused
• individual effort and reward	➡ individual and team effort and reward
• management knows best	➡ all together know best
• success as personal success	➡ success as the success of others
• best for organization (focused on bottom line)	➡ best for organization in society

How to use this leadership tool

"Leadership defines what the future should look like, aligns people with that vision, and inspires them to make it happen despite the obstacles."

—John Kotter, *LEADING CHANGE*

Use this matrix to rate your management and leadership skills. Keep in mind that this is not either-or, and that powerful leaders need both management and leadership expertise. Use the right-hand column to plan how you will make improvements in two or three of these skill areas. This could include planning to overcome a weakness or limitation, or further developing an existing management or leadership strength.

WEB WORKSHEET

Management	Rating (1 = weak, 7 = outstanding)	Leadership	Rating (1 = weak, 7 = outstanding)	Action plans
success based on predictability	1 2 3 4 5 6 7	success based on adaptation	1 2 3 4 5 6 7	
goals	1 2 3 4 5 6 7	vision and values	1 2 3 4 5 6 7	
plans	1 2 3 4 5 6 7	energy	1 2 3 4 5 6 7	
defining vision and purpose statement	1 2 3 4 5 6 7	lives vision and purpose	1 2 3 4 5 6 7	
defining value statements	1 2 3 4 5 6 7	modeling values	1 2 3 4 5 6 7	
do things right	1 2 3 4 5 6 7	do the right things	1 2 3 4 5 6 7	
top-down strategy	1 2 3 4 5 6 7	all, at all levels, strategic	1 2 3 4 5 6 7	
measurement of activities	1 2 3 4 5 6 7	measurement of results	1 2 3 4 5 6 7	
short-term results emphasized	1 2 3 4 5 6 7	long-term results, big picture	1 2 3 4 5 6 7	
linear, rational, analytical	1 2 3 4 5 6 7	whole systems, intuitive	1 2 3 4 5 6 7	

"head stuff" (compliance)	1 2 3 4 5 6 7	"heart stuff" (commitment)	1 2 3 4 5 6 7	
controls	1 2 3 4 5 6 7	inspires, reframes, coaches	1 2 3 4 5 6 7	
one best management style	1 2 3 4 5 6 7	multiple, situational styles	1 2 3 4 5 6 7	
techniques	1 2 3 4 5 6 7	principles	1 2 3 4 5 6 7	
content	1 2 3 4 5 6 7	context and process	1 2 3 4 5 6 7	
quality control	1 2 3 4 5 6 7	everyone responsible for quality	1 2 3 4 5 6 7	
inward-looking	1 2 3 4 5 6 7	customer-focused	1 2 3 4 5 6 7	
individual effort and reward	1 2 3 4 5 6 7	individual and team effort and reward	1 2 3 4 5 6 7	
management knows best	1 2 3 4 5 6 7	all together know best	1 2 3 4 5 6 7	
success as personal success	1 2 3 4 5 6 7	success as the success of others	1 2 3 4 5 6 7	
best for organization	1 2 3 4 5 6 7	best for organization in society	1 2 3 4 5 6 7	

Related leadership tools

1.1 Twenty-First Century Leader	2.3 Directional Statements	4.1 Organizational Design
2.1 Systems Thinking	2.8 Balanced Scorecard	9.1 Leadership Versatility

For further assistance

Boyett, Joseph H., and Jimmie T. Boyett. *The Guru Guide: The Best Ideas of the Top Management Thinkers*. John Wiley & Sons, 1998.

Crainer, Stuart. *The Ultimate Book of Business Gurus: 110 Thinkers Who Really Made a Difference,* Ultimate Business Series. Amacom, 1998.

Drucker, Peter. *The Frontiers of Management: Where Tomorrow's Decisions Are Being Shaped Today*. Harper & Row, 1986.

Drucker, Peter. *Managing in Turbulent Times*. Harper & Row, 1980.

Grove, Andy. *High Output Management*. Vintage Books, 1983.

Grove, Andy. *Only the Paranoid Survive: How to Exploit the Crisis Points That Challenge Every Company and Career*. Currency Doubleday, 1996.

Kotter, John. *Leading Change*. Harvard Business School Press, 1996.

1.3 HOW EFFECTIVE LEADERS ACT: AN OVERVIEW

Inspired by Geoffrey Bellman, Warren Bennis, Bert Nanus, and Debra Benton.

Leadership is an incredibly complex and varied topic, encompassing everything from interpersonal relationships to corporate strategy. This tool moves you above your day-to-day leadership activities, to take a bird's-eye view of leadership fundamentals. A leader's theory is no small matter. It has a lot to do with his or her long-term success as a leader. Think hard about your own leadership style, strengths, and development needs as you read this overview of how effective leaders think and act.

Leadership competencies	Specific skills required
Leaders focus attention on results by:	❑ knowing what they want and focusing on results ❑ challenging others with an inspiring, realistic, and shared vision ❑ seeking consensus and commitment to goals ❑ balancing idealism and realism ❑ demonstrating business skills [☛ 1.7 Results-Based Leaders, 13.3 Accountability]
Leaders create an effective working atmosphere by:	❑ being accountable for the norms that drive behaviors in their workgroups ❑ designing and managing the people side of the work environment, which provides context and meaning for people ❑ making ideas tangible, and communicating facts and concepts in understandable and encouraging ways ❑ emphasizing *why*, versus simply telling people *how* (thus enabling people to make decisions without constantly having to appeal to a higher authority) [☛ 4.1 Organizational Design]
Leaders manage themselves and model how others can do the same by:	❑ setting aside personal issues and getting on with the job ❑ approaching problems and relationships in the present, rather than from the context of past difficulties ❑ trusting others even when this involves a level of risk (Withholding trust is sometimes necessary for self-protection, but the price is too high if it means always being on guard.) ❑ being able to function without constant approval and recognition from others ❑ honestly assessing the fit between people's skills and the requirements of the job ❑ understanding people's strengths, and finding ways to compensate for their limitations ❑ treating people in the workgroup with the same courteous attention they extend to strangers ❑ understanding the importance of accepting people as they are, while insisting on performance [☛ 1.5 Seven Habits, 1.4 Leader Principles, 12.2 Trust]
Leaders encourage teamwork by:	❑ using consensus as opposed to command, coercion, or compromise ❑ accepting conflict as inevitable, and mediating conflict on rational grounds ❑ supporting decisions based on knowledge and technical competence, rather than on personal whims or the prerogatives of rank ❑ encouraging emotional expression while emphasizing task accomplishment [☛ 10.1 HiPo Teams, 10.2 Team IQ, 10.6 Group Leader Skills]

How to use this leadership tool

"What I'm talking about is self-invention. Imagination. That's basically how we get to know ourselves. People who cannot invent and reinvent themselves must be content with borrowed postures, secondhand ideas, and 'fitting in' instead of 'standing out.'"

—Warren Bennis, *AN INVENTED LIFE*

WEB WORKSHEET

Sharpen your thinking by challenging these one-liners on leadership. Cite reasons why you agree or disagree. Your answers on the chart will provide a profile of your leadership thinking, values, and style. After you've completed the chart, take time to review your responses. What do they tell you about your leadership strengths, and about limitations or development needs? Ask a trusted coworker how he or she interprets these responses, and for suggestions on your leadership strengths and development needs.

	I agree because...	I disagree because...
Leadership is a people business. [☛ 1.2 Manage or Lead?]		
Leaders make people hopeful. [☛ 4.5 Culture]		
Power is the currency of leaders. [☛ 9.9 Power]		
Learning is essential fuel for leaders. [☛ 14.6 Learning Styles]		
Leaders are only as powerful as the ideas they communicate. [☛ 8.1 Conversations]		
Leadership is mainly a function of character. [☛ 1.5 Seven Habits]		

FOUR STEPS TO IMPROVING YOUR LEADERSHIP SKILLS:

1. In which area of leadership do you feel you most need to improve?

2. How might you go about making those improvements?

3. Develop a brief action plan for making those improvements. It doesn't have to be elaborate. A few simple steps will do.

4. Now, follow through with this plan. You'll be surprised at how leadership skills can be developed with just a little work and discipline.

RELATED LEADERSHIP TOOLS

1.4 Leader Principles	4.1 Organizational Design	9.2 Situational Leadership
1.6 Boards of Play	9.1 Leadership Versatility	14.7 Personal Preferences

FOR FURTHER ASSISTANCE

Bellman, Geoffrey. *Getting Things Done When You Are Not in Charge*. Simon & Schuster, 1992.

Bennis, Warren. *An Invented Life: Reflections on Leadership and Change*. Addison-Wesley, 1993.

Bennis, Warren, and Bert Nanus. *Leaders: The Strategies for Taking Charge*. Harper & Row, 1985.

Benton, Debra. *How to Think Like a CEO: The 22 Vital Traits You Need to Be the Person at the Top*. Warner Books, 1996.

1.4 PRINCIPLES TO GUIDE YOUR USE OF LEADERSHIP TECHNIQUES

Inspired by Geoffrey Bellman, Peter Block, Stephen Covey, Gene Dalton, Paul Thompson, Ralph Kilmann, David Ulrich, Jack Zenger, and Norman Smallwood.

While leadership techniques and how-tos are helpful, they fail you in the long run unless they are based on some firm foundations or principles. This table summarizes important principles for leaders. Use these as a springboard for developing your beliefs and thinking as a powerful leader in your organization.

PRINCIPLES UNDERLYING LEADERSHIP TECHNIQUES

Principle	The dangers of ignoring this principle	Positive steps to enact this principle
Model the behavior you expect from others: Be recursive. [☞ 1.8 Recursive Leadership]	If what you say is different from what you do (i.e., the audio doesn't match the video), others will quickly sense this. They will mistrust you, even if they can't specifically say why they have doubts.	The best way to encourage exemplary behavior is to model the behavior you want from others. If you want feedback, accept feedback. If you want openness, be open. If you want results, produce leadership results.
Think strategically as well as tactically. See the big picture and align your efforts with it, but also attend to details and get things done. [☞ 3.1 Strategy]	Ineffective leaders are often too detail-oriented. This can lead to losing sight of the big picture while micromanaging others. On the other hand, talking big and not delivering is also ineffective. A balance of strategic and tactical thinking is required.	If you are too detail-oriented, ask yourself "Why?" Ask big-picture questions. Alternatively, if you are a big-picture leader, but have trouble paying attention to details, work toward balancing your perspective by focusing on tactics.
Value accountability. Think of yourself as running a business within your organization—Team, Inc.	Leaders who have not defined their accountabilities are often frustrated by low-value activities. They blame executives for "not making good use of my skills."	If you were an independent business delivering your function within your organization, what would you stop? Start? Continue doing? [☞ 13.3 Accountability]
Be results-oriented—build organizational capital and growth; and people-oriented—build human capital and growth. [☞ 1.7 Results-Based Leaders]	Emphasizing results at the expense of people is a short-term tactic at best. Emphasizing people at the expense of business results bodes poorly for the long-term survival of the organization.	Typically, operating and financial measures need and receive a lot of attention. Expending an equal effort on assessing and developing people best ensures long-term organizational success. [☞ 13.9 Human Capital]
Manage complexity and cope with ambiguity. [☞ 6.3 Complex Situations]	Lack of tolerance for ambiguity and complexity pushes you and others to suboptimal, narrowly drawn problem definitions, solutions, and roles. [☞ 7.1 Problem Framing]	Take time to explore issues that might be too narrowly defined. Help ambiguity-phobic others by summarizing content and process frequently.

Challenge and support, but don't protect or compete with your own employees.	Leverage as a leader comes not only from getting results yourself, but also from helping others to achieve results. [☛ 1.7 Results-Based Leaders]	You will be valued as a leader and considered easier to work with if you see your success as the success of others. [☛ 13.10 Careers]
Understand your personal need for control, and the control needs of others. [☛ 9.4 Leader Impact]	Leaders' dysfunctional behaviors can usually be traced back to their need for control. Leaders need to let go and either trust their people or find new people. Leadership will be stressful unless you believe people want to do a great job.	Believe in people. Get feedback and coaching. It is extremely difficult to assess the impact of one's own behavior. Learn about the use and abuse of power. Your finest success is when your people have learned how to create their own success.
Don't blame others. From others' perspective, there is always a rationale for doing what they are doing.	Without this principle, you may tend to attribute negative motivations to others or push your own agenda on others. Either way, you become a very poor listener.	Refrain from categorizing people or groups as "They are all ...." If a person is "acting weird," talk privately with that person. People's behavior is always rational—as they see it. "Seek first to understand ...." [☛ 1.5 Seven Habits]
Listen for content and for process. [☛ 8.7 Active Listening]	Don't be content-bound. When talking about a situation, be as conscious of the process—*how* the situation is being worked—as you are about the content—*what* is being worked on.	Be aware of content *and* process. Many leaders think mainly in terms of their function and job—the content. Process concerns how content gets translated into results. Effective leaders are also aware of the emotions of others in a situation, and can respond with empathy when needed.
Surface and deal with conflict and resistance. [☛ 5.9 Resistance]	Resistance and conflict don't go away if ignored or suppressed. They just surface in other, more harmful ways.	Be clear about where you stand on issues. This takes self-awareness and courage. It also involves a level of discomfort, but that's the price leaders must pay to ensure an effective working environment.
Improve systems and processes. [☛ 2.1 Systems Thinking]	Joseph Juran notes that approximately 85% of problems can be corrected only by changing systems and processes. Thus, fewer than 15% can be remedied by training or changing people.	Remove systemic barriers to results. For example, if you want your Systems Analysts to be more client-focused, consider relocating them into the client's workspace.
Build partnerships with your people. The best leadership situations have a 50-50 feel. [☛ 9.10 Networking]	One-up leadership, whereby the boss does the thinking, is at best a short-term tactic in modern, knowledge-based organizations.	Encourage others to express their thoughts and feelings. Encourage neither dependence nor independence, but interdependence.
Be an expert in leadership as well as in your functional or technical field.	Without self-knowledge and self-awareness, you are condemned, like history, to repeat your past. [☛ 12.4 Feedback]	Learn leadership skills. Learn coaching skills. Watch and model leaders who are strategic and who get both business and people results. [☛ 13.1 Coaching]

How to use this leadership tool

"Without principles we are leaves in the wind pushed in every direction by every new idea."

—David Bly

Clarifying your personal leadership principles will:

✔ Develop your integrity as a leader.

✔ Clarify your leadership values, limits, and ethics.

✔ Help you explain your actions to others, including why you can't do something they might expect of you.

✔ Help you discuss underlying principles and needs, and avoid getting stuck on a position or arguing alternatives.

✔ Help guide your decisions and choices.

✔ Help you coach others.

✔ Help you create unique responses in novel situations.

WEB WORKSHEET

Don't be limited by the list of leadership principles in the table already provided. Prepare your own principles list. Since principles tend to be broad, overarching statements, make this list tangible by noting actions that you will start doing, stop doing, and continue doing to demonstrate each leadership principle within your workgroup or team.

Your leadership principle	Actions you will START doing to demonstrate this principle	Actions you will STOP doing to demonstrate this principle	Actions you will CONTINUE doing to demonstrate this principle

RELATED LEADERSHIP TOOLS

1.5 Seven Habits	1.11 Integrity	13.1 Coaching
1.8 Recursive Leadership	9.1 Leadership Versatility	15.3 JoHari Window

FOR FURTHER ASSISTANCE

Bellman, Geoffrey. *Getting Things Done When You Are Not in Charge*. Simon & Schuster, 1992.

Block, Peter. *The Empowered Manager: Positive Political Skills at Work*. Jossey Bass, 1987.

Block, Peter. *Stewardship: Choosing Service Over Self-Interest*. Berrett-Koehler, 1993.

Covey, Stephen. *The Seven Habits of Highly Effective People: Powerful Lessons in Personal Change*. Simon & Schuster, 1989.

Dalton, Gene, and Paul Thompson. *Novations: Strategies for Career Management*. Scott, Foresman and Company, 1986.

Kilmann, Ralph. *Beyond the Quick Fix: Managing Five Tracks to Organizational Success*. Jossey-Bass, 1984.

Ulrich, David, Jack Zenger, and Norman Smallwood. *Results-Based Leadership*. Harvard Business School Press, 1999.

1.5

THE BASIC HABITS AND PRACTICES OF SUCCESSFUL LEADERS

Inspired by Stephen Covey.

Stephen Covey notes that from the Enlightenment of the 1700s until the 1930s, a *character ethic* of leadership prevailed. This ethic held that leaders' characteristics (e.g., integrity, courage, patience, humility) were the basis of their success. Since the 1930s, however, a *personality ethic* has held sway. As a result, human and public relations skills, image management, positive attitudes, techniques, and quick fixes have dominated leadership thinking. Covey urges a return to the character ethic, arguing that skills and techniques are ineffective unless grounded in a leader's values, principles, and character.

Note to readers: The authors are acutely aware of the character versus personality critique. As a result, a number of tools described in this book examine the principles underlying leadership how-tos and techniques. When principles—guidelines for leadership conduct such as fairness, integrity, dignity—are deeply understood, accepted, and integrated with a leader's beliefs and thinking, the leader is then able to use leadership tools and techniques in highly congruent and effective ways. For an implicit critique of Covey's approach, see ☛ 1.7 Results-Based Leaders.

LEADERSHIP HABITS AND PRACTICES

Leadership habit	Related leader beliefs, thinking, and practices
Exercise initiative. (Be proactive.)	❑ Take responsibility for your own life, rather than blaming others. ❑ Know that you can "act, or be acted on." ❑ Work with the things you can do something about—within your "circle of influence." [☛ 9.4 Leader Impact] ❑ Lead by taking the lead, not only in your organization but also in your personal life. ❑ Encourage and coach others to foster these habits.
Create the future. (Begin with the end in mind.)	❑ Take the time to envision the future and refine what you are trying to accomplish. [☛ 2.4 Visioning] ❑ Value people who look at the big picture. ❑ Be continually aware that doing the right things comes before doing things right. [☛ 13.5 Time Management] ❑ Be aware that the faster your environment is changing, the more you will feel like controlling efficiencies. Yet your purpose, priorities, and direction need consideration.
Keep perspective. (Put first things first.)	❑ Have a clear mission statement that provides meaning, purpose, and direction. [☛ 2.3 Directional Statements] ❑ Ensure that your actions are aligned with your mission and based on values and principles you are proud of, not upon moods, feelings, and circumstances. ❑ Remember, the most important things in life are usually not urgent, are easy not to do, and are often avoided. [☛ 13.5 Time Management] ❑ Say "no" to the unimportant, no matter how urgent.

Foster interdependence. (Think win–win.)	❑ Seek agreements or solutions that are mutually beneficial to all parties. ❑ Encourage and foster relationships of mutual benefit. [☛ 9.5 Negotiation] ❑ Work from an abundance mind-set. Seek solutions that enlarge the pie. [☛ 14.1 Scarcity and Abundance]
Show empathy. (Seek first to understand, then to be understood.)	❑ Exercise patience and thoughtfulness, reflecting your understanding of what others have said, before seeking to be understood by them. ❑ Diagnose before you prescribe. ❑ Remember, it's impossible to influence people without first understanding them. [☛ 8.7 Active Listening]
Value differences. (Synergize.)	❑ Creativity is based in differences and seeing things in new ways. Foster a climate in which people will share their ideas and be open to each other. [☛ 6.7 Creativity and Innovation] ❑ Value different opinions and perspectives when seeking solutions. [☛ 14.7 Personal Preferences]
Continually improve. (Sharpen your saw.)	❑ Continuously renew the physical, intellectual, emotional, spiritual, and social dimensions of your life. ❑ Formulate a personal program to keep balance in your life, and encourage others to do the same. ❑ Continually become more self-aware through personal development activities (e.g., learning more about leadership, examining your actions to discover underlying principles, getting feedback and coaching).

HOW TO USE THIS LEADERSHIP TOOL

"Your attitude determines your attitude."

—Stephen Covey, *THE SEVEN HABITS OF HIGHLY EFFECTIVE PEOPLE*

It's one thing to know what to do; it's another thing to do it. Covey speaks of a positive learning spiral: committing and doing, which leads to learning, which leads to making more intelligent commitments and more effective action, which leads to additional learning, and so on. Use this workspace to begin your positive learning spiral.

WEB WORKSHEET

Leadership habit	Your strengths relative to this habit	Your development needs relative to this habit	Steps you will take to further develop your strengths, and to overcome your weaknesses
Exercise initiative. (Be proactive.)		[☛ 3.1 Strategy]	
Create the future. (Begin with the end in mind.)		[☛ 2.4 Visioning]	

Keep perspective. (Put first things first.)		[☛ 9.4 Leader Impact]	
Foster interdependence. (Think win–win.)		[☛ 10.1 HiPo Teams]	
Show empathy. (Seek first to understand, then to be understood.)		[☛ 8.7 Active Listening]	
Value differences. (Synergize.)		[☛ 14.7 Personal Preferences]	
Continually improve. (Sharpen your saw.)		[☛ 3.2 Sigmoid Curve]	

Related leadership tools

1.8 Recursive Leadership	4.4 Employee Involvement	9.1 Leadership Versatility
1.9 Paradigms	4.7 Job Satisfaction	9.4 Leader Impact
2.3 Directional Statements	5.1 Change Equation	13.5 Time Management

For further assistance

Covey, Stephen. *The Seven Habits of Highly Effective People: Powerful Lessons in Personal Change.* Simon & Schuster, 1989.

1.6 LEADERSHIP: THE BOARDS OF PLAY

Inspired by Will McWhinney, Bernie Novokowsky, Doug Smith, and Jim Webber.

Leadership fads and their terminology are tossed around like so much confetti—empowerment, quality, reengineering, values, goals, vision, networking, strategic advantage, transformation, to mention but a few. Often, proponents of each management theory sell the value of their own approach while pointing out deficiencies in other approaches. On occasion, a theorist comes along who tries to integrate these theories into a larger model.

This tool presents such a model, a way of looking at leadership in a novel way—as a board game (e.g., chessboard, Monopoly, or checkers game board). This model has four boards of play, each with its own rules, customs, and stakes. Playing a board game in a social setting is one way to learn a lot about players and leadership.

➡ The "games" leaders select depend on their worldviews and personalities. Some leaders expect others to define the rules and get very annoyed when rules are not clear or when they are violated; others want to define or redefine the rules to suit their needs.

➡ All leaders implicitly or explicitly select a board of play, based upon assumptions they make about their freedom of action, ranging from accepting and playing within all the rules (Board 1) to accepting no rules—trying to create a whole new game (Board 4).

➡ Leaders who can "play" at higher board levels necessarily have more power and influence than those at the lower levels.

Boards of play ➡	Supervision 1	Management 2	Leadership 3	Breakthrough leadership 4
Strategy of the leader	Work within policies—the "rules."	Establish policies—the "rules"; gain advantage.	Motivate through vision, values, and purpose.	Create new standards, strategic advantage, and paradigms.
Goal of leadership action	Enforce rules established by others.	Set the rules for others to follow within established organizational norms.	Determine the norms—what really matters inside the organization.	Invent new and better ways of organizing through new purposes, meanings, and strategies.
Success measure	Rules are followed.	New rules are established and enforced.	The organization works well within accepted benchmarks.	A new organizational paradigm or benchmark is set.

Major concerns as a leader	How to supervise competently	How to establish a power base to set the rules and control rewards	How to establish or change what is important to the organization	How to change the whole system, be the best at what you do
Leadership processes	Techniques and standards of supervision	Techniques of power and control, particularly over Board 1 supervisors	Understanding the big picture, coaching, empowerment, and group action	Visioning and systemic change, changing the paradigm
Sample tools from this book that would appeal	☛ 9.7 Selling Wheel ☛ 12.4 Feedback ☛ 13.7 Documenting Performance ☛ 14.5 On-Job Training	☛ 2.7 Goal Statements ☛ 5.7 Stakeholder Groups ☛ 13.3 Accountability	☛ 2.5 Values ☛ 2.6 Clarifying Purpose ☛ 2.8 Balanced Scorecard ☛ 7.1 Problem Framing ☛ 13.10 Careers	☛ 1.9 Paradigms ☛ 1.10 The GAS Model ☛ 2.1 Systems Thinking ☛ 2.4 Visioning ☛ 3.2 Sigmoid Curve

Hᴏᴡ ᴛᴏ ᴜsᴇ ᴛʜɪs ʟᴇᴀᴅᴇʀsʜɪᴘ ᴛᴏᴏʟ

"Games are consciously or implicitly played all the time. Expertise, power, value, and meaning are constant issues in our lives."
—Will McWhinney et al., *CREATING PATHS OF CHANGE*

This model can be helpful in a number of ways:

- for your own personal development—At which board do you presently lead (or want to lead), and what does this mean for you?
- to coach others—At what board is a protege operating and what is he or she capable of?
- to lead change—Change is more challenging at the higher boards of leadership.
- to design development events for others—The training and development needed at each board is dramatically different.

WEB WORKSHEET

For your own personal development, complete this worksheet:

1. Reading the descriptions of each board, on which board do you currently lead? What's your evidence? How might others have the same assessment of you?

2. Are you satisfied with leadership at this level for now?
   —If you are satisfied, what is your definition of success?

   —If you are satisfied, what development do you need to lead successfully at this board?

3. If you are dissatisfied, what skills do you need to develop in order to move to the next board?

RELATED LEADERSHIP TOOLS

1.2 Manage or Lead?	1.9 Paradigms	3.1 Strategy
1.4 Leader Principles	2.4 Visioning	13.10 Careers

FOR FURTHER ASSISTANCE

McWhinney, Will, ed. *Creating Paths of Change: Managing Issues and Resolving Problems in Organizations.* Sage Publishing, 1997.

1.7

THE LEADERSHIP RESULTS EQUATION

Inspired by Dave Ulrich, Jack Zenger, and Norm Smallwood.

Much has been written about the attributes of a successful leader—those hard-to-define terms such as character, habits, skills, motives, personal traits, and style. Yet neither leadership attributes nor financial results are sufficient in themselves. Besides having the "right stuff" as an effective leader, you need to use that stuff to produce business results. This tool will help you ascertain your own leadership attributes and make optimum use of those attributes to achieve four areas of results. The four areas go beyond financial measures to include organizational and employee results, customer results, and shareholder results. A leader is successful only when meaningful results are achieved in all four areas. Thus the equation:

Attributes × Business Results ⟹ Effective Leadership

Both leadership attributes and business results are necessary, and feed off each other.

Leadership attributes	Business results
What you **are**: ✔ values ✔ motives ✔ character ✔ traits	Organizational and employee results: ✔ aligning organizational culture with strategy ✔ maintaining strategic focus ✔ leading and managing people ✔ developing individual and organizational capabilities
What you **know**: ✔ abilities, skills ✔ technical and professional knowledge ✔ business knowledge	Customer results (internal or external): ✔ understanding your customer base ✔ customizing for customer needs ✔ creating long-term relationships
What you **do**: ✔ leadership behaviors ✔ competencies ✔ leadership style	Shareholder results (external investors, internal sponsors): ✔ responding to the organizational environment ✔ getting the numbers ✔ managing financial capital

In their best seller, *Results-Based Leadership,* David Ulrich et al. define a "Model of Balanced Outcomes."

	Process-centric	
Organization Results		Investor Results
Internal Focus	———————————	**External Focus**
Employee Results		Customer Results
	People-centric	

Leadership starts at the top, be this the top of organizations, business units, or project teams. Effective leaders:

- ❏ Clearly define results. [☞ 2.7 Goal Statements]
- ❏ Balance short- and long-term results in four areas: organizational, employees, customers, investors. [☞ 2.8 Balanced Scorecard]
- ❏ Are accountable, and hold others accountable, for results. [☞ 13.3 Accountability]
- ❏ Identify and apply the leadership attributes and practices needed to achieve results.
- ❏ Assess competency gaps for individuals and groups, and provide training to fill those gaps. [☞ 14.3 Needs Analysis]
- ❏ Realign systems (e.g., compensation programs) to develop desired leadership attributes and produce business results (Not infrequently, old systems set up barriers to employee performance.) [☞ 2.1 Systems Thinking, 5.6 Aligning Systems]
- ❏ Communicate, communicate, communicate (including plenty of two-way communication so others can provide feedback for midcourse corrections). [☞ 8.2 Direct Communication]
- ❏ Consistently model the attributes and behaviors they encourage others to practice. [☞ 1.8 Recursive Leadership]
- ❏ Follow through on promises and action plans. (The difference between a fad and a sustained success is ongoing follow-through.) [☞ 13.3 Accountability]

How to use this leadership tool

"It is faddish to think of leaders as people who master competencies and emanate character. Leaders do much more than demonstrate character. ... Effective leaders get results."
—Dave Ulrich, Jack Zenger, and Norm Smallwood, *RESULTS-BASED LEADERSHIP*

Effective leaders balance results in four areas (remember, these are more than financial measures): organizational results, employee results, customer or client results, and investor or stakeholder results. The point is to nurture the goose that is expected to lay the golden eggs. Thus, a results-based leader:

- ➡ Clearly sets out the balanced results expected—organizational, employee, customer, and investor.
- ➡ Defines the leadership attributes needed to achieve those results.
- ➡ Ensures that organizational systems (e.g., work design, compensation) are aligned to achieve these results.
- ➡ Follows through by rewarding achievement and holding all leaders in the organization accountable for desired results.

Use this matrix to spark your thinking about results-based leadership.

---

1. Clearly set out the balanced results expected.

   For **organizational** results, consider:
   - ❑ determining the organizational capabilities needed
   - ❑ aligning systems and business processes to produce results

   For **employee** results, consider:
   - ❑ determining the human capabilities needed
   - ❑ building employee commitment to results
   - ❑ designing or redesigning work processes and systems to support desired results

   For **customer or client** results, consider:
   - ❑ defining who your customers and clients are and are not [☛ 3.6 Strategic Relationships]
   - ❑ clearly determining how you add value for your customers
   - ❑ ensuring customer or client service systems are working effectively

   For **investor** results, consider these areas:
   - ❑ setting profit or revenue growth targets
   - ❑ managing costs

   Next steps:

   [☛ 2.1 Systems Thinking, 2.8 Balanced Scorecard, 5.7 Stakeholder Groups]

---

2. Define the leadership attributes needed to achieve those results. Consider:
   - ❑ competencies required—clearly linked to balanced business results
   - ❑ capabilities needed to design results systems and engage employees

   Next steps:

   [☛ 10.3 Team Competencies, 13.8 Competencies]

---

3. Ensure that organizational systems, and all leaders in the organization, are aligned with desired results. Consider:
   - ❑ work design and business processes
   - ❑ rewards and compensation systems
   - ❑ training in results-based leadership at all levels in the organization

   Next steps:

   [☛ 2.1 Systems Thinking, 2.2 7S Model, 4.1 Organizational Design, 4.3 Reengineering]

---

4. Follow through by holding leaders accountable for desired results.
   ❑ Use accountability agreements.
   ❑ Follow through on business plans and goals.
   ❑ Evaluate and reward achievement at all levels in the organization.

Next steps:

[☛ 13.3 Accountability]

RELATED LEADERSHIP TOOLS

1.2 Manage or Lead?	2.1 Systems Thinking	3.1 Strategy
1.8 Recursive Leadership	2.7 Goal Statements	13.3 Accountability

FOR FURTHER ASSISTANCE

Ulrich, David, Jack Zenger, and Norman Smallwood. *Results-Based Leadership.* Harvard Business School Press, 1999.

1.8

Recursive Leadership:
The Logic of Leadership

Inspired by Douglas Hofstader, Peter Block, and Geoff Bellman.

Children often delight in the game, "What's wrong with this picture?" whereby they find drawings of the moon and stars in the same sky as the sun. Please play along with this leadership version. Spurred on by a new emphasis on organizational creativity and innovation, Kelly, the leader of a professional group, announces at the next staff meeting: "Management says we need to be more creative and innovative. This new direction will help us prosper. So come back next week with your most creative ideas." The group members are excited to hear that percolating ideas will now be able to bubble up and improve their rather staid organization. At the next meeting, the first idea is met with, "This would cost a lot"; the second with, "I wonder whether they would go for this." The third never even made it to the table. What's wrong with this leadership picture?

This tool, in a novel way, extends a mathematical and computing science term, *recursion*, to explore some aspects of effective leadership. Recursion means to use a problem as part of its own solution. Recursion is perhaps easier to define by using an example of *non*recursion, like sending out a four-page memo on how to reduce paper communication! The meaning of recursion will become clearer through the examples in this tool.

The Most Effective Leadership Behavior—Recursion

This tool deals with just two aspects of recursive leadership:

1. Model the *behavior* you want from others.

    As a leader, the best way to encourage exemplary behavior in others is to model the behavior you want them to emulate. If you want openness, be open. If what you say is different from what you do, people quickly sense this, even if they can't put their finger on it. In his book, *The Ultimate Book of Business Gurus,* Stuart Crainer suggests that reengineering efforts often failed because " ... reengineering usually failed to impinge on management. Not surprisingly, managers were all too willing to impose the rigors of a process-based view of the business on others, but often unwilling to inflict it upon themselves."

2. Ensure the *process* is recursive, or congruent, with the *content*.

    If leaders want more creativity and innovation, they must design innovative and creative systems to deal with the ideas, including rejection! If "People are our most valuable resource" is touted, all processes and changes must have the valuable input of people built-in.

RECURSIVE MAXIM #1

The best way to elicit model behavior is to model the behavior you want from others.

    People are quick to sense disconnects between what is said versus what is actually being done.

Nonrecursive	Recursive
Others will find it hard to: • Listen to a leader who is not listening to them. • Accept feedback from a leader who does not accept feedback. • Give recognition to a leader who does not give them recognition. • Share confidences with a leader who cannot keep confidences. • Think highly of a leader who does not think highly of them. • Be innovative and creative with a leader who is not creative about creativity.	If you want others: ✔ to accept change—be open to change yourself. ✔ to consider you a leader—assume leadership roles. ✔ to be strategic with your time—be strategic with theirs. ✔ to open up—ask open-ended questions and be open to their answers. ✔ not to have hidden agendas with you—don't have hidden agendas with them. ✔ to be reasonable with you—be reasonable with them. ✔ to accept your inadequacies—admit to your own and accept their inadequacies. ✔ to exhibit model behavior—model model behavior.

    Many leadership gurus talk about authenticity as a basis for effective leadership. At the root of authenticity is a set of espoused leadership processes enacted in a recursively consistent way. Recursive thinking continually challenges a leader to ask, "Are what I say and what I do congruent with what I say I'm about?" Acting recursively minimizes disconnects. Recursion is at the heart of integrity. [☞ 1.11 Integrity]

RECURSIVE MAXIM #2

One reason a leadership tool fails is because the process isn't recursive with the content.

    Many of the tools in this book have had a roller-coaster ride. One example is management by objectives (MBO), with its slow ride up to acceptance, its giddy ride down, then up again, while gurus and leaders debated how to use the tool effectively. Finally, in frustration, MBO ground to a halt as leaders got off and ran to find another leadership tool. Recursively, it could be asked, "Do we truly understand the *goal* of a goal-setting program like MBO?"

    If a leadership tool is to succeed, it should be turned back on itself to ensure that the process mirrors itself. You may find as you read through this table that it reads like a series of mirrors reflecting one another.

Some leadership tools	If you want the tool to succeed:
Strategy clarification	✔ Have a clear strategy for the strategy clarification. ✔ Be strategic about clarifying and introducing a strategy. ✔ Be strategic about revising the strategy.
Goal setting	✔ Have a clear goal for setting goals. ✔ The point of goal setting is to have the end—the goal—drive the means. Don't let the process of producing goal statements overwhelm the end—results.
Value clarification	✔ Mirror the values while clarifying and communicating the values. For example, if a value is teamwork, use teamwork to clarify and introduce the values.

Creativity and innovation	✔ Be creative and innovative about how you elicit and deal with creativity and innovation. ✔ Be creative about rejecting unsuitable ideas.
Teamwork	✔ Use a team to introduce teams. ✔ Have the leadership operate as a team. ✔ Introduce teamwork in ways that are congruent with how you want your team to act.
Quality	✔ Ensure the quality program is designed as a *quality* quality program. ✔ Use quality tools to measure the success of and improve the quality program.
Accountability	✔ Be accountable for the accountability process. ✔ Visibly model your accountability statements.

These are a few recursive actions you could take to ensure congruence between the tool and the process used to formulate, introduce, and sustain it. The key technique is to ask the recursive question, "If XYZ is such a good leadership tool, if we turned it back on itself, what would it tell us about how to understand it, introduce it, and sustain it?"

HOW TO USE THIS LEADERSHIP TOOL

Recursive sayings:
Headline in the *Economist,* December 1999:
"*Rethinking Thinking*"
Marshall McLuhan: "*The medium is the message.*"
Roseanne of TV fame "*… Nobody gives you power. You just take it.*"
Groucho Marx made a career of recursive humor: "*Sincerity is the key to success. If you can fake that, you've got it made.*"

Some upsides of recursive leadership behavior:

✔ People will be more likely to accept you warts and all, because they know you are willing to accept them warts and all.

✔ One of the most powerful ways to elicit model behavior in others is to model the behavior you expect in others. People more often than not will mirror back your behavior.

Like all leadership models, there are downsides to recursive behavior:

✘ Recursive behavior doesn't always work. Some, for example, will take openness as a sign of weakness and try to exploit it. This leads us to a leadership principle: Nothing works all of the time when it comes to human behavior. Think about it: If behavior x always elicited behavior y on the part of others, you could then manipulate others' behavior (and be manipulated!).

✘ Recursive behavior sets a very high, perhaps ideal, standard of leadership conduct.

WEB WORKSHEET

Take a few minutes to apply recursion to your leadership role.

The behavior you expect in others	How you will model the behavior
"We need more teamwork around here."	*My leadership team needs to do team building first.* *My role with respect to my team needs to model how I expect other leaders to interact with their teams.*

A leadership tool you have or wish to use	How the tool needs to mirror itself
"We need more teamwork around here."	*Build an effective team to plan and introduce teams.* *Form a team to ensure that organizational systems support teamwork, not, as in most organizations, individual work.*

RELATED LEADERSHIP TOOLS

1.4 Leader Principles	1.10 The GAS Model	6.1 Logic Errors
1.9 Paradigms	1.11 Integrity	14.2 Rethinking Your Thinking

FOR FURTHER ASSISTANCE

Bellman, Geoffrey. *The Consultant's Calling: Bring Who You Are to What You Do.* Jossey-Bass, 1990.

Bellman, Geoffrey. *Getting Things Done When You Are Not in Charge.* Simon & Schuster, 1992.

Block, Peter. *Flawless Consulting: A Guide to Getting Your Expertise Used.* University Associates, 1978.

Hiebert, Murray. *Powerful Professionals: Getting Your Expertise Used Inside Organizations.* Recursion Press, 1999.

Hofstadter, Douglas R. *Godel, Escher, Bach: An Eternal Golden Braid.* Basic Books, 1999.

1.9 Understanding the Thinking Behind Your Thinking

Inspired by Stephen Covey, Peter Drucker, Thomas Kuhn, Peter Senge, Stephen Weinburg, Marvin Weisbord, and many others.

Is there a leader who hasn't heard of the word *paradigm*? Probably the most familiar paradigm shift in history was moving from thinking that the world was flat, to the stunning realization that it was round! Yet many explorers of the day continued business as usual, working within the "flat earth" paradigm. Needless to say, the explorers who adopted the new "round earth" paradigm were able to take advantage of huge economic expansion opportunities. Does any of this sound like the present-day paradigm shift to e-commerce?

The paradigm shifting process that Stephen Weinburg describes within scientific research is not dissimilar to paradigm shifts within the leadership field. He notes, "There are periods of 'normal science' ... (when) scientists tend to agree about what phenomena are relevant and what constitutes an explanation of these phenomena. ... Near the end of a period of 'normal science' a crisis occurs. ... There is alarm and confusion. Strange ideas fill the scientific literature. Eventually there is a revolution. Scientists become converted to a new way of looking at nature, resulting eventually in a new period of normal science. The 'paradigm' has shifted." Some of the major paradigm shifts within leadership have included participative management, planning and business strategy, and the changing nature of work and employment.

Leaders today need to understand their own mental maps or personal paradigms, and become efficient at making paradigm shifts. It's important to understand your personal and leadership paradigms because:

✔ If you don't understand the thinking behind your leadership ideas and tools and their limitations, they will almost certainly fail. (If you don't learn from history, you're bound to repeat it.)

✔ By understanding the paradigm behind a leadership tool, you are better able to refine and adapt it to your unique set of circumstances (and also challenge others who espouse easy answers to complex problems).

✔ True improvement and growth result from regularly challenging and revising your leadership paradigms.

The workplace change paradigm

Marvin Weisbord describes the paradigm shift in how work and processes are designed, and who is involved.

Work design paradigm	Elements of the paradigm	What challenged the paradigm?
About 1900: **Experts solve problems.**	• Fredrick Taylor's scientific management • Study, subdivide, and standardize work so that anyone can do it.	• The Hawthorne studies of the 1930s showed that productivity increased when workers were involved.
About 1950: **Everybody solves problems.**	• The Human Relations Movement and participative management studies show people can be more productive when they are involved.	• The knowledge that motivated people can be defeated by poorly designed systems. • Studies show that a combination of involved workers and well-designed work systems produces better results.
About 1965: **Experts improve systems.**	• The rise of the systems thinking and quality movements • Eric Trist and Fred Emory's sociotechnical design • Success of quality gurus with Japanese industry	• Success of Japanese management style of using quality tools combined with worker participation. • Rise of technical complexity and the knowledge worker—no expert could understand it all.
About 1985: **Everybody improves whole systems.**	• Open-book management • The total quality movement combining quality tools with teamwork • Systems thinking	• Rise of new economy, the Internet, and e-commerce • The changing employment contract, loss of corporate loyalty, and worker specialization and contracting out

PARADIGMS AND CHANGE

It is new entrants, not established players, who most often initiate the shift to a new paradigm. Defenders of traditional approaches can always point out problems with the new paradigm, as new paradigms seldom solve more than a few of the problems that confronted the old paradigm. Allegiance to the new paradigm is often a matter of faith, and cannot be forced. For this reason, the transition between competing paradigms cannot be made incrementally. A shift of underlying assumptions is required. Inevitably, as we enter the twenty-first century, new paradigms of organization and leadership are already in the process of being sorted out.

HOW TO USE THIS LEADERSHIP TOOL

"For a social discipline, such as management, the assumptions are actually a good deal more important than are the paradigms for a natural science. The paradigm—that is, the prevailing general theory—has no impact on the natural universe. Whether the paradigm states that the sun rotates around the earth, or that, on the contrary, the earth rotates around the sun, has no effect on sun and earth. But a social discipline, such as management, deals with the behavior of people and human institutions. The social universe has no 'natural laws' as the physical sciences do. It is thus subject to continuous change. This means that assumptions that were valid yesterday can become invalid and, indeed, totally misleading in no time at all."

—Peter Drucker, *FORBES MAGAZINE,* October 5, 1998

Often, paradigm shifts are not easily identified. Symptoms that an organizational paradigm shift may be happening are:

➡ Change seems overwhelming.

➡ People feel a loss of control over their lives, jobs, or careers.

➡ People who used to be confident are now feeling lost, confused, and baffled or threatened by what seem to be "new rules."

Even when identified, paradigm shifts can seem revolutionary, with people disagreeing about problems. With different underlying assumptions, people in the old and new paradigms live in different worlds. Thus, a principle or method that is impossible to grasp by one group is intuitively obvious to another group.

WEB WORKSHEET

Use the workspace provided to reflect on and prepare for paradigm change within your workgroup, organization, or industry.

As you read and hear strange ideas about the new economy, changing leadership, organizational issues, the changing marketplace, and so on, what issues do you feel the most uneasy about?
What do other people suggest, and what does your reaction to changing circumstances suggest to you, about your current leadership paradigm?
Is your organization or workgroup currently experiencing a paradigm shift? How would you describe this shift?
What are elements of your current leadership paradigm? How is it changing? [☛ 1.1 Twenty-First-Century Leader, 1.4 Leader Principles]
What people or groups, including you, may be feeling a loss as a result of these changes? What might they or you be losing? [☛ 5.8 Human Transitions]
Given that you support these changes, what steps might you or your workgroup take to ensure that resistance to needed changes is minimized, and that every opportunity is provided for the changes to succeed? [☛ 5.1 Change Equation]

RELATED LEADERSHIP TOOLS

1.1 Twenty-First-Century Leader	1.6 Boards of Play	3.1 Strategy
1.4 Leader Principles	2.1 Systems Thinking	3.2 Sigmoid Curve

FOR FURTHER ASSISTANCE

Covey, Stephen. *The Seven Habits of Highly Effective People: Powerful Lessons in Personal Change.* Simon & Schuster, 1989.

Drucker, Peter F. *Forbes Magazine,* October 5, 1998. http://www.forbes.com/forbes/98/1005/6207152a.htm (A wonderful review of leadership paradigms by the "*The* Sage of Management.")

Kuhn, Thomas S. *The Structure of Scientific Revolutions.* University of Chicago Press, 1996.

Senge, Peter M. *The Fifth Discipline: The Art and Practice of the Learning Organization.* Doubleday, 1990.

Senge, Peter M., Richard Ross, Bryan Smith, Charlotte Roberts, and Art Kleiner. *The Fifth Discipline Fieldbook: Strategies and Tools for Building a Learning Organization.* Currency Doubleday, 1994.

Weinberg, Steven. "The Revolution That Didn't Happen." *New York Review of Books*, October 8, 1998. http://www.nybooks.com/nyrev/WWWarchdisplay.cgi? 19981008048F.

Weisbord, Marvin Ross. *Productive Workplaces: Organizing and Managing for Dignity, Meaning, and Community.* Jossey-Bass, 1989.

1.10 THE GAS MODEL: DESIGNING PRACTICAL ORGANIZATIONAL PROCESSES

Inspired by Karl Weick.

Leadership processes in organizations are often so elegantly designed, they are not usable! For instance:

- An organization spent days crafting a mission, key result, and goal statements for every department and individual employee. These were tidily assembled into large binders, which subsequently were rarely opened.
- A task force spent countless hours developing a performance management system that was never implemented in any meaningful way.
- An enthusiastic executive returns from a time management training seminar, hastily demands that all employees in the department start using the process taught in the seminar, then wonders why others are not as enthusiastic.

This tool will help you optimally design, or redesign, leadership processes. It guides leaders in making the necessary trade-offs to ensure that processes are practical and usable.

The ideal leadership process is threefold: It is simultaneously general, accurate, and simple (GAS).

1. It is General in its use (i.e., it works over a wide range of circumstances, beneficial for executives, yet useful for frontline workers).
2. It is Accurate or precise in its use (i.e., it accurately describes the unique situations in all departments—past, present, and future—without being exclusive or limiting to any one department).
3. It is Simple to use (i.e., no one will need much training to use the process).

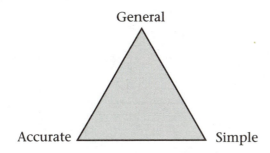

An example is an organization that wants a **simple**-to-use career program—no need for large information binders and arduous training programs. If the career program is **general**, it can be used in all parts and levels of the organization (e.g., systems analysts, engineers, librarians, accountants, and so on). If it is **accurate**, the process will precisely describe the career development paths of all positions in the company, without being specific to any one discipline or profession. Here's the catch: It is impossible to maximize all three dimensions (general, accurate, simple) when designing the process. Trade-offs are inevitable. For example, as accuracy improves, the process becomes less and less simple (i.e., the binder of detailed information begins to pile up).

The catch to the General-Accurate-Simple (GAS) model is that you can have only two of the three! If you design a process that is General and Simple, some may challenge its Accuracy by saying, "You need to be more specific for my department by adding...." This leads to elaborating on the process to make it more Accurate. If you make the process Accurate and Simple for one department, it will be less General for other departments. Thus, leaders must inevitably make trade-offs and consider the most useful balance between these three dimensions when designing a process.

In case you think that only leadership models are subject to the GAS model, consider one of the most powerful formulas in physics, Newton's second law: $F = ma$. It only works well when the velocity of the object is far from the speed of light. As velocity approaches the speed of light, you need to use Einstein's insights on relativity—no longer simple, but more accurate.

How to use this leadership tool

"I think [many leadership models] are uninformative and pedestrian partly because people have tried to make them general and accurate and simple. In trying to accommodate all three of these aims, none have been realized vigorously; the result has been bland assertions."

—Karl Weick, *THE SOCIAL PSYCHOLOGY OF LEARNING*

Think of a leadership process that you will be designing or redesigning in the near future (e.g., performance management, strategic planning, goal setting, accountability, career development, compensation, and so on). Assess this process in terms of the GAS model. What trade-offs are needed so that the process is useful and usable in your organization?

WEB WORKSHEET

Name of leadership process: _____

Level of *Generality* needed and why	
Level of *Accuracy* needed and why	

Level of *Simplicity* needed and why	
Trade-offs required and why	

RELATED LEADERSHIP TOOLS

1.8 Recursive Leadership	2.8 Balanced Scorecard	6.5 Force-Field Analysis
2.1 Systems Thinking	4.1 Organizational Design	7.4 Polarities

FOR FURTHER ASSISTANCE

Weick, Karl. *The Social Psychology of Organizing*. McGraw-Hill College Division, 1979.

1.11   INTEGRITY: GUT-LEVEL ETHICS

Contributed by Layton Fisher and inspired by Gay Hendricks and Kate Ludeman.

Integrity and its cousin, ethical behavior, are at the core of long-term successful leadership. Personal integrity, particularly of leaders, is the source and foundation of organizational integrity and ethics. This tool takes the cerebral concept of ethics and places it where you can understand and act on it—at gut level.

Think back to a gathering of some type, a meeting or even a dinner with friends, a time when you noticed something in your body telling you, "Something isn't right here!" You feel tension rise within you. You lose your sense of ease and ability to act spontaneously. A question of integrity has surfaced. Someone's opinion or behavior is hard for you to accept.

Integrity boils down to:

✔ being authentic with yourself,

✔ being authentic with others, and

✔ doing what you say you will do.

BEING AUTHENTIC WITH YOURSELF AS A LEADER

You will respect yourself more when your feelings and your actions are in alignment or congruent. Biologically, the human brain is set up such that external stimuli come first through the primordial limbic brain. Put simply, things are *felt* before they are relayed to the thinking center of the brain and brought into consciousness. To better understand your feelings, tune into your body's signals—dry throat, shoulder tension, or a lump in your stomach—any of which may be trying to tell you that something is out of whack here.

➡ First, you sense an emotion such as fear, anger, or sadness.

➡ Second, you need to name the emotion, to acknowledge the emotion to yourself: "I'm angry," "I'm scared," or "I'm sad." This is necessary because, although feelings live in the body, dealing with them requires that you bring them into consciousness.

➡ Third, to act on your feeling, it's necessary to think about what might have triggered or caused this feeling. For example, "I'm apprehensive right now because I hear us agreeing to an action I believe to be at odds with our policy. This could cause our employees to lose trust in us."

The right opening to speak up can sometimes pass quickly in organizations, and people often regret their silence and having missed the opportunity to lead. Stay connected to your feelings; acting with integrity creates a powerful model for others to trust their own feelings and speak their own truths.

BEING AUTHENTIC WITH OTHERS AS A LEADER

This means there's congruence between what you say and how you act (the audio matches the video). Are there distortions, untruths, or omissions in your communications with others: Big or little? Active or passive? If yes, first acknowledge this to yourself, then clear up any potential misunderstandings with the appropriate other person(s). For example, "Bernie, even though I assured you that your budget would not be cut, I already knew that corporate was planning a cut, and I knew that it would apply to everyone. I'm sorry I didn't make that clear." This kind of action can surprise you. Although you may fear you have betrayed a trust, Bernie may be grateful and trust may be enhanced in the long run.

DOING WHAT YOU SAY YOU WILL DO—KEEPING YOUR PROMISES AS A LEADER

This is about keeping your promises and agreements—delivering on what you said you would do (or not do). There's an old joke that having someone to blame is nearly as good as having a solution to the problem! Indeed, in this age of spin-doctoring, a story is sometimes offered as a replacement for good performance. However, there is less and less room for habitual excuse-makers in organizations today. Clarify agreements (put the important ones in writing), keep your agreements, and make only those agreements that you are committed to keeping. If, for some legitimate reason, you can't keep an agreement, renegotiate promptly. Finally, accept responsibility if you fail to meet an agreement. In this way, you contribute to developing a culture of integrity within your organization. That's a leadership contribution and a legacy you can be proud of.

HOW TO USE THIS LEADERSHIP TOOL

"There is no such thing as a minor lapse of integrity."
—Tom Peters, *THE TOM PETERS SEMINAR*

WEB WORKSHEET

Most leaders are well-intentioned and want to act in an integral and ethical way. Yet, while we judge ourselves by our intentions, others only know us through their interpretation of our behavior. Answer the questions presented here to examine your intentions and integrity. After you have answered the questions to your own satisfaction, you may wish to work with a trusted leadership coach. In this way, you'll have an opportunity to more clearly understand how others might be viewing your behavior, despite your intentions.

Being authentic with yourself as a leader
When and under what circumstances are you at ease with yourself and with the way you deal with other people?
What are your leadership pinch points—leadership situations in which you feel out of sync with yourself?
Are there situations in your life (business, leadership, home life) in which you feel you are living a lie? Briefly describe one such situation.

What actions will you take to begin living and leading more authentically?

Being authentic with others as a leader

Where are there distortions in your communications with others—colleagues, reports, customers, and so on?

When have you been guilty of spin-doctoring an event to make yourself look better?

What do you need to do to square yourself with these people? What is your biggest fear when you speak the truth with these people?

[☛ 1.8 Recursive Leadership]

Doing what you say you will do and keeping your promises as a leader

When do you avoid accountability for your actions (e.g., making excuses, laying blame)?

Which past agreements remain unfulfilled and need to be renegotiated?

What do you need to do in order to be clearer about your agreements and to follow through?

Related leadership tools

1.4 Leader Principles	2.5 Values	15.1 Balance
1.5 Seven Habits	12.2 Trust	15.2 Emotional Intelligence
1.8 Recursive Leadership	13.3 Accountability	15.7 Stress

For further assistance

Hendricks, Gay, and Kate Ludeman. *The Corporate Mystic: A Guidebook for Visionaries with Their Feet on the Ground.* Bantam, 1996.

2

Tools for Big-Picture Thinking

One organizational guru, Eliot Jaques, proposes that leadership compensation systems be based on the length of time a leader needs to look into the future. Another guru, Peter Senge, says another variable, breadth, should be factored in. Together, they make the case for this section—the need for successful leaders to understand and use big-picture thinking tools.

2.1

Introduction to Systems Thinking for Leaders

Inspired by Peter Scholtes and Peter Senge.

"All the empowered, motivated, teamed-up, self-directed, incentivized, accountable, reengineered, and reinvented people you can muster cannot compensate for a dysfunctional system," says Peter Scholtes, systems thinking proponent. In this book, we choose more middle ground—although systems are extremely important and the most leveraged place to improve, we contend that leaders lead much more than well-oiled systems. In fact, most leaders cannot change most of the systems in which they lead! No one would propose that his or her organization is the perfect system, because systems are composed of imperfect people. Then there is the example of motivated, self-directed, accountable people trying to make the best of a bad system in the TV series *M*A*S*H*.

This tool will introduce you to the elements of systems thinking and analysis. As leaders, we suggest that you look to systems improvement first; however, we also urge you to find, refine, and use the other tools in this book, as needed.

What is systems thinking?

A system is a collection of interrelated and interdependent processes and subsystems which, together, produce a result. Any system, other than perhaps the universe itself, is part of a larger system. What you consider a system is somewhat arbitrary. For example, the Financial Services department in an organization could be considered a system, with Budgeting, Reporting, Accounts Receivable, and Accounts Payable as subsystems. Each of these subsystems, Accounts Payable for example, has additional systems within it. It may sound confusing, but where you draw the line determines the system you want to examine. Where you draw the line sets boundaries for the system, and makes it what is called a closed system. In the past, departments acted like closed systems and created what were often called stovepipes or functional silos. Departments that acted like closed systems acted as if the organization was set up to do accounting, systems, engineering, and so forth. One characteristic of modern leadership is the opening up of systems to thoroughly consider how one organizational system—financial services, for example—fits into the larger system. Wal-Mart, for example, revolutionized the retail business by considering its suppliers part of its customer service system.

Systems thinking is looking for patterns inside and outside the system, then understanding and optimizing the overall system. Your thinking about a system changes depending on your purpose for examining it. Separating a subsystem from the larger system (drawing a box around it in order to isolate it) is a useful step in getting a manageable picture of the subsystem itself, before removing the box to see where the subsystem fits into the larger picture. Seeing and diagramming a system like your organization is a very creative process. Some conceptualizations of systems can lead to better results than others.

To illustrate systems thinking, we use the example of a car as a system. If you consult an automobile repair manual, a car is composed of dozens of subsystems—motor, electrical system, transmission, sound system, steering system, braking system—and hundreds of parts—radio, CD or DVD, speakers, and wiring (also part of the electrical system).

The car-as-a-system example	Some implications for leaders
➡ A system—the car—is much more than the sum of its parts. One could put all the parts of a car into a garage and not have a car. Often, with the breakdown of a single part, the whole system breaks down.	✔ The whole organizational system is greater than the sum of its parts. The interrelations and interdependencies are as important as the parts (the subsystems). A single poorly integrated subsystem weakens the whole organization. (People systems are more robust than mechanical systems, because people can and will work around poor systems).
➡ Each system is a subsystem of a larger system. A car would not be a useful system without a system of roads and fueling stations. For example, one difficulty with electrical cars is the lack of recharging stations.	✔ As leader of a subsystem, remember that you are always part of the larger system, which *also* includes external systems of suppliers, customers, clients, competitors, consultants, governments, and society.
➡ Each subsystem of a great car is actually **suboptimized**! For example, the world's best transmission would be too big, too heavy, or too expensive for the world's best car. The trick is to suboptimize each subsystem to optimize the whole system.	✔ The need for suboptimized subsystems is at the heart of many leadership problems. Each leader has to suboptimize his or her subsystem if the whole organization is to be optimal. As Peter Senge puts it, "… in systems … in order for you to succeed, others must succeed as well."
➡ To change one subsystem of a car—for example, to change from two-wheel to all-wheel drive—requires a number of changes in other systems, including transmission, wheel assembly, brakes, and so on.	✔ Any major change requires changes in many other interacting systems to make it work. Change more often sputters or fails because it conflicts with existing systems set up to support another result! [☛ 4.1 Organizational Design]

A typical organizational system can be illustrated, at a high level, as:

Purpose	Inputs	Value-Adding Processes	Results	Benefits to Stakeholders
A system is driven by its purpose and goals. (A car designed for fuel efficiency would need quite different system thinking than would a racing car.)	Every system depends on quality inputs—suppliers, services, and raw materials from other systems.	An organization, team, or business unit must have its internal systems fine-tuned to add value to the inputs and produce results.	Results are measured against targets, customer acceptance, quality standards, competitors, and so on.	Stakeholders can include clients, customers, employees, investors, the community, the country, and so on.

> *"... most of the problems faced by mankind concern ... our inability to grasp and manage the increasingly complex systems of our world."*
> —Peter Senge, *THE FIFTH DISCIPLINE*

Every organizational subsystem is part of a larger system. Any organization's success depends on the success of its subsystems. A pertinent example is the design of a leadership development system. Let's assume you want to design or redesign your leadership development system so it is more effective.

1. The first step is to set a clear purpose and goals for the system.

2. Since there is no one best way to illustrate a system, the next two steps are probably best done iteratively:

  ⟹ Diagram the Leadership Development system, drawing a boundary around it, in order to get the results you need. This closed-system diagram would include the major subsystems and processes needed to increase leadership effectiveness; for example, a needs assessment process, an administrative subsystem, an evaluation and feedback subsystem, a delivery subsystem, and so forth. Don't go too far down this road before you look at the larger system.

  ⟹ Next, diagram the Leadership Development system in terms of how it fits with other subsystems and with the organizational system as a whole.

One ***partial and simple*** illustration of external connections is shown here:

3. Now, analyze the system diagrams for bottlenecks, breakdowns, and leverage points. For example, much leadership training is not nearly as effective as it could be, for some of these systemic reasons:

  • There's no point in designing a closed leadership development system that is not supported by, and does not support, other organizational systems. However, leadership development professionals, in response to other systems' resistance, often try to design even more elegant leadership development systems, thereby increasing resistance from those interacting systems! Remember, in systems, more of the same rarely works.

- Looking around the interacting systems, note where there will be support and where there will be problems. You may find that much leadership development is disconnected from organizational strategy. For example, training often leads to frustration when the trainee can see a better way of working, yet is unable to implement it! Often, the compensation system works against development. If a leader, for instance, wants to initiate the team concept and the current compensation is firmly tied to individual performance, the team concept will struggle.

- After bottlenecks are identified, the systems designer is faced with:

    a. working to change the interacting systems to make them more supportive, or

    b. suboptimizing the leadership development system so it will work better within the larger system, or

    c. both (a) and (b).

WEB WORKSHEET

Y OUR APPLICATION

1. Think of a system within your area of responsibility.

2. Write the purpose and goals for the system as you would like it to be.

[☛ 2.6 Clarifying Purpose, 2.7 Goal Statements]

3. Diagram first the internal system (the closed system, with its own internal processes); then the external system (the open system, showing how the closed system fits with other organizational systems).
Don't worry about drawing a perfect diagram initially; the diagram will always be imperfect. Be willing to go through a number of drafts until you get one that is helpful to you and others.

4. As above, examine the subsystems to optimize the system.

[☛5.6 Aligning Systems]

RELATED LEADERSHIP TOOLS

2.2 7S model	4.3 Reengineering	5.6 Aligning Systems
4.1 Organizational Design	5.1 Change Equation	5.7 Stakeholder Groups

FOR FURTHER ASSISTANCE

Block, Peter. *Stewardship: Choosing Service Over Self-Interest.* Berrett-Koehler, 1993.

Kotter, John. *Leading Change.* Harvard Business School Press, 1996.

Senge, Peter M. *The Fifth Discipline: The Art and Practice of the Learning Organization.* Doubleday, 1990.

Senge, Peter, Richard Ross, Bryan Smith, Charlotte Roberts, and Art Kleiner. *The Fifth Discipline Fieldbook: Strategies and Tools for Building a Learning Organization.* Currency Doubleday, 1994.

2.2 THE 7S MODEL: ALIGNING FOR SUCCESS

Inspired by Stuart Crainer, Tracey Goss, Richard Pascale, Anthony Athos, Tom Peters, and Robert Waterman.

The *7S model* is one of many frameworks that will encourage leaders to think systemically, particularly when planning large systems or systemwide change within an organization (e.g., starting up a project, redesigning a workgroup or team, coaching other leaders to make changes within the organization). Peters and Waterman observed that leaders using this model got "more done because they could pay more attention with all seven S's instead of just two." (Traditionally, the only two S's that leaders *did* pay attention to were strategy and structure.)

Your organization is full of interacting systems—sales, accounting, promotions, compensation, inventory, performance assessment, and development, just to mention a few. Within each of these systems are more systems; for example, accounting may have systems for budgeting, invoicing, accounts payable, expense accounts, and so on. In an ideal situation, all these systems are aligned to achieve well-defined goals with spectacular results. The less than ideal is more common; a normal organization continually wrestles with misaligned systems. Much of a leader's energy is expended in trying to accomplish something while dealing with organizational systems that seem designed for different purposes.

Sometimes referred to as the hard S's, the three more rational, understandable or visible, measurable, and formal aspects of organization design are:

Structure—how people are organized to do the work; division of roles and responsibilities.
(Information) Systems—information and how it is shared; measurement.
Strategy—the direction and goals of the organization or business unit.

Sometimes known as the soft S's, and four aspects often ignored to the peril of change programs, are:

Staff—people; the demographics of those who work in the organization.
Skills—competencies and skills needed to run the organization.
Style—how the organization is led (e.g., participatory, team, top-down).
Shared values—values espoused and practiced by the organization (e.g., entrepreneurship, innovation).

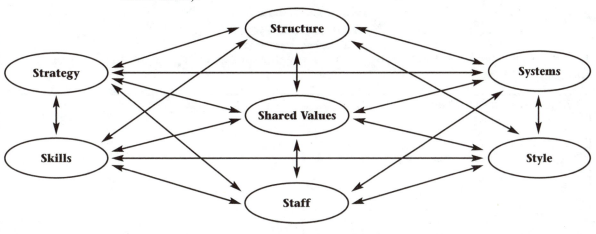

This graphical illustration of a misaligned organization speaks volumes about the need for alignment!

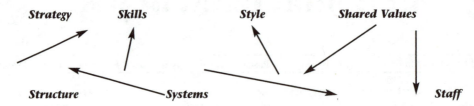

HOW TO USE THIS LEADERSHIP TOOL

"In retrospect, what our framework (the 7S model) has really done is remind the world of professional managers that 'soft is hard.' It has enabled us to say, in effect, 'All that stuff you have been dismissing for so long as intractable, irrational, intuitive, informal organization can be managed.'"

—Tom Peters and Robert Waterman, *IN SEARCH OF EXCELLENCE*

If your organization is struggling, it could be because of a misalignment among the 7 S's—one or more of the S's is not supporting the others. Often, restructuring is the first or only solution considered. (We suggest that this solution, used in isolation from the other 6 S's, has a lot in common with reshuffling the chairs on the *Titanic*.) Don't attempt change by focusing on only one or two of the 7 S's. Rather, use this tool to examine organizational change from a systemic point of view.

Another application for this tool is in planning change. Change often fails because it is not supported by other interacting systems. Many leaders try to push through change by concentrating on the excellence of the change itself. More often, it is more effective and economical to concentrate effort on aligning those subsystems that may impede or support the proposed change. In planning change, leaders need to identify the 7 S's, starting most often with Strategy, and ask:

? Which S's support our Strategy?

? Which S's (more specifically which parts of any S) might inhibit or be barriers to our Strategy?

? What can we do to turn around or reduce the barriers?

WEB WORKSHEET

Use the space here to systemically plan an organizational change with the help of the 7S model.

The initiative you need to plan:

Strategy	How will this initiative support the direction and goals of the organization? Of my workgroup?
	[☛ 2.3 Directional Statements]
Structure	How would people be most appropriately organized to support and achieve this initiative (e.g., teams, matrix structure, cross-functional project groups, organizational chart, and so on)?
	[☛ 4.1 Organizational Design]
Systems	What information, processes, communication, and measurements will need to be adjusted to support this initiative?
	[☛ 5.6 Aligning Systems]
Shared values	How does this initiative fit with the shared values of the organization? Of my workgroup?
	[☛ 2.5 Values, 4.5 Culture]
Style	What leadership style supports (or hinders) this initiative? Ideally, what leadership style would fit best with this initiative?
	[☛ 9.1 Leadership Versatility]
Staff	What kinds of people are needed to support this initiative? Who should be on the project team?
Skills	What knowledge and skills will be needed within the organization to support and achieve this initiative? What knowledge and skills currently exist, and what will need to be built?
	[☛ 13.8 Competencies]

RELATED LEADERSHIP TOOLS

1.9 Paradigms	3.3 Environmental Scan	5.2 Major Change
2.1 Systems Thinking	5.1 Change Equation	5.7 Stakeholder Groups

FOR FURTHER ASSISTANCE

Crainer, Stuart. *The Ultimate Business Library: 50 Books That Shaped Management Thinking.* Amacom, 1997. (Tells the story of how Pascale and Athos contributed to the model.)

Goss, Tracey, Richard Pascale, and Anthony Athos. "The Reinvention Roller Coaster: Risking the Present for a Powerful Future." *Harvard Business Review.* 1993.

Peters, Thomas, and Robert H. Waterman. *In Search of Excellence: Lessons from America's Best-Run Companies.* Harper & Row, 1981.

2.3

DIRECTIONAL STATEMENTS:
THREE LEVELS OF CLARITY

Inspired by Alan Wilkins.

A key responsibility and ongoing challenge for leaders involves defining a clear direction for their workgroup, department, or organization, and aligning action with this organizational direction. Yet there remains considerable confusion as to how this is best achieved. The Babel of terms is bewildering—mission, purpose, strategy, values, beliefs, goals, objectives, vision, to mention but a few.

Workgroups or organizations often go to considerable effort to produce a set of directional statements, only to find that they lack practical impact, or even worse, that they have become a source of scorn (witness the popularity of *Dilbert* cartoons!). This tool will help you:

✔ Determine the directional statements that will provide focus and energy for your workgroup.

✔ Develop directional statements that are congruent with your organization's mission, and that lead to commitment and results on behalf of your clients.

✔ Help everyone understand the words, logic, and meaning of your directional statements.

Three levels of directional thinking and statements are shown in the table:

1. *High-level statements* encapsulate an overall reason for being, key values, and long-term direction. Like a constitution, these big-picture statements are expected to inspire and endure over a long time. They need to be concise, yet packed with meaning and capable of capturing people's interest within a few minutes. These statements guide long-term direction.

2. *Mid-level statements* determine direction and priorities for a shorter time frame—a few months to a few years. Like a rudder on a ship, these statements guide immediate direction.

3. *Action-level statements*—the "how to's"—determine how you will actually go about accomplishing the goals set out in the mid- and high-level statements. These statements guide action and follow-through.

Levels of Statements		Flow of Statements		

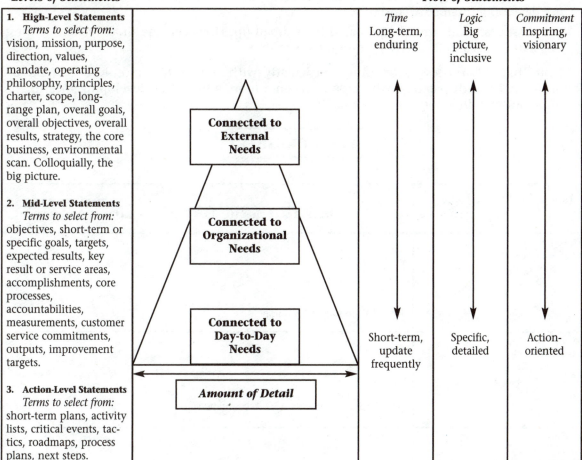

Levels of Statements

1. High-Level Statements
Terms to select from: vision, mission, purpose, direction, values, mandate, operating philosophy, principles, charter, scope, long-range plan, overall goals, overall objectives, overall results, strategy, the core business, environmental scan. Colloquially, the big picture.

2. Mid-Level Statements
Terms to select from: objectives, short-term or specific goals, targets, expected results, key result or service areas, accomplishments, core processes, accountabilities, measurements, customer service commitments, outputs, improvement targets.

3. Action-Level Statements
Terms to select from: short-term plans, activity lists, critical events, tactics, roadmaps, process plans, next steps.

Connected to External Needs

Connected to Organizational Needs

Connected to Day-to-Day Needs

Amount of Detail

Flow of Statements

Time Long-term, enduring — Short-term, update frequently

Logic Big picture, inclusive — Specific, detailed

Commitment Inspiring, visionary — Action-oriented

H OW TO USE THIS LEADERSHIP TOOL

"Requiring everyone to continually 'nest his or her vision' in new practices or a continuation of the old … can produce increased understanding of what is worth doing and what is not."
—Alan Wilkins, *DEVELOPING CORPORATE CHARACTER*

If you, as a leader, don't provide any structure, people will feel that there is no mechanism or process through which they can contribute. If you provide too much detail and structure, however, people will feel that "It's a done deal," and their contributions are not required. Thus, we suggest this minimal level of structure for designing directional statements:

❶ As the leader, start by defining your *givens*—the minimum specifications of either content or process that you feel are essential elements of the directional statements.

❷ Explain and discuss your thinking with your workgroup. Then ask each member of your workgroup to draft each level of directional statement within the agreed guidelines on his or her own. The table provided here will assist in this process.

❸ Next, have the group come together as a whole to review these drafts, test assumptions, develop refinements, and seek synergies.

❹ Final drafts can then be prepared by a subgroup. However, the final version of these statements should have full group consensus.

Note that this process is ongoing, particularly with respect to action-level statements. You'll find that, with practice, workgroups become more efficient at developing meaningful and motivational directional statements.

WEB WORKSHEET

Statement level	Selected term(s)	Draft of statement(s)	Next steps to complete statement
High-Level Statements		[☛ 2.4 Visioning, 2.5 Values]	
Mid-Level Statements		[☛ 2.7 Goal Statements, 13.3 Accountability]	
Action-Level Statements		[☛ 10.12 RASCI Planning]	

RELATED LEADERSHIP TOOLS

2.4 Visioning	2.7 Goal Statements	13.3 Accountability
2.6 Clarifying Purpose	11.1 Process Cycle	13.4 MBO

FOR FURTHER ASSISTANCE

Wilkins, Alan. *Developing Corporate Character: How to Successfully Change an Organization without Destroying It.* Jossey-Bass, 1989.

2.4   VISIONING AND VISION STATEMENTS

Inspired by Peter Block, John Kotter, and Peter Senge.

A key distinction of a leader is the ability to shape the future. The starting point for this is a clear vision. Sports psychologists are clear: World-class athletes spend considerable time visualizing the superior performances they desire to attain. This tool will assist you with visioning, then writing a compelling vision statement. The vision of this tool is to inspire you to create, with others, an inspiring vision!

Some principles for establishing a powerful vision are:

✔ It is different from goals and objectives (time-limited targets aligned with the vision).

✔ It needs to inspire and motivate the hearts and minds of others, creating a picture of a better future and a shared sense of direction, while enrolling others in aligned action.

✔ It pushes people beyond their comfortable routines, while respecting the past, by being rooted in the realities of customers, shareholders, employees, markets, and other environmental forces.

✔ It needs to be strategic, based in customer and client needs, the touchstone for future decisions and plans, encouraging accountable actions that are congruent with the vision.

✔ It may never be totally achieved; neither is it pie-in-the-sky, turning off the concrete-thinking people needed to attain the vision.

✔ It can be explained in five minutes or less; if it can't, you will have lost the attention and interest of others.

It is dangerous to use an existing vision as an example of a well-crafted vision, because successful organizations ebb and flow. Your best bet for current exemplars is to search the Web sites of organizations you admire. One example is Ford Motor Company:

"Our vision is to be the world's leading automotive company, from the viewpoint of our customers, shareholders, and employees. To achieve that vision, we're rebuilding our company around a simple premise: Everything we do must maximize the quality and value of our products for our customers, or we shouldn't do it. By creating the greatest value for our customers at the lowest cost to Ford, we'll increase our company's value to our shareholders."

How does a vision statement fit with other statements?

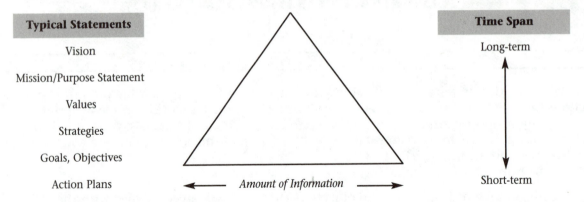

Typical Statements		Time Span
Vision		Long-term
Mission/Purpose Statement		
Values		
Strategies		
Goals, Objectives		
Action Plans	← *Amount of Information* →	Short-term

If you lead a unit or a project inside a larger organization, your vision should be nested inside the larger organizational vision.

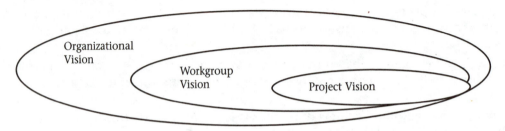

How to use this leadership tool

In Jack Welch's GE, "There is no room for anyone who is not an 'A' player ... with a vision and the ability to articulate that vision to others so vividly and powerfully that it becomes their vision."

—Mikel Harry and Richard Schroeder, *SIX SIGMA*

Creating a vision statement can be a messy process. Most vision statements start with an individual and are refined through a number of iterations. It takes time and energy to develop and communicate a statement, garner support, and, most importantly, achieve aligned action. Don't get bogged down. Remember Shaun Murphy's saying, "It's better to have vision than a vision statement."

1. First draft by an individual leader:
   - Note the principles for establishing a vision, and the reality checks listed in the next section.
   - Be clear about your givens and where you need help. (You may have difficulty enrolling others if you are too rigid about your statement. Conversely, a vision-by-committee will rarely be engaging.)

2. Vet with some key stakeholders:
   - Explain what you are trying to do with a vision statement and why.
   - Verbally present your emerging vision.
   - Ask for participation and feedback.
   - Explain your process.

     [☛ 5.7 Stakeholder Groups, 10.7 Getting Participation]
3. Redraft:
   - Check for system and environmental alignment: Where will current realities and systems be out of sync and give rise to cynical reactions?

     [☛ 2.2 7S Model, 5.6 Aligning Systems]
4. Refine with a larger group of stakeholders:
   - Start the systems alignment and action process.
   - See Change Leadership tools: a vision significantly different from the current one starts a series of changes to support the new vision.

     [☛5.1 Change Equation]
5. Publicize through a multiple process:
   - First and foremost, through personal explanations.
   - Continue and sustain the changes that flow from the vision.

     [☛8.3 Organizational Communication]

"Where is this real world everybody keeps talking about?"
© Ashleigh Brilliant

Visioning reality checks

❑ Can I and others explain this vision to any stakeholder in five minutes or less?

❑ With what other visions—previous or other leaders or stakeholders—might this be in conflict? (Note that these visions may be implicit—not clearly written or stated—but driving action nonetheless.)
   - If you lead a unit within a larger organization, do these visions nest? (See diagram.)

❑ If this vision were made real, how would it affect:
   - customers, users, and clients?
   - shareholders, stockholders, and stakeholders?
   - employees?

❑ Would this pass the Bulletin Board test?
   - What would people say if you could hear their thoughts and personal conversations as they read it for the first time? (On the other hand, cynics are always with us. You can't be sidetracked by them.)
   - What reservations would the stakeholders have? How could they be dealt with?

❑ Am I willing to lead the changes that flow from the new vision?

RELATED LEADERSHIP TOOLS

1.10 The GAS Model	2.3 Directional Statements	3.2 Sigmoid Curve
2.2 7S Model	2.6 Clarifying Purpose	5.1 Change Equation

FOR FURTHER ASSISTANCE

Block, Peter. *Stewardship: Choosing Service Over Self-Interest.* Berrett-Koehler, 1993.

Kotter, John. *Leading Change.* Harvard Business School Press, 1996.

Senge, Peter M. *The Fifth Discipline: The Art and Practice of the Learning Organization.* Doubleday, 1990.

Senge, Peter, Richard Ross, Bryan Smith, Charlotte Roberts, and Art Kleiner. *The Fifth Discipline Fieldbook: Strategies and Tools for Building a Learning Organization.* Currency Doubleday, 1994.

2.5   VALUES AND LEADERSHIP

Inspired by Ken Blanchard, Michael O'Connor, James Kouzes, Barry Posner, Patricia Jones, Larry Kahaner, and James O'Toole.

"Values comprise the things that are most important to us. They are the deep-seated, pervasive standards that influence almost every aspect of our lives: our moral judgements, our responses to others, our commitments to personal and organizational goals," say Kouzes and Posner in their best-seller, *The Leadership Challenge.* "However silently, values give direction to the hundreds of decisions made at all levels of the organization every day." The values of an organization's leaders, particularly senior leaders, form the bedrock of that organization's culture. This tool provides guidance for clarifying and living your values.

The benefits of clarifying organizational values include:

✔ They encourage and set standards for ethical behavior throughout the organization.

✔ They provide a constant guideline or touchstone for decision making, often reducing conflict and stress.

✔ They encourage personal effectiveness by creating overarching guidelines about working with employees, customers or clients, and other stakeholders.

✔ They help attract and retain people who are prepared to support and work within the stated values.

The disadvantages of clarifying organizational values include:

✘ Leaders are obligated to model the stated values; leaders must scrupulously behave within declared values.

✘ They can engender cynicism, unless everyone in the organization is held accountable for upholding declared values.

STEPS FOR DEFINING AND LEADING WITH EXPLICIT VALUES

Step ❶ Initiation by senior management	❏ Values work absolutely must be actively supported and lived from the top. ❏ There must be a clear rationale, tied to organizational success, for clarifying values. ❏ Every leader must be prepared to model the stated values. ❏ The process of introduction must be congruent with the values; if you hold that "employees are our most valued resource," then employees must be consulted!
Step ❷ Defining and clarifying values	❏ Involve stakeholders (e.g., leaders, employees, customers, clients, suppliers). Use focus groups, team meetings, and surveys. ❏ The first draft of values should reflect the givens of senior management. ❏ Gather information as to what stakeholders currently see as implied values. ❏ Gather feedback on givens and proposals for additional values. ❏ Analyze the gaps between implied values and desired values. ❏ Finalize value statements and publish them, along with operational and measurable indicators of success.

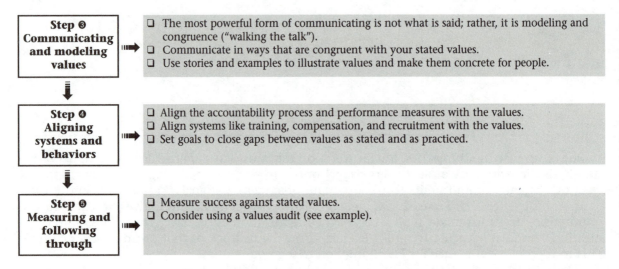

Step ❸ Communicating and modeling values	❏ The most powerful form of communicating is not what is said; rather, it is modeling and congruence ("walking the talk"). ❏ Communicate in ways that are congruent with your stated values. ❏ Use stories and examples to illustrate values and make them concrete for people.
Step ❹ Aligning systems and behaviors	❏ Align the accountability process and performance measures with the values. ❏ Align systems like training, compensation, and recruitment with the values. ❏ Set goals to close gaps between values as stated and as practiced.
Step ❺ Measuring and following through	❏ Measure success against stated values. ❏ Consider using a values audit (see example).

EXAMPLES OF VALUE STATEMENTS

To help you get a sense of the power and impact of values, search the Web sites of organizations you admire and find their value and belief statements. Here are two examples of values-based organizations, one commercial, one not-for-profit.

Example 1:

> "The Body Shop produced an externally and independently verified Values Report in its three value areas—Social, Environmental, and Animal Protection. You can view the report, summary and methodology, all on-line. [We] are proud to announce that out of the 100 international company reports evaluated by SustainAbility for the United Nations Environmental Programme, our Values Report scored the highest rating for the second year running. SustainAbility refers to the Values Report 1997 as '…unusual in its efforts to integrate social and environmental reporting with considerable stakeholder engagement.'"

Example 2:

> The World Association of Girl Guides and Girl Scouts diplays its values statement prominently on its Web site:

> "Girl Guiding/Girl Scouting is based on a core set of values that are found in the Girl Guide/Girl Scout Promise and Law. Each Girl Guide and Girl Scout promises to do her best to her faith and to others, and in so doing she realizes her fullest potential as a responsible citizen."

HOW TO USE THIS LEADERSHIP TOOL

> "Employees … are very critical when wide gaps exist between (stated) values and actions. They watch to see how stated values are reinforced and how these values influence actions."
>
> —James Kouzes and Barry Posner, *THE LEADERSHIP CHALLENGE*

Don't be concerned that terms such as *values, beliefs, principles,* and *philosophy* are often used interchangeably. Authors tend to protect their definitions. Stephen Covey, for example, downplays the term *values* in favor of the term *principles.* He writes that, "Principles are not *values.*

A gang of thieves can share values, but they are in violation of … fundamental principles."
Consistent with the values of this book, we simply encourage you to clarify your deep-seated
beliefs, whether you call them values or not; then, practice them!

EXAMPLES OF VALUES CATEGORIES

Here are just a few examples of values categories. Consider these as you embark on a values-
clarification process for your workgroup or organization.

❑ Integrity
❑ Fairness
❑ Honesty
❑ Corporate citizenship
❑ Operational
   excellence
❑ Quality—no rejects
	❑ Development of
	   people
	❑ Dignity
	❑ Equal opportunity
	❑ Customer service
	❑ Respect of diversity
	❑ Cooperation
	❑ Accountability
	❑ Hard work
		❑ Environmental
		   responsibility
		❑ Safety
		❑ Participation
		❑ Reliability
		❑ Teamwork
		❑ Consensus-seeking
			❑ Organizational
			   growth
			❑ Innovation
			❑ Financial success
			❑ Shareholder value
			❑ Ethical behavior *(see
			   behavioral example)*

AN EXAMPLE OF A BEHAVIORAL VALUES DESCRIPTION

The difficulty with words and phrases like those provided in the values list is that they are overly general. To be actionable, value statements need to be stated in behavioral terms. Here is an
example.

Ethical Behavior
General statement: Everyone in our organization will strictly uphold the highest ethical standards.
Some measurable and observable levels of implementation success:
- Never accepting gifts of more than $25 from vendors, suppliers, or anyone who could possibly benefit from
  association with the Company, unless the gift is clearly on a reciprocal basis.
- In cultures where gift exchange is an accepted practice, exercising care and prudent judgment.
- Under no conditions will we offer or accept a kickback to or from anyone.
- Ensure that all employees understand the Company's policy concerning ethical behavior.
- Always discuss potential ethical concerns, or conflicts of interest, with a manager or team leader.

WEB WORKSHEET

IDENTIFYING AND CLOSING YOUR VALUES GAPS

The values you currently espouse
Assume you will be unable to communicate with your organization over the next six months. Write a one-page memo that tells people how you want the organization to be led in your absence. A condensed statement of this sort would include many of your values.

The values you currently practice
To ferret out your values-in-practice, think of a) where you spend your time and energy, b) how you react to stressful situations, and c) what behaviors you reward.

Actions you will take to close the gap between your espoused values and the values that you currently practice

[☞ 1.8 Recursive Leadership]

RELATED LEADERSHIP TOOLS

1.2 Manage or Lead?	2.1 Systems Thinking	2.3 Directional Statements
1.6 Boards of Play	2.2 7S model	2.4 Visioning

FOR FURTHER ASSISTANCE

Blanchard, Kenneth H., and Michael O'Connor. *Managing by Values.* Berrett-Koehler, 1997.

Jones, Patricia, and Larry Kahaner. *Say It and Live It: The 50 Corporate Mission Statements That Hit the Mark.* Doubleday, 1995.

Kouzes, James M., and Barry Z. Posner. *The Leadership Challenge: How to Keep Getting Extraordinary Things Done in Organizations.* Jossey-Bass Publishers, 1996.

O'Toole, James. *Leading Change: The Argument for Values-Based Leadership.* Ballantine, 1996.

2.6 CLARIFYING PURPOSE: HARNESSING PEOPLE POWER IN ORGANIZATIONS

Inspired by John Jones, Patricia Jones, Larry Kahaner, and numerous other sources.

Creation of meaning or purpose is what distinguishes *leadership* from *management*. People want meaning in their work lives. They want to know *why*: to what end and for what purpose they are working so hard. History shows us people will do almost anything for leaders who lead people by defining an engaging purpose. In the process of clarifying purpose, leaders help people grow, expand their thinking, and become contributors to new initiatives. In their book, *Built to Last,* about companies that outperformed the stock market by 50 to 1 over the last 50 years, Collins and Porras identified as the number-one factor "an enduring sense of purpose." Alternatively, when change fails, it's invariably because people can't see the purpose, the why, underlying the change, and thus cannot meaningfully commit themselves to supporting the new initiative.

WHAT IS A PURPOSE?

- A purpose is a reason for being—why this organization, unit, or project exists.
- A purpose statement is a high-level description of the direction and value of your activities to your clients or customers, to your workgroup or organization, and to yourself.
- Purpose clearly and concisely answers the question: *"How does this proposed unit or activity add value for our customers, our stakeholders, and our organization?"*
- Similar terms used are: rationale, mission, overall goal, direction, vision, scope, intent, strategy, wavelength, big picture, meaning, or *why*.

WHY IS PURPOSE IMPORTANT?

- ✔ A clear purpose helps keep a workgroup committed, on track, and on schedule. Anyone in the group should be able to tell anyone else the *why* of any activity.
- ✔ A clear purpose reduces frustration, and the potential for conflict, by aligning members of a workgroup around a reason for being.

CHARACTERISTICS OF AN EFFECTIVE PURPOSE STATEMENT

- ❑ It motivates aligned action.
- ❑ It is well-understood and concise. It can be explained to any stakeholder in three minutes or less, and every member of the organization has a personal understanding of the organization's purpose.
- ❑ It guides plans, decisions, and activities in the face of ambiguity.
- ❑ It is enduring. Thus, modifying a purpose statement signifies a new direction.

Nested purposes

A specific purpose keeps a workgroup or team in touch with the larger organizational purpose. Each purpose should be aligned and nested within a larger purpose.

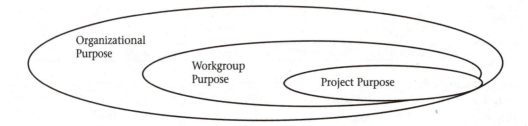

How to use this leadership tool

"The conviction that life has a purpose is rooted in every fiber of man, it is property of the human substance. Free men give many names to this purpose, and many think and talk about its nature."

—Primo Levi

Use this tool to write a purpose statement for your organization, for your workgroup or team, for a specific project or project team, for a decision, or for a personal or life issue.

WEB WORKSHEET

Two steps are important in developing a purpose statement:

Step 1: Determine why you need a purpose statement. Discuss the need for a clear purpose statement (i.e., the purpose of a purpose statement). Work with your group to discover and define why it needs a clear purpose statement. Outline the pitfalls of *not* having a clear purpose statement. Don't skip this step. It's important for people to understand why they are spending time defining and writing a purpose statement.

> Briefly summarize why you and your group think that it is important to have a purpose statement.

Step 2: Commit to implementing your purpose statement. Use whichever of these three scenarios best suits your unique situation.

    A. If you have a purpose statement already drafted, stay open to improvement. Present it as a draft, and seek input from all workgroup or team members. Commitment to a purpose comes as a result of allowing others to influence in meaningful ways, not simply through directing, informing, or sharing information.

B. If you have a mandated statement of purpose from senior management, work with your group to develop a deeper understanding of this purpose and how it might be modified, if necessary. (Be prepared to explain to senior management why this modification is important.)

C. If a purpose statement is not yet prepared, work with your group to develop one. This statement may evolve over a number of meetings. Ask the group to suggest a draft purpose statement. You might start by brainstorming words and phrases. Discuss suggestions and changes. The time to seek closure is when the purpose statement provides *clarity* to guide *action*.

Jot down the key steps you will need to take to ensure that your workgroup has a purpose statement that everyone can commit to aligning with and implementing.

Related leadership tools

1.3 Leadership	1.6 Boards of Play	2.7 Goal Statements
1.5 Seven Habits	2.3 Directional Statements	10.7 Getting Participation

For further assistance

Jones, John. *"Criteria for Effective Goal Setting: The SPIRO Model."* In William Pfeiffer and John Jones, eds. *The 1972 Annual Handbook for Group Facilitators.* University Associates, 1972. 132–133.

Jones, Patricia, and Larry Kahaner. *Say It and Live It: The 50 Corporate Mission Statements That Hit the Mark.* Doubleday, 1995.

2.7 WRITING CLEAR GOAL STATEMENTS

Inspired by Russell Ackoff, Shaun Murphy, and David Irvine.

The goal of writing goals is not to have well-crafted goal statements. It's to inspire and guide action. Goal setting is likely one of the oldest of management tools. It's unlikely that the pyramid builders said, "Let's drag millions of huge, finely carved rocks many miles, and see what we can build!" The key reason for writing goals is that the end result will be clear before the means are decided.

Writing goals can be a challenge for leaders. What seems simple in concept can be a minefield of logical booby traps! It's easy to get bogged down with long-winded, well-intentioned, but obtuse goal statements. Keep in mind that it's better to achieve great results than to write great goal statements.

> *"It's more important to have great goals, than great goal statements."*
> —Shaun Murphy

There are many goal-setting models in use today, and the terminology can seem confusing (e.g., goals, objectives, key result areas, key measures, performance standards, and on and on). Don't be confused. Your goal in writing goals is: a clear, concise, measurable or observable *goal* statement. Write only as much in the intent and action plan categories as needed to clarify the intent behind the goal and the actions required to achieve the goal. Since you'll need to go back and forth a little, we suggest using the format provided here:

Intent	Goal	Action plan
What is the direction in which you are heading?	How will you know when you get there? (Your goal must be measurable or observable.)	In general, how will you get there? What steps are required?

Intent: The intent statement explains the overall direction and purpose of your goal. It is a broader statement than the goal statement, so it's okay to include evaluative words and phrases such as maximize, optimize, effectively, efficiently, and so on. Words and phrases such as these are unhelpful in a goal statement, but they do convey your overall purpose, direction, or intent.

Goal: Keep it simple. A sentence is the norm. *It absolutely, positively must be measurable or observable.* For example, "Complete the project XYZ report by March 16," or, "Have the project XYZ report approved by the Board by April 27th." This is by far the hardest of the three levels to write well. You may also find that your goals, if they're measurable or observable, are at best only an approximation of what you really intend. This is normal. Finally, don't use any empty evaluative words. None! Not one *effectively* or *efficiently*! It's tough, so just start with a first draft. You can come back and improve on it later.

Action Plan: As you write your intent and goal statements, a hodgepodge of ideas for achieving your goals will likely come rushing out at you. Don't lose these thoughts. Note them under action plans. Your notes should include key requirements for achieving the goal: sequencing, scheduling, steps, milestones, resources needed, who needs to be involved, assumptions, time demands, and so on. Keep it simple; your focus here is on writing a clear goal statement. You can focus on writing clear action plans later.

These acronyms have received wide publication, and may be helpful as you write your goal statement. Goals should be:

The ACORN model	The SPIRO model	The SMART model
A = accurate C = consistent with higher-level objectives O = stated as outputs R = realistic N = numeric	S = specific P = payoff-oriented I = inspiring R = realistic O = observable	S = specific M = measurable A = attainable and actionable R = realistic T = time-limited

HOW TO USE THIS LEADERSHIP TOOL

"What is the use of running when you are on the wrong road?"
—German proverb

Inherent in the goal-setting process is the notion of ends and means chains. That is, goals are hierarchical, with lower-level goals being the means to achieve higher-level goals. Take, for example, the goal of bringing a new technological innovation into production. The immediate goal is market penetration. A higher-level goal is increasing market share. An even higher-level goal is increasing division revenues, and so on. Thus, the goal of "market penetration" is only a means to the higher-level goal of "increasing market share," and this in turn is only a means to "increasing division revenues," and so on.

If it helps, think of your intent statement as being a higher-level goal, and of your goal statement as being a lower-level goal. Now, from this perspective, write a couple of clear goal statements. As you work, write the intent statement, or *why* it's important to achieve this goal. In addition, as you write these statements, note even lower-level goals—action plans that will help you accomplish your goal.

WEB WORKSHEET

Use the workspace here to draft a couple of clear goal statements. As you work, make comments in the intent (higher-level goal) and the action plan (lower-level goals) categories. Although you will make notes in all three categories or goal levels, make the focus of your effort the writing of a couple of clear, measurable or observable goal statements. Clarifying intent and writing action plans are usually easy once clear goal statements have been written.

Goal #1

Intent	

Goal	
Key Action Items	

Goal #2

Intent	
Goal	
Key Action Items	

Goal #3

Intent	
Goal	
Key Action Items	

RELATED LEADERSHIP TOOLS

1.6 Boards of Play	2.6 Clarifying Purpose	13.3 Accountability
2.3 Directional Statements	2.8 Balanced Scorecard	13.5 Time Management

FOR FURTHER ASSISTANCE

Ackoff, Russell Lincoln. *Creating the Corporate Future: Plan or Be Planned For.* Wiley, 1981.

Klatt, Bruce, Shaun Murphy, and David Irvine. *Accountability: Getting a Grip on Results,* 2nd ed. Stoddart, 1998.

2.8 MEASURING SUCCESS: THE BALANCED SCORECARD

Inspired by Robert S. Kaplan, David Norton, Joseph and Jimmie Boyett,
David Ulrich, Jack Zenger, and Norman Smallwood.

Until recently, most organizational hard performance scorecard numbers were traditional financials, like sales, return on capital, profitability, and so on. These numbers were aggregated to help senior executives make corporatewide decisions. More recently, many organizations are expanding these financial measures in two ways:

1. balancing harder financial and production measures with softer measures like customer satisfaction and environmental protection; [☞ 1.7 Results-Based Leaders]

2. generating and sharing significant measures with leaders at all levels. [☞ 4.6 Open-Book Leadership]

Measures and scorecards are necessary, encapsulated in the sayings "What gets measured, gets done" and "Hard drives out soft." The most common traditional business measure is money, for the individual as well as for the organization: salary, stock options, bonuses, assets. Recently, however, demand has arisen for other, more balanced measures *and* for more balanced lifestyles, as a result of the impact of such phenomena as the quality movement, the information age, knowledge workers, virtual e-commerce, and environmental awareness.

Besides finding balanced measures for the success of your organization, business unit, project, or yourself, this tool speaks for more balanced measures of success for individual and team performance. It is a challenge to find the right balance of success measures for performance management. For instance, some organizations have set up bonus systems to reward individuals who excelled—only to see them excel at the expense of others! People are smart about working the system.

This tool presents a number of measures in a number of categories to help you choose, for yourself personally and for your organization, a more balanced set of success measures. The difficulty is to select a small set of numbers that are significant and representative of the success of the organization, as well as being significant to the individual using them. Some suggestions are provided here for selecting the best measures. As you look at these measures, consider which would be appropriate for each level of your organization: executives, business unit leaders, and project leaders.

Scorecard measurement areas	Some potential measures
Financial Success Measures (Traditional measures extended to many more leaders.)	Operating income, return on capital, sales, sales growth, profit margin, profitability, revenue per unit, unit costs, and the like.
Strategic Measures (The measures of success supporting the direction of the organization.)	Look to your strategic direction statements for measures. Some measures may include innovation, growth, new markets, new product development, organizational capabilities, and the like.
Stakeholder Measures (Customers, clients, suppliers, regulators, unions, and other business partners.)	Customer or client satisfaction, retention, growth, service, returns and warranty claims, on-time delivery, value-added measures, and the like. Supplier satisfaction, quality, on-time delivery, rejects. Regulatory disputes, legislation influence, and the like.

Internal Process Measures	Key business process success indicators, production numbers, quality measures, reject rates, reduced cycle times, cost reductions, new products, inventory turnover, process redesign and optimization, and the like.
Employee and Community Measures	Employee satisfaction, commitment measures, work climate, productivity measures, turnover, return per employee, capability development, grievance rate, suggestion rate, diversity, life balance measures. Community may include environmental and community relations measures.

There are no magic measures. They will be different for each organization, depending on the organization and its direction. They will be very different for profit-making and not-for-profit organizations.

How to use this leadership tool

Innovating companies today are using their Balanced Scorecards to

(1) gain consensus and clarity about their strategic objectives,

(2) communicate strategic objectives to business units, departments, teams, and individuals,

(3) align strategic planning, resource allocation, and budgeting processes, and,

(4) obtain feedback and learn about the effectiveness of their strategic plan and its implementation.

—Robert S. Kaplan, *THE BALANCED SCORECARD*

Now that you have seen the range of measures that may be used to produce a balanced scorecard, the question is which measures to use. Here are some guidelines:

➡ Keep the number of measures relatively small, so they are easy to keep in mind.

➡ To be balanced, measures should come from most of the categories in the table.

➡ The measures should be tightly connected to your organizational direction, strategy, and goals.

➡ The cause–effect relationships should be relatively tight. "If we do X, we should increase the measure of Y on the balanced scorecard, which is a measure of organizational success."

➡ The measures should measure what you want to be really good at.

➡ The measures should not conflict with the values of the organization.

➡ The measures should not act at cross-purposes with one another. Pursuing one measure should not beggar another. One group pursuing its measures should not be able to do that at the expense of others. There is a saying in leadership: "Expecting A but rewarding B." Avoid it.

➡ The measures need to be intelligible for the level of person expected to use them. Teach people business literacy skills. Jack Stack suggests that, for many people, the measures need to be told in the form of stories.

➡ You need to be able to publicize the data for these measures on a regular basis. The numbers need to be current and published regularly to have meaning. The measures need to be prominently publicized and discussed at regular intervals.

➡ The measures should balance short-term payoffs with long-term growth.

WEB WORKSHEET

Think about a balanced scorecard for yourself, your workgroup or team, your business unit, or your organization. A process for doing this will surely involve a number of iterations. This process could be done by you as an individual or by a working group, depending on the nature of the scorecard and the culture of the organization.

1. Make a quick first pass by jotting measure areas in the matrix provided. Don't worry about being right or wrong at this point.
2. After the first pass, check your work against the guidelines listed previously and revise it.
3. When you have a preliminary list, informally check and refine your thinking with a few stakeholders.
4. Now work with a wider group of people to get the measures right.
5. Communicate not only your balanced scorecard, but why and how the measures were chosen.

Scorecard measure area	Who the measure is for	The few specific, significant measures

RELATED LEADERSHIP TOOLS

1.7 Results-Based Leaders	2.5 Values	3.1 Strategy
2.1 Systems Thinking	2.7 Goal Statements	4.6 Open-Book Leadership

FOR FURTHER ASSISTANCE

Boyett, Joseph H., and Jimmie T. Boyett. *The Guru Guide: The Best Ideas of the Top Management Thinkers*. John Wiley & Sons, 1998.

Kaplan, Robert S., and David P. Norton. *The Balanced Scorecard: Translating Strategy into Action*. Harvard Business School Press, 1996.

Ulrich, David, Jack Zenger, and Norman Smallwood. *Results-Based Leadership*. Harvard Business School Press, 1999.

3

Tools for Strategic Thinking

With the business environment changing so rapidly in this dot-com age of sound bites and e-commerce, successful leaders need to look well beyond routine and day-to-day operational tactics. Providing "more of the same" is not a tenable strategy. Thus, every leader, and ideally every employee, needs to think and act strategically. To help you sharpen your thinking and skills as leader and organizational strategist, these tools summarize the most prominent perspectives on strategy of the past 20 years.

3.1

THE LEADER AS STRATEGIST

Inspired by Joseph and Jimmie Boyett, Michael Porter, Gary Hamel, C. K. Prahalad, Lee Perry et al., and many others.

With the business environment changing so rapidly in this dot-com age of sound bites and e-commerce, leaders need to look well beyond the routine and day-to-day operational tactics in order to be successful. Thus, every leader, and ideally every employee, needs to think and act strategically. Yet this is no simple matter. That's why few leadership topics have stirred as much debate as has strategy. This tool summarizes and compares the most prominent perspectives on strategy of the past 20 years. It will help you sharpen your thinking and skills as a leader and an organizational strategist.

PERSPECTIVES ON STRATEGY, 1980–2000

Strategy guru	Contributions or concepts
Michael Porter	Defined three core concepts of strategy: 1. the basic competitive forces (new entrants, new substitute products or services, rivalry among competitors, increased bargaining power of suppliers and buyers); 2. the generic competitive strategies (cost leadership, differentiation of products or services, market segmentation focus); 3. the value chain (from raw material supply to operations, marketing, distribution, and after-sales service).
The Boston Consulting Group	Outlined a Growth/Share Matrix in which an organization defined its products and services as: ➡ *Stars*—high market share and high growth; ➡ *Cash Cows*—high market share and low growth; ➡ *Question Marks*—low market share with potential high growth; and ➡ *Dogs*—low market share and low growth.
Gary Hamel and C. K. Prahalad	Argued that competitive advantage starts with customers and intellectual leadership. ➡ Think beyond the technology of your products and services per se, to their use (i.e., think beyond "cell phone," to the ability to communicate with others from anywhere on earth). ➡ Think beyond your business units and people, to core competencies—knowledge, skills, and technologies that benefit designated customers.
Henry Mintzberg	Mintzberg sees strategy as impermanent and evolving, and notes that "strategy is the organization's 'conception' of how to deal with its environment for a time." As such, Mintzberg views strategic planning as onerous, slow, overly analytical, and too formalized for today's fast-moving, knowledge-based organizations. Rather, he stresses strategic thinking: a more experimental, organic, discontinuous, and evolving process of clarifying and adapting strategy in real time.
Lee Perry, Randy Stott, and Norm Smallwood	Like Mintzberg, Perry, Stott, and Smallwood see strategy as ubiquitous and evolving. They emphasize: ➡ making strategic assumptions explicit; ➡ strategic improvising in small offensive thrusts, and by everyone; ➡ understanding competitive advantage and disadvantage, and matching capabilities with opportunities; ➡ performance measurement, and reducing human energy loss through strategic alignment.

Michael Tracey and Fred Wiersma	Identified three value disciplines, only one of which can be the basis of an organization's strategy: 1. *Operational excellence*—quality, price, and ease of purchase that no competitor can match. 2. *Product leadership*—providing the best possible product(s) to as many customers as possible. 3. *Customer intimacy*—understanding your customers and delivering exactly what they want.
James Moore	Challenged competition as the basis of strategic thinking. "Competitive advantage in the new world stems from knowing when and how to build ecosystems … ." Like a biological ecosystem, strategies evolve over four stages: 1. pioneering or creating a new product or service niche; 2. expansion of the ecosystem by working with partners to attain niche dominance; 3. maintaining authority in the ecosystem, often by cost-cutting and restructuring; 4. finally, as in biological ecosystems, death and renewal due to the changing environment.
Adam Brandenburger	Framed strategy as games theory with changing rules of competition, including changes to how value is added, what tactics are used, how scope is defined, and so on.

How to use this leadership tool

"As Kierkegaard once observed, life is lived forward but understood backward. Managers may have to live strategy in the future, but they must understand it through the past."

—Henry Mintzberg, MINTZBERG ON MANAGEMENT

Strategies are abstractions until they are delivered at the mundane, day-to-day level of operating a business (i.e., waiting on customers). At this point, your strategy may seem obvious to insiders, but what outsiders, including competitors, will miss is the deep level of understanding and commitment behind the strategy. Leaders achieve this level of understanding and commitment by involving as many people as possible in building and adapting a strategy, and by talking with their people on a regular basis about the implications behind the strategy. Use the workspace here to plan or review your organization's strategy, and to plan how you will continually communicate the strategy within your organization.

WEB WORSKHEET

Element of strategic thinking	Things to think about	Your action plan
Be strategic about your strategy.	❑ Keep it simple. Strategy needs to be a template for decision making. People need to carry it in their heads and have a deep sense of what is and isn't strategic for the organization. ❑ Design and adapt your strategy-making process to your specific situation. [☞ 1.8 Recursive Leadership]	
Have a competitive edge (i.e., be very good at something).	❑ Be better at providing a product or service than your competitors (e.g., at GE, Jack Welch insists on being in the top two, or dropping a product line). ❑ At what product(s) or service(s) will you excel?	

	In what ways will your organization have a competitive edge with its product(s)/service(s)?	
Think outside the box.	We know that this phrase has been badly overworked. Nonetheless, managers are often so caught up in the demands of their roles and profession, and so immersed in a given way of thinking, that they know little outside their organizations and their work. ❑ Seek many opinions and perspectives. ❑ Read and consult with people outside your industry, organization, and area of expertise. [☛ 6.7 Creativity and Innovation]	
Think of your organization from the point of view of others	❑ Talk to and understand the perspectives of your customers, suppliers, employees, and other stakeholders. ❑ Learn about competitors, their directions, and their core competencies. [☛ 5.7 Stakeholder Groups]	
Let your strategy evolve.	❑ Senior management needs to elucidate a strategic framework that gives others ample opportunity for strategic improvising.	
Have everyone in your organization think strategically.	❑ Don't isolate strategic thinking to senior managers or to a strategic planning group. ❑ Have all business and staff units clarify their strategies. ❑ Model strategic thinking and challenge others to think strategically. [☛ 10.7 Getting Participation]	
Align systems to support your strategy.	❑ Your organizational systems are perfectly aligned to achieve your current results. In many ways, the hardest part of strategy implementation is re-jigging your systems to support the new strategy. [☛ 5.6 Aligning Systems]	

Related leadership tools

1.6 Boards of Play	2.3 Directional Statements	2.6 Clarifying Purpose
1.10 The GAS Model	2.4 Visioning	3.2 Sigmoid Curve
2.1 Systems Thinking	2.5 Values	

For further reading

Boyett, Joseph H., and Jimmie T. Boyett. *The Guru Guide: The Best Ideas of the Top Management Thinkers.* John Wiley & Sons, 1998.

Hamel, Gary, and C. K. Prahalad. *Competing for the Future.* Harvard Business School Press, 1996.

Mintzberg, Henry. *The Rise and Fall of Strategic Planning: Reconceiving Roles for Planning, Plans, and Planners.* The Free Press, 1994.

Mintzberg, Henry, Bruce Ahlstrand, and Joseph Lampel. *Strategy Safari: A Guided Tour through the Wilds of Strategic Management.* Simon & Schuster, 1998.

Perry, Lee Tom, Randall G. Stott, and W. Norman Smallwood. *Real-Time Strategy: Improvising Team-Based Planning for a Fast-Changing World,* Portable MBA Series. John Wiley & Sons, 1993.

Porter, Michael E. *Competitive Advantage: Creating and Sustaining Superior Performance.* Free Press, 1998.

Porter, Michael E. *Competitive Strategy: Techniques for Analyzing Industries and Competitors.* Free Press, 1998.

3.2 THE SIGMOID CURVE: ANTICIPATING AND PREPARING FOR CHANGE DESPITE CURRENT SUCCESS

Inspired by Charles Handy.

Everything has its ups, downs, and plateaus. Nothing lasts forever, including success. So, to succeed in the long term, leaders need to anticipate and start working toward a new future—strange as it may sound—even before that future actually begins to take shape. This tool provides a way of thinking about the future that cautions you not to take success for granted. It suggests the need to begin planning for change during times when things are on the upturn—be it of a product, service, investment, or even the success of your own leadership career!

Consider these ups and downs: Apple Macintosh—a product's ups and downs; the Soviet Empire—a country's life cycle; romantic relationships—Shakespeare's observation, "The course of true love never did run smooth."

> *"A good life is probably a succession of sigmoid curves, each new curve started before the first curve fades."*
> —Charles Handy. *THE AGE OF PARADOX*

Such ups and downs can be illustrated by two intersecting curves, known as the Sigmoid Curves. The word *sigmoid* means a double curve in an S shape.

The Sigmoid Curve   **Successive Sigmoid Curves**

Curve *A* represents the current and projected life cycle. Notice that the curve has a slow start, an acceleration to a plateau, and then a tailing off. The second curve represents a future success scenario. Like a booster rocket on a spacecraft, you must plan to jettison the first rocket and ignite the next, to take you into a new orbit. The trick is:

⇒ to plan the abandonment of the first curve while things are still going well;

⇒ to make the most of the first curve (curve A) before making a major commitment to the second curve (curve B); and

⇒ to realize that, for a while, new ideas need to coexist with the old.

The fact that you are reading this book probably means you are somewhere on curve *A* looking for improvement, possibly to your own career. The appropriate place to start thinking about the second curve is while you are still approaching the peak of curve *A* (i.e., while you are still ascending on the curve). For most people, however, real energy for change comes only when they are looking disaster in the face (e.g., being laid off, failing to meet a business goal, their product or service no longer selling). These disasters typically take place after Curve *A* has peaked and is tailing off. Being complacent while on the crest of curve *A*, they didn't see them coming! The Japanese word *kaizen*, or continuous improvement, is based on the assumption that there is no perfect answer in a changing world, and that complacency is the enemy of long-term success.

> *"One of the paradoxes of success is that the things … which got you there, are seldom those that keep you there."*
> —Charles Handy, *THE AGE OF PARADOX*

Leaders are concerned that the first curve will turn down before they are able to find the second curve. Leaders need to anticipate and get on to the second curve as soon as possible, or preferably before the first curve begins its downturn. But few want their peaceful existence on the first curve to be disturbed until after the downturn begins! By then, however, it may be too late. The trick is to find the second curve while still keeping the first one going. This requires personal flexibility and tolerance for change and ambiguity.

How to use this leadership tool

> *A stranger at the side of the road gives you these directions: "It's easy to find. Just keep going the way you are and after a while you'll come across a small bridge with Davy's Bar on the far side. You can't miss it. Then, a half mile before you get there, turn to your right and go up the hill."*
> —Charles Handy, *THE AGE OF PARADOX*

In this fast-moving world, sigmoid curves are increasingly accelerated. Today, business strategies often need to be replaced within two or three years, and product life cycles are shorter than in the past. Consider some of the products, services, or strategies to which you presently attribute your success as a leader. Graph where each of these might presently be on the first sigmoid curve here. (You may also wish to use this tool to examine your career or work relationships.)

WEB WORKSHEET

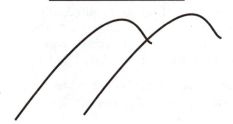

Reflect on the significance of where you have placed your mark on the first sigmoid curve, be it in reference to your career, your group's product or service, or a work relationship. What steps do you need to consider taking so you can prepare for the second curve, without prematurely leaving your current success (on the first curve) behind?

How can you use the concept of the sigmoid curve to help ensure your success as a leader? What changing demands are being made of leaders in your organization, and how can you adapt your thinking and approach to meet these leadership demands?

RELATED LEADERSHIP TOOLS

1.1 Twenty-First-Century Leader	2.1 Systems Thinking	3.3 Environmental Scan
1.9 Paradigms	3.1 Strategy	3.6 Strategic Relationships

FOR FURTHER ASSISTANCE

Handy, Charles. *The Age of Paradox*. Harvard Business School Press, 1995.

3.3

SWOT: STRENGTHS, WEAKNESSES, OPPORTUNITIES, AND THREATS

Inspired by Alexander Hiam, David Ulrich et al., Peter Drucker, and others.

In preparation for formulating strategy, leaders need to examine the current state of their organizations, both inside and out. A common preliminary step to strategy clarification is an Environmental Scan or SWOT—brainstorming and assessing the **S**trengths, **W**eaknesses, **O**pportunities, and **T**hreats to your organization, business unit, or team. Besides using SWOT *within* your organization, it also needs to be carried out looking at your organization *from the outside*. Peter Drucker boldly states, "Executives of any large organization are woefully ignorant of the outside.... When it comes to outside data, we are still very largely in the anecdotal stage."

Make sure the data is thoroughly clarified, since you will make strategic decisions based on this data.

✔ Strategy must be built on reliable and clear assumptions, not on hunches and unstated assumptions.

✔ Good strategy capitalizes on the current strengths and opportunities, as well as shoring up weaknesses and preparing for threats.

Although the concept of SWOT seems simple, its execution can be challenging. SWOT data is best generated within your workgroup, so you can assess the quality of the data, the group's understanding of the data, and the depth of the group's commitment to formulating strategy. It also helps to approach SWOT from many perspectives (e.g., an internal perspective, the perspective of customers or competitors, short-term and long-term perspectives, and so on).

Key strengths	Key opportunities
(clearly listed and prioritized)	*(clearly listed and prioritized)*
Key weaknesses	**Key threats**
(clearly listed and prioritized)	*(clearly listed and prioritized)*

Checklist of possible places to look for SWOT items

Economics	Outputs	Stakeholders	Marketplace
❑ Financial Resources: – debt – liquidity – reserves – investment – effect of inflation – expected economics ❑ Costs: – overhead – production costs – supplies ❑ Profitability ❑ Investor Confidence	❑ Products/Services: – product life cycle – growth – market share ❑ Product/Service Mix: – breadth – spin-offs – focus ❑ Product Quality ❑ Competitiveness ❑ Production Capability ❑ Technology: – up-to-date – leading-edge – R & D	❑ People: – current capabilities – ability to retrain – flexibility/diversity – commitment ❑ Core Competencies ❑ Systems: – human resources – logistics – coordination – information – communication ❑ Government/ Legislation ❑ Unions ❑ Other Stakeholders	❑ Customers: – stability – new possibilities – service ❑ Market: – concentration – state of the industry ❑ Competitors: – strength – new directions ❑ Suppliers: – security of supply – cost of supply ❑ Risk/benefit of world events, e.g., price of petroleum

This list could go on forever. A creative piece of strategy clarification is to isolate the critical few. This checklist will definitely need refinement—a large corporation would use quite different factors from a non-profit; an executive group would use quite different factors from a small professional services team. [If the information is overwhelming, you may wish to use some data organization technique like ☞ 7.8 Affinity Diagrams or 10.11 Priority Setting.]

An effective SWOT, and the subsequent strategy, are closely related to what Peter Drucker calls a "Theory of Business Specifications." Drucker specifies four interlocking elements.

Peter Drucker's
Theory of Business Specifications

1. The assumptions about environment, mission, and core competencies must fit reality.
2. The assumptions in all three areas have to fit one another.
3. The theory of business must be known and understood throughout the organization.
4. The theory of the business has to be tested constantly.

Reprinted with permission from Peter Drucker, *Managing in a Time of Great Change* (Truman Talley Books, 1995), pp. 30–31.

How to use this leadership tool

"… ignorance of an organization's past can undermine the development of strategies for its future."
Henry Mintzberg et al., *STRATEGY SAFARI*

If a strategy is not based on good data, internal and external, it will probably fail. The old maxim of computer programming, GIGO—garbage in, garbage out—applies equally well to strategy clarification. Having said this, there is always still room for creativity and informed hunches. After all, strategy evolves as much as or even more than it can be made deliberate. Nonetheless, even creative and highly improvised strategies work best when grounded in realistic data.

WEB WORKSHEET

A SWOT is often carried out as a preliminary step to strategy clarification. SWOT data doesn't have to be 100 percent factual and objective—avoid analysis paralysis—but it should be based on some form of footing (e.g., experience, group consensus, survey data, market trends, and so on). In preparation for a SWOT meeting, ask the members of your workgroup to independently complete this matrix.

Strengths	Opportunities
(clearly listed and with data as needed)	*(clearly listed and with data as needed)*
Weaknesses	**Threats**
(clearly listed and with data as needed)	*(clearly listed and with data as needed)*

RELATED LEADERSHIP TOOLS

1.9 Paradigms	3.2 Sigmoid Curve	3.5 Strategic Resourcing
3.1 Strategy	3.4 Business-Unit Strategy	3.8 Strategic Alliances

FOR FURTHER ASSISTANCE

Drucker, Peter. *Managing in a Time of Great Change*. Truman Talley Books, 1995.

Hiam, Alexander. *The Vest-Pocket CEO: Decision-Making Tools for Executives*. Prentice Hall, 1991.

Ulrich, David, Jack Zenger, and Norman Smallwood. *Results-Based Leadership*. Harvard Business School Press, 1999.

3.4 THE FUNDAMENTALS OF BUSINESS-UNIT STRATEGY

Inspired by Anil K. Gupta.

Strategic thinking is the bedrock of effective leadership, and it's almost impossible for a leader to overemphasize this activity. Yet, while much has been written for senior executives about defining corporate strategy, much less emphasis has been placed on thinking strategically at the business-unit level. Corporate strategy deals with broad issues like what business to be in and how to exploit synergies across divisional businesses. Business-unit strategy focuses on how to compete within a market defined by the corporation. Strategy formulation at the business-unit level has a twofold purpose: a) to provide focus so that the business unit can sustain and develop its internal (and perhaps external) market position, and b) to enable the business unit to adapt faster than its external (and perhaps internal) competitors. Business-unit strategy has five critical elements. Depending on the nature of your business unit, these elements will need adaptation.

Defining Business-Unit Scope

Who are our target clients or customers?
- By demographics—Clients or customers can be identified by age, income levels, psychological characteristics, and so on.
- By market segment—Clients or customers can be identified by industry classification, company size, country, and so on.
- Prioritize these client or customer groups: Which customer groups will yield the most value?

What client or customer needs are we trying to fulfill?
- Define in terms of the underlying generic problem faced by the client or customer, rather than in terms of your products or services (e.g., not courier services; rather "the urgent transfer of documents").

What core competencies are required to fulfill these client or customer needs?
- Examples include product technology, process management, project management, marketing innovation, and so on.
- How can your business unit capitalize on corporate competencies?

Business-Unit Goals

Financial goals (e.g., sales volume, growth in revenue base, cash flow, profitability, growth in assets):
- What financial success measures will you use to report to the corporation?

Market position and customer satisfaction goals (e.g., market share, new customer initiatives):
- While both market position and profitability are important, long-term financial success is ultimately a consequence of winning in the marketplace.

Internal business-unit goals (e.g., cycle time reduction, employee satisfaction).

Innovation and learning goals (e.g., percent of sales from new services).

Relative Competitive Advantage

Define dimensions on which we intend to be superior to external competitors.
- Where will you be clearly superior? Where you will remain at par or accept being at a disadvantage to competitors?

Define client- or customer-relevant outputs.
- What matters in your marketplace (e.g., price, delivery time, quality, technology, aesthetics)?
- These may be relative to competitor's outputs rather than absolute, or they may change over time (e.g., the cheap quartz watch keeps better time than an expensive mechanical watch).
- In what way will you differentiate your service or product (e.g., cost leadership, reliability)?

This work requires understanding the overall organization's dominant skills and relative weaknesses.
- Decide what work to do internally, and what to farm out (e.g., alliances, joint ventures, contracting).
- Reliance on others to perform essential activities, at which they are superior, may strengthen your overall bundle of products, services, and prices. However, this carries risks (e.g., nonperformance, profit skimming, competition).

Managing the Value Chain

List the drivers of customer value, cost structure, and asset investment for each business activity (e.g., research, design, assembly, marketing, distribution). Ensure integration across value-chain activities, including those performed by business partners and contractors. This may include reduced development or delivery cycle times, more customization, smaller inventories, more effective communication, lower costs, and so on (e.g., electronic data exchange between a supplier like Procter & Gamble and a retailer like Wal-Mart).

How to use this leadership tool

"Once a business unit has defined the type of competitive advantage that it intends to establish, it faces the challenge of actually creating the intended advantage, a process that has two parts: 1. designing the value constellation, and … 2. managing the value chain."

—Anil K. Gupta, in *THE PORTABLE MBA IN STRATEGY*

Focusing strategy at the right level can be a challenging task. For example, should a paper goods business unit focus on "paper goods," or one level down, on "diapers, towels, and tissues"? You can define strategy too precisely; for example a wristwatch business-unit strategy (circa 1970): "the production of mechanical, pin-levered watches." This missed the now-burgeoning market for electronic watches. On the other hand, if you define strategy too broadly, it doesn't provide the crisp focus needed to guide day-to-day business decisions. The challenge of finding the right level is defining business-unit scope. Indeed, challenges surface through all five stages of business-unit strategy, and a lack of superiority along any critical dimension of relative competitive advantage will sooner or later result in your business unit being unable to sustain its current market position.

WEB WORKSHEET

Use the workspace provided here to sketch out some opening thoughts about your business unit's strategy. This process will evolve as you work, and will take some time. Involve team members early and often in this process. Invite and encourage them to influence the strategy in meaningful ways. Implementation is next to impossible if people in the business unit don't deeply understand or aren't fully committed to the strategy.

Defining Business-Unit Scope

Business-Unit Goals

[☞ 2.7 Goal Statements]

Relative Competitive Advantage

Designing the Value Constellation

[☞ 5.7 Stakeholder Groups]

Managing the Value Chain

Related leadership tools

2.6 Clarifying Purpose	3.2 Sigmoid Curve	3.5 Strategic Resourcing
2.7 Goal Statements	3.3 Environmental Scan	3.6 Strategic Relationships

For further assistance

Fahey, Liam, and Robert Randall, eds. *The Portable MBA in Strategy.* John Wiley & Sons, 1994.

3.5 STRATEGIC RESOURCING: DEFINING HIGH-VALUE WORK FOR SERVICE GROUPS

Inspired by Jon Younger, Randy Stott, and Norm Smallwood.

More and more, organizations expect their internal service groups to compete for work within their own organizations against the very best external service providers. Thus, it's essential that internal service groups have a clear and focused business strategy. This demands a profound sense of clarity about what they do (and don't do) and how their service contributes to the success of the organization. This tool will help your service group understand where it needs to concentrate its time and energy.

Sharpen your group's strategy by organizing the services you provide into the following four categories.

High Value-Added: Work that is key to the current and future success of the organization.

Business Necessity: Necessary work, but not core to organizational success (e.g., expense reports).

Unique: Work that must be staffed internally because it is proprietary to your organization, or for reasons of security, government regulation, policy, and so on.

Generic: Work that could be provided by other internal or external service groups.

THE STRATEGIC RESOURCING MODEL

		Contribution to Organizational Strategy	
		High Value-Added	**Business Necessity**
Technology and Expertise	*Unique— Must Be Done by Your Service Group*	**Market Actively** Be the best!	**Maintain Efficiently** Keep it running effectively.
	Generic— Can Be Done by Others	**Broker and Coach** Find and work with the best in class.	**Contract Out** Find providers of worry-free service and monitor them.

As a *partial* example, a Human Resources group in a large organization saw their strategy as:

	High Value-Added	*Business Necessity*
Unique	*Change leadership* *People and organization effectiveness* *Compensation program design*	*Compensation administration* *Benefits administration* *Reporting*
Generic	*Special expertise projects*	*Training programs* *Award programs*

Your service group will be considered a powerful contributor to your organization to the degree that you operate from the Market Actively box. We call this work Market Actively because it is the responsibility of your service group to show how your work activities add value to your organization; thus the need to market these activities enthusiastically. However, beware that Market Actively work can often become Generic or Business Necessity work over time; thus the ongoing challenge of keeping your service group focused on work that is high value-added. Only by doing this will your group be recognized for its high value contributions to the organization.

A couple of other caveats are also in order here. First, while every service group has essential work that must be done, far too many of these groups allow Business Necessity work to dominate their activities. The goal is to do this *must do* work as efficiently as possible, thereby freeing up time and energy for higher-value work. Second, be careful about asking clients and customers, "What would you like from us?" because they will often ask for more of the same (i.e., Maintain Efficiently activities). Again, while this work must be done, it will not enhance your group's standing as a strategic contributor to the organization.

How to use this leadership tool

"You do not merely want to be considered just the best of the best. You want to be considered the only ones who do what you do."

—Jerry Garcia

It often happens that individuals or groups become so busy doing necessary but routine work, that when high value-added projects arise in their organizations, these are actually outsourced to external service providers! This Strategic Resourcing model will help you initiate a review of your group's current work activities and plan a more value-added business strategy for your service group. Don't be dismayed if you are able to identify only a few High Value-Added activities.

Use this tool to begin improving your group's strategy and focus. This will lead to contracting out some lower-value activities, and training others in the organization to do some of your Business Necessity work. Most importantly, it will help you define the High Value-Added work that your group most needs to Market Actively.

WEB WORKSHEET

Ask yourself and then involve your group in asking these questions. Note responses in the workspace provided.

- Which activities in our group are presently directed at generic work, and could be done by others?
- Which activities in our group involve Maintain Efficiently work, and distract us from doing High Value-Added work? (Note: If there is debate over whether an activity is

High Value-Added or Business Necessity, we suggest you place it in the Business Necessity column initially, then discuss how to increase its added value.)

- Which activities in our group are Market Actively work and deserve more of our time and energy?

Contribution to Organizational Strategy

		High Value-Added	Business Necessity
Technology	*Unique— Best Done by Group*		
and Expertise	*Generic— Can Be Done by Others*		

RELATED LEADERSHIP TOOLS

3.1 Strategy	3.3 Environmental Scan	3.6 Strategic Relationships
3.2 Sigmoid Curve	3.4 Business-Unit Strategy	3.9 Marketing Services

FOR FURTHER ASSISTANCE

Hiebert, Murray. *Powerful Professionals: Getting Your Expertise Used Inside Organizations.* Recursion Press, 1999.

STRATEGIC RESOURCING MODEL WORKSHEET

1. Make a quick draft of key activities of your group for yourself.
2. Check your analysis with your leadership team.
3. If dissatisfied, work with a representative task force to determine where to spend your group's time and energy.
4. Prepare a plan of change. Get understanding and commitment of key stakeholders.

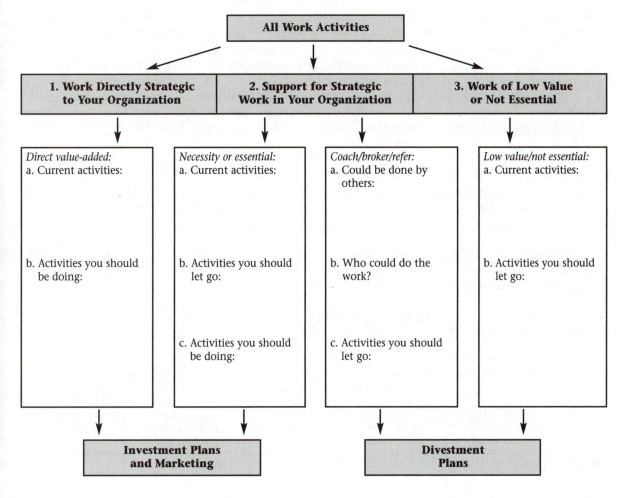

3.6

STRATEGIC RELATIONSHIPS: ANALYZING
YOUR CLIENT BASE

Inspired by a number of sources, including the work of the Novations Group.

Every leader provides products or services to someone—clients or customers, internal or external. Yet not all clients or customers are of equal value. Leaders and their workgroups need to regularly examine their client or customer base—those to whom they provide services—to ensure they are offering the highest value-added services and products to the right people. A good generalization is that 20 percent of your clients will require 80 percent of your time and energy. Which clients or customers are getting your group's high valued-added work? Which should be getting this work? These are important questions for workgroup success. This tool will help you rethink your products and services, and your client or customer base.

This tool starts with the assumption that you and your workgroup have already figured out how to focus on high value-added work. [If you haven't, use tool ☞ 3.4 Business-Unit Strategy or 3.5 Strategic Resourcing.] Given this assumption, consider these questions:

- ✔ Currently, who *are* your major clients or customers?
- ✔ Who *should be* your major clients or customers?
- ✔ Is the type of work that your group does for your major clients or customers high value-added work?
- ✔ What work *should* your group be doing that it is not presently doing?

This matrix will help you and your workgroup rethink strategic relationships with current and desired clients or customers. (In italics is a *partial* example for a Finance Department in a medium-size organization.)

INCREASING VALUE-ADDED WORK

	Low value activities	Necessary, but nonstrategic current activities	Activities that we do, but should be done by others	Current high value-added activities	High value-added work that we need to market actively
Your current clients/ customers	*All departments: lease car administration*	*Budget Process Management* *Accounts Payable* *Accounts Receivable*	*All departments: expense claim auditing*	*Executives: monthly financial health reports*	*Current Business Unit managers: Financial information and decision tools*
Clients/ customers you should have			*Procurement: Inventory financial management*	*Executives: Future activities evaluation*	*New Business Unit managers and all project and team leaders: Financial literacy*

How to use this leadership tool

WEB WORKSHEET

Follow these steps to analyze your client or customer base.

1. *Do some thinking for yourself.* Although you need a reasonably clear idea of what should go in the planning matrix that follows, be careful not to close your thinking to input from others. Do you have any givens—those things that you cannot compromise? Leaders need to be decisive regarding their client or customer bases and the group's product and service mix so that people know the group's direction. However, don't be so decisive that you become inflexible, and group members feel that they can't challenge established practices or contribute new ideas. [☞ 3.3 Environmental Scan]

2. *Involve others.* Sooner or later, your workgroup or team needs to agree to, and commit to, a strategy for providing products and services to specified clients or customers. The only path to commitment is involving group members and allowing them to influence strategic decisions. If your group is very large, you may need to assemble a task force—ideally, the best strategic thinkers from your group—to represent the group in this strategic decision-making process. You will want to lead this group, as strategic thinking is crucial to your success. You need to involve others, but this work cannot be delegated. [☞ 10.7 Getting Participation]

3. *Decide how you will proceed.* Depending on the lead time available, and how big a break with tradition you expect to make, this process may be done quick and dirty at some risk; or, more ideally, over a series of meetings with input from clients, senior management, and others not on the task force. [☞ 5.1 Change Equation]

4. *Complete this matrix.* Write in key names and key activities. Remember the 80-20 rule. Don't get caught up in detail and analysis paralysis. Plan action steps after you have completed this matrix. For example: What can you do to add more customers or clients to the high value-added side of this matrix? What steps can you take to reduce low-value activities?

	Low-value current activities	Necessary, but nonstrategic current activities	Activities that we do, but should be done by others	Current high value-added activities	High value-added work that we need to market actively
Your current clients/ customers					
Clients/ customers you should have					

RELATED LEADERSHIP TOOLS

2.1 Systems Thinking	3.4 Business-Unit Strategy	3.7 RAIR Logic
3.2 Sigmoid Curve	3.5 Strategic Resourcing	5.7 Stakeholder Groups

FOR FURTHER ASSISTANCE

Hiebert, Murray. *Powerful Professionals: Getting Your Expertise Used Inside Organizations*. Recursion Press, 1999.

3.7 RAIR LOGIC: ALIGNING CUSTOMERS, STRATEGY, CULTURE, AND LEADERSHIP

Inspired by Norman Chorn and Ivan Nurick.

Business strategy aligns organizations with their customers and markets; aligning the organization with its business strategy starts with leadership. Leadership influences, guides, and fosters people's thinking and behavior, and over time creates the organization's culture. Needless to say, to succeed in the long term, an organization's culture ("how things are done around here") must be fully aligned with its business strategy. This tool provides a way of checking to ensure alignment among your organization's leadership style, culture, business strategy, and customer needs or markets. [☛ 4.5 Culture]

For the most part, customers and clients operate from four predictable and describable sets of **RAIR** preferences (**R**espond, **A**ssure, **I**nnovate, **R**elate). The table presented here outlines these preferences, and recommends the appropriate strategy, organizational culture, and leadership style for each. One or two of these preferences often dominate customer or client demand within an industry or market, although all four usually exist to varying degrees in most business environments. These preferences provide a useful way for a leader to focus business strategy on the needs of customers and clients, as well as to align the organization's culture and leadership style in support of this business strategy.

The elements of strategic alignment

Customer Needs → Business Strategy → People → Organization Culture →

Respond indicates a predominately "thinking" customer or client preference for products and services; *assure* a "sensing" preference; *innovate* an intuitive or "intuiting" preference; and *relate* a "feeling" preference. These four categories are based upon the Myers-Briggs type indicator. [☛ 14.7 Personal Preferences]

	Respond *thinking predominates*	**Assure** *sensing predominates*	**Innovative** *intuitiung predominates*	**Relate** *feeling predominates*
Customer or client needs	➡ customer-led demand ➡ fast turnaround ➡ responsiveness ➡ on-time performance	➡ consistency ➡ reliability ➡ predictability ➡ efficient administration ➡ guarantees ➡ dependability	➡ supplier leadership ➡ new ways of delivering products or services ➡ leading-edge technology ➡ creative responses	➡ understanding ➡ insight ➡ consideration ➡ empathy ➡ acceptance ➡ sharing ➡ guidance ➡ trusting
Appropriate strategy	➡ have products available ➡ respond promptly to customers' requests ➡ get things done fast	➡ develop accurate, decisive, exact, and systematic approaches to serving customers	➡ take calculated risks ➡ develop innovative options for delivering products and service	➡ develop methods of: relating cooperating challenging supporting customers

Appropriate organizational culture	➠ responsive ➠ action and growth-oriented	➠ systematic ➠ consistent ➠ reliable	➠ develop new approaches ➠ seek change	➠ involving ➠ consultative ➠ consensus-seeking
Appropriate leadership style	➠ active ➠ assertive ➠ forceful ➠ driving ➠ pragmatic	➠ hierarchical ➠ managerial ➠ administrative	➠ imaginative ➠ adaptable ➠ visionary ➠ conceptual	➠ involving ➠ supportive ➠ consensus-seeking ➠ caring

HOW TO USE THIS LEADERSHIP TOOL

"The key to success is to ensure that your strategies, capabilities and approach to leadership [are] internally consistent and aligned with the requirements of the operating environment. … This is accomplished by focusing upon the dominant logic within each of these elements and aligning each element to achieve balance (equilibrium) within the whole business system."

—Norman Chorn and Ivan Nurick, *STRATEGIC ALIGNMENT*

Use the table and categories provided to assess the appropriateness and alignment of your current market environment (customer needs), business strategy, organizational culture, and style of leadership within your business unit or organization. Next, repeat the process, responding not to the current situation, but rather to what each of these elements could and should become. Assess gaps between the current situation and the ideal or future scenario, and plan action to close these alignment gaps. Keep in mind that organizational change requires culture change, and culture change requires change in leadership style; yet neither should be undertaken without a clear business strategy. [☛ 3.3 Environmental Scan, 5.1 Change Equation]

WEB WORKSHEET

Current situation	Ideal future scenario (achieve within _____ years)
Current customer needs are:	Customer needs will be:
Current strategy:	Ideal future strategy:
Current organizational culture:	Ideal future organizational culture:
Current leadership style:	Ideal future leadership style:

Given the information you have provided, number your current and ideal future alignment logics (with 1 being most dominant, and 4 being least dominant or not relevant at all).

Current situation	Ideal future scenario *(in _____ years)*
☐ *Respond* (thinking style)	☐ *Respond* (thinking style)
☐ *Assure* (sensing style)	☐ *Assure* (sensing style)
☐ *Innovate* (intuiting style)	☐ *Innovate* (intuiting style)
☐ *Relate* (feelings style)	☐ *Relate* (feelings style)

RELATED LEADERSHIP TOOLS

3.1 Strategy	3.5 Strategic Resourcing	5.6 Aligning Systems
3.4 Business-Unit Strategy	3.6 Strategic Relationships	14.7 Personal Preferences

FOR FURTHER ASSISTANCE

Chorn, Norman, and Ivan Nurick. *Strategic Alignment: The Science of Aligning Customers, Strategy, Culture and Leadership.*

3.8 PARTNERING FOR SUCCESS: JOINT VENTURES AND STRATEGIC ALLIANCES

Contributed by Mel Blitzer and inspired by Michael Schrage.

As we enter the second millennium, organizations large and small, private and public, local and transnational are joining forces—forming alliances—from the most informal of agreements through to joint ventures and mergers. Known as strategic alliances, collaborative relationships, or cooperative ventures, these arrangements help organizations to:

✔ Face the challenges of a complex, constantly shifting business environment.

✔ Keep pace with technological innovation.

✔ Meet the pressures of globalization.

At the development and implementation stage, strategic alliances can become quite complex, especially when the organizations involved have little history of working with each other. This is when having an alliancing model like the one presented here can be invaluable in helping to sort out and track the alliance development process.

THE STRATEGIC ALLIANCE DEVELOPMENT CYCLE

Conceptual and technical collaboration form the basis of successful alliances.

Conceptual collaboration:

➡ The overarching intent of the proposed alliance is developed. People devise concepts, ideas, themes, and strategies, and outline the nature and possible solutions to organizational problems. A useful analogy is a group of people planning to build a house together. Conceptual collaboration would give everyone a clear idea and picture of how the house will look. This may go as far as detailed blueprints of the house.

Technical collaboration:

➡ The alliance is built based on the agreed project concept or blueprint. This involves bringing people with complementary skills together to accomplish a specific task—in our analogy, building a house.

When combined, conceptual and technical collaboration can be used to construct a four-stage model of alliancing.

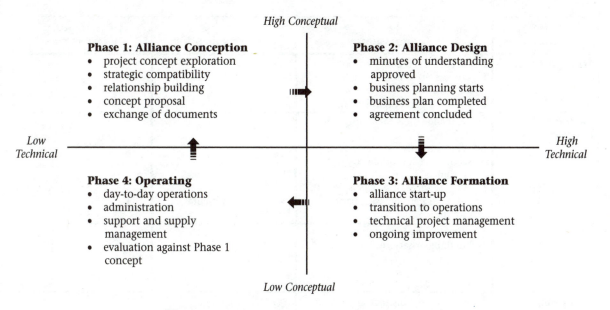

How to use this leadership tool

"Like romances, alliances are built on hopes and dreams—what might happen if certain opportunities are pursued."

—Rosabeth Moss Kanter, HARVARD BUSINESS REVIEW

Establishing mutually beneficial alliances or partnerships requires that you a) assess your own organization to determine what kind of alliance, if any, will further your strategic business interests, and b) do a similar assessment of your potential partner organization(s) to determine compatibility between that organization and your organization. Ask yourself these essential alliancing questions:

? Why should your organization be involved in partnering (e.g., a joint venture, a strategic alliance)?

? How will creating a joint venture or alliance provide synergies for your organization and your partner's?

Like any good marriage, a solid, long-term, mutually beneficial relationship between organizations begins with a good understanding of yourself and your intended partner. A thorough self-assessment can help you determine whether an alliance might further your business interests.

WEB WORKSHEET

Use the workspace here to assess your organization and your proposed partner organization(s) for strategic fit. Whether or not you ultimately form an alliance with another organization(s), this analysis will serve as useful strategic architecture for your organization.

Strategic dimension	Key questions	Your organization	Your proposed alliance partner
Strategic intent	? Where is each company going? ? What is the vision for each business? ? Is there a good high-level fit?	[☛ 2.4 Visioning]	
Customers/ markets	? Who and where are traditional markets? ? What attributes of products or services are important to customers? ? What services or products does the customer perceive each partner offering?	[☛ 3.3 Environmental Scan]	
Businesses	? What are the logical groupings or bundling of services or products?		
Core products/ services	? What are the distinct services or products of each company that are a direct result of competitive competencies?	[☛ 3.1 Strategy]	
Core competencies	? What are the core competencies, capabilities, and skills that will carry each company toward its intent?	[☛ 13.8 Competencies]	
Support and supply	? What critical internal support and external supply functions enable the core business of each company?		
Current and future issues	? What challenges and critical issues does each organization face? ? What do the SWOT analyses look like?	[☛ 3.3 Environmental Scan]	
Stakeholders	? Who are the stakeholders in the success or failure of each company? ? Who has an interest in what you do? ? What do the stakeholder maps look like?	[☛ 5.7 Stakeholder Groups]	
Culture	? How do the societal and corporate cultures affect the organization design and management style of each company? ? Is there a good cultural fit?	[☛ 4.5 Culture]	

RELATED LEADERSHIP TOOLS

2.3 Directional Statements   2.8 Balanced Scorecard   3.3 Environmental Scan
2.5 Values   3.1 Strategy   6.5 Force-Field Analysis

FOR FURTHER ASSISTANCE

Bleeke, Joel, and David Ernst, eds. *Collaborating to Compete: Using Strategic Alliances and Acquisitions in the Global Marketplace.* John Wiley & Sons, 1993.

Doz, Yves L., and Gary Hamel. *Alliance Advantage: The Art of Creating Value through Partnering.* Harvard Business School Press, 1998.

Lorange, Peter, and Johan Roos. *Strategic Alliances: Formation, Implementation and Evolution.* Blackwell Publishers, 1992.

Lynch, Robert Porter. *Business Alliances Guide: The Hidden Competitive Weapon.* John Wiley & Sons, 1993.

Schrage, Michael. *Shared Minds: The New Technologies of Collaboration.* Random House, 1990.

3.9 MARKETING A PROFESSIONAL SERVICE GROUP

Inspired by Novations Group and Tom Peters.

Professional service groups (e.g., IT, HR, Legal) within many large organizations are often being deregulated internally. No longer are operating managers obligated to use these internal services. Thus, *internal* service groups are expected to compete with *external* service groups for work within their own organizations. This tool will help you market your internal professional services group within your organization.

Use these steps and questions when developing a marketing plan for your internal professional services group. Involve others early and often in preparing this marketing plan: first, your internal service professionals; then, your clients (e.g., operating professionals who use your group's internal services, senior managers who sponsor your group's internal services).

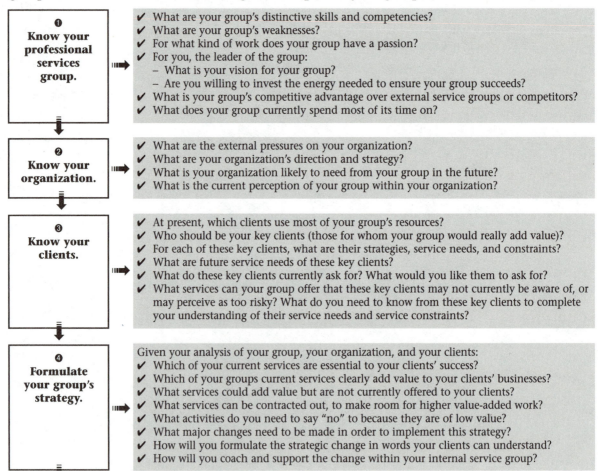

❶ Know your professional services group.

- ✔ What are your group's distinctive skills and competencies?
- ✔ What are your group's weaknesses?
- ✔ For what kind of work does your group have a passion?
- ✔ For you, the leader of the group:
  - – What is your vision for your group?
  - – Are you willing to invest the energy needed to ensure your group succeeds?
- ✔ What is your group's competitive advantage over external service groups or competitors?
- ✔ What does your group currently spend most of its time on?

❷ Know your organization.

- ✔ What are the external pressures on your organization?
- ✔ What are your organization's direction and strategy?
- ✔ What is your organization likely to need from your group in the future?
- ✔ What is the current perception of your group within your organization?

❸ Know your clients.

- ✔ At present, which clients use most of your group's resources?
- ✔ Who should be your key clients (those for whom your group would really add value)?
- ✔ For each of these key clients, what are their strategies, service needs, and constraints?
- ✔ What are future service needs of these key clients?
- ✔ What do these key clients currently ask for? What would you like them to ask for?
- ✔ What services can your group offer that these key clients may not currently be aware of, or may perceive as too risky? What do you need to know from these key clients to complete your understanding of their service needs and service constraints?

❹ Formulate your group's strategy.

Given your analysis of your group, your organization, and your clients:
- ✔ Which of your current services are essential to your clients' success?
- ✔ Which of your groups current services clearly add value to your clients' businesses?
- ✔ What services could add value but are not currently offered to your clients?
- ✔ What services can be contracted out, to make room for higher value-added work?
- ✔ What activities do you need to say "no" to because they are of low value?
- ✔ What major changes need to be made in order to implement this strategy?
- ✔ How will you formulate the strategic change in words your clients can understand?
- ✔ How will you coach and support the change within your internal service group?

❺ Integrate this strategy into a marketing plan.	✔ What are the long-term marketing goals for your internal professional service group? ✔ What are the short-term marketing goals for your group? ✔ What is your plan for marketing your group's professional services? ✔ How will you communicate with your clients in a way that supports their acceptance? ✔ How will you get feedback in order to take corrective action on the inevitable problems that will crop up as you implement your new marketing plan?

HOW TO USE THIS LEADERSHIP TOOL

"Business-ing = The process of turning every job into a business, every worker into a businessperson, a business unit of one."

—Tom Peters, *CIRCLE OF INNOVATION*

Developing a marketing plan for your internal professional services group needs the involvement and support of all members in the group. If you don't provide enough structure, people will feel there is no mechanism or process through which they can contribute to developing the marketing plan. On the other hand, if you provide too much detail and structure, people will think "It's a done deal" and their contribution is not required. We suggest this minimal level of structure for preparing a marketing plan. (Some of these steps will need adjustment depending on the size of your professional services group.)

WEB WORKSHEET

1. Present the benefits for preparing a marketing plan. [☛ 9.7 Selling Wheel]

2. As the group's leader, define your givens—your overall goals for having a marketing plan, the minimum specifications of the marketing plan (e.g., "We must continue to service the Northern Operations Business Unit"), and elements of the process that must be used in developing the marketing plan (e.g., "We will need to involve all senior service professionals in our group; our clients need to be consulted"). [☛ 2.3 Directional Statements, 2.7 Goal Statements]

3. Explain and discuss your thinking with members of your internal services group. Ask key members (or all members) to challenge and refine your givens, and to add their own ideas.

4. Prepare a first draft of the marketing plan (either alone or with the help of others).

5. Next, have the group come together as a whole to review drafts of the marketing plan, test assumptions, develop refinements, and seek synergies. [☛ 10.7 Getting Participation]

6. Depending on the size of your group, you may wish to form a task force representing all stakeholders inside your group, to work on further developing the marketing plan.

7. The task force can then prepare a final draft. However, this draft should have full group support.

8. Finally, you or your task force need to go out and talk with your clients and further refine your plan.

GETTING THE PROCESS STARTED

As a way to begin the process of developing a marketing plan, use the workspace here to capture your initial thoughts under each of the five steps. Of the thoughts you jot down, note:

➠ which you consider to be givens or nonnegotiables (and thus provide clear direction to your group);

➠ which are preferences, to which you have no firm commitment as yet; and

➠ which are raw ideas that you will use to stimulate the group's thinking as they work on developing a marketing plan.

❶ Know your professional services group.	
❷ Know your organization.	
❸ Know your clients.	
❹ Formulate your group's strategy.	
❺ Integrate this strategy into a marketing plan.	

Related leadership tools

1.6 Boards of Play

3.2 Sigmoid Curve

3.5 Strategic Resourcing

3.6 Strategic Relationships

4.9 Professional Expertise

13.11 Delivering Expertise

For further assistance

Hiebert, Murray. *Powerful Professionals: Getting Your Expertise Used Inside Organizations*. Recursion Press, 1999.

Peters, Thomas J., and Dean LeBaron. *The Circle of Innovation: You Can't Shrink Your Way to Greatness*. Knopf. 1997.

4

TOOLS FOR DESIGNING PRODUCTIVE PROCESSES AND ORGANIZATIONS

A poor process or dysfunctional organization will diminish the contribution of even the most motivated employees (and leaders!). As Peter Scholtes says, "All the empowered, motivated, teamed-up, self-directed, incentivized, accountable, reengineered, and reinvented people you can muster cannot compensate for a dysfunctional system." This section provides an overview of some key tools leaders require to design effective processes and organizations that will maximize the contributions of people.

4.1

Designing Productive Organizations

Inspired by Bernie Novokowsky, Peter Drucker, Jay Galbraith, David Hanna, Susan Mohrman, and Thomas Cummings.

"Structure is a very powerful shaper of behavior. It's like the strange pumpkin I once saw at a country fair. It had been grown in a four-cornered Mason jar. The jar had since been broken and removed. The remaining pumpkin was shaped exactly like a small Mason jar. Beside it was a pumpkin from the same batch of seeds that was allowed to grow without constraints. It was five times bigger. Organization structures and systems have the same effect on the people in them. They either limit or liberate their performance potential."

—Jim Clemmer, *PATHWAYS TO PERFORMANCE*

When it comes to designing an organizational structure there is no such thing as "one size fits all." On this matter, Peter Drucker, arguably the most distinguished organizational guru of our time, is unequivocal: "There is no such thing as the one right organization [design]. There are only organizations, each of which has distinct strengths, distinct limitations, and specific applications." This tool will provide you with the overall design of an organization, division, or workgroup, including a systemic model for organizational design.

Organizational design needs to:

1. *Support organizational aims.* An organization's high-level thinking as expressed in its vision, mission, and values must lead to solid business results. For example, if customer service is a highly valued organizational aim, then the organization must be widely organized to deliver outstanding customer service. [☛ 2.5 Values, 2.6 Clarifying Purpose]

2. *Be systemic.* Many organizational designs fall short because the elements of the design don't fit with and support each other. Nor do they support the larger system. A good organization design facilitates: a) access to information, b) decision making by those with the best information, and c) the ability to take appropriate action in the face of change. [☛ 2.1 Systems Thinking]

3. *Focus from the outside-in.*

Organization design starts with an assessment	Key questions
➠ Clarify customer/client needs. ➠ Map stakeholder groups. ➠ Understand relevant environmental forces. [☛ 3.3 Environmental Scan]	✔ Who does this organization serve? ✔ Who are the groups who have a stake in success? ✔ What are the driving or competitive forces in the society around the organization?

4. *Be easy to understand and communicate.* The organization should be readily understandable: inside (to employees) and outside (to customers and other stakeholders). People need to be able to work the system quickly and easily. [☛5.1 Change Equation, 8.3 Organizational Communication]

5. *Be flexible.* Only stone-age organizations can be cast in stone. Organizations need to be able to turn on a dime so they can reorganize to deal with environmental changes or to capture opportunities. [☛ 1.10 GAS Model]

An organizational design model

All of the following design elements must be in place and aligned to support each other. We suggest you design last what is often designed first—organizational structure. Each double-headed arrow represents the need for mutual support among the design elements.

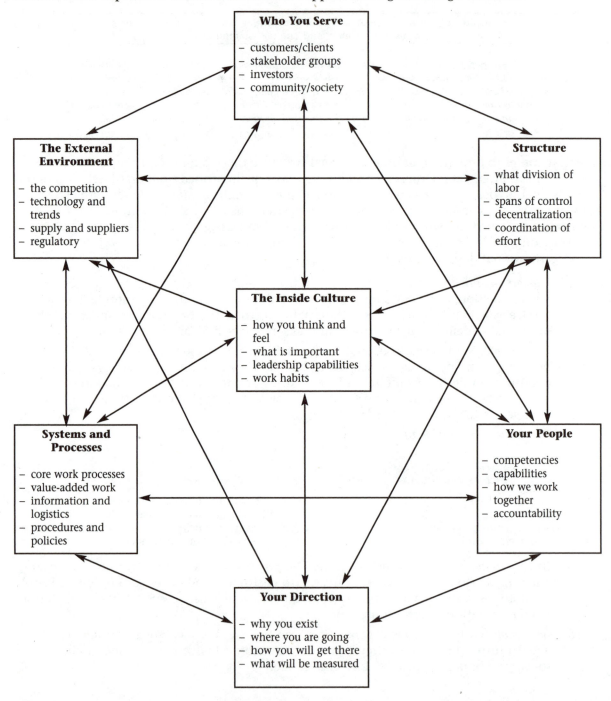

Who You Serve
- customers/clients
- stakeholder groups
- investors
- community/society

The External Environment
- the competition
- technology and trends
- supply and suppliers
- regulatory

Structure
- what division of labor
- spans of control
- decentralization
- coordination of effort

The Inside Culture
- how you think and feel
- what is important
- leadership capabilities
- work habits

Systems and Processes
- core work processes
- value-added work
- information and logistics
- procedures and policies

Your People
- competencies
- capabilities
- how we work together
- accountability

Your Direction
- why you exist
- where you are going
- how you will get there
- what will be measured

"... Organization is not absolute. As such, a given organizational structure fits certain tasks in certain conditions and at certain times."
—Peter Drucker, "MANAGEMENT'S NEW PARADIGM," *FORBES*

Mathematicians know that modeling a seven-body, mutually interacting system like the one shown here is a daunting task. Ultimately, the seven boxes will need to be balanced by trial and error. To get started, jot down your first ideas for the design or redesign of your part of the organization. (You'll need a pencil and eraser!) A suggested process is:

1. Refine the captions of each box to suit your organizational culture.

2. Work from the big picture and givens to details and the less-understood.

3. Jot in the data as you think it ought to be for the redesigned organization. Start a list of information that you need to add to the data and measurements.

4. Next, step back and assess how each box fits with and supports every other box. Adjust your data and expectations to make the whole work. Remember the principle of systems thinking illustrated in the performance of a great car: It doesn't have the world's most powerful engine. Rather, it has the engine that best integrates with all the other characteristics of the vehicle, and thereby maximizes the overall performance design features of the car as a whole.

5. Unless you want to design a top-down organization, involve others early and often to refine your assumptions, add new ideas and data, and build commitment to the final design.

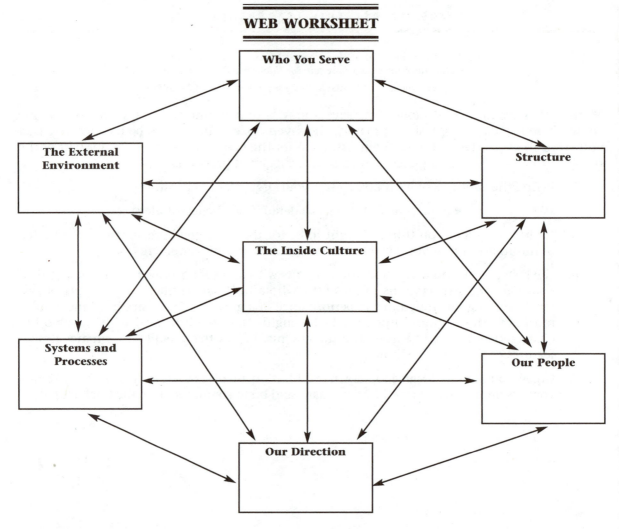

WEB WORKSHEET

Who You Serve

The External Environment

Structure

The Inside Culture

Systems and Processes

Our People

Our Direction

Copyright McGraw-Hill 2000. Original purchasers of this book are permitted to photocopy or customize this worksheet by downloading it from *www.books.mcgraw-hill.com/training/download*. The document can then be opened, edited, and printed using Microsoft Word or other word processing software.

RELATED LEADERSHIP TOOLS

2.1 Systems Thinking	2.3 Directional Statements	5.6 Aligning Systems
2.2 7S Model	4.3 Reengineering	5.7 Stakeholder Groups

FOR FURTHER ASSISTANCE

Drucker, Peter. *Managing in Turbulent Times*. Harper & Row, 1980.

Galbraith, Jay. *Designing Complex Organizations*. Addison-Wesley, 1973.

Hanna, David P. *Designing Organizations for High Performance*. Addison-Wesley, 1988.

Mohrman, Susan. A., and Thomas G. Cummings. *Self-Designing Organizations: Learning How to Create High Performance*. Addison-Wesley, 1989.

4.2

HIERARCHY: LEADERSHIP LEVELS
IN AN ORGANIZATION

Inspired by Peter Drucker, Elliot Jaques, and Peter Senge.

These days, it seems a little out of fashion to say *hierarchy* and *leadership* in the same sentence. Yet management hierarchies remain at the heart of most organizations. As Peter Senge notes, "There are some people who say the future organization is going to have no hierarchy. I don't agree." Peter Drucker is even blunter: "… One hears today about 'the end of hierarchy.' This is blatant nonsense. In any institution there has to be a final authority, that is, a 'boss'—someone who can make the final decision and who can expect to be obeyed." This tool provides a practical model to help you consider hierarchical levels and spans of control.

Maverick organizational theorist Elliot Jaques argues that the more senior the leader, the longer the time span (the farther into the future) he or she is responsible for managing. For example:

⟹ A retail chain store, frontline junior salesperson's time span is from here-and-now customer service to perhaps a few weeks into the future, depending on the store's reordering cycle.

⟹ The chain store manager's time perspective may range from here-and-now decisions to a time span beyond next season's promotion plan and the annual lease renewal.

⟹ The chain store CEO must be looking several years ahead to plan the direction and focus of the organization in the changing business environment.

Jaques argues that the longer the time perspective that the individual is responsible for, the higher the leadership level, and the more the individual should be rewarded. In Jaques' words, "Time-span measurement of a leadership role requires nothing more than eliciting the assignments which a manager is putting into that role, and sorting out those tasks or task sequences with the longest target completion time." Extending Jaques' time-based model, Peter Senge argues that the justification for hierarchy is breadth. This ladder notion concerns understanding and dealing with the impacts of decisions within organizations.

Here is a broad-brush matrix combining organizational level with time and breadth perspectives.

Organizational level	Time perspective required	Breadth perspective required
Senior executive	Must look 10 or more years ahead to assess the impact of decisions.	Must look at the broad system and wide impacts (internal and external) of decisions—on business, society, competitors, workforce, and so on. Must keep organization healthy in its wider environment.
Vice president	Must look ahead from 3 to 10 years.	Must understand and deal with all impacts and influences inside and outside the organization.

Mid-level leader	In the range of 1 to 5 years.	Must understand and deal with all internal impacts and outside impacts in functional area.
Frontline leader	In the range of 6 months to 1 year.	Must understand and deal with immediate internal impacts and outside impacts in functional area.
Senior professional	In the range of 2 to 5 years.	Must understand and deal with all internal impacts and outside impacts in professional or specialty and functional area.
Junior professional	Up to 1 year.	Must understand and deal with the immediate impact of their work.
Frontline nonprofessional	Up to a few weeks.	Must understand and deal with the immediate impact of their work.

In addition to considering the time-span and breadth perspectives of hierarchy, today's organizations also try to keep the number of management levels to a minimum (to keep their hierarchies as flat as possible).

HOW TO USE THIS LEADERSHIP TOOL

"There is wisdom in the old proverb of the Roman law that a slave who has three masters is a free man. It is a very old principle of human relations that no one should be put into a conflict of loyalties—and having more than one master creates such a conflict."

—Peter Drucker, "MANAGEMENT'S NEW PARADIGM," *FORBES*

You may find using time span and breadth an intriguing alternative to the more traditional job evaluation and description methods of linking compensation categories to jobs. Advantages of using the notions of time span and breadth include:

✔ They emphasize thinking longer-term and more broadly.

✔ They get around issues related to amount of turf and number of reports that have traditionally been troublesome in determining compensation levels.

✔ They lend legitimacy to employees who may have no reports and a small budget, yet are expected to think long-term and widely.

✔ They provide a way of thinking about leadership levels that transcends organizational functions and disciplines.

WEB WORKSHEET

Suggested uses of the following matrix:

1. The process of clarifying an optimal hierarchy is always iterative. Use the matrix provided earlier as a guide.

2. Jot in the typical *What?* (results), by when (time spans), and the breadth of decisions. Then estimate the appropriate responsibility level. Note typical examples. These will be helpful in explaining how you arrived at a given responsibility level for each role.

3. You will almost certainly need to rework this matrix a number of times before you get the groupings clear.

What outputs? Goals, output, results (Use concrete examples.)	By when? Time horizon required (Use concrete examples.)	With what impact? Breadth perspective required (Use concrete examples.)	Organizational level
[☞ 2.7 Goal Statements]		[☞ 2.1 Systems Thinking]	

RELATED LEADERSHIP TOOLS

1.6 Boards of Play	2.1 Systems Thinking	13.3 Accountability
1.7 Results-Based Leaders	4.1 Organizational Design	13.10 Careers

FOR FURTHER ASSISTANCE

Drucker, Peter. *The Practice of Management,* 2nd ed. Harperbusiness, 1993.

Jaques, Elliot. *Requisite Organization: A Total System for Effective Managerial Organization and Managerial Leadership for the Twenty-First Century.* Cason Hall & Co., 1996.

Peter Senge, interview in Gibson, Rowan, ed. *Rethinking the Future: Rethinking Business, Principles, Competition, Control and Complexity, Leadership, Markets, and the World.* Nicholas Brealey, 1999.

4.3   Business Process Reengineering

Inspired by Cheryl Currid, Michael Hammer, James Champy, and Steven Stanton.

Reengineering advocates have lauded successes including American Express "… reducing its annual costs by $1 billion …"; AT&T turning a "… nine-figure loss to a nine-figure profit…"; a financial firm reducing its new customer processing time from 6 to 14 days, to a few hours; and a life insurance company reducing the application process from a three-week period to less than one hour. On the other hand, Michael Hammer concedes that many organizations undertook reengineering efforts "… only to abandon them with little or no positive results." However, like all the leadership tools, reengineering, in the proper circumstances, can achieve remarkable results; improperly used, it can be a very expensive failure.

Some organizations use phrases like "business process design" or "process redesign" instead of reengineering. However, the official definition of reengineering, according to Michael Hammer and James Champy, is "the fundamental rethinking and *radical redesign* of business *processes* to bring about *dramatic* improvements in performance." (Italics are Hammer's.) The next section highlights core processes that leaders need to consider if they intend to undertake business process reengineering.

The core process of process reengineering

Four steps or questions are at the core of the reengineering process.

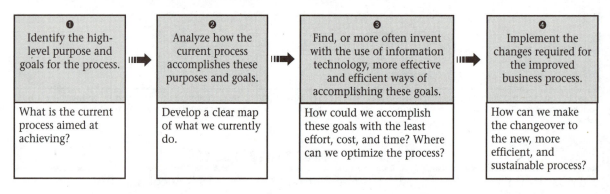

❶ Identify the high-level purpose and goals for the process.	❷ Analyze how the current process accomplishes these purposes and goals.	❸ Find, or more often invent with the use of information technology, more effective and efficient ways of accomplishing these goals.	❹ Implement the changes required for the improved business process.
What is the current process aimed at achieving?	Develop a clear map of what we currently do.	How could we accomplish these goals with the least effort, cost, and time? Where can we optimize the process?	How can we make the changeover to the new, more efficient, and sustainable process?

The principles of process reengineering

The reengineering principles listed here have a profound effect on the leadership culture within an organization. They move it from top-down control to a more involving and democratic culture. Ironically, although castigated for its antihumane aspects, many reengineering failures are actually due to leaders being unwilling to give up control (i.e., this work often becomes bogged down when people in power have strong vested interests in the status quo).

1. *Honor the past.* Invariably, current business processes are the way they are for historical reasons. These processes were elaborated over time due to breakdowns in the past, not because people were stupid. [☞ 4.5 Culture]

2. *Redesign processes to get results.* Assess where work can be done in parallel, then integrated at crucial points. Results must justify means—redesigning functions, tasks, and jobs. [☞ 2.2 7S Model]

3. *Combine several jobs or functions into one.* Reengineering cuts across traditional functions.

4. *Maximize use of information technology.* Automate, but also harness information technologies to do things in ways that couldn't be done at all in the past. (Most reengineering efforts are highly dependent on the use of information technologies.)

5. *Capture data only once, if possible.* Capture data electronically when it is created.

6. *Push work and decisions as far down to frontline workers as possible.* Reengineered employee benefits programs have employees accessing their own information and making the changes on-line, for example. [☞ 9.2 Situational Leadership]

7. *Minimize handoffs.* These are often a source of errors, delays, and conflict.

8. *Make controls and reconciliation everyone's responsibility.* As with TQM, minimize the need for checking by others. [☞ 7.7 Quality Tools]

9. *Emphasize change leadership.* With the focus on process redesign, the need to help people make the human transition to new processes and roles is often ignored. [☞ 5.1 Change Equation]

How to Use This Leadership Tool

"We have found that many tasks that employees performed had nothing to do with meeting customer needs— that is, creating a product high in quality, supplying that product at a fair price, and providing excellent service. Many tasks were done simply to satisfy the internal demands of the company's own organization."

—Michael Hammer and James Champy, *REENGINEERING THE CORPORATION*

This table describes a typical reengineering process. Also, because reengineering has met with skepticism and failure as well as success, a checklist of dos and don'ts is provided.

WEB WORKSHEET

❶ Get Started.	❷ Analyze current processes.	❸ Find (invent) more effective and efficient ways of accomplishing goals.	❹ Implement sustainable changes and capture the benefits.
❑ Be absolutely clear about the purpose and goals of the project. ❑ Be sure you have top management support.	❑ Start by mapping the current process. ❑ Work with the people who currently work within the process, to map the process.	This is the most creative phase of the redesign process and can take considerable time and research. ❑ Use these questions to redesign the process:	This state involves the introduction of change. Consider adding some new people to the team who are expert at change leadership.

❑ Form a steering committee. ❑ Select a core process. ❑ Determine the process redesign owner. ❑ Form a redesign team, with key stakeholders represented.	❑ Get baseline measures on the effectiveness of the process. ❑ Map where breakdowns, errors, conflict, etc., typically occur.	• How could we accomplish these goals with the least effort, time, and expense? • Where can we optimize the process? • Where could information technology help us be more efficient? When a new process design prototype is completed, test and refine the prototype. Be prepared for people not wanting to share information for fear of job loss, "It can't be done," "It won't work," etc.	❑ Obtain senior managements' unequivocal support one more time. The more significant the change, the more support and perseverance will be required. ❑ Thoroughly plan the change required, both technical changes and human changes. (See Section 5, Tools for Leading Change.) ❑ Ensure that all systems are aligned to support the change.

SOME DOS

✔ Get the unequivocal support of top management. Business process reengineering is a revolutionary, quantum leap process. [☛ 5.4 Change Scale]

✔ Spend as much time on the people side as you do on the technical issues of redesign. Also, be attentive to the politics. [☛ 5.8 Human Transitions]

✔ Get the time and budget to do it right. Process mapping, innovative redesign, and systemwide change take considerable time and effort. [☛ 5.2 Major Change]

✔ Look at the organization as an outside customer or client would. Work from an objective and nonvested perspective. [☛ 5.7 Stakeholder Groups]

✔ Be clear about goals and results. The redesign is driven by clear goals, not by the tasks involved. [☛ 2.3 Directional Statements]

✔ Get lots of technical help, especially at the redesign phase.

✔ Question everything. Sacred cows will dump all over the redesign.

✔ Get commitment and buy-in, early and often. Breakthrough changes require a lot of coordinated effort and support. [☛ 5.1 Change Equation, 5.2 Major Change]

✔ Use a lot of two-way communication. Don't wait until the change is announced to bring people on board. [☛ 8.3 Organizational Communication]

✔ Map the wider system that the redesigned process needs to fit into. (Failure to have your recommendations accepted is often related to a lack of support, rather than to a technical problem with the recommendations themselves.) [☛ 2.1 Systems Thinking, 4.1 Organizational Design, 5.6 Aligning Systems]

- ✔ Find the best possible people for the redesign team. Think beyond technical aspects to issues of change leadership. [☞ 10.1 HiPo Teams]
- ✔ Proceed boldly but carefully with unproven technology. Relying on vaporware has its dangers.

SOME DON'TS

- ✘ Don't get frustrated. You will meet resistance when you change "the way things are done around here."
- ✘ Don't let senior management off the hook. They, not the project team, need to own the final outcome.

RELATED LEADERSHIP TOOLS

2.1 Systems Thinking	4.1 Organizational Design	5.4 Change Scale
2.6 Clarifying Purpose	4.4 Employee Involvement	5.6 Aligning Systems
2.7 Goal Statements	5.2 Major Change	5.8 Human Transitions

FOR FURTHER ASSISTANCE

Currid, Cheryl C. *The Reengineering Toolkit: 15 Tools and Technologies for Reengineering Your Organization*. Prima Pub, 1996.

Hammer, Michael, and James Champy. *Reengineering the Corporation: A Manifesto for Business*. Harperbusiness, 1994.

Hammer, Michael, and Steven A. Stanton. *The Reengineering Revolution: A Handbook*. Harperbusiness, 1995.

4.4

EMPLOYEE INVOLVEMENT:
A RANGE OF POSSIBILITIES

Inspired by Edward Lawler, Victor Vroom, and Philip Yetton.

Modern organizations are being pressured to involve employees more substantively than in the past. Changing the level of involvement can be a challenging task. As the saying goes, "The system is perfectly aligned to produce what it is now producing." The upshot is that the current level of involvement is thoroughly entrenched by custom, culture, values, expectations, styles, and tradition. Here are some sobering reasons, however, for changing the traditional levels of involvement:

⟼ *Increasing complexity of organizations, systems, and stakeholders*—some examples are the complexity of e-commerce, off-shore competition, and alliances with suppliers, contractors, and customers.

⟼ *Increasing complexity of work* prevents an individual leader from knowing or even understanding it all—technology, information, legislation, internationalization, multiple cultures, shorter cycle times. No longer can there be a General Manager, knowledgeable and skilled in all areas of work. The modern leader needs to marshal advice and resources, involving many source people. [☛ 1.1 Twenty-First-Century Leader, 1.2 Manage or Lead?]

⟼ *The rise of the knowledge worker.* Traditionally, leaders did the thinking; followers did the work unthinkingly, to drive out variance. Today, workers are expected to think thoroughly about their work and how it fits into the big picture. [☛ 4.9 Professional Expertise, 7.7 Quality Tools]

⟼ *The need for innovation to succeed.* Creativity and innovation are more likely surpressed in authoritarian leadership styles and more likely to thrive in high-involvement work cultures.

⟼ *Workers want more say in their work.* Today's highly educated workforce is less likely to "do as they're told." [☛2.5 Values, 4.5 Culture]

Given this backdrop, leaders feel pressured to dramatically increase employee involvement. The question is, "What kind of involvement, and by whom, will enhance the work situation?"

This tool outlines a range of levels of employee involvement and provides a checklist for choosing and implementing the appropriate level.

A RANGE OF INVOLVEMENT LEVELS

	Level 1 **Authoritarian or top-down**	Level 2 **As-needed involvement**	Level 3 **Joint problem solving**	Level 4 **Joint leadership**	Level 5 **Self-directed teams or contractors**
Leader role	Mainly one-way, rule-based direction and close daily supervision (i.e., "Just do as you're told"). Often done in a loving but parental mode.	Supervisors have an open-door policy and invite employee input on an as-needed basis.	Supervisors involve employees in problem solving, as part of project teams, task forces, and committees. Leader makes final decisions.	Leaders share responsibility for work but are still accountable for employee processes and results. Decisions are made jointly and by consensus.	Leaders work as facilitators and coaches. Leaders are accountable only for the overall direction and integration of work. Leaders rarely veto decisions.
Employee role	Employees are not involved in significant decisions. Employees involved only when needed.	Employees provide data and help to identify and solve problems on an invitational basis.	Employees help to identify and solve problems, as well as recommend solutions.	Employees are often organized into natural work teams and are involved in setting business goals. Employees identify, define, and solve problems; get leader approval; then implement solutions.	Workers determine the direction and conditions of their work unit (i.e., they manage change). Employees fully accountable for processes and results.
Activities	Employees understand and follow the rules and, in the worst cases, use grievance procedures to resolve problems.	Employees may participate in problem-solving groups, complete surveys, and provide input into suggestion systems. Leaders make all significant decisions.	Employees work in task forces, project groups, and quality groups.	Employees and leaders work within partnership or team structures.	Work is by independent individuals (e.g., contractors) or in self-managing teams (e.g., they are involved in hiring and terminating team members).

GUIDELINES FOR CHOOSING A LEVEL OF INVOLVEMENT

There is no absolute best involvement level, but there are optimal levels to produce the best results and allow employees to attain satisfaction. Here are some guidelines that will help you choose an appropriate level.

The guideline	What to look for	Remarks
The results required	➡ The optimal level of involvement starts with a clear statement of results. Involvement is generally a means, not an end in itself. [☞ 1.7 Results-Based Leaders]	Involvement can also be valued in its own right—think of democracy, which is probably inefficient in many respects. [☞ 4.6 Open-Book Leadership]
The maturity of the workers	➡ Some workforces are more than prepared to take on responsibility, and are pressuring leaders to let it happen. However, if the workforce doesn't have the knowledge, skills, or values for self-direction, there is no point in establishing self-managed teams. ➡ The rise of knowledge work is pushing toward more substantive involvement by workers. [☞ 9.2 Situational Leadership]	Leaders need to be careful with this one. Leaders and organizational cultures can create dependencies or, alternately, can encourage self-dependency. Dozens of studies show that most, but not all, workers can take on more responsibility with coaching, some pushing, and lots of positive feedback. [☞ 4.5 Culture]
The nature of the work	Among other things, if the work: ➡ requires a high level of innovation or quality, ➡ is very technical, ➡ is nonroutine, or ➡ requires a team approach because no one person has all the answers, then higher levels of involvement are called for.	In general, the nature of work is driving a higher involvement of workers.
Your natural style	Assess your own personal style for: ➡ the amount of control you can give up, and ➡ the amount of risk you can bear.	Research shows effective leaders adapt their styles to the situation. [☞ 9.1 Leadership Versatility] You probably need coaching or assistance if the level of involvement needed is "not you." [☞ 13.1 Coaching]
The culture of the organization	➡ Organizations often have cultures that are rooted in past practices and events. These cultures are notoriously hard to change. [☞ 2.5 Values, 4.5 Culture]	The easiest and best time to establish the level of involvement is in new, "green field" situations. Remember that current systems generally support the current level of involvement.

HOW TO USE THIS LEADERSHIP TOOL

"Leaders need an ability to look through a variety of lenses. We need to look through the lens of a follower. We need to look through the lens of a new reality. We need to look through the lens of hard experience and failure. We need to look through the lens of unfairness and mortality. We need to look hard at our future."

—Max De Pree, *LEADERSHIP JAZZ*

If you want to, or need to, change the level of involvement, adapt and use these suggestions.

GUIDELINES FOR TRANSITION

❑ *The change must start with you, the leader.* Think through and list the behaviors you will continue to use, stop using, and start using. You must change first! [☛ 15.2 Emotional Intelligence, 15.5 Habits]

❑ *Scrupulously model the behaviors you expect from others,* especially during transitions to a higher-involvement culture. Workers are rightfully critical and skeptical of leaders who don't "walk their talk." [☛ 1.8 Recursive Leadership]

❑ *Make the process model the outcome;* make it recursive. You can request and encourage, but not dictate, involvement. Involve employees in the change to the level anticipated after the change. [☛ 1.8 Recursive Leadership]

❑ *Get coaching help.* As a leader, you will need assistance to learn new skills, such as group leadership. Notoriously poor judges of their own behavior, leaders often need feedback to ensure congruence between what they espouse and what they actually do. A coach will provide encouragement when things are not going as well as expected. [☛10.6 Group Leader Skills, 12.4 Feedback, 13.1 Coaching]

❑ *Use change leadership tools* to plan, implement, and follow through on the change. [☛ 5.1 Change Equation]

❑ *Current systems generally support the current level of involvement.* Poor, unsupportive systems will defeat the most enthusiastic leaders and workers. [☛ 2.1 Systems Thinking, 4.1 Organizational Design]

❑ *Two-way communication is key.* Research shows that employees feel communicated with at about one-third the level that leaders feel they have communicated. [☛ 8.2 Direct Communication, 8.3 Organizational Communication]

❑ *Train the workers in group and team skills.* Yes, workers need to do things differently as well. Workers have been left to last in this list of guidelines. Generally, they will be only too willing to do what needs to be done if the conditions are right. [☛ 10.1 HiPo Teams, 10.3 Team Competencies]

❑ *Help people through the transition.* If people have been asked for years to act in a certain manner, it will take some time and effort to make the change. [☛ 5.8 Human Transitions]

WEB WORKSHEET

STARTING ACTION PLANS

Now go back and look at the levels of involvement and guidelines for choosing the level. Make a preliminary action plan in the space provided here. This plan is preliminary, in the sense that you will want to involve others in fleshing out and implementing these plans.

1. What is the probable level of involvement required so that your organization will produce the kind of results it needs in the future?

2. Change starts with you, the leader. What do you need to:
   - start doing?

   - stop doing?

   - continue doing?

3. What systems, external driving forces, and cultural expectations will:
   - support the change?

   - impede the change?

4. What are the specific next steps to take?

Related leadership tools

1.8 Recursive Leadership	4.6 Open-Book Leadership	9.1 Leadership Versatility
4.1 Organizational Design	4.7 Job Satisfaction	9.2 Situational Leadership

For further assistance

Lawler, Edward E. *High-Involvement Management: Participative Strategies for Improving Performance.* Jossey-Bass Publishers, 1986.

Vroom, Victor, and Philip Yetton. *Leadership and Decision Making.* University of Pittsburgh Press, 1973.

4.5 ORGANIZATIONAL CULTURE: SAIL OR ANCHOR?

Inspired by Terrence Deal, Allen Kennedy, John Kotter, Edgar Schein, Marvin Weisbord, and Alan Wilkins.

Organizational culture has had a meteoric ride, from its roots in anthropology, to a refit for corporate and organizational cultures, to fad status in the 1980s, to fading status in the 1990s. Today, speaking too loudly about culture risks places you into the passé leader group. Yet, like many leadership tools, it provides valuable insights and lessons.

In simple terms, culture is "the way things are done around here." In *Leading Change,* John Kotter defines culture as "… the norms of behavior and shared values among a group of people." To people who have bought in, a culture is nearly invisible, because it contains all the assumptions that are made about what it is okay and not okay to talk about, how to talk about it, what to do, and what not to do. People often notice a strong organizational culture *only* when they become frustrated by having to interact with a *different* organizational culture.

While taking a quasi-anthropological-cultural approach, this tool outlines the basics of organizational culture, its importance, and how leaders can work with it.

A BRIEF HISTORY OF CULTURE

From the story told by Noel Tichy and Stafford Sherman of how Jack Welch changed the culture of GE, "A corporate culture is the sum of the unwritten norms, beliefs, and values that define appropriate behavior." Anyone who thinks culture is not important should work with Jack Welch at GE for a while!

Michael Dell voices ambivalence about culture. "I'm often asked how we at Dell manage to maintain the attitude of a challenger even as we continue to grow at record speeds. Culture is by far one of the most enigmatic facets of management that I have encountered. It's also one of the most important. Once a reporter asked me which of our competitors represented the biggest threat to Dell. I said, 'The greatest threat to Dell wouldn't come from a competitor. It would come from our people.'"

The pivotal book on culture is *Corporate Cultures: The Rites and Rituals of Corporate Life.* Written by Terrence Deal and Allen Kennedy in 1982, it told lots of stories outlining the basics of corporate culture, its impact, and how to reshape it. Rejecting culture as a useful term in 1989, Alan Wilkins wrote in *Developing Corporate Character,* "I use the term *character* rather than *culture* for several reasons that are related to why we have so often failed at culture change in organizations. First, culture has been trivialized because so many have written about 'managing culture,' 'managing myths,' or 'creating meaning' without serious attention to how difficult it is to manipulate these complex social processes. Second, culture has been used to think about almost everything organizational, and therefore it has lost its special meaning." So much for the corporate culture into which the concept of "corporate culture" was introduced!

Why is understanding organizational culture so important?

➡ If fish could think, they would assume water is the perfect and natural environment for life. Because cultures are largely invisible to the people inside them, they are rarely questioned, simply assumed. Appropriate assumptions will cause the organization to thrive; inappropriate assumptions will cause it to wither—often working harder at what no longer works. [☞ 1.9 Paradigms]

⇒ Cultures are notoriously hard to change. The starting point is understanding the current culture. [☞ 5.2 Major Change]

⇒ Increasingly, organizations are working internationally. Not understanding your own organizational culture and how it may differ from other international cultures can be disastrous for your organizational success, and devastating for the employees who represent your organization. [☞ 8.9 Cross-Cultural]

⇒ Organizations are becoming increasingly diverse. If the diversity is to be a source of increased effectiveness, the current organizational culture must be prepared.

⇒ Many mergers or takeovers looked great from a financial and asset point of view, yet became disasters when the organizational cultures could not be so easily merged.

What are some elements of organizational culture? Here are some common elements, with a short explanation.

Element	What this element includes
Heroes	Think of IBM and you think of Tom Watson Sr.; GE and Jack Welch; Mary Kay Cosmetics and Mary Kay Ash; and so forth. Every organization has its strong heroes, who also define the stories and meaning of the culture.
Stories	Often called myths, these are the stories that are told during coffee breaks and other informal situations. For example, one consulting organization revelled in how much its members travelled. Travel stories abounded, for example, super-frequent travellers holding up planes at the gate. What does that tell you about what is important in that organization?
Rituals	Meetings are but one bastion of rituals—from who attends what, to who can be late and who cannot be late, to who starts the meeting, to how discussion is closed. Other rituals—and all organizations have them—include humor, beer and pizza Fridays, clothing, and all-employee communication meetings.
The formal versus the informal organization	Read a part of your organization's Policy Manual and ask yourself, "What is actually done around here compared to official policy?" Every organization has an informal culture-in-practice, usually much stronger than the formal espoused culture.
Branding	As this book is being written, the "in" culture term is branding. Does this tell you something about leadership culture? The term is refitted from advertising and the consumer industry, where products and services like Ford, Heinz, Microsoft, and Andersen Consulting can capitalize on their brands.
Meaning	Creating meaning is best explained through the story of three medieval stonemasons cutting stones for a cathedral. When asked, "What are you doing?" the first answered, "I am cutting a stone." The second said, "I am shaping a keystone to support the main arch." The third answered, "I am building an edifice to God." A key skill of leaders compared to managers is the ability to create meaning, often tying even what might seem a trivial task to the success of the organization. It's sobering to think that people will do almost anything for leaders who can create meaning. [☞ 1.6 Boards of Play, 2.6 Clarifying Purpose]

HOW TO USE THIS LEADERSHIP TOOL

"Do we have corporate cultures that are anchors on change? Or cultures that enable us to adapt to the changing environment?"

—John Kotter, *RETHINKING THE FUTURE*

Organizational culture can be devilishly difficult to clarify. People working inside the organization, like fish in water, will have a hard time understanding their own assumptions. People external to the organization will bring their own cultural assumptions to bear. All culture gurus remark on how difficult it is to change a culture. Yet all is not lost: Cultures do change.

What, then, can be done, particularly in a brief handbook like this? One simple and effective method is to start the process in an entertaining but insightful way. The process described here is best done in a group setting. (One aspect of the emerging leadership culture is the skill of leading groups!)

WEB WORKSHEET

1. In a large-group setting, explain why you are doing this and establish trust. It can be very threatening to surface cultural assumptions, the values of leaders, and unspoken assumptions. On the other hand, if the trusting and nondefensive conditions are established, people will take great glee in surfacing assumptions and contradictions that get in the way of effectiveness. Be careful! If management has not been open in the past, they may take the brunt of the implied criticism. [☛10.6 Group Leader Skills, 10.7 Getting Participation]

2. Have groups of 5 to 8 discuss and list on flip chart pages "What's okay" and "What's not okay" to do around here. Encourage and protect openness. Make the groups large enough and diverse enough so no one person can be fingered. Here is a partial example of a group report. [☛ 10.9 Visible Information]

What is okay to do or think around here	What is not okay to do or think around here
– to come late for meetings – to speak openly about how to improve your own job – to present your ideas in a logical way – to propose cost-cutting etc.	– to end-run your immediate manager – to challenge management – to raise emotional issues – to deal with conflict openly – to propose spending to make more money etc.

In the large group, have the subgroups report out. Remind the group that what is reported is okay and not a reflection on any individual. Have the group look for commonalties and themes; record these on a flip chart.

3. Depending on your purpose and needs and the level of openness and trust established, you may wish to go the next step in the group. Remind people what direction your organization and group are trying to take. Then ask the groups to complete a second session. "If that is the direction we want to take, what do we need to start, stop, and continue doing around here?" Here is a partial example report.

Need to Start	Need to Stop	Need to Continue
– dealing with difficult interpersonal issues – to openly surface conflict – make it okay to critique management etc.	– coming late for meetings – punishing people for speaking openly etc.	– logical presentations (with some emotion added!) – cost-cutting ideas etc.

4. In the full group, have subgroups report out.

5. Finally, prioritize and prepare action plans with the large group. [☛ 10.11 Priority Setting, 10.12 RASCI Planning]

Keep in mind that organizational cultures are closely aligned with values [☛ 2.5 Values] and beliefs. Similar principles apply to business unit cultures, professional (e.g., engineering or accounting) cultures, union cultures, government cultures, even East Coast versus West Coast culture, teenage culture, and so on.

R ELATED LEADERSHIP TOOLS

1.4 Leader Principles	1.8 Recursive Leadership	2.5 Values
1.6 Boards of Play	2.3 Directional Statements	8.9 Cross-Cultural

F OR FURTHER ASSISTANCE

Deal, Terrence E., and Allan A. Kennedy. *Corporate Cultures: The Rites and Rituals of Corporate Life.* Perseus Books, 2000. Reissue.

Kotter, John. "Cultures and Coalitions." In Gibson, Rowan, ed. *Rethinking the Future: Rethinking Business, Principles, Competition, Control and Complexity, Leadership, Markets, and the World.* Nicholas Brealey, 1999.

Schein, Edgar H. "Are you corporate cultured?" *Personnel Journal.* November, 1986. 83–96.

Schein, Edgar H. *Organizational Culture and Leadership,* 2nd ed. Jossey-Bass, 1997.

Weisbord, Marvin Ross. *Productive Workplaces: Organizing and Managing for Dignity, Meaning, and Community.* Jossey-Bass, 1989.

Wilkins, Alan L. *Developing Corporate Character: How to Successfully Change an Organization without Destroying It.* Jossey-Bass, 1989.

4.6

OPEN-BOOK LEADERSHIP: DEVELOPING ENTREPRENEURIAL THINKING

Inspired by Jack Stack.

Although the ideas behind open-book management had been around for years, Jack Stack took them to new levels in his book, *The Great Game of Business*. "The more people know about a company, the better a company will perform. This is an ironclad rule," says Stack. Open-book refers to sharing corporate and business-unit information—financial, production, quality—and any other information that would help employees adopt a more entrepreneurial and business-thinking orientation. This tool contains guidelines for adopting open-book management.

Open-book management is designed to assist and encourage employees to act like owners. It does this by:

1. giving employees the corporate, financial, and production information they need;
2. teaching employees how to understand and use this information; and
3. providing employees with a financial stake in the company's performance.

It is possible to underinform or overinform employees. If you provide too much information, employees drown in the details. If you provide too little, employees can't develop a full understanding of the business. Either way, employees are disempowered. You need to provide employees with critical information only; that is, information that will help them to better understand your business, to take calculated risks, to make intelligent business decisions, and to feel that they are trusted and valued and play a meaningful role within the organization.

Information	The range of business information that your employees might benefit from knowing (Note: Select and provide employees with the critical numbers only.)
Big picture	strategy and direction, business climate, share price, competition, customers' businesses and needs, overall business success measures, trends
Financial	balance sheets, income sheets, assets, cash flow, expense accounting, taxation, net present value, cost of materials, labor costs, project financials, business unit financials, overhead, standard costs
Production	volume, rate, cost per unit, materials costing, production goals (and why), quality measures
Business unit/ project	profit and loss, investment financing, cost of goals, production costs, overhead costs, competitors' information, sales and marketing information
Sales/ marketing	revenue, volume, rate, cost of sales, competitors' pricing, markups, customer service indicators, marketing and sales strategies, sales forecasts
Organizational	safety, lost-time accidents, attendance, environmental, union agreements
Bonus/reward programs	what is available, how they work, how they balance interdependencies with individual rewards, their size and why

In Jack Stack's Springfield Remanufacturing Corp., selected critical numbers are encapsulated into a Weekly Scorecard, which is *partially* reproduced here to give you a glimpse into what open-book means in practice. Needless to say, these numbers are not just distributed on paper but are questioned, discussed, and used to establish priorities and plans.

SPRINGFIELD REMANUFACTURING CORP.
PROJECTED INCOME STATEMENT   DATE: _____
U.S. DIVISIONS
(000) Omitted

MONTHLY CONSOLIDATED INCOME

		PLAN	CURRENT	NEXT	MONTH 2	MONTH 3	MONTH 4	MONTH 5
SALES	U.S.							
PROJECTIONS	CAN.							

SALES:

	PLAN	MAPLE	WILLOW	MARSH-FIELD	NEW STREAM	TOTAL	PERCENT
GROSS SALES-CANADA							
GROSS SALES U.S.							
BEHIND SCHEDULE							
AVAILABLE-TO-SHIP							
PROJ. END BEHIND SCHEDULE							
RETURNS/DISC/ ALLOWANCES							
NET SALES SHIPMENTS							
STD. COST-OF-GOODS-SOLD							
GROSS STD. INCOME							
MEMO: INVENTORY RECEIPTS							
MANUFACTURING VARIANCES							
PUR PRICE/RECLASS/ FREIGHT							
MAT'L USEAGE/SCRAP							
INV. ADJUSTMENT							
LABOR PERFORMANCE							
O/H SPENDING							
OVERHEAD ABSORPTION							
OVERHEAD VARIANCE							
TOTAL MFG. VARIANCES							
CONTRIBUTION MARGIN							
EXPENSES							
ENGINEERING							
SALES & MARKETING							
GEN'L ADMIN							
ESOP CONTRIBUTION							
WARRANTY-CLAIMS PAID							
WARRANTY-ALLOWED VARIANCE							
WARRANTY ACTUAL							
TOTAL WARRANTY EXPENSE							
TOTAL EXPENSES							

From *The Great Game of Business* by Jack Stack, copyright 1992 by The Great Game of Business, Inc. Used by permission of Doubleday, a division of Random House, Inc.

THE DOS AND DONTS OF OPEN-BOOK LEADERSHIP

✔ *Do* define and relentlessly communicate the big picture—what results you expect, your strategy and priorities, interdependencies among groups, rewards for achieving results, and so on. [☛ 8.3 Organizational Communication]

✔ *Do* educate and train your employees in appropriate business skills—the nature of the business, the external pressures, the basics of making money, customer needs and service, understanding and using financial data, production measures, and what all those numbers mean for the organization and for themselves. [☛ 14.3 Needs Analysis]

✔ *Do* redesign your information and accounting systems so employees can understand and use the data these systems generate to make informed decisions. Too often, these systems are designed exclusively for senior management and for external reporting. [☛ 2.1 Systems Thinking]

✔ *Do* give up control over the numbers. Information is a form of power. Open-book leadership must be combined with a participative leadership style and with teamwork.

✔ *Do* ensure that other organizational systems are aligned to support open-book leadership. [☛ 5.6 Aligning Systems]

✔ *Do* combine open-book leadership with rewards that are linked to performance. Use a mix of individual, team, and organizational rewards, while ensuring that the overall success of the organization is not compromised.

✔ *Do* discuss regularly the meaning and trending of the numbers, then set new targets as conditions change.

✔ *Do* make open-book leadership fun. Make the numbers come alive with stories and examples.

✘ *Don't* use information to manipulate others. Rather, use it to create understanding and to reward success.

✘ *Don't* go halfway. Don't provide only half the numbers needed, or fail to fairly reward performance.

HOW TO USE THIS LEADERSHIP TOOL

"Let your people know whatever you know about the company, the division, the department, the particular task at hand. … Don't use information to intimidate, control, or manipulate people. … When you share the numbers and bring them alive, you turn them into tools people can use to help themselves as they go about business every day."

—Jack Stack, *THE GREAT GAME OF BUSINESS*

Sharing the numbers is only one small part of leadership. Use this checklist to assess your readiness to be an open-book leader. Plan actions to improve your leadership practices in those areas where you consider yourself to be underperforming as a leader. Your action plans might also include ways of building on present strengths as a leader.

WEB WORKSHEET

Leadership practices	Actions effective leaders take	Action plans to improve your leadership practices
Teach and coach business literacy.	❑ Explain why and how money is made and wealth is created. ❑ Explain why and how profits are made. ❑ Explain which critical numbers are important. ❑ Understand and help others understand the business and its competitive environment. ❑ Help workers understand customer needs and customer service. ❑ Explain the numbers in a straightforward way. ❑ Teach and model accountability. [☛ 13.3 Accountability]	
Stay close to your people.	❑ Get out onto the "shop floor" where the work is done. ❑ Teach and model interdependence. ❑ Trust people to do what is best for the company. ❑ Inspire confidence and excitement. ❑ Be open and honest. ❑ Model total integrity with people. ❑ Give and receive tough feedback. [☛ 8.2 Direct Communication]	
Tell the truth.	❑ Know how much you can tell others and explain why. ❑ Know what can't be shared and explain why. ❑ Be up-front about jobs and security. ❑ Minimize mixed messages. ❑ Use down-to-earth explanations; listen well. [☛ 12.2 Trust]	
Align systems.	❑ Get appropriate and timely information to workers to support their decision making. ❑ Design appropriate rewards so everyone wins. ❑ Use an appropriate leadership style; encourage others to take responsibility and make decisions. ❑ Understand interdependencies, so that one group doesn't win at the expense of another. ❑ Break down functional stovepipes. [☛ 9.1 Leadership Versatility, 9.2 Situational Leadership]	
Lead by example.	❑ Be a great communicator, storyteller, educator, coach, and counselor. ❑ Live by "My success is the success of others." ❑ Do not talk down or over their heads. ❑ Be credible on the "shop floor." ❑ Act as an external border guard, fending off external annoyances so people can do their work. [☛ 1.8 Recursive Leadership]	

Communicate the big picture.	❑ Define and understand the big picture, then share it in an appropriate way. ❑ Do not overdo the big picture and confuse people; do not underdo it and lose credibility. ❑ Be able to share corporate confidential information.	

RELATED LEADERSHIP TOOLS

1.8 Recursive Leadership   4.1 Organizational Design   4.7 Job Satisfaction

2.1 Systems thinking   4.4 Employee Involvement   8.3 Organizational Communication

FOR FURTHER ASSISTANCE

Stack, Jack, and Bo Burlingham. *The Great Game of Business*. Doubleday, 1994.

4.7   JOB SATISFACTION: INVOLVING WORKGROUPS IN DESIGNING JOBS

Inspired by Merrelyn Emery and Terry Golbeck.

This tool will help you engage employees in assessing the challenge, opportunity, and meaning they get from their work.

Employee job satisfaction is not an end in itself; however, it needs to be acknowledged that individual performance is highly correlated with job satisfaction. Leaders can't wave magic wands and make everybody happy, but they can design jobs for maximum employee satisfaction and productivity.

Job satisfaction can be operationally defined as meeting the employee needs listed in the table. When these needs are met, people usually report more satisfaction with their organizations, their leaders, and their overall work experience, and, not surprisingly, better organizational results are usually achieved.

Employee need:	What it means:
• Opportunities for decision making	✔ Leaders need to delegate so employees can make decisions that they can call their own. ✔ Leaders need to provide employees with a decision-making framework—too much direction and they feel controlled, too little and they flounder. [☛ 9.2 Situational Leadership]
• Opportunities to continuously learn on-the-job	✔ Leaders need to coach by giving timely feedback on work behavior and performance. ✔ Leaders need to establish challenging but achievable goals. [☛ 13.1 Coaching]
• Opportunities for variety in work	✔ Leaders need to ensure that employees have a level of variety in their work, to help employees maintain interest and to avoid boredom and fatigue. [☛ 4.7 Job Satisfaction]
• Support and respect from coworkers	✔ Leaders must not pit employees against one another. ✔ Leaders must avoid setting up win–lose situations.
• Meaningful work	✔ Leaders need to provide whole jobs and involvement in the whole product (i.e., a sense that employees are building homes, not just putting on the doorknobs). ✔ Leaders must remind employees of the purpose, the *why* of the job, and regularly demonstrate to employees that they value and appreciate their contributions. [☛ 4.4 Employee Involvement]
• A job that leads to a desirable future, rather than to a dead end	✔ Leaders need to recognize that learning and improvement are basic human needs. ✔ A desirable future does not necessarily have to be a promotion or even a guarantee of job security, but it must encourage skill improvement and personal growth. [☛ 2.4 Visioning]

How to use this leadership tool

"Nobody can implement commitment for you."

—Marvin Weisbord, *PRODUCTIVE WORKPLACES*

Use this tool to assess job satisfaction—and even to redesign jobs—in your workgroup. Ask each member of the group to complete the questionnaire provided here, in preparation for a group discussion of job satisfaction and job design. Depending on the level of trust in the group, you could collect questionnaire responses and report these back in aggregate and anonymous form, or each individual group member could speak about his or her own questionnaire responses.

WEB WORKSHEET

Seek mutual agreement on improvement areas, as evidenced by cumulative questionnaire results. Listen, respect differences, and provide direct feedback as part of this group dialogue process. Carried out effectively, this process will lead to the enthusiastic involvement of group members in redesigning their jobs and working to improve their job satisfaction, individual performance, and overall organizational results.

Job Satisfaction Questionnaire

Personal needs

- Rate from –5 to +5, with 0 being best (the perfect amount), +5 being far too much, and –5 being far too little.

	Rate from –5 to +5
1. Opportunities for decision making • You have organizational support for making decisions in your work area. • You understand the goals and direction of the organization, and have the information you require to make informed decisions.	–5 | | | 0 | | | +5
2. Opportunities to continuously learn on-the-job • Your work is challenging. • You receive timely and supportive feedback on your performance. • Training is encouraged and provided.	–5 | | | 0 | | | +5
3. Opportunities for variety in work • Your work provides ample variety.	–5 | | | 0 | | | +5

Work climate

- Rate the following from 0 to 10, with 10 being the best, and 0 being the worst.

	Rate from 0 to 10
4. Support and respect from coworkers • You are not expected to compete against your coworkers, and you can count on their support.	0 | | | 5 | | | 10

5. Meaningful work
   • Your work has worth and quality, and provides a sense of involvement.
   • You know how your job fits within the whole system, and how your performance contributes to the success of the organization.
	0 | | | | 5 | | | | 10

6. A job that leads to a desirable future, not a dead-end • You are able to learn, develop your skills, and grow as a person within your job.	0 | | | | 5 | | | | 10

RELATED LEADERSHIP TOOLS

4.1 Organizational Design	9.2 Situational Leadership	13.3 Accountability
4.4 Employee Involvement	10.4 Team Commitment	

FOR FURTHER ASSISTANCE

Emery, Merrelyn. *Searching: The Theory and Practice of Making Cultural Change.* John Benjamins Publishing Co., 1999.

4.8 REVITALIZING THE BOARD OF DIRECTORS IN A NONPROFIT ORGANIZATION

Inspired by John Carver.

Leaders in nonprofit organizations benefit considerably when their Board of Directors is well designed, has a clear role and process for governing, and has a clearly defined relationship with the management team. It's a mistake to think that a strong Board will get in your way as a leader. It's most often the weak Boards that meddle in operations. Strong leaders need strong Boards. Organizational success starts with clear roles and accountabilities for both. This tool outlines a systematic approach to Board design, and emphasizes the central role of the Board in developing and overseeing policy in the four areas listed.

1. Define a clear mission.

What is a clear mission?
- A mission is the organization's contribution to the world. What products and services are provided and to what customers?
- The mission statement is brief and worded in terms of results, not activities. It drives all goals and activities. [☛ 2.3 Directional Statements]

Some tips and pitfalls:
- Aim for practical and cost-effective measures of success. However, the fact that results are measurable doesn't make them valuable. Imprecise measures of the right things beat highly precise measures of the wrong things.
- The Board should focus on the *why*, not the *how*; on ends (mission and high-level goals), not on means (operational activities). Boards that meddle in means disempower their CEO and management team.

2. Clarify the relationship between the Board and the Chief Executive Officer (CEO).

Things to clarify:
- Power that is passed to the CEO (or Executive Director) in the form of expectations, limitations, and accountabilities.
- How the CEO's use of that power is evaluated; what will be evaluated and how.

Key elements of the Board's role:
- The Board is responsible for its own development, job design, discipline, and performance.
- One of the most important tasks of a Board is the choice of CEO.
- The CEO has a right to expect the Board to be clear about its expectations and limitations, and to speak with one voice.

Key elements of the CEO's role:
- The CEO is responsible to the Board for achievement of organizational goals and for following Board policies.
- The CEO needs a strong Board, strategic direction and goals, but a free hand for managing operations, within policies and parameters.
- The CEO must influence the organization's culture, must set a high level of ethics and prudence, and must achieve results. [☛ 4.5 Culture]

Potential pitfalls:
- Ensure there is no overlap of tasks for which management is accountable. Shared accountability is often shirked. [☛ 13.3 Accountability]
- If boundaries aren't defined, the Board will likely forage in whatever individual interests and fears occur to them.

3. Clarify limitations on the CEO's and the management team's activities.

Things to clarify:
- Having clearly prescribed the results expected (the ends), next clarify only the boundaries or limits on the CEO and management team practices, activities, and methods. [☛ 2.7 Goal Statements]
- Identify specific areas of Board concern. State exactly what is *not* prudent and ethical.
- Consider where expert input might be needed, such as technical matters (e.g., legal or finance).

Potential pitfalls:
- Boards can choose to be understanding of performance shortfalls, but should never bend an inch on integrity. [☛ 1.11 Integrity]

4. Clarify Board processes.

Things to clarify:
- How the Board represents its shareholders, membership, or ownership.
- How the Board works together and leads strategically. [☛ 3.1 Strategy]
- Members need to speak with one voice (supporting decisions only when you win the vote is not supporting the process).
- To determine whether an issue is a Board or CEO issue, ask: "How is the issue at hand related to current policy?" "Does the policy suffice to deal with the concern?" If not, make new policy.
- Evaluation of results is the only way to evaluate CEO performance.

Potential pitfalls:
- Denying, ignoring, or smoothing over differences, or allowing personality to dominate in confrontation. [☛ 12.7 Dealing with Conflict]
- Dealing with dysfunctional behavior is more difficult if the Board has not previously determined what constitutes dysfunctional behavior. (Thus, it is important to create a set of ground rules for the Board.) [☛ 10.8 Ground Rules]

How to use this leadership tool

"When the Board addresses the right things it finds it doesn't have to address many things."
—John Carver, *BOARDS THAT MAKE A DIFFERENCE*

This tool represents a considerable challenge for a CEO and his or her Board of Directors. There is no divine point at which to set the boundary between Board and CEO responsibility. By necessity, Board policy making is fluid and stops at whatever point the Board is willing to have the CEO make interpretations and decisions. Thus, unless the Board wishes to do the CEO's job (which is always a mistake), Board policies will always leave room for CEO interpretation. (Note that Board policies will not substitute for a lack of trust between the Board and the CEO.) In addition, Board policies need to be explicit, current, in simple language, encompassing, brief (a page or less), accessible, and distinct from operating policies.

When developed and practiced with a reasonable level of discipline, the policy governance approach works like magic. However, it does take considerable effort to develop and maintain a full set of Board policies in all four areas. Because of the effort required, Boards need to be committed to this approach at the outset.

When embarking on a major task such as this, it's good to remind yourself how one eats an elephant—one bite at a time. This work will take from several months to a year or longer. If need be, you can complete a good first draft of these policies in one or two workshops, with the help of someone trained in the use of Carver's policy governance model. Don't be intimidated. The work is well worth the effort. Start fresh. Don't use old policies. And don't choose policies from a catalog! However, you might consider comparing the policies that you and your

Board develop with policies of other organizations. Once developed, these policies will be living documents, requiring some rework from time to time.

WEB WORKSHEET

1. Define a clear mission.

[☛ 2.3 Directional Statements]

2. Clarify the relationship between the Board and the leadership team.

[☛ 10.8 Ground Rules]

3. Clarify Board expectations for and limitations on the CEO and the leadership team.

[☛ 13.3 Accountability]

4. Clarify Board processes.

RELATED LEADERSHIP TOOLS

1.2 Manage or Lead?	2.6 Clarifying Purpose	10.8 Ground Rules
2.1 Systems Thinking	4.1 Organizational Design	13.3 Accountability

FOR FURTHER ASSISTANCE

Carver, John. *Boards That Make a Difference: A New Design for Leadership in Nonprofit and Public Organizations.* Jossey-Bass, 1991.

4.9 Using Professional Expertise: A Modern Leadership Skill

Inspired by William Bridges, Peter Drucker, Robert Reich, and thousands of consulting workshop participants.

Today's leaders need to use the high-quality advice of many expert specialists in order to effectively manage their piece of the business. There used to be a position known as General Manager—someone who generally knew everything in his or her field of work. In the new economy, such people are rare birds. Now, leaders must seek expert advice on information technology, finance, human resource management, legal issues, public relations, economics, environment, health and safety—the list goes on and on. The purpose of this tool is to help leaders obtain and use knowledge workers' professional advice more effectively.

In a nutshell …

Working with Information Systems (IS) professionals from the head office, the Regional Manager of a large retail chain said, "When a new IS professional comes into the region, either I, myself or one of my managers is happy to spend some time helping the new analyst understand our operations. I am no IS expert and need advice on the best use of Information Technology (IT) systems. If the professional continues to expect me to 'hold his or her hand' I get annoyed, because we need value-added advice. On the other hand, the real *problem* IS people are those who come in and try to tell me how to run my business. That's my job! I need to understand how IT can help us, but our own management needs to make the decisions and live with them. We need both inputs on the table—IS and Operations. The best IS professionals understand this give-and-take approach."

Think of how much time *you* spend seeking good specialist advice. Think of how frustrating it is not to get the effective and innovative advice you need. While professionals need to *deliver* their expertise effectively, you, as leader, also need to do some things to ensure you *receive* the best possible advice [☛ 13.11 Delivering Expertise]. The best leader–professional relationships are business partnerships in which neither party feels one up nor one down over the project. The professional "knowing better" than the business leader is dysfunctional, because no professional can understand or be accountable for your operation the way you can. The opposite approach is also dysfunctional, because you, as leader, can't possibly master every area of changing professional knowledge, yet you need innovative solutions to your problems.

Thus, modern professionals need to be business partners and consultants for you:

Leader too aggressive	Business Partner	Leader too passive
←		→
"I'll tell the professional."	"Let's find the best solution together."	"Tell me what to do."

Effective Use of Professional Expertise: Some Dos

In order to be a better business partner, you and the professional need to:

❑ Take the time up front to clarify your underlying needs. Pressures on you, especially time pressures, often push you to ask for solutions rather than identifying your underlying needs. A professional cannot help you find the best solution without understanding your underlying needs.

❑ Talk with your professionals about how they can add value to your organization. Unfortunately, many professionals are techies, focused on the technical excellence of projects, not on the business results. One of the biggest complaints of the clients of professionals is, "They don't understand my business." Take time to discuss your business direction, needs, and constraints.

❑ Involve professionals early in business decisions. The sooner professionals are at the table to hear the context of your business and decisions, the better they can help you with what you really need—business solutions, not technical solutions. Invite professionals to meetings where problems and strategies are being discussed that are pertinent to their expertise.

❑ On occasion, have a taking stock meeting focused on improving the partnership—the consulting relationship—using the checklist provided in the Web Worksheet. Ask questions like, "What is working?" and "What could be improved?" Paradoxically, the busier everyone is, the more imperative it is to get off the treadmill and step back to look at the bigger picture.

❑ Clarify expectations more clearly. Research shows that 80 percent of conflict arises from unclear expectations. Business partners want to avoid having to say, "That's not what I need."

❑ With the professional, read and discuss another tool in this book, ☛ 13.11 Delivering Expertise. It provides specific models for delivering one's expertise.

HOW TO USE THIS LEADERSHIP TOOL

"Because the 'players' in an information-based organization are specialists, they cannot be told how to do their work. There are probably few orchestra leaders who could coax even one note out of a French horn, let alone show the horn player how to do it. But the conductor can focus the horn player's skill and knowledge on the musicians' joint performance. And this focus is what the leaders of an information-based business must be able to achieve."

—Peter Drucker, "THE COMING OF THE NEW ORGANIZATION,"
HARVARD BUSINESS REVIEW

To get the kind of professional advice you need in order to lead a modern organization, you need to periodically sit down with your key support professionals and discuss what works well and how both of you can improve the relationship.

Position this meeting as a 50-50 partnership-building meeting. You expect value-added support from professionals, and professionals expect support from you. Select from this checklist those items the two of you will discuss at such a meeting. Keep in mind that both professionals and clients are often more adept at the first group, Logical Review Items, than they are at the second group, Relationship Review Items.

WEB WORKSHEET

CHECKLIST FOR PROFESSIONAL EXPERT—LEADER CLIENT MEETINGS

Use this checklist to highlight those items that are most helpful to you.

Logical Review Items:

❑ What past and current results are you each happy with?

- ❑ What concerns do you each have about past and current activities?
- ❑ What is the leader's business direction and strategy for a) the next year, and b) the next five years?
- ❑ Discuss changes, direction, and strategies in the larger organization and their potential impact on professional services.
- ❑ What is happening in the professional's area of expertise that might be helpful to you and your customers?
- ❑ What new methods and technology are available that may improve your productivity?
- ❑ How does the above translate into priorities for the professional in the short and long terms?
- ❑ Document priorities.
- ❑ Clarify and document performance goals. [☛ 2.7 Goal Statements]
- ❑ How will success and results be measured?
- ❑ Any other business or professional issues needing clarification or resolution?
- ❑ Any other loose ends needing clarification?
- ❑ What systemic changes must take place to support the changes discussed and planned? [☛ 2.1 System Thinking]
- ❑ Recontract for services and support.

The Relationship Review Items:
- ❑ What worked well in the relationship?
- ❑ What could be improved in the future?
- ❑ Give and receive feedback on each person's personal performance.
- ❑ What worked well in communication? [☛ 8.1 Conversations]
- ❑ How could communication be improved in the future?
- ❑ Discuss and negotiate higher-impact roles.
- ❑ Discuss learning: What have we learned that we could use on future projects?
- ❑ Discuss longer-term relationship strategies.
- ❑ Discuss the level of ownership of project results and commitment in the client's organization.
- ❑ Discuss concerns, if any, about the people side of change. [☛ 5.8 Human Transitions]
- ❑ In the complex stakeholder system, who else needs to have this kind of discussion? [☛ 5.7 Stakeholder Groups]
- ❑ How will we celebrate successes?

MEETING COMMITMENTS AND ACTION PLANS

As a result of this meeting, document what each will do.

Leader's action commitments	Professional's action commitments

RELATED LEADERSHIP TOOLS

3.1 Strategy   8.1 Conversations   13.10 Careers

4.7 Job Satisfaction   13.3 Accountability   13.11 Delivering Expertise

FOR FURTHER ASSISTANCE

Bridges, William. *JobShift: How to Prosper in a Workplace without Jobs.* Addison-Wesley, 1994.

Drucker, Peter F. *Managing in a Time of Great Change.* Plume, 1998.

Hiebert, Murray. *Powerful Professionals: Getting Your Expertise Used Inside Your Organization.* Recursion Press, 1999.

Reich, Robert. *The Work of Nations: Preparing Ourselves for Twenty-First-Century Capitalism.* Vintage Books, 1991.

4.10

SURVEYING EMPLOYEES: LEADING THE SURVEY PROCESS

Inspired by Joe Folkman, John Jones, William Bearley, and Leland Verheyen.

Employee surveys provide an important way of gathering information, particularly in large organizations. This tool looks at managing the overall survey process, from planning and involving stakeholders, to responding to and acting on survey results. It is important to distinguish between formal academic survey standards (with, for example, control groups and elegant statistical analysis) and an employee survey process in which the emphasis is on change, results, and with much more focus on what happens after the survey results are tabulated.

Plan the survey process.

❑ Start by defining a clear vision of what you're trying to do. Have a clear and primary purpose for surveying the employees (e.g., to discover and delineate a critical issue, or to set the stage for a specific change). Secondary purposes might include providing feedback to managers, assessing progress or trends, or better understanding employees. [☛ 2.3 Directional Statements]

❑ Discuss how data will be collected, who will see it, and how results will be fed back; how management anticipates responding to results; and who will make those decisions.

❑ Plan to maximize participation, response rates, and follow-ups (news bulletins, inclusion in meetings). Response rates can vary from 25% to 90%, depending on such factors as organizational climate, survey length, importance of issues, confidentiality assurances, and fear of reprisals.

❑ Since there is no ideal time to conduct the survey (e.g., people too busy, units are short-staffed, too many other changes), seek a workable time rather than an ideal time.

❑ Consider surveying all employees versus simply sampling. While appropriate for statistical purposes, sampling is usually not appropriate for purposes of acceptance, commitment, and buy-in to change.

Involve survey stakeholders early and often.

❑ Building commitment to survey projects is never completed until the expected changes are "the way we do things around here." Be prepared to constantly reposition and resell the survey idea at all levels and all stages.

❑ Know that people expect change, so set realistic expectations about what might happen as a result of the survey (something specific between "All issues will be resolved" and "Nothing ever happens as a result of these surveys"). [☛ 5.1 Change Equation]

❑ Think of yourself as working with survey participants, not survey subjects (of doing something *with* and *for* them, not *to* them). With management, use *we* from the beginning if you want *our* results at the end. Often, the survey task force owns the survey design, then wonders why management doesn't own the data and results, much less the employees' owning them.

❑ Involve as many potential survey contributors as possible in planning the survey process. Although people are rarely enthusiastic about the idea of a survey, at least initially, don't simply assume that they will be negative. [☛ 4.4 Employee Involvement]

❑ Ask potential survey contributors, up front, for their help in making something meaningful happen.

Act on survey results and changes promptly.

❑ After it's been collected, analyze the data quickly (e.g., within a week or two).
❑ Considerable value is lost if you don't provide a feedback and discussion process. Have an objective facilitator(s) lead mini focus groups or interviews to understand the data patterns and cross-validate survey findings.
❑ Coach managers to receive and act on survey results quickly and nondefensively. [☛ 12.4 Feedback]
❑ Share all the data, not just a summary (e.g., use an internal Web site). Report response rate, positive responses, negative responses, and exceptionally high and low responses.
❑ Use pictures to support conclusions (e.g., graphs, bar charts). Don't overwhelm employees with statistics and analysis.
❑ Act on survey results quickly. Focus on implementation, not analysis. Analysis paralysis is the bane of survey projects.

Questionnaire design

❑ Make questions as concrete as possible. Base questions on behaviors (what you can see or measure). Minimize questions about attitudes and feelings.
❑ Target for 50 to 60 items. Make it easy to administer, easy to respond to, easy to analyze, and easy to resurvey in the future.
❑ Target completion time for less than 45 minutes.
❑ Test the questionnaire design using focus groups (12 to 15 employees). Several drafts are usually required before systemwide use.
❑ Ask more than one behavioral question to survey complex topics like morale and leadership.
❑ Before asking a question, ask, "If the responses to this question are negative, are we willing to do something about it?" If the answer is "no," don't ask the question.
❑ Organize questions into sections. (This makes completion, analysis, and feedback easier.)
❑ Consider including space for write-in comments. Although difficult to analyze, they allow participants to say what they want, and they generate considerable interest.
❑ Consider using a captive survey process whereby employees are scheduled to complete the survey in a designated room during the workday. This increases response rates from around 50% (when surveys are returned by mail) to 90% (for captive surveys).

Questionnaire demographics

❑ A demographic is a group of participants sharing a set of characteristics. One such group might be "all engineers with over 15 years of experience." Demographic information greatly enhances interpretation of survey results.
❑ On the downside, the more demographic information that is requested on a survey, the more employees may fear being personally identified. Anonymity is best ensured when demographic group size exceeds ten. However, in demographic groups that are larger than 250, findings can become overgeneralized and meaningful information can be obscured.
❑ Attitudinal data is social data, influenced by culture and history. As such, the major value of attitudinal data lies in comparisons among workgroups; hence the importance of demographic categories on the survey instrument. For example, the biggest influences on morale and job satisfaction are almost always the department you work in and the boss you work for. After them come your job and your peers.

H OW TO USE THIS LEADERSHIP TOOL

"Ever since Elton Mayo found that worker productivity can be affected by human as well as technical considerations, employee attitudes, opinions, and behaviors have been closely examined in the workplace."

—Leland G. Verheyen, "How to Develop an Employee Attitude Survey,"
TRAINING AND DEVELOPMENT JOURNAL

WEB WORKSHEET

Use the workspace here to draft the attributes of an employee survey that you will be using within your business unit or organization.

Plan the survey process.
The primary purpose of this survey is to: [☛ 2.3 Directional Statements, 2.6 Clarifying Purpose]   Secondary purposes include: Steps you can take to maximize response rates:

Involve survey stakeholders early and often.
Steps you will take to continually sell the survey project: [☛ 5.7 Stakeholder Groups]   How will you set employee expectations for the survey project?

Act on survey results and changes promptly.
How you will clarify and cross-validate the survey results?   Steps you will take to ensure managers act on survey results promptly and nondefensively: [☛ 5.1 Change Equation]

Questionnaire design
What elements of questionnaire design will be particularly important to the success of your survey?

Questionnaire demographics
What demographic information will be particularly important for interpreting your survey results?   What demographic information would you like to collect, but won't, because it would risk endangering employee anonymity?

RELATED LEADERSHIP TOOLS

1.10 The GAS Model	5.1 Change Equation	8.3 Organizational Communication
2.1 Systems Thinking	5.7 Stakeholder Groups	12.4 Feedback

FOR FURTHER ASSISTANCE

Folkman, Joe. *Employee Surveys That Make a Difference*. Executive Excellence Publishing, 1998.

Jones, John E., and William L. Bearley. *Surveying Employees: A Practical Guidebook*. Human Resource Development Press, 1996.

Verheyen, Leland. "How to Develop an Employee Attitude Survey." *Training and Development Journal*. August 1988, 72–76.

5 TOOLS FOR LEADING CHANGE

As if you didn't already know it, change is a defining characteristic of the early twenty-first century. Leadership gurus are unanimous:

"… if you don't change, you die."
—Strategy guru C.K. Prahalad

"Business @ the speed of light."
—Bill Gates

"… change is now happening exponentially."
—Reengineering guru Michael Hammer

"We are, by any technical definition, operating out of control."
—Systems guru Peter Senge

And, as a good transition to this chapter,

"You can't stumble backwards into the future."
—Charles Handy

5.1 LEADING CHANGE: A CHANGE EQUATION

Inspired by John Kotter, Gene Dalton, and Peter Scholtes.

Leadership at its essence is leading change. This tool presents a straightforward equation that you can use to plan a change and to explain the need for specific actions to support a change. In a mathematical equation in which the variables are multiplied together, if one variable is small or zero, then the product is small or zero, no matter how large the other variables. All are needed!

SUSTAINABLE CHANGE =				
Big picture ×	**Buy-in** ×	**Skills & tools** ×	**Manage risks** ×	**Action**
❏ Prepare a vision, one that you can explain in five minutes or less. ❏ Always communicate the change in a wider context. Answer the question "Why?" and address the fit with the organizational direction. ❏ Use metaphors, stories, and examples to illustrate; people need a good illustration to understand the change. ❏ Prepare an interdependency analysis; often, change has many interlinking systems, which can foil change. ❏ Find and exploit synergies with other initiatives.	❏ The best way to gain the acceptance of others is by involving them early and often. ❏ Communicate, communicate. (Research shows that others feel leaders have communicated less than half as much as leaders think they have.) ❏ Use multiple types of communication. ❏ Use two-way communication; ask for feedback. ❏ Prepare a stakeholder map, as each group sees it. ❏ Build and organize allies early; often, support is only asked for at the action phase. ❏ Recognize and thank people for their support when you get it.	❏ Always provide for training in new skills. ❏ Understand that productivity often initially drops (just when you want gains). ❏ Ensure that your change is user-friendly. ❏ Do not overlook the skills that other leaders will need to explain the change to their people. Provide coaching and training materials for other leaders and their people. ❏ Ensure that people affected have the right equipment at the right time.	❏ Treat others' reservations as normal; risks are a natural side effect of change. Don't resist resistance. ❏ Anticipate as many risks and reservations as you can. ❏ Learn how people need to transition internally. ❏ Never underestimate the power of the status quo and the need for people to protect their turf. ❏ Recognize the power and influence of the rumor; a void will get filled. ❏ Own up to inconsistencies and problems; say "I'm sorry" and correct them. Hiding gaffes and risks rarely works.	❏ Prepare short-term action plans that generate small wins. ❏ Recognize and celebrate successes. ❏ Always model the behavior you expect in others; walk your talk. ❏ Minimize "happy talk." It makes people cynical. ❏ Undermine cynics with quick wins. ❏ Keep your cool and your sense of humor. Implementing major change in organizations is a challenge for anyone. ❏ Communicate frequently and on a consistently scheduled basis.

How to use this leadership tool

"Usually whatever we propose to change is part of a larger system. It is important, therefore, to look at the systemic implications of any proposed change."

—Peter Scholtes, *THE TEAM HANDBOOK*

Think of a change that you are leading or involved with, and use the previous checklist to guide you as you plan critical change activities on this worksheet. If needed, modify the terminology provided here (e.g., big picture, buy-in) to fit the current terminology used in your organization.

WEB WORKSHEET

Equation variable:	Actions to take in this area:
Big picture	[☛ 2.4 Visioning, 2.6 Clarifying Purpose, 3.1 Strategy]
Buy-in	[☛ 5.7 Stakeholder Groups, 9.8 Selling Large Projects]
Skills & tools	
Manage risks	
Action	

Related leadership tools

5.2 Major Change   5.6 Aligning Systems   5.9 Resistance

5.3 Change Readiness   5.7 Stakeholder Groups   9.8 Selling Large Projects

For further assistance

Hiebert, Murray. *Powerful Professionals: Getting Your Expertise Used Inside Organizations*. Recursion Press, 1999.

Kotter, John. *Leading Change*. Harvard Business School Press, 1996.

Scholtes, Peter R. *The Team Handbook: How to Use Teams to Improve Quality*. Joiner Associates, 1988.

5.2 Leading Major Change in Your Organization

Inspired by John Kotter, David Ulrich, Jack Zenger, Norm Smallwood, and Karl Weick.

Nothing demands that leaders truly lead like large-scale change within a department or organization. This tool provides an essential framework for leading major change. In his best-seller, *Leading Change,* John Kotter defined an Eight-Stage Process of Creating Major Change, adapted here.

Change success stage	What to do ...
1. **Establish a sense of urgency.** *result = a shared need*	✔ Complacency, often crudely described as being "fat and happy," is the enemy of change. The hardest systems to change are those perceived to be working adequately: If it ain't broke, don't fix it. (Would you want to fly with an airline with that motto?) Leaders need to create a sense of urgency that drives the need for change. Two typical urgency issues are competition and financial issues. Keep in mind that what resonates with senior management may not with frontline workers.
2. **Create a guiding coalition.** *result = accountability*	✔ Change starts at the top, but needs to be widely led. Establish a cross-organizational team to lead the change, along with a strong and committed leader. This team should contain both commitment leaders (the heart side of change) and strategic leaders (the head side).
3. **Develop a vision and strategy.** *result = anticipation*	✔ People are inspired by vision. People don't get excited about what they don't understand. Write a vision and strategy for change so that it passes the 5-minute test. If you cannot clearly state the vision and strategy of the change in 5 minutes, you will lose people and energy. Everyone needs to know What? Why? and How?
4. **Communicate the change vision and strategy.** *result = commitment*	✔ Use every means you can to communicate why and what the change is about. The standard advertising dictum is that it takes hearing a communication seven times before people become clearly aware of what you are talking about. Also, a more subtle form of communication must take place: All leaders must model the change they expect in others. One "Aw, shit" wipes out one thousand "Way to go's." For example, if you are introducing cost reduction and the change leaders are not scrupulously cost conscious themselves, cynicism will reign.
5. **Clear the way for broad-based action.** *result = systemic alignment*	✔ Look at the change systemically. Most change fails not because it wasn't the right thing to do, but because interacting systems impeded the change. Recognize that current systems are set up to maintain the status quo. Encourage new ideas and risk-taking within the strategic framework. Light many fires of change across the organization.
6. **Generate and recognizing small wins.** *result = momentum*	✔ How do you eat an elephant? One bite at the time. When the change is large, set many short-term mileposts, and celebrate their achievement. Recognize behavior and results that are aligned with the change. Recognize people who dismantle barriers to the change.
7. **Consolidate the small wins.** *result = a culture of success*	✔ Success builds more success. Results build from results. Use the credibility of small wins to continue the push to the big win—the overall change. Measure and build a feeling of progress toward the vision.
8. **Anchor the new approaches in the culture and systems.** *result = sustained change*	✔ What you want people to say about the new change is, "This is the way things are done around here." Connect the change with organizational success. Align all systems with the change.

HOW TO USE THIS LEADERSHIP TOOL

"Successful change of any magnitude goes through all eight stages ... Although one operates in multiple phases at once, skipping even a single step or getting too far ahead without a solid base almost always creates problems."

—John Kotter, *LEADING CHANGE*

Think of a major change that you are involved with in your department or organization. Use the workspace here to plan how you will lead this major change.

WEB WORKSHEET

Change success factor	Your action plans
1. **Establish a sense of urgency.** *result = a shared need* [☞ 2.6 Clarifying Purpose]	
2. **Set up a guiding coalition.** *result = accountability* [☞ 5.7 Stakeholder Groups]	
3. **Establish a vision and strategy.** *result = anticipation* [☞ 2.4 Visioning, 3.1 Strategy]	
4. **Communicate the change vision and strategy.** *result = commitment* [☞ 8.2 Direct Communication]	
5. **Clear the way for broad-based action.** *result = systemic alignment* [☞ 5.6 Aligning Systems]	
6. **Look for and recognize small wins.** *result = momentum*	
7. **Consolidate the small wins.** *result = a culture of success*	
8. **Anchor the changes in the culture and systems.** *result = sustained change* [☞ 5.6 Aligning Systems]	

RELATED LEADERSHIP TOOLS

5.1 Change Equation	5.6 Aligning Systems	5.9 Resistance
5.3 Change Readiness	5.7 Stakeholder Groups	9.8 Selling Large Projects

FOR FURTHER ASSISTANCE

Kotter, John. *Leading Change*. Harvard Business School Press, 1996.

Ulrich, David, Jack Zenger, and Norman Smallwood. *Results-Based Leadership*. Harvard Business School Press, 1999.

Weick, Karl E. *The Social Psychology of Organizing*. Random House, 1969.

5.3 ASSESSING READINESS FOR CHANGE

Inspired by John Kotter, Gene Dalton, Peter Scholtes, and others.

Is your organization, department, or workgroup ready for change? This tool will help you assess the always-difficult question of change readiness. Check the one box in each *row* that best describes your change project.

		Low-hanging fruit *Ready for change.*	**Usual hurdles** *Change will require energy and effort.*	**Brick walls** *Entrenched against change*
1.	Nature of the Problem or Opportunity	❑ Problem is visible and hurting.	❑ Problem causes concern for some, but not others.	❑ Many don't agree there is a problem.
2.	Cause of the Problem	❑ Underlying cause(s) can be isolated and fixed.	❑ Multiple underlying causes; current talk is about symptoms.	❑ Underlying causes are unknown; it is seen as threatening to surface or discuss causes.
3.	Benefit and Risk	❑ Clear benefits and very few disadvantages.	❑ Clear benefits with some risks.	❑ Considerable risk; benefits uncertain and intangible.
4.	Support of Primary Sponsors	❑ Strong management sponsor; widespread support.	❑ Support by some stakeholder groups, but not by others.	❑ The change is supported by only a few people and/or opposed by some.
5.	Support from Other Stakeholders	❑ Stakeholder groups are supportive, while the change does not threaten them.	❑ Some stakeholders benefit by the status quo, while some are threatened.	❑ Change threatens some groups' reasons for being or they benefit from the status quo.
6.	Systemic Barriers	❑ Interlinking systems would not require additional changes.	❑ Some straightforward changes needed in interlinking systems.	❑ Would require a number of changes in a number of interlinking systems.
7.	Funding	❑ Funding available.	❑ Need some additional funding.	❑ Need considerable or unbudgeted funding.
8.	Payout (ROI)	❑ Quick and measurable payout.	❑ Medium-term payout, reasonably measurable.	❑ Payoff is not obvious, benefits not measurable.
9.	Speed of Implementation	❑ Can be implemented quickly, with little disruption.	❑ Implementation within a few weeks to a few months, or can be phased in.	❑ Full implementation would take months to years; or the change is abrupt and severe.
10.	Impact on People	❑ Very little skill training or restructuring needed.	❑ Some retraining and/or restructuring needed.	❑ A considerable amount of training and/or restructuring needed.
11.	Within your Influence	❑ You can personally coach or troubleshoot the change.	❑ You need the leadership of a few others and you can indirectly coach the change.	❑ You need the leadership of many managers and others; or change is out of your hands.
	Add Total Number of Checkmarks:	A.	B.	C.

Your Change Readiness Index = (A_____ × 1) + (B_____ × 2) + (C_____ × 3) = _____

- If the Readiness Index is less than 14, go for it. It's a winner!
- If the Readiness Index is 14 to 18, you will need to plan thoroughly and anticipate difficulties.
- If the Readiness Index is 19 or above, you will have considerable difficulty implementing the change. It will require time and effort to build support and reduce the barriers to change.

HOW TO USE THIS LEADERSHIP TOOL

"When all is said and done, more is said than done."

—Vince Lombardi

By way of example, a process improvement task force thought it would go for big system changes with visible payoffs. After using this tool, it became obvious that others in the organization were not ready to embrace this level of change. As a result, the task force wisely decided to do a number of smaller, quick-hit projects, to gain credibility and experience. A side benefit was that during these start-up phases, the ground was laid for the future success of larger, more complex change projects.

WEB WORKSHEET

Think of the proposed change in your leadership area, then use this tool to:

1. Assist you in assessing the difficulty of the change.
2. Guide you in deciding how much time and effort will be needed to support the change.
3. Help you determine whether you should sponsor the change at this time or at all.

Another good use of this tool is when project teams or task forces are making recommendations. The tool can be used to assess the difficulty of implementing the recommended changes.

Proposed change	Readiness index score	Critical actions needed to reduce barriers to the change?

RELATED LEADERSHIP TOOLS

5.1 Change Equation   5.5 Change Window   6.5 Force-Field Analysis
5.2 Major Change   5.9 Resistance   9.7 Selling Wheel

FOR FURTHER ASSISTANCE

Hiebert, Murray. *Powerful Professionals: Getting Your Expertise Used Inside Organizations*. Recursion Press, 1999.

Kotter, John. *Leading Change*. Harvard Business School Press, 1996.

Scholtes, Peter. *The Team Handbook: How to Use Teams to Improve Quality*. Joiner Associates, 1988.

5.4   LEADING CHANGE: SMALL WINS OR BREAKTHROUGHS?

Inspired by Michael Hammer, James Champy, Robert Schaffer, and Karl Weick.

Change in organizations is a complex phenomenon; no single approach will work consistently over a wide range of change situations. Leaders need to consider the magnitude of any given organizational change and whether it can be introduced in chunks or must be completed in one quantum leap. Note that in some change situations you may be able to strategize an all-or-nothing change yet implement it in manageable pieces, thereby reconciling the two approaches contrasted here and gaining the benefits of both while avoiding the problems of both.

The small wins approach	OR	The breakthrough approach
Other phrases used:		**Other phrases used:**
➡ Incremental change ➡ Continuous improvement ➡ Adaptation ➡ Chunking ➡ Simplification		➡ (Radical) Transformation ➡ Discontinuous change ➡ Reinvention ➡ Frame-breaking ➡ Reengineering
✔ Start with subprojects that are likely to succeed. Build success on success. ✔ Small changes allow the system to absorb the overall, larger change. ✔ Small changes allow people to adapt and adjust emotionally, enabling them to become better prepared for additional changes. ✔ It is easier to involve people in small, specific changes. ✔ Have an overall goal and strategy, then implement small projects and move incrementally to attain that overall goal.		✔ Improvement is more than the sum of its parts. You can't tinker your way to breakthrough change. ✔ With a quantum leap change, no one can cling to the past. ✔ Change is better introduced as one large change, rather than "death by a thousand cuts." ✔ You must look at the whole system. Most large-scale changes fail because the recommended change wasn't supported by the other systems it needed to interact with.
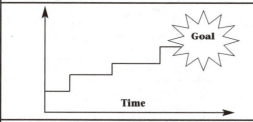		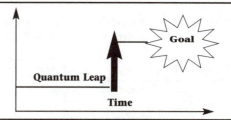
In the small wins corner From *High-Impact Consulting* by Robert Schaffer: To avoid one of what Schaffer calls the "Five Fatal Flaws" of consulting: *"Instead of aiming for 'one big solution' that will require a long cycle time and huge up-front investment, high-impact consulting divides projects into increments, with rapid cycle times, for quicker results."*		**In the all-or-nothing corner** From *Reengineering the Corporation* by Hammer and Champy: *"Reengineering, we are convinced, can't be carried out in small and cautious steps. It is an all-or-nothing proposition that produces dramatically impressive results. Most companies have no choice but to muster the courage to do it. For many, reengineering is the only hope for breaking away from the ineffective, antiquated ways of conducting business."*

"Never underestimate the magnitude of the forces that reinforce complacency and help maintain the status quo."

—John Kotter, *LEADING CHANGE*

There is no easy answer here, and it would be misleading to characterize these approaches as either-or. Breakthrough change is difficult, and there are times when no number of small wins will ever add up to the large-systems change that is necessary for your organization. This is because the status quo in organizations has a way of powerfully rejecting, absorbing, or corrupting incremental changes. To quote a popular phrase, "Your organization is perfectly aligned to get the results that it is currently getting."

WEB WORKSHEET

Small wins approach		Breakthrough approach
	OR	

Small wins approach	Breakthrough approach
Where/when to use: ✔ Senior management is not ready for or supportive of breakthrough change. ✔ You need to build credibility for change. ✔ Risks of failure are catastrophic. ✔ The sum of incremental changes will add up to a large-scale change.	Where/when to use: ✔ Your back is against the wall: Change or go out of business. ✔ You have tried "more of the same" and it isn't getting the overall results needed.
Checklist of things to consider: ❑ Clarify the overall change goal or vision before you break the change into chunks. ❑ Be sure that small wins will move you toward the overall change that is required. ❑ Turn over chunks to project teams.	Checklist of things to consider: ❑ This kind of change requires commitment at the highest level. ❑ Must be led by a strong steering committee. ❑ Requires a crisis or a sense of urgency. ❑ Requires the breakup of current functions; some leaders will not succeed. ❑ Since many old systems will no longer support the change, you must do thorough systems and stakeholder analyses. [☛ 5.6 Aligning Systems, 5.7 Stakeholder Groups]

Think of some needed changes in your leadership area. Use the workspace provided here to assess whether a Small Wins or a Breakthrough approach would be most appropriate.

Potential change	Small wins approach	Breakthrough approach
	Benefits of this approach:	Benefits of this approach:

	Downsides of this approach:	Downsides of this approach:

RELATED LEADERSHIP TOOLS

2.1 Systems Thinking	5.1 Change Equation	5.6 Aligning Systems
3.2 Sigmoid Curve	5.3 Change Readiness	5.7 Stakeholder Groups

FOR FURTHER ASSISTANCE

Hammer, Michael, and James Champy. *Reengineering the Corporation: A Manifesto for Business.*

Schaffer, Robert H. *High-Impact Consulting: How Clients and Consultants Can Leverage.* Jossey-Bass Publishers, 1997.

Weick, Karl. *The Social Psychology of Organizing.* McGraw-Hill College Division, 1979.

5.5 CHANGE WINDOW: A BALANCED APPROACH TO WINNING SUPPORT FOR CHANGE

Inspired by Marvin Weisbord and numerous other sources.

"Resistance to change" is by far the most quoted reason why change doesn't succeed. Yet if you ask people, "How could we improve things around here?" more often than not they will rhyme off a number of changes they would like to see. They perceive that the upsides of *their* desired changes will outweigh any downsides. All change is double-edged, and involves a range of benefits, disadvantages, and risks. This tool will help you plan change in a balanced and holistic way, with a view to increasing the commitment of others to the change.

THE CHANGE WINDOW

Current situation	Recommended change
❹ Advantages, pros, benefits of the way things presently are: **Comfort of the familiar** *(Even if the current situation is painful, many find comfort in the familiar: "The devil you know is better than the devil you don't know.")*	❷ Advantages, pros, benefits of the recommended change. **Benefits of the change** *(A leader often sees and stresses only the benefits of the change.)*
❶ Risks, disadvantages, and downsides of the way things presently are. **Problems with status quo** *(The need for change often starts here. It is much harder to start change when things are perceived to be going well.)*	❸ Risks, disadvantages, and downsides of the recommended change. **Reservations and concerns about the change** *(People's first reaction is often to experience and express the downsides of the change.)*

POINTS TO CONSIDER

- People are often skeptical of change because they have been sold a bill of goods in the past. That is, emphasis was placed on the *need* for change and the *benefits* of change, while little attention was paid to the *risks, limitations,* or *disadvantages* of the change.
- The point of the Change Window is to put needs, benefits, risks, and reservations into perspective. Leaders seeking long-term commitment to a change must clarify issues in all four quadrants.

- Real or not, if a person *perceives* a risk, it is real to him or her. Benefits and disadvantages must be discussed from the *other person's* point of view.
- Leaders usually focus on quadrants ❶ (the need) and ❷ (the benefits of the change).
- Employees often focus on quadrants ❸ (the perceived dangers and discomfort of change) and ❹ (the comfort of the familiar).
- By using this Change Window, you will be able to tell in which quadrant a person's concerns and questions are located. In this way, you'll gain insight into how best to respond to these questions.
- Finally, leaders need to understand that people often circle through these four quadrants a few times before they are willing to commit to supporting a given change. Thus, patience, persistence, and a willingness to hear people's concerns are critical for the successful implementation of change within organizations.

HOW TO USE THIS LEADERSHIP TOOL

Calvin: *"I thrive on change."*

Hobbes: *"You? You threw a fit this morning because your mom put less jelly on your toast than yesterday!"*

Calvin: *"I thrive on making **other** people change."*

—Bill Waterson

Think of a change that you are initiating or being asked to support within your organization. With this change in mind, complete the Change Window. Do this from the perspective of others in your workgroup, or from the perspective of a specific group of key stakeholders to this change.

WEB WORKSHEET

1. Start by making notes in quadrant ❶ about the need for the change.
2. Next, in quadrant ❷, summarize the benefits of the change.
3. In quadrant ❸, note the reservations and downsides of the change as others would see them.
4. Finally, in quadrant ❹, jot down why people might prefer the current situation.

Whenever possible, involve your workgroup in completing these quadrants. This will support a more lasting commitment to the change initiative.

Current situation	Recommended change
❹ Advangates of the current situation	❷ Advantages of the recommended change [☛ 9.7 *Selling Wheel*]
❶ Disadvantages of the current situation	❸ Risks of the recommended change [☛ 5.9 *Resistance*]

1. On balance, quadrants ❶ and ❷ must outweigh ❸ and ❹ for others to embrace the change. After you have made notes in each of the four quadrants, ask yourself, "Which areas seem to need the most work in order for this change to succeed?"

2. Additional uses for the Change Window include:
   - as a presentation tool to provide a balanced perspective on a change; and
   - as a coaching tool to help others present change in a more balanced way.

RELATED LEADERSHIP TOOLS

5.1 Change Equation	5.3 Change Readiness	6.5 Force-Field Analysis
5.2 Major Change	5.9 Resistance	9.7 Selling Wheel

FOR FURTHER ASSISTANCE

Hiebert, Murray. *Powerful Professionals: Getting Your Expertise Used Inside Organizations.* Recursion Press, 1999.

Weisbord, Marvin Ross. *Productive Workplaces: Organizing and Managing for Dignity, Meaning, and Community.* Jossey-Bass, 1989.

5.6 ALIGNING SYSTEMS: BUILDING SYSTEMS COMPATIBILITY INTO CHANGE PLANS

Inspired by numerous sources, including John Kotter, Tom Peters, Robert Waterman, and Peter Senge.

Leaders sometimes try to push through change by improving the technical excellence of the change itself, while ignoring the many other interacting systems that impact on the success of the change (e.g., structure, leadership style, skills, and so on). In these cases, the change often sputters or fails not because the change itself was faulty or misguided, but because it was not supported by the many other interacting systems within the organization. The idea behind this tool is simple but powerful. It stresses the importance of understanding and aligning change initiatives with existing interacting systems; or alternatively, of redesigning these interacting systems to support the change initiative. Only then can change initiatives add sustainable and lasting value within organizations.

SYSTEMATIC CHANGE PRINCIPLES

- Change often fails because it was not supported by other interacting systems.
- For successful change, leaders need to identify those systems that interact with the change.
  - Which interacting systems will support or accelerate the change?
  - Which interacting systems will inhibit or act as barriers to your recommended change?
  - What can be done to reduce, eliminate, or even turn around these barriers?

By way of example, many a task force has sought to produce an elegant career development process for their organization. Yet these efforts have sometimes been abandoned because people ask questions such as, "Will my compensation parallel my career development?" In this way, change fails because interacting systems (e.g., the compensation program) were not aligned with the proposed change.

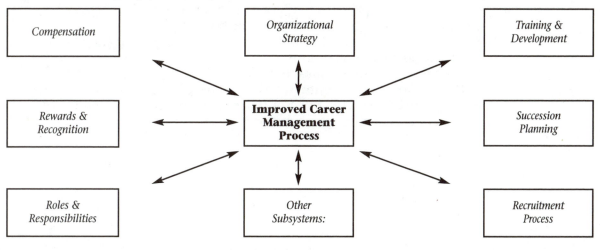

Past experience in your organization may have shown that attempts to change a particular process have been met with resistance, often even scuttled. Using this tool, a team or workgroup can draw an interacting systems map, then use the map to improve the original change proposal. They can then modify the change and action plans to deal with incompatibilities and conflicts among interacting systems. The interacting systems map can ultimately be used as part of a successful change presentation.

Place the proposed change in the center of a large sheet of paper or display board. Then place all the other systems that interlink with the change around the center. Draw arrows to illustrate connections. Next, consider each interacting system, and ask: "Will this interacting system support or hinder the proposed changes?"

? For systems that are supportive of the change, ask: "How can we enhance or use this support to ensure successful change?"

? For systems that are barriers to the change, ask: "How can we reduce this barrier to minimize its disruption to the proposed change?" or "How can we redesign our change proposal to minimize the negative effect of this barrier?"

? For systems whose impact on the proposed change is unknown, ask: "How can we get information about this system, to ensure it does not get in the way of our proposed change?"

Hᴏᴡ ᴛᴏ ᴜsᴇ ᴛʜɪs ʟᴇᴀᴅᴇʀsʜɪᴘ ᴛᴏᴏʟ

"More than 95 percent of your organization's problems derive from your systems, processes, and methods, not from your individual workers. Your people are doing their best, but their best efforts cannot compensate for your inadequate and dysfunctional systems."

—Peter Scholtes, *THE LEADER'S HANDBOOK*

1. On the worksheet provided, identify the systems that are likely to interact with your change proposal.
   ? Which systems will support the proposed change?
   ? Which systems will inhibit or be barriers to the recommended change?
   ? What can you do to reduce, eliminate, or turn around these barriers?

2. A tool such as this works best if it is adapted to each change task force's unique needs. For example, consider the following steps:
   • Post sheets of flip chart paper to produce a large square.
   • Place the recommended change in the middle box.
     – Diagram all the subsystems that will interact with the recommended change.
     – Draw lines to show interrelationships.
     – Circle the supporting subsystems in green.
     – Circle the unknown impact subsystems in yellow.
     – Circle the subsystems that conflict or that you are concerned about in red.
     – Write action plans next to each subsystem.

ALIGNING SYSTEMS WORKSHEET

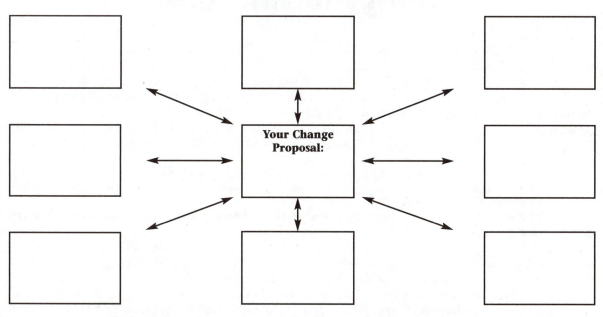

Your Change Proposal:

ACTIONS NEEDED TO ENSURE SYSTEMS ALIGNMENT

1. Which interlinking systems will support or be neutral to the change?

2. Which interlinking systems will impede the change?

3. Which interlinking systems will have unknown effects?

4. What actions are needed to deal with the systems identified in 2 and 3?

RELATED LEADERSHIP TOOLS

2.1 Systems Thinking	5.1 Change Equation	5.7 Stakeholder Groups
2.2 7S Model	5.3 Change Readiness	9.7 Selling Wheel

FOR FURTHER ASSISTANCE

Kotter, John. *Leading Change*. Harvard Business School Press, 1996.

Peters, Thomas, and Robert H. Waterman. *In Search of Excellence: Lessons from America's Best-Run Companies*. Harper & Row, 1981.

Senge, Peter M. *The Fifth Discipline: The Art and Practice of the Learning Organization*. Doubleday, 1990.

5.7 STAKEHOLDER GROUPS: UNDERSTANDING AND MAPPING STAKEHOLDER SYSTEMS

Inspired by Stephen Heiman, Diane Sanchez, Tad Tuleja, Robert Miller, and John Kotter.

Increasingly, projects and change initiatives in organizations have multiple stakeholders, and rarely do changes or recommendations have an impact on only a single interest group. Thus, to have your ideas accepted and implemented, it's crucial to determine who these stakeholder groups are and what role each plays in the change process. This tool will help you identify, organize, and map the different stakeholder groups and their different perspectives.

FIVE TYPICAL STAKEHOLDER GROUPS

1. **Contact or working stakeholder(s):**
   The people who represent sponsor-stakeholders; they may work directly with you on a project team.
   The contact stakeholder may be an individual or a group, a task force or a committee. Often they represent other stakeholder groups. These stakeholders are project-oriented, busy people who usually wish to minimize their time and energy spent on the project. A contact stakeholder's typical question is: *"How can we successfully finish this project on time and within budget, and get acceptance for implementation?"* Contrast this question with those of the remaining stakeholder types.

2. **Sponsor, financial funder, or decision stakeholder(s):**
   The individual or group that has the authority to approve the project.
   Often senior managers or management committees, these stakeholders approve the budget and free up resources for implementation. Their basic question is: *"Is this proposal organizationally and financially sound?"* Their perspective often takes in more than any one particular project. They are concerned about your project's impact on the organization. Beware of the rampant myth about this group, that if you get the top-level stakeholder's approval, the project is a shoo-in. Not true! Their commitment is certainly necessary, but alone it's often not sufficient.

3. **End-user stakeholder(s):**
   The group of stakeholders who will actually implement the changes and make them work on the job.
   Their basic question is: *"Will this really work under my practical conditions and will it make my job easier?"* Note how different this question is from that of the sponsor stakeholder. Often, leaders tend to be more comfortable working with one or two particular stakeholder groups and not with others. This can be costly. To succeed today, leaders need to work equally well with the full range of often diverse stakeholder groups.

4. **Indirect stakeholder(s):**
   They are able to say, "No, your proposal does not fit our organizational policy or requirements."
   The least obvious stakeholders, these are people who cannot directly approve your proposal, but who can say "no" or can hold up your project. The basic question of indirect stakeholders is: *"Does this proposal meet the standards and policies we control?"*

Examples are groups such as purchasing, legal, human resources, regulatory or governmental compliance groups, safety, systems groups, and so on. Rather than considering these groups as roadblocks, you need to understand that they are rightfully trying to uphold the standards of the organization.

5. **Coach stakeholder(s):**
   They help you understand and work within the informal stakeholder system.
   The most unusual stakeholders, these people are particularly needed if you work at arm's length from other stakeholder groups (e.g., from head office to field). They can come from any level of the organization and be any person, from highly-placed executives who may coach you, right through to an office clerk. The role of coaches is to help you and your project get approval. Their basic question is: *"How can we get the job done?"* These people will help you navigate around obstacles in other stakeholder systems, and help you understand unwritten rules: "how things work around here." They will also give you blunt feedback about what is and is not working. The more complex the project, the more valuable coaches become.

TYPES OF STAKEHOLDER MAPS

Stakeholder maps can range from simple box-and-arrow arrangements to very creative drawings. Keep in mind the issue is clarity of stakeholders and how to deal with them. Creative maps can lead to creative discussions and actions. Henry Mintzberg in his book *Mintzberg on Management* drew a very creative map of an organization.

Internal and External Influencers of an Organization

Reprinted with permission from Henry Mintzberg's *Mintzberg on Management*. The Free Press, a Division of Macmillan, Inc., 1989, p.100.

How to use this leadership tool

"Now that we've reached agreement, all we need is to get everybody else to agree with us."

© Ashleigh Brilliant

The roles, interests, and influences of various stakeholder groups come into focus when mapped around a given change proposal or project. You can draw a map using the stakeholder categories on the worksheet provided or by drawing freehand. You'll find these guidelines helpful, regardless of how you draw your map.

1. *Sketch out a first draft of your stakeholder map.*
   - Involve others on the project team in this mapping and planning process.
   - Group people into stakeholder groups on the basis of whether they would generally see your project in the same way. You may be surprised when an unexpected interest group surfaces using this mapping process. However, this is a good thing. Now you can plan to consider the new stakeholder group's interests. This will pay dividends later, when you request project approval and begin to seek out allies for implementing the project.
   - Consider the stakeholders of your stakeholders. They can often help or hinder your projects.
   - Draw arrows showing relationships and affinities among stakeholder groups.

2. *Complete your stakeholder map.*
   Ask these questions about each stakeholder group:
   - **?** Who are they? Give them a collective name that makes sense in your organization.
   - **?** What are their concerns compared to the other stakeholder groups? How critical are these concerns to the project's success?
   - **?** What is their current status? Are they informed and up to date? Are they supportive? Are any offside?
   - **?** What benefits would they see in this project? (Are they able to answer the question, "What's in it for me?"?)
   - **?** What problems would they see with this proposal or project? What reservations might they see with the project? What are their major concerns about the project? How might they be unsupportive of the project?
   - **?** Prioritize the significant stakeholder groups for this project. Not all interest groups are in need of equal attention.
   - **?** Are you giving each interest group sufficient emphasis?

Related leadership tools

2.1 Systems Thinking	5.9 Resistance	9.7 Selling Wheel
5.1 Change Equation	6.3 Complex Situations	9.8 Selling Large Projects

For further assistance

Heiman, Stephen E., Diane Sanchez, Tad Tuleja, and Robert B. Miller. *The New Strategic Selling: The Unique Sales System Proven Successful by the World's Best Companies*. Warner Books, 1998.

Hiebert, Murray. *Powerful Professionals: Getting Your Expertise Used Inside Your Organization*. Recursion Press, 1999.

Kotter, John. *Leading Change*. Harvard Business School Press, 1996.

Stakeholder Group Map Worksheet

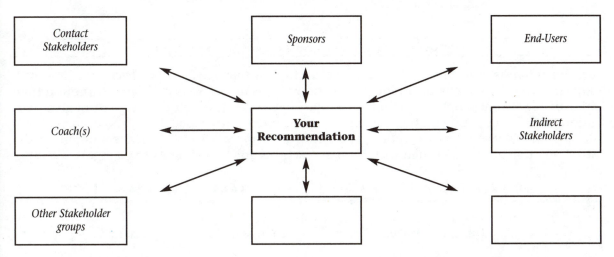

Contact Stakeholders		Sponsors		End-Users
Coach(s)		**Your Recommendation**		Indirect Stakeholders
Other Stakeholder groups				

Action planning to improve stakeholder support

1. What is their priority, compared to that of the other groups? How critical are they to the project's success? Not all client groups are in need of equal attention.

2. Characterize each stakeholder group into this matrix:

Friends	Fence-sitters	Foes	Foreign
• Already support the change. • Tend to spend too much time with these groups, but cannot be ignored.	• Could support the change or not, depending on the work you do with them. • The most important group to work with and sell the change to.	• Will probably never support the change. • Don't butt your head against a brick wall. • If you have too many of these, you need to get more support or reconsider the change.	• Don't know where these groups stand. • Need to find out where they stand; ignorance is not bliss, but dangerous.

3. For the Fence-Sitters, how do you ensure they stay on board and, if possible, assist the change?

4. For the Foes, what reservations and risks would they see? How can you deal with these risks?

5. For the Foreign, how will you find out where they stand?

6. What are your next steps to improve your stakeholder situation?

5.8 HUMAN TRANSITIONS: HELPING PEOPLE WORK THROUGH MAJOR CHANGE

Inspired by William Bridges, Susan Campbell, and Virginia Satir.

Leaders often assume that if change is logical from a management perspective, people will adjust. The process of change inside people, however, is more like distress and disruption than adjustment. Before people can accept and adjust to change, they frequently go through a transition period. This period is often evidenced by low morale, increased stress, and decreased productivity. This tool offers a practical, straightforward approach to help leaders minimize the stress and downtime associated with human reactions and adjustments to change.

THE CRITICAL DIFFERENCE BETWEEN CHANGE AND TRANSITION

Change:

- The actual physical move, restructure, or change of location, procedures, equipment, and so on.
- This change takes place outside the person, and relatively quickly (e.g., being moved to another city, getting a new manager).

Transition:

- The human reorientation that people go through in coming to terms with a change (e.g., coming to feel like a new city is home or that a new manager is a trusted colleague).
- This inner transition often takes much longer than the outside or physical change. The transition is internal and emotional (i.e., feelings-based). It requires a new way of understanding and looking at things.

For example, your staff may have complained about their obsolete desktop computers and software. Finally, you, their leader, have the budget and priority to have the Systems Department make the change. The switchover—the change—is brief, often less than an hour per desktop. But what do you, as their leader, hear after the change? Often complaints! This time it's about the new desktop systems: "The new keyboards don't feel right and some keys are in new places." Or "The new operating system doesn't look the same as the old one. Where are my critical files?" And so on. Although the physical change was relatively quick, the emotional transition that takes place inside of people—becoming proficient and feeling at ease with the new equipment—may take a number of weeks. Given this situation, your initial reaction, as their leader, might be to interpret staff complaints as ingratitude. But wait! Understanding the nature of human transitions will help you accept these complaints as the natural responses to change they are.

Downsizing and layoffs are all too common, and many people in the North American workforce have had personal experience with this type of transition. Here is an example of how one company managed this change and the human transition that accompanied it, with sensitivity and respect for its workforce.

1. The first meeting: Endings. They announced the change and the upcoming layoffs. The meeting was focused on letting go of the past, listening to employees, and inviting people to express their feelings.
2. The next meeting, a week later, created the inevitable Turmoil as the new organizational structure was reviewed with employees. The focus was on the transition from letting go to beginning a new future.
3. The final meeting, a month later, focused on New Beginnings. Plans were made and goals clarified.

One person in the organization expressed her feelings about the three-step process this way: "I've been through downsizing before and never want to go through one of these exercises again, but this was by far the least traumatic. Normally, at the first meeting, managers, uneasy with the emotions of layoffs, would quickly shift the meeting discussion to the 'bright future ahead,' while employees listening could only think of the traumatic present."

LEADING THE PEOPLE SIDE OF CHANGE

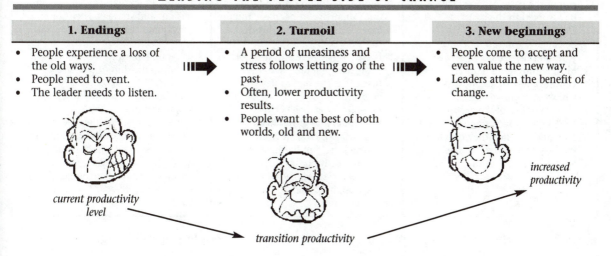

1. Endings	2. Turmoil	3. New beginnings
• People experience a loss of the old ways. • People need to vent. • The leader needs to listen.	• A period of uneasiness and stress follows letting go of the past. • Often, lower productivity results. • People want the best of both worlds, old and new.	• People come to accept and even value the new way. • Leaders attain the benefit of change.

current productivity level

transition productivity

increased productivity

Productivity goes down during the turmoil phase, as people struggle to learn and master the new way of doing things. If they don't understand the human need for transitional space or time, leaders might panic as productivity temporarily drops. They then begin another change, on top of the old change, in an attempt to fix things and regain lost productivity. This can create additional turmoil and stress, and possibly an additional decrease in productivity.

HOW TO USE THIS LEADERSHIP TOOL

"Some changes are so slow you don't notice them, others are so fast they don't notice you."
© Ashleigh Brilliant

Leaders cannot force transitions, but they can facilitate and expedite them. Use this checklist to plan effective people transition in your organization.

Endings	Turmoil period	New beginnings
❏ Do not assume others have moved with you or are in the same phase of transition. Often, you, as leader, are at the New Beginnings stage and wonder why others are not there with you. ❏ It's natural for people to gripe, to wish for the good old days, the past, the way things were. ❏ People need to express their feelings at Endings. Help them do that: – Ask people about their feelings. – Protect persons who vent. – Express your own feelings. ❏ Your role is to listen, to empathize, not sympathize. ❏ Honor the past. Acknowledge what had worked in the past. ❏ Do not take peoples' venting personally. You can fix things, but you can't fix people. ❏ Most Endings end naturally. After venting a few times, most people will want to move on. ❏ Use the power of the group. Endings are much more powerful and quicker when they occur publicly and in a group session. ❏ Support is a key feature: Listen and lead.	❏ It's natural and okay to be in turmoil: – *Emotionally:* confusion, stress, vacillation, blaming others – *Thinking:* asking why, resisting suggestions, second-guessing – *Behaviorally:* "just going through the motions" ❏ Some people will try to recapture the way things were; others will want to rush ahead to the future. ❏ Transitions can't be forced, but they can be led. Turmoil takes some time, but be definite about a time limit. ❏ Insist on the rational change while personally supporting your people. Be tough on the problem but supportive of people. "Tough love" is an apt phrase during transitions. ❏ Focus on the here and now, on short-term, familiar activities. Insist that the day-to-day work gets done. ❏ Mantain a balance between individual and group work: – *Individual:* Deal with individual issues, help individuals through the transition. – *Group:* Harness the power of the group; help the group through the change.	❏ Declare the transition over. Announce New Beginnings. ❏ Celebrate or otherwise symbolically mark the New Beginnings. ❏ Recognize new beginnings: – *Emotionally:* new energy, new spirit, focus outward – *Thinking:* setting new goals, looking ahead, focusing on results – *Behaviorally:* talk of future, focus on productivity ❏ Help group members look beyond the day-to-day (which you encouraged during the Turmoil period). Formulate expectations, state them clearly, and follow up. ❏ Clarify longer-range goals, results, vision, and strategy. Focus on a target and marshal work toward that target. ❏ A group will need to (re)consider: – group mission or purpose, – goals, – roles and accountabilities, and – ground rules. ❏ Check for systems alignment. One of the major reasons for the failure of change to take hold is that other interacting organizational systems do not support the change.

What are the key actions you will take to facilitate the people side of change?

Related leadership tools

5.1 Change Equation	5.6 Aligning Systems	8.2 Direct Communication
5.3 Change Readiness	5.7 Stakeholder Groups	9.1 Leadership Versatility

For further assistance

Bridges, William. *Transitions: Making Sense of Life's Changes.* Addison-Wesley, 1980.

Campbell, Susan M. *From Chaos to Confidence: Survival Strategies for the New Workplace.* Simon & Schuster, 1995.

Hiebert, Murray. *Powerful Professionals: Getting Your Expertise Used Inside Your Organization.* Recursion Press, 1999.

Satir, Virginia. *The New Peoplemaking.* Science and Behavior Books, 1988.

5.9 SURFACING AND DEALING WITH RESISTANCE

Inspired by Peter Block.

Resistance: a strange, loaded word with negative and emotional baggage. But resistance is, believe it or not, a completely natural human experience. Resistance is how we protect ourselves from being had. When presented with significant change, most people think of the reasons why this new idea won't work. It's pretty natural to want to stay in and defend the status quo, even when the current way of doing things isn't working very well. As change agents, leaders need to understand and deal early with resistance, be it direct or indirect. It doesn't go away until you deal with it honestly. This tool will help you do that.

Resistance can often be positive, in the sense that:

- You know your request has been heard and people are perhaps striving to understand how to make it work without upsetting their environment too much; or
- It may represent a legitimate commitment to another alternative or to a different way of thinking.

However, indirect resistance is often camouflaged, and can look like a sincere response. Only when resistance is direct, sincere, and in the open does it become possible to discuss and deal with real concerns.

Here are some common examples of behaviors that could be either sincere responses or forms of *indirect* resistance.

Signs of direct resistance	Signs of indirect resistance
• People tell you their real concerns, and how they feel, openly and honestly. • They maintain eye contact and use "I" statements. (Pay attention to cultural differences.) • Bluntness may feel hurtful at the time, but is actually the more honest and easier form of resistance to deal with. • You know exactly where you stand; the issue is clear. ▼ • Leads to honest negotiation or conflict resolution. • You can put your energy into the real issue.	• People ask for more and more detail, endlessly questioning. • They are not able to find a good time to implement, or continually assert a rigid timetable. • They intellectualize, debate definitions and concepts, or talk in apparently rational terms, but not about the real concerns. • They decide "The problem has gone away," or press for solutions too soon. • They say someone else is the problem, using third-party language: *we* or *they* statements. • You have a gut feeling that something's wrong. • You don't know where you stand. ▼ • Leads to misdirected energy and frustration. • You will be led to put energy into side issues.

Leaders need to know how to surface indirect resistance and turn it into direct resistance. Begin by *not* assuming or mind reading. You could be wrong! What looks like resistance could be a genuine request or comment. Use the process known as the "two good-faith responses technique" to surface indirect resistance:

1. Initially, treat the other people's comments in good faith and respond accordingly. For example, if they ask for more information, provide it. If they ask for more information a second time, once again, provide it.

2. After having given two good-faith responses, at the third request, you should respond differently. Now it's time to recognize and name the resistance.

3. Name what you think is the resistance in a way that invites the other people to be open with you, without forcing or threatening. (Pushing too hard at this point will only drive their indirect resistance further underground.) For example, you might ask something like, "Pat, each time you've asked for more information, I've provided it, and you still seem to need more. Is there something else that's troubling you?"

4. Having asked this question, now be quiet. Give the other person time to reflect. He or she will need a few moments to prepare a response. At this point, the other person may be willing to discuss real concerns. You've done all that you can, and now it's the other person's choice.

How to use this leadership tool

"Resistance is a predictable, natural, emotional reaction against the process of being helped and against the process of having to face up to difficult organizational problems. ... It is not a reflection of the conversation [you] are having ... on an objective, logical, or rational level."

—Peter Block, *FLAWLESS CONSULTING*

Although not a guarantee, the "two good-faith responses technique" is a powerful approach to opening up direct communication. More often than not, it helps to surface indirect resistance. Used sincerely, this technique can reduce hidden agendas and help people deal more directly and honestly with each other.

Each situation is unique. In some situations, you might want to give three or even four good-faith responses; in others, only one such response might be appropriate. Think of a situation in which you might be experiencing indirect resistance—you are getting the runaround, or feeling put off. Use the workspace here to plan how you might use the "two good-faith responses technique" to surface indirect resistance and to help the people concerned to become more direct in their dealings with you.

WEB WORKSHEET

Describe the form that this individual's indirect resistance is taking (e.g., asking for more information, saying "It's not in the budget," etc.).

How will you gently challenge this person to come clean and tell you his or her real concerns? What specifically might you say? (It's important that this challenge is not so weak that it's missed by the other person, or so strong that it drives the other person's indirect resistance even further underground. In crucial situations, you may wish to practice phrasing your challenge with a trusted coach.)

If, despite your good-faith responses, the other person is still not willing to be direct with you, what alternatives do you have and what steps might you take next?

RELATED LEADERSHIP TOOLS

| 8.5 Metacommunicating | 12.1 The Relationship Bank | 12.6 Confrontation |
| 8.7 Active Listening | 12.4 Feedback | 12.7 Dealing with Conflict |

FOR FURTHER ASSISTANCE

Block, Peter. *Flawless Consulting: A Guide to Getting Your Expertise Used*. University Associates, 1978.

Hiebert, Murray. *Powerful Professionals: Getting Your Expertise Used Inside Organizations*. Recursion Press, 1999.

5.10

APPRECIATIVE INQUIRY:
BUILDING CHANGE ON SUCCESS

Inspired by Suresh Srivastva, David Cooperrider, Martin Seligman, Tom Pitman, and Gervase Bushe.

Effective leadership has become synonymous with the ability to facilitate strategic and lasting change in organizations (i.e., improvements that stick). Appreciative inquiry is a process for doing this. However, it entails a shift away from traditional management thinking and, as such, it is often defined in contrast to problem solving (see table). Because appreciative inquiry is such a departure from the assumptions of traditional management processes, it can be a challenging concept to grasp fully. Yet this is a learning curve with a potentially huge payoff.

Those who use appreciative inquiry claim it helps them achieve extraordinary results, while detractors claim it's somewhat naive and overly optimistic about human nature. Appreciative inquiry is not for everyone. It tends to resonate with leaders who think laterally as well as linearly, who have a generally positive and hopeful view of human nature, and who are able to tolerate a degree of ambiguity as the process unfolds. The columns and examples in this table will help you determine whether appreciative inquiry fits with your leadership style.

Problem solving	Appreciative inquiry
• Improvement is not sought unless a problem is identified.	• A "possibility blueprint" is developed outlining what might, should, and will be in the future.
• Problems are defined. (The focus is on what's *not* working.)	• Success is defined. (The focus is on what is already working well.)
• Possible causes are analyzed (based on how the problem has been defined).	• Possible futures are envisioned (based on current successes).
• Data collection seeks to discover what has gone wrong and where people have failed.	• Data collection seeks to confirm and value past successes, and takes place within a climate of mutual inquiry (a learning community).
• Solutions are defined (to fix the problem).	• An ideal future is defined (what should be).
• Action plans are outlined.	• Innovation is encouraged to achieve the defined ideal future.

Key assumptions and strategies of appreciative inquiry include:

✔ Many things are currently working well in most organizations. Change and future success is best built on these positive foundations. You cannot "fix" your way to success; you have to build success on success.

✔ People will support change when they feel understood and valued, when they understand the need for the change, and when they feel able to influence the direction and pace of the change.

✔ Multiple realities exist within organizations and workgroups. Different stakeholders can see the organization and the recommended change in remarkably different ways.

✔ Real communication is possible only when groups value their differences.

✔ The language we use influences our reality—the way we see things. Leaders who look for problems will find problems. Leaders who look for successes will find successes.

> *"… three umpires disagreed on the tack of calling balls and strikes. The first one says, 'I call them as they is.' The second one says, 'I calls them as I see them.' The third and cleverest umpire says, 'They ain't nothing 'till I calls them.'"*
>
> —H. W. Simons

Appreciative inquiry differs from traditional visioning work in that the envisioned future is grounded in past and current successes. In this way, the system maintains the best of the past by articulating what has been achieved, then continuing and adapting these successes into the future.

How to use this leadership tool

> *"While traditional problem-solving processes separate, dissect, and pull apart, appreciative inquiry processes generate affirming images which integrate, synthesize, and pull people together."*
>
> —Tom Pitman and Gervase Bushe, *OD PRACTITIONER*

An organization has been through a number of tremendous changes in a period of three years: a merger, a restructuring, and an accompanying downsizing. People have become disillusioned at even the hint of further change. Yet you, as a leader, have been told, and you know instinctively, that further change is needed. Instead of using the traditional leadership processes that have been used over the past three years (asking, "What problems are you having?"; focusing on deficiencies; defining problems; and fixing what's broken), you may want to use appreciative inquiry (asking, "What's working well around here?"; multiplying hope and energy by surfacing the organization's history of success).

WEB WORKSHEET

Use the workspace provided here to plan your approach to a difficult organizational issue using an appreciative inquiry process.

How might you approach the system (the group, department, and so on) in order to:
• Build working relationships with group members?

- Explore the strengths and past successes of the system and its members?

- Involve the entire system in a search for solutions, in a way that recognizes and values the organization's strengths and potential?

RELATED LEADERSHIP TOOLS

5.9 Resistance	10.6 Group Leader Skills	14.6 Learning Styles
8.7 Active Listening	14.1 Scarcity and Abundance	14.7 Personal Preferences

FOR FURTHER ASSISTANCE

Cooperrider, David L., and Suresh Srivastva. "Appreciative Inquiry into Organizational Life." *Research in Organization Change and Development*, vol. 1, 1987. 129–169.

Pitman, Tom, and Gervase Bushe. "Appreciative Process: A Method of Transformational Change." *OD Practitioner*. September 1991. 1–4.

Seligman, Martin. *Learned Optimism: How to Change Your Mind and Your Life*. Pocket Books, 1990.

6

TOOLS FOR CRITICAL THINKING AND INNOVATION

In any leader's competency tool kit are many thinking and innovation tools to improve your own thinking and to help you coach others to improve theirs. This section emphasizes tools that help leaders deal with a most valued and demanding skill—sorting out complex situations.

6.1

THE BS DETECTOR KIT:
RECOGNIZING ERRORS OF LOGIC

Inspired by John Paulos and Carl Sagan.

Leaders need tools for detecting erroneous logic. Not only is this tool interesting reading, but by occasionally reviewing the fallacies pointed out here, you will sharpen your instincts for detecting logical errors in your own thinking and in that of others.

LOGICAL FALLACIES

Logic error	What it is	Example
Attacking the person, not the problem—*ad hominem*	Attacking the arguer rather than the argument or the facts	*"You're a typical engineer; you'll never understand human needs."*
Vague terms	Using vague terms rather than stating the real, concrete issue	*"We have a communications problem" rather than, "You and I haven't spoken since the incident."*
Defining the problem as a solution	Presenting a solution to an as-yet undefined problem	*"We need to send all our Systems Analysts to an interpersonal skills workshop."*
An either-or false dichotomy	Presenting only two alternatives when a range is available	*"Either you take the transfer or you'll have no career here."*
Confusing association and correlation with causation	Causation cannot be assumed just because something routinely happens after a certain event.	*"We have a lot more absences on Mondays because people get paid on Fridays."*
Sequence means cause	Just because two thing happened in sequence, that doesn't necessarily mean one is causing the other.	*"Chris seemed upset after getting negative feedback yesterday. Now he called in sick today."*
The statistic of small numbers—over-generalizing	Making general inferences from a very small sample	*"I talked to a couple of customers and nobody likes the new design."*
Misunderstanding the nature of statistics	Making incorrect statistical inferences	*"Over half of the statistics you hear are wrong."*
Incorrect conclusions—*non sequitur* (It does not follow.)	Drawing incorrect conclusions from data	*"We have more lost-time accidents this month. Our new safety program isn't working."*
Pleading	Appealing to some authority or law to support an argument	*"It's human nature for people to … (e.g., be selfish, want to help)."*
Blindly trusting authority	An argument that amounts to little more than "Trust me"	*"If you work hard, the company will take care of you."*
Selective observation	Using only selected pieces of evidence to support your argument	*"Twice this week, Terry has been whispering on the phone. Someone must be getting fired."*

Inconsistency	Applying an argument only where it suits your interests and/or needs	A leader giving others feedback because *"It's good for them"* when the same leader does not accept feedback.
Caricaturing	Making fun of a person or position rather than dealing with real issues	*"All accountants are dull and analysis-retentive."*
Slippery slope (domino theory)	Assuming that if you do something once, it will escalate	*"If we allow one person to do this, they'll all want to do it."*
Appealing to ignorance	The claim that whatever has not been proven false must be true, and vice versa	*"We haven't heard from marketing, so they can't be promoting our product."*
Short-term versus long-term; tactics versus strategy	Assuming short-term actions will make long-term sense, or vice versa	*"If we all work harder, our jobs will be more secure."*
Weasel words	Using aphorisms to disguise unpleasant realities	*"We need to rationalize our operations by rightsizing our resources."*

How to use this leadership tool

"On occasion we're gullible because we're caught up in powerful emotions, for example, anger, wonder, fear, greed, and grief."

—Carl Sagan, *THE DEMON-HAUNTED WORLD: SCIENCE AS A CANDLE IN THE DARK*

We suggest four levels of application for this leadership tool.

1. As a reminder, review the list of fallacies outlined from time to time.

2. Think of your own examples when you have experienced these errors of logic. Doing so will ground this tool for you and make each category of logic error more understandable and meaningful. You might wish to involve your workgroup in using this tool. They too could benefit from developing their instincts for detecting logical fallacies.

3. Use the appropriate steps to test and detect logical fallacies in management decisions:

   ❑ Take the time to analyze a problem before taking action. (Many leaders claim that they don't have time to do it right the first time, but seem to find time to fix up things that go wrong.)

   ❑ Learn how to use problem-solving and decision-making tools. [☛ 7.2 Problem Solving]

   ❑ Learn and use the Quality tools like causal analysis, fishbone diagrams, and so on. [☛ 7.7 Quality Tools]

   ❑ Seek independent confirmation of your decisions.

   ❑ Search out alternative hypotheses; remember that human behavior is complex and often multicausal.

   ❑ Don't assume the first solution is the best solution; seek out and explore other options.

   ❑ Quantify information whenever possible (this aids in decision making).

- ❑ If there's a chain of argument, ensure that every link in the chain works.

- ❑ When two hypotheses explain the data equally well, choose the simpler of the two; (this is known as Occam's razor).

- ❑ Determine whether the hypothesis can be falsified. (It is far easier to prove something wrong than right!)

- ❑ Learn group leadership skills. (They are designed to help you minimize errors of logic.)

4. Think of a decision that you or your workgroup is currently facing. Check (✓) which errors of logic you might be particularly vulnerable to making, given your own past history of decision making and the circumstances of this particular decision.

__Attacking the person, not the problem	__The statistics of small numbers	__Inconsistency
__Vague terms	__Misunderstanding the nature of statistics	__Caricaturing
__Defining the problem as a solution	__Incorrect conclusions—*non sequitur* (It does not follow.)	__Slippery slope (domino theory)
__An either-or false dichotomy	__Pleading	__Appealing to ignorance
__Confusing association and correlation with causation	__Blindly trusting authority	__Short-term versus long-term; tactics versus strategy
__Sequence means cause	__Selective observation	__Weasel words

What specific actions can you or your workgroup take to avoid making these errors of logic?

Related leadership tools

1.9 Paradigms   6.4 Discussing Messes   7.1 Problem Framing

6.2 Assumption Analysis   6.6 Six-Hat Thinking   7.3 Finding Cause

For further assistance

Paulos, John. *Innumeracy: Mathematical Illiteracy and Its Consequences,* 2nd ed. Vintage Books, 1990.

Sagan, Carl. *The Demon-Haunted World: Science As a Candle in the Dark.* Ballantine Books, 1996.

6.2 ASSUMPTION ANALYSIS: TESTING DECISIONS BY EXAMINING THEIR UNDERLYING BIASES

Inspired by Ralph Kilmann.

Leaders can improve their decision making by first outlining options for action, then examining the assumptions held by supporters of these options. This tool will help you surface and challenge your own and other people's assumptions, as a way of ensuring quality of decisions in complex and dynamic business environments.

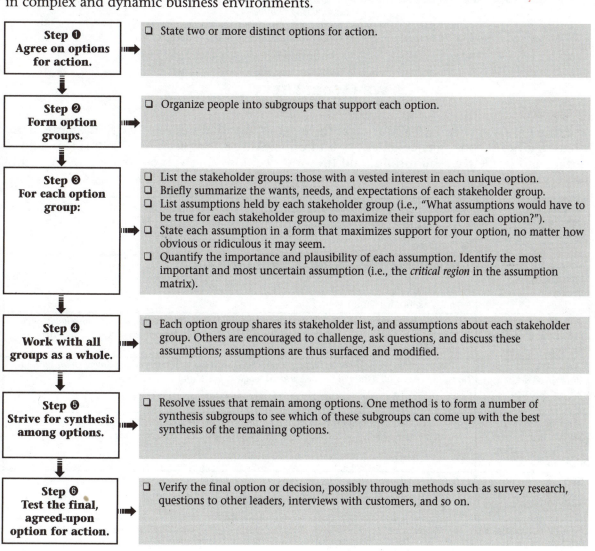

Step ❶
Agree on options for action.

❑ State two or more distinct options for action.

Step ❷
Form option groups.

❑ Organize people into subgroups that support each option.

Step ❸
For each option group:

❑ List the stakeholder groups: those with a vested interest in each unique option.
❑ Briefly summarize the wants, needs, and expectations of each stakeholder group.
❑ List assumptions held by each stakeholder group (i.e., "What assumptions would have to be true for each stakeholder group to maximize their support for each option?").
❑ State each assumption in a form that maximizes support for your option, no matter how obvious or ridiculous it may seem.
❑ Quantify the importance and plausibility of each assumption. Identify the most important and most uncertain assumption (i.e., the *critical region* in the assumption matrix).

Step ❹
Work with all groups as a whole.

❑ Each option group shares its stakeholder list, and assumptions about each stakeholder group. Others are encouraged to challenge, ask questions, and discuss these assumptions; assumptions are thus surfaced and modified.

Step ❺
Strive for synthesis among options.

❑ Resolve issues that remain among options. One method is to form a number of synthesis subgroups to see which of these subgroups can come up with the best synthesis of the remaining options.

Step ❻
Test the final, agreed-upon option for action.

❑ Verify the final option or decision, possibly through methods such as survey research, questions to other leaders, interviews with customers, and so on.

ASSUMPTION MATRIX

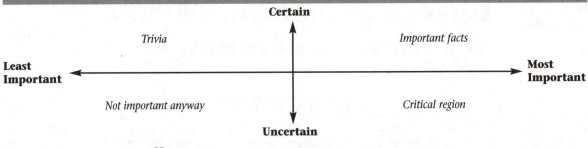

HOW TO USE THIS LEADERSHIP TOOL

"Decision Trap Number 4:
Overconfidence in Your Judgment. Failing to collect key factual information
because you are too sure of your assumptions and options."

—Russo and Schoemaker, *DECISION TRAPS*

WEB WORKSHEET

Use this approach to surface and analyze the assumptions that underlie decisions, particularly when significant consequences might result from making a poor decision. Use this template to surface and challenge assumptions, and thus test decisions that you or your group are in the process of making.

Step ❶ Determine options.	*What options or alternatives seem possible, given the circumstances of this situation?* [☛ 7.1 Problem Framing]
Step ❷ Form option groups.	*What subgroups or individuals seem to support each option?* [☛ 5.7 Stakeholder Groups]
Step ❸ Form each option group.	*Have each option group surface and state the assumptions that must be true for each stakeholder group, in order for their option to be optimal. (Do this no matter how obvious, interesting, or absurd these assumptions may appear.)*
Step ❹ Work with the whole group.	*Have each option group share its findings from step 3 with the group as a whole. Invite challenge and support to ensure all assumptions are surfaced, made explicit, and stated clearly.* [☛ 10.9 Visible Information]
Step ❺ Strive for synthesis among options.	*Given the assumptions that have surfaced and corresponding implications for each option, strive to arrive at a better option. Use a synthesis of the research that has been completed for each of the original options.*
Step ❻ Test the final option.	*What steps will you take to verify the selected or final option with key stakeholder groups? (Use Assumption Matrix to test and verify.)*

RELATED LEADERSHIP TOOLS

5.7 Stakeholder Groups   6.5 Force-Field Analysis   7.5 Decision Making

6.1 Logic Errors   6.6 Six-Hat Thinking   10.6 Group Leader Skills

FOR FURTHER ASSISTANCE

Kilmann, Ralph. *Beyond the Quick Fix: Managing Five Tracks to Organizational Success.* Jossey-Bass, 1984.

6.3 SORTING OUT COMPLEX SITUATIONS

Inspired by Benjamin Kepner, Charles Tregoe, and George Campbell.

Dealing with complex situations is crucial to your success as a leader. Often presented as generalities and couched in simple phrases like "the systems problem" or "the communications problem," we call these "big fuzzies." Your leader's antennae should be tweaked when you hear problems described in such general terms as the "maintenance problem" or the "supplier problem." Rarely can such complex concerns be traced to a single cause or resolved with a single solution, yet ineffective quick fixes are often suggested to solve these multifaceted problems. One indicator of the need for this tool is that, when these quick-fix actions are taken, the problem does not disappear. In fact, it may get worse after the quick-fix "solution" has been applied!

This tool will help you deal with the multicausal nature of big fuzzies; their need to be broken into their constituent parts, then prioritized; and subsequently, how to plan action for the highest-priority areas.

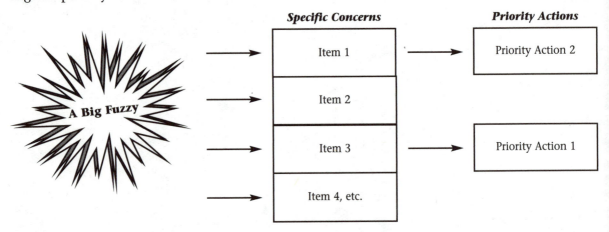

Use these four steps to turn your big fuzzies into prioritized action plans.

Process step	How to's
1. Persuade your work-group to take a different approach to the problem.	✔ Explain the complexity of the concern and the need to use this process to develop a full understanding of the problem situation. This may include widening or narrowing the problem frame. The outcome for this step is a clear, manageable frame for the problem and an action plan for working the problem. [☞ 7.1 Problem Framing]

2. Brainstorm, making the elements of the problem visible.	✔ Have the group brainstorm the elements of the big fuzzy, making the information visible to all (e.g., flip chart, whiteboard). A powerful question is, "Can you give me an example of ...?" This encourages concrete and actionable concerns. Don't evaluate, debate, or discuss at this stage. Encourage questions for clarification only. Until the group has assigned priorities, you don't even know whether debate is necessary. [☞ 6.6 Six-Hat Thinking, 6.9 Brainstorming, 10.9 Visible Information]
3. Evaluate and assign priorities.	✔ It may be helpful to first discuss your priority-setting criteria. It may also be helpful to categorize or group the issues in some way, but be careful! Grouping at too high a level can lead to overgeneralized, rather than specific, action plans. [☞ 10.11 Priority Setting]
4. Plan action on the top priorities.	✔ For each high-priority item, determine what will be done, who will do it, how it will be done, timelines, and follow-up actions. [☞ 10.12 RASCI Planning]

How to use this leadership tool

Question: *"How do you eat an elephant?"*
Answer: *"One bite at a time."*

An illustration of the use of the Sorting Out Complex Situations tool was in a company where, over several months, the "communications problem" kept cropping up in conversations and on meeting agendas. At the CEO's suggestion, the newsletter was beefed up. Employees were still disgruntled. Some leaders suggested a motivation workshop, others an employee survey, while still others suggested an all-employee meeting to clear the air. Use of this tool prevented the need for all of these costly "solutions." A cross-section of employees was asked to help better define the problem. Their concerns covered a wide range, from "The automated answering system is losing telephone messages" to "I can't talk to my boss." No single action could possibly have alleviated such a wide range of concerns. The concerns were prioritized and the most important ones were dealt with.

When you hear a big fuzzy coupled with name-to-blame, your antennae should go up. This occurs when people label problems without giving them much thought. For example: the "engineering problem" (projects are behind schedule), the "personnel problem" (too many people are leaving the company), the "purchasing problem" (inventory is too high), and so on. In these cases, the problem needs to be renamed. Implied blame needs to be removed from particular groups or functions and defined more practically and concretely, in order to render the problem less emotional. Name the problem, not the person or department.

Keeping all of this in mind, begin by tackling one big fuzzy in your organization that needs to be sorted out. Start by getting together a small group of interested stakeholders with varying perspectives (e.g., 5 to 9 people), and use the chart provided to help you and your group prioritize elements and plan action.

WEB WORKSHEET

Brainstorm and list the elements of the big fuzzy, asking for clarifying examples.	Establish which elements have highest priority.	Plan action for dealing with each high-priority element.
[☛ 6.9 Brainstorming]	[☛ 10.11 Priority Setting]	[☛ 10.12 RASCI Planning]

Related leadership tools

6.4 Discussing Messes	7.1 Problem Framing	10.9 Visible Information
6.5 Force-Field Analysis	10.6 Group Leader Skills	10.11 Priority Setting

For further assistance

Campbell, George. *Facilitation Skills Workshop.* Vector Consulting Associates, 1991.

Kepner, Charles H., and Benjamin B. Tregoe. *The New Rational Manager.* Princeton Research Press, 1981.

6.4 DEALING VERBALLY WITH COMPLEXITY

Inspired by the thousands of participants in the *Consulting Skills for Professionals* workshops.

A challenging leadership situation is when someone approaches you with a mess. Often, these messy problem statements contain implied general, but ineffective, solutions: "The maintenance problem occurred again last night" or, "We've got the systems snafu again" or, "Absenteeism is up again. I told you we needed to send our supervisors to a leadership workshop!" Your chief verbal tool in dealing with such complexity is questioning, even though most people don't think much about types of questions or their implications. This tool will provide an on-the-spot, effective questioning strategy. The model presented illustrates the use of three levels of questions. Actual sample questions and a questioning sequence are outlined later in this tool.

THE HOURGLASS MODEL FOR SORTING OUT A COMPLEX SITUATION

Type of question	Mental model	Why these questions?	What you are doing?
❶ Triage Questions	Complex situation → Immediate needs dealt with	*Triage* is the medical term for sorting out priorities when multiple casualties come into a medical facility. Triage questions do *not* fix the underlying problems. They alleviate the immediate symptoms, establishing "In what order do we treat the casualties?" or "What needs attention first?" They are the classic Band-Aid™ questions.	• Fixing the immediate hurts. (See the Danger!—caveat section.) • Putting on Band-Aids™. • Finding quick fixes. • Buying time. • Not dealing with underlying issues and causes. • Relieving immediate pressure before being able to look at the big picture.
❷ Big-Picture Questions	Longer-term issues dealt with	Big-picture or open-ended questions: • Help everyone step back and look at the overall situation. • Help get at underlying causes, systemic issues, and longer-term needs. Many leaders find it difficult to ask big-picture questions, because a. They are afraid of the answers! Big-picture questions may make the problem look worse and move you outside your comfort zone. b. It may feel better to have a poor solution than none at all!	• Establishing rapport by helping the person talk it out. • Asking open-ended questions to broaden and get at the context of the problem. • Getting at the underlying issues. • Getting at the context, causes, and related systemic issues. • Setting yourself and the others up to deal with the longer-term solutions.
❸ Closing Questions		Once you have the big picture sorted out, you are in a most strategic place for a leader. You and others can now decide on priorities and plans to ensure that the problem does not recur.	• Narrowing the scope of the problem by jointly establishing priorities and action plans. • Clarifying responsibilities and next steps.

Danger!—caveat

 In cases in which *only* triage issues—usually symptoms—are dealt with, the problem will almost certainly recur. When immediate needs are met, the temptation for others is to say, "Thank you" and move on. If this happens, you leave yourself in a low-leverage situation. If you sense this may happen, start by asking larger, big-picture questions. You can always revert to triage, if needed.

Dealing with ambiguity with others

To capture the benefits of big-picture questions, you must be able to manage the increased ambiguity they produce. One technique is this: On hearing the answer to a big-picture question, always paraphrase or summarize what you have heard. The benefits of using this technique are:

- It shows you are listening, able to track the complexity, and willing to handle messy situations.
- Others can correct any misconceptions you may be receiving.
- Summarizing has the highly desirable effect of reducing ambiguity.
- Summarizing helps others to go to the next deeper level, where underlying causes and barriers are situated.

How to use this leadership tool

"Nothing undermines openness more surely than certainty. Once we feel as if we have 'the answer,' all motivation to question our thinking disappears."

—Peter Senge, *THE FIFTH DISCIPLINE*

To help you with the practical application of the Hourglass Model, here is an example of the hourglass from everyday life. Because of its universal appeal, the example of a parent–child situation is used for illustration. We do **not** mean to imply that parent–child relationships are the same as leader–other relationships!

Picture a five- or six-year-old child playing in a playground near home. The child comes running home to the parent. The child is crying, scratched, bruised, and has a minor cut. What would an effective parent do? Triage, of course. First the parent would soothe the cries, treat the cut, and put bandages on the scrapes. Then would the parent send the child back to the playground? (Often children are anxious to get back.) No! An effective parent would probably sit down with the child and ask big-picture questions about how the situation arose and how the accident happened. After discussing the bigger picture of how the child got hurt, an effective parent would probably complete the conversation with both parent and child agreeing to carry out some actions designed to keep the child away from further harm.

To help you get started with the hourglass application, here is a questioning sequence you might use, starting with someone stating a complex issue:

Step 1: Summarize and Outline Your Process

a. Summarize or paraphrase what you have heard so far:

"What I understand so far is … ."

b. Outline your process:

"In the time we have available, I suggest we first look at the most immediate need(s), then step back and have you help me understand the big picture, and end with the best plan of action."

Step 2: Triage

a. Transition:

"Let's spend the next _____ minutes on the immediate needs."

b. Typical triage questions:

"What is your most immediate concern?"

"Does anything need attention right now?"

"How much flexibility do we have with the deadline?"

"What issues cannot wait and need to be addressed right now?"

c. Clarify a plan for the triage issues:

After discussing the most immediate concern(s), end the discussion with, *"So, what we will do to deal with the most immediate concern is ... ."*

Step 3: Big Picture

a. Transition:

"Now that we have dealt with the most immediate need, let's step back and look at the big picture. You have mentioned these concerns so far ... ." (Summarize the first-pass list of concerns.)

b. Typical big-picture questions:

"Just so I understand the big picture, can you tell me some more about the situation?"

"Give me some examples of the situation."

"So I can understand the situation, what were the original goals for the project?"

"How did this situation get started?"

"What end result is required?"

c. Go deeper, if required:

After summarizing, or better, making visible what you have heard so far, ask, *"Is there anything else about the situation that would help me understand it better?"*

Step 4: Close on Longer-Term Actions

a. Transition:

(Assuming you have been asking big-picture questions and summarizing client concerns:)

b. Typical closing questions:

"Given the concerns we have discussed, it appears to me that your highest-priority concerns are x, y, and z. Is that the way you see it?"

c. Negotiate action plans:

When you and the other agree on the action plans, propose your own role: *"From these priorities, I think I could be most helpful by ... . Does that work for you?"*

d. Agree to longer-term actions to deal with the priority concerns.

Related leadership tools

6.3 Complex Situations

8.7 Active Listening

9.1 Leadership Versatility

10.6 Group Leader Skills

10.9 Visible Information

10.11 Priority Setting

For further assistance

Hiebert, Murray. *Powerful Professionals: Getting Your Expertise Used Inside Organizations.* Recursion Press, 1999.

6.5

FORCE-FIELD ANALYSIS:
ORGANIZING AND UNDERSTANDING COMPLEXITY

Inspired by Kurt Lewin, Marvin Weisbord, and others.

Dealing with complexity is a way of life for leaders. There are few simple answers where human beings are involved. One indication of a complex problem is that the actions taken to solve the problem have had little or no effect, or have caused yet another problem. This tool compares the driving and restraining forces behind a leadership problem to magnetic or electrical fields. (Remember your high school physics?) In doing so, it helps leaders to analyze and act on problems that are difficult to measure. It does this by helping leaders organize and simplify a problem, and thus to understand:

- the many forces relevant to understanding a complex situation;
- the multiple causes of a complex problem;
- where to act first when multiple actions are available; and
- how to introduce change into an existing system.

Problems reach a state of equilibrium such that the driving forces and the restraining forces come into a form of balance or stalemate (e.g., habits, norms, organizational culture, established practices, and so on). If you want improvement (positive change), this balance must be upset: The driving forces must become stronger than the restraining forces. Often, this is best achieved by reducing the restraining forces first, and increasing the driving forces second. This sequence is recommended because removing restraining forces can allow the driving forces to have more impact, while simply adding driving forces can result in increased resistance. To illustrate, consider a common leadership situation—unproductive meetings.

Desired goal: Productive meetings (e.g., an increase in measurable or observable results from the meeting, decreased meeting time, increased participation).

Current situation: People come late and leave early, or don't show up at all. People come to the meetings without preparing. People complain about side conversations. Much of the meeting is spent debating what was decided at the last meeting.

FORCE-FIELD ANALYSIS

(Note: The length of the arrow indicates the relative strength of the driving or restraining force.)

Driving forces (toward better meetings)	Restraining forces (holding us back from better meetings)
Need for meeting results	Lack of agreed-to meeting process
Concern by senior management	Lack of meeting leadership skills
Personal frustration	Poor preparation for meetings
Projects behind schedule	Too many meetings
People uninformed	No ground rules
Need for teamwork	No consequences if late or no-show
	No written purpose or goals; just topics

HINTS

- This tool is easy to use with groups. Use a flip chart, overhead, or whiteboard and have meeting participants brainstorm their perceptions of driving and restraining forces.
- After you have completed the force-field diagram, indicate the relative strength of the forces by using a 1 to 5 scale, or by the different lengths of the arrows (as shown in the example).
- Then, prioritize action by either adding more forces on the driving side or removing or reducing forces on the restraining side. It's often more effective to remove or reduce restraints and barriers than it is to push the change harder by adding more driving forces. In general, you are usually more effective as a *pull* leader than as a *push* leader.

HOW TO USE THIS LEADERSHIP TOOL

"The forces driving toward and those restraining problem resolution reach an equilibrium. … You 'move' a problem by increasing drives or reducing restraints. Lewin believed the latter was better, because driving forces attract more restraints while reducing restraints permits existing drives to prevail."

—Marvin Weisbord, PRODUCTIVE WORKPLACES

The value of this tool lies in its simplicity. There is a process a leader might use in a group.

1. Get agreement that the situation is complex and needs to be better organized to be understood. Briefly introduce the idea of force-field analysis, perhaps using an example.
2. Use a visual medium—whiteboard, flip chart, overhead projector—and clarify the Desired Goal and the Current Situation. The more exact the situation description, the more valuable the resulting analysis. [☛ 7.1 Problem Framing]
3. Draw a line down the center of the visual. Write "Driving Forces" on one side and "Restraining Forces" on the other.
4. Ask people to brainstorm the forces on either side, while a scribe records them as key words on the visual. Remind participants to describe the forces as they are now, not as they could be. When the brainstorming is complete, clarify and refine the forces as needed, until consensus is reached on the forces that have been arrayed on either side. [☛ 6.9 Brainstorming]
5. If helpful, assess the relative strength of the forces by a numerical system (1 to 5 usually works) or by the length of the arrows (see example).
6. Starting with the restraining forces, look for the most leverage—where the force is strong and where decreasing its strength is relatively easy.
7. Next, look at the driving forces. Agree on those forces that are most highly leveraged for success; that is, where you'll get most improvement for effort expended (the biggest bang for the buck).
8. Complete the analysis by planning action (e.g., who will do what by when). [☛ 10.12 RASCI Planning]

WEB WORKSHEET

Use this worksheet to analyze a problem or opportunity in your work area.

Desired goal: _____

Current situation: _____

Force-Field Analysis Worksheet:

Driving forces	Restraining forces

RELATED LEADERSHIP TOOLS

2.1 Systems Thinking	6.3 Complex Situations	10.6 Group Leader Skills
5.7 Stakeholder Groups	6.9 Brainstorming	10.9 Visible Information

FOR FURTHER ASSISTANCE

Weisbord, Marvin Ross. *Productive Workplaces: Organizing and Managing for Dignity, Meaning, and Community.* Jossey-Bass, 1989.

6.6 Optimizing Your Thinking—A Hat 6-Pack

Inspired by Edward de Bono.

Thinking hats provide a metaphor for creative and flexible thinking about a problem or opportunity. The hats ensure that issues are approached from a range of different, and even diametrically opposed, perspectives. Individuals and groups are asked to take the attitude suggested by each of the imaginary hats. At first this may feel artificial, but it helps to unscramble thinking, surface hidden assumptions, keep discussion from drifting, generate a wide range of innovative possibilities, and, most importantly, lead to better decisions and plans.

Hat color	Typical lead-in	Color significance	Thinking attributes	Benefits of this type of thinking	Problems if overused
White	*"What are the facts here?"*	*Purity, neutrality*	Facts, figures, information, objective, neutral; like solving a math problem	Is logical. Can be explained to others. Increases chances of success.	Undervalues intuition and feelings. May stifle creativity. Low energy, lack of heart, enthusiasm, buy-in.
Red	*"Tell it like it is." "Where do you stand?"*	*Seeing red*	Emotions, intuition, taste, hunch; feelings (e.g., euphoria, fear, apathy)	Legitimizes emotions. (No need to justify feelings; they just are.) Energizes.	Erratic action. "All heart, no head." Danger of personalizing conflict.
Black	*"It won't work because … ."*	*Black cloud*	Devil's advocate. What is wrong, why it won't work, risks. Points out errors. BS detector.	Tests thinking. Increases the chances of the decision actually working.	Negative, judgmental, depressing. Inaction. Pessimism.
Yellow	*"Let's make it happen!"*	*Sunshine*	Constructive, generative, dreams, hopes, visions. Probes and explores benefits.	Optimism, positive. Energizing. Teamwork.	Skepticism when it doesn't work.
Green	*"There must be a better way."*	*Fertile*	Creative, movement, new ideas, new approaches. Search for alternatives, options, new ways of understanding. Cuts across old patterns and old habits.	Can come up with a much better way of doing something. Ensures best process is used.	Many ideas, few decisions and actions. Going off half-cocked.
Blue	*"Let's step back and think about how to do this."*	*Cool, the sky (the big picture)*	Focuses thinking. In control, rational, thinking about thinking. Facilitates (calls for the use of all the other hats).	Ensures best use of people's time. Helps reduce decision-making time.	Inaction—too much time spent on how to do something versus doing it. Arguments over process.

			Defines, sets boundaries for discussion, shapes the questions, summarizes.		

HOW TO USE THIS LEADERSHIP TOOL

"The main difficulty with thinking is confusion. We try to do too much at once. Emotions, information, logic, hope and creativity all crowd in on us. It is like juggling with too many balls."

—Edward de Bono, *SIX THINKING HATS*

Think of a problem that you are currently facing, one for which you could use different viewpoints or perspectives. Use the attributes required by each of the six thinking hats to increase the chances of assessing and resolving this problem successfully. Use the workspace provided to plan how someone with an attribute from each thinking hat would approach this problem.

If you use thinking hats in meetings, you will also want to think about the sequence of thinking hats, and the balance of airtime for each type of thinking. If you seek to ensure full airing of an issue or problem, you should include a person from each of the six hats of thinking. A group of black hats is unlikely to really agree to do something innovative or new. This tool can also help you in understanding where another person is coming from in a group, and why you may be agreeing or at odds.

WEB WORKSHEET

Blue (process, summarize)	[☛ 11.1 Process Cycle]
White (facts, objective)	[☛ 6.1 Logic Errors, 6.2 Assumption Analysis, 10.9 Visible Information]
Red (emotions, feelings)	[☛ 8.6 Communication 101, 10.5 Group Disturbances, 12.7 Dealing with Conflict]
Black (risks, problems)	[☛ 5.9 Resistance, 7.6 Potential Problems]
Yellow (optimism, positive)	[☛ 2.4 Visioning, 14.1 Scarcity and Abundance]

Green (creative, new ideas)	
	[☛ 6.7 Creativity and Innovation, 6.8 Mind Mapping]

RELATED LEADERSHIP TOOLS

6.1 Logic Errors	8.6 Communication 101	14.1 Scarcity and Abundance
6.2 Assumption Analysis	10.8 Ground Rules	14.7 Personal Preferences

FOR FURTHER ASSISTANCE

de Bono, Edward. *Six Thinking Hats*. Little/Brown, 1985.

6.7

CREATIVITY AND INNOVATION:
THE LEADER'S ROLE

Inspired by Edward de Bono, Gerald Nadler, Shozo Hibino, Mihaly Csikszentmihalyi, and Roger Von Oech.

In the world of *Fast Company,* "more of the same" or even "getting better at the same" rarely works. Would you want to fly with an airline whose motto was, "If it ain't broke, don't fix it"? One of Jack Welch's famous one-liners is, "If it ain't broke, break it." Writing about the new economy, Lester Thurow is blunt: "Businesses must be willing to destroy the old while it is still successful if they wish to build the new that will become successful. ... Both creation and destruction are essential to driving the economy forward." In other words, no creativity, no survival!

This tool will give you an overview of some typical creativity tools and their implementation.

We use a distinction made by some creativity gurus:

Creativity is the process of generating new ideas.

Innovation is creating the conditions for creativity and for implementing the best ideas.

Many books and workshops rightfully focus on creativity (generation of new ideas); yet in most organizations the *bottleneck* is actually innovation (getting a new idea accepted and producing results). Most organizations are designed to continue on the path they have set (implicitly or explicitly). Your role as leader is crucial in encouraging a culture that can generate ideas; high-grading and selling those ideas; and ensuring successful implementation and results.

CREATIVITY TECHNIQUES

Creativity experts have designed and promoted thousands of techniques. Here is a sample list.

Technique	What is it?	Some how to's:
Lateral Thinking	Exploring many different ways of looking at an issue, rather than accepting the first logical definition and solution.	✔ Encourage low-probability thinking, rather than what de Bono calls high-probability but uncreative (vertical) thinking. ✔ Always ask for the second right answer.
Brainstorming or Mental Popcorn	Assigning a defined period to no-evaluation thinking, when novel or unusual contributions are encouraged.	✔ Probably the most used (some would say abused) technique in groups and teams. ✔ A step in a process in which "mental popcorn" is used for the purpose of increasing the scope of thought. [☞ 6.9 Brainstorming]
Reframing	Exploring a set of assumptions about the scope of an issue and the range of solutions available.	✔ Make it acceptable to challenge the often narrow assumptions that are embedded in a problem definition. ✔ Ask questions that broaden or narrow the scope of the issue. [☞ 7.1 Problem Framing]

Using Metaphors	Using metaphors helps people explore novel approaches and new options.	✔ Sports metaphors are commonly used to describe situations: kick-off, coach, and heavyweights. ✔ To help create more options, use a new or novel metaphor, like "Suppose our customers are fish … ."
Blue-Skying/ No Constraints/ What if …	Imagining how the issue could be dealt with if you had no constraints or barriers to deal with.	✔ Ask people to set aside all the barriers, impediments, and problems and think of the ideal solution. "What if we had all the money we need … ." ✔ Then take this idea and make it work as best you can.
Using Humor	Because it is based on unexpected twists, humor is a great way to loosen up, in order to generate new ideas.	✔ Use humor to break out of conventional thinking (e.g., "How many management consultants does it take to change a light bulb?") ✔ Be careful. Sarcastic humor can shut down creativity.
Six-Hat Thinking	Another of de Bono's techniques places creative (green hat) thinking in the context of legitimizing other modes.	✔ Six-Hat Thinking is particularly effective in equalizing various group members' thinking. [☛ 6.6 Six-Hat Thinking]
Mind Mapping	Taking a situation, especially a complex issue, and mapping all its interconnections.	✔ On a whiteboard, name the complex issue in the center, place all related items around it, then connect these issues with appropriate arrows. [☛ 6.8 Mind Mapping]

INNOVATION PROCESSES

Leaders have tremendous control over the first part of the innovation process: encouraging new ideas (or *not discouraging* new ideas). The second part of innovation—high-grading and stickhandling a new idea into action—is the most challenging of all. These are dealt with in the application section.

HOW TO USE THIS LEADERSHIP TOOL

"It's easier to be a result of the past than a cause of the future."

—Ashleigh Brilliant

As a leader, the culture you establish is crucial. You have the most control over encouragement of a culture of creativity in your area of influence. Most workers have a wealth of creative ideas to improve their work and the organization, if only they are give a chance to express those ideas and work them through. In our experience, 3M is one organization that is working hard at creating a culture that lives up to its innovation motto.

WEB WORKSHEET

THE INNOVATION ASSESSMENT AND ACTION PLAN

Part 1: Encouraging Innovation in Your Area of Influence (workgroup, team, business unit, or organization)

Rate yourself on these questions and plan action as required.

Innovation assessment question	Your personal assessment	Action plan to improve
How creative is your own thinking style?		[☛ 14.7 Personal Preferences]
How threatened are you by someone else generating a new idea?		[☛ 15.6 Defenses]
How prepared are you to deal with the ambiguity and risk new ideas bring?		
How often do you use negative phrases like, "We've tried that," "It won't work here," "They won't go for it," or "If it ain't broke, don't fix it"?		
How skilled are you at encouraging new ideas?		
How skilled are you at encouraging participation?		[☛ 10.7 Getting Participation]
How many creativity techniques are used by yourself and your workgroup?		
How well do you deal with failure? (No new idea is foolproof.)		
How conscious and skilled are you at understanding problem frames and reframing?		[☛ 7.1 Problem Framing]
How skilled are you at border guarding—providing creativity and innovation space for individuals and groups?		
How often do you explicitly discuss creativity and innovation with your workgroup?		[☛ 10.8 Ground Rules]
How balanced are you in your lifestyle: learning, reading, and contributing outside your profession and worklife so you have "lateral-thinking" life experiences?		[☛ 15.1 Balance]

Part 2: Taking a Creative Idea to Action

Now assess your skills at taking a good idea to implementation and producing results. Plan actions as appropriate.

Innovation assessment question	Your personal assessment	Action plan to improve
How skilled are you at massaging an idea to make it more workable and results-oriented?		
How conscious are you of establishing an innovation culture?		[☛ 4.5 Culture]
How skilled are you at selling a new idea?		[☛ 9.7 Selling Wheel]

How skilled are you as a change leader?		[☞ 5.1 Change Equation]
How skilled are you at systems thinking, at the core of issue identification and successful innovation?		[☞ 2.1 Systems Thinking]

RELATED LEADERSHIP TOOLS

2.1 Systems Thinking	4.4 Employee Involvement	7.1 Problem Framing
3.2 Sigmoid Curve	6.6 Six-Hat Thinking	9.1 Leadership Versatility

FOR FURTHER ASSISTANCE

3M Web Site, http://www.mmm.com
If you want to get a feel for an organization that has innovation at its core, explore this Web site.

Csikszentmihalyi, Mihaly. *Flow: The Psychology of Optimal Experience,* 2nd ed. HarperCollins, 1991.

de Bono, Edward. *Six Thinking Hats.* Little/Brown, 1985.

Nadler, Gerald, and Shozo Hibino. *Breakthrough Thinking: The Seven Principles of Creative Problem Solving,* 2nd ed. Prima Pub, 1998.

Von Oech, Roger. *A Whack on the Side of the Head: How You Can Be More Creative,* 2nd ed. Warner Books, 1998.

Note: There are tons of creativity and innovation resources available. Be creative and visit your favorite on-line bookstore, using the keywords "creativity" or "innovation" to explore the range for yourself.

6.8 MIND MAPPING: A BREAKTHROUGH TOOL

Inspired by Tony Buzan, Will McWhinney, Bernie Novokowsky, Jim Webber, and Doug Smith.

Many concerns faced by leaders are complex and fuzzy and have multiple causes and solutions. Mind mapping is a creative, real-time, energizing method for illustrating issue complexity and systemic interrelations. Mind mapping promotes creative problem solving by helping participants to visualize data (helpful for visual learners); to see interrelationships among data elements; and to look at new solutions. Done well, this mind mapping tool can lead to breakthroughs by reframing an issue or finding a better solution.

There are five typical steps to producing a mind map:

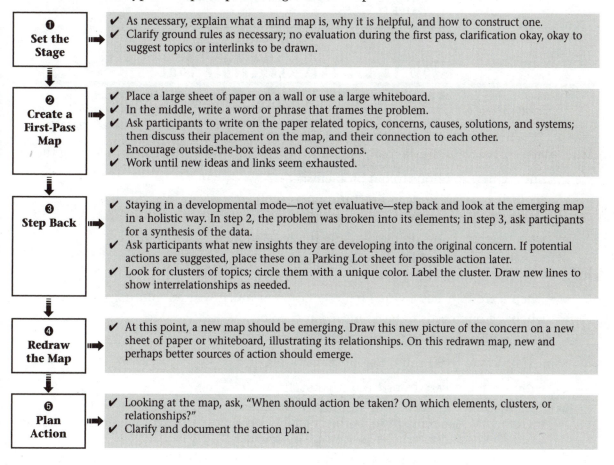

❶ Set the Stage
- ✔ As necessary, explain what a mind map is, why it is helpful, and how to construct one.
- ✔ Clarify ground rules as necessary; no evaluation during the first pass, clarification okay, okay to suggest topics or interlinks to be drawn.

❷ Create a First-Pass Map
- ✔ Place a large sheet of paper on a wall or use a large whiteboard.
- ✔ In the middle, write a word or phrase that frames the problem.
- ✔ Ask participants to write on the paper related topics, concerns, causes, solutions, and systems; then discuss their placement on the map, and their connection to each other.
- ✔ Encourage outside-the-box ideas and connections.
- ✔ Work until new ideas and links seem exhausted.

❸ Step Back
- ✔ Staying in a developmental mode—not yet evaluative—step back and look at the emerging map in a holistic way. In step 2, the problem was broken into its elements; in step 3, ask participants for a synthesis of the data.
- ✔ Ask participants what new insights they are developing into the original concern. If potential actions are suggested, place these on a Parking Lot sheet for possible action later.
- ✔ Look for clusters of topics; circle them with a unique color. Label the cluster. Draw new lines to show interrelationships as needed.

❹ Redraw the Map
- ✔ At this point, a new map should be emerging. Draw this new picture of the concern on a new sheet of paper or whiteboard, illustrating its relationships. On this redrawn map, new and perhaps better sources of action should emerge.

❺ Plan Action
- ✔ Looking at the map, ask, "When should action be taken? On which elements, clusters, or relationships?"
- ✔ Clarify and document the action plan.

PARTIAL EXAMPLE: LEADERSHIP DEVELOPMENT

This partial example illustrates (without color!) what an original map would look like for a group working on leadership development.

HOW TO USE THIS LEADERSHIP TOOL

"Mind mapping promotes free association of ideas and 'pops' new meanings for familiar concepts. It provides paths around our normal self-censoring and supports joint intuitive right-brain work within a group."

—Will McWhinney *et al.*, *CREATING PATHS OF CHANGE*

Mind mapping is a versatile, helpful, and engaging tool to use in situations including these:

- ✔ finding new solutions to old problems;
- ✔ analyzing, organizing, and picturing new problems;
- ✔ reorganizing and revitalizing an old concern;
- ✔ when concerns are complex—many interrelated items;
- ✔ to help a group to think more systemically;
- ✔ focusing priorities on areas of most leverage;
- ✔ when a group needs a visual representation of much written information;
- ✔ when a group needs to be energized and unlock its creative side;
- ✔ to help plan action in the most effective area.

Some pointers to make mind mapping work in a group:

- ❑ Group size can vary from 1 (do it yourself) to 50.
- ❑ Time needed can vary from 15 minutes to quickly map a situation, to long-term: an incremental map remains in a project team's meeting space, with members encouraged to add items and interlinks as they are discovered.
- ❑ If you use the incremental chart, at meetings, discuss what is emerging and rechart as needed.

Think of a situation in which mind mapping may help you illustrate a problem; then use the space provided to plan action.

The central focus:

RELATED LEADERSHIP TOOLS

2.1 Systems Thinking　　　6.5 Force-Field Analysis　　　10.6 Group Leader Skills

6.3 Complex Situations　　6.6 Six-Hat Thinking　　　　10.9 Visible Information

FOR FURTHER ASSISTANCE

Buzan, Tony. *The Brain User's Guide: A Handbook for Sorting Out Your Life.*

McWhinney, Will, ed. *Creating Paths of Change: Managing Issues and Resolving Problems in Organizations.* Sage Publishing, 1997.

6.9 BRAINSTORMING: GENERATING IDEAS QUICKLY

Inspired by numerous sources.

Brainstorming is a commonly used group process and innovation tool. It's usually used to generate a lot of ideas quickly. Teams and groups use it because it's an understood and acceptable process in most organizations, and because it generates short bursts of energy and lots of ideas.

WHY USE BRAINSTORMING?

- ✔ It's a quick way of getting lots of information on the table.
- ✔ It increases participation, which leads to commitment.
- ✔ It leads to creative ideas and solutions.
- ✔ It leads to synergy, whereby new ideas are built on each other; participants begin to put together previously unrelated ideas.
- ✔ It's fun and energizing.
- ✔ It's more efficient than debating one idea at a time. Generating a number of ideas in a group, and then evaluating and debating to find the best ideas(s), is effective and time-efficient.

DEVELOPMENTAL VERSUS EVALUATIVE THINKING

For brainstorming to be effective, leaders need to ensure that their workgroup or team distinguishes between two kinds of thinking, developmental and evaluative. (Note: The references to "hat" thinking can be understood by reviewing ☞ 6.6 Six-Hat thinking.)

Type of thinking		Techniques	Ground rules
Developmental • Used to get many ideas in the open. **Evaluative** • Used to determine the best plan of action.		*Developmental:* • Brainstorming • Lateral thinking • Green- and yellow-hat thinking *Evaluative:* • Priority setting • White-, red-, and black-hat thinking • Decision making	*Developmental:* • No criticism. • Build on others' ideas. • Out-of-the-box thinking encouraged. • Quantity more important than quality. *Evaluative:* • Clarification, concerns, and questioning okay. • Debate is okay. • Seek closure on the best ideas or actions.

How to Brainstorm

1. Ask the workgroup or team to brainstorm; explain the goal of brainstorming, and why it will be helpful. Try to illustrate by giving an example or telling a story of the power of brainstorming.

2. Agree to a definition or statement of the concern for which ideas will be brainstormed.

3. Depending on the team or workgroup, highlight key ground rules (e.g., "Don't evaluate while brainstorming.") [☞ 10.8 Ground Rules]

4. Have someone visibly and succinctly record all ideas on a whiteboard or flip chart. Use only key words to keep the ideas moving. You need to record only enough words to reconstruct the thought. [☞ 10.9 Visible Information]

5. Work intensely for a short period of time.

6. Clarification questions are okay, but don't slow down the brainstorming process with long explanations.

7. Invite everyone to contribute. Encourage fun and out-of-the-box ideas. Humor unleashes innovative ideas. [☞ 10.7 Getting Participation]

8. Don't evaluate ideas until brainstorming is finished (the most important ground rule when brainstorming).

Hints

❏ Some distinguish between unstructured brainstorming, as described here, and structured brainstorming, whereby participants may write down ideas first and then express ideas in round-robin fashion. See the next section for variations.

❏ If a group member wants to change a word or the nuance of another participant's brainstorm idea, treat the amendment like a new idea, and write it using the new words. Otherwise, it may feel like evaluation.

❏ Brainstorming has been used extensively in organizations. As such, it may have developed dysfunctional norms in some organizations. In these situations, use an alternative process and call it something else.

How to Use This Leadership Tool

"The effects of leaping to conclusions are common problems for most groups. Norman Maier ... discusses ... the tendency of groups to settle on the first proposed solution that is minimally acceptable. ... Once groups jell around one solution it is unlikely that other solutions, even higher quality solutions, will receive appropriate consideration."

—L. Perry, R. Stott, and N. Smallwood, *REAL-TIME STRATEGY*

Brainstorming is one of the best-known and most widely used leadership tools today. A couple of variations on this technique are:

- Use a more structured approach. Ask each participant to jot down a few ideas on a sheet of paper, and then go around the room with each person presenting one idea at a time, in round-robin fashion, until all the ideas have been presented. No evaluation takes place until all ideas are expressed. However, clarifying and building or expanding on another person's ideas are both okay.

- Ask people to post their ideas on a wall (large Post-It™ Notes can be very helpful). Ideas can then be sorted into categories, and the best categories can be evaluated first. [☞ 7.8 Affinity Diagrams]

Use the space provided here to brainstorm where you might use brainstorming as a leadership tool:

Situations in which you and your workgroup need to generate more ideas (be they obvious, interesting, or absurd):
How you will explain the need for and benefits of brainstorming to your workgroup: [☞ 9.7 Selling Wheel]
Potential disadvantages of brainstorming in your workgroup, and how you will minimize these:
Ground rules you will suggest or clarify to ensure that brainstorming is effective in your workgroup: [☞ 10.8 Ground Rules]

RELATED LEADERSHIP TOOLS

6.6 Six-Hat Thinking	7.1 Problem Framing	10.8 Ground Rules
6.8 Mind Mapping	10.6 Group Leader Skills	10.9 Visible Information

FOR FURTHER ASSISTANCE

Klatt, Bruce. *The Ultimate Training Workshop Handbook: A Comprehensive Guide to Leading Successful Workshops and Training Programs.* McGraw-Hill, 1999.

7

TOOLS FOR PROBLEM SOLVING, DECISION MAKING, AND QUALITY

Solving problems effectively and making great decisions are at the heart of leadership. Effective leaders, like effective professionals and tradespeople, have a full tool kit of leadership tools. Among the most useful are the problem-solving and decision-making tools described in this section.

7.1 REFRAMING: WORKING THE *REAL* PROBLEM

Inspired by Roger Fisher, William Ury, Edward Russo,
Paul Schoemaker, Paul Watzlawick, et al., and Norm Smallwood.

Far too often problem-solving efforts fall flat because leaders work the wrong problem. A problem presented to a leader is often summarized into a complaint or a frustration. It frequently takes a lot of probing by the leader to get to the genuine problem definition. Problems can be defined too narrowly, too broadly, or in a way that leads to an inferior set of solutions.

This tool helps leaders put the presented problem into a new frame—in other words, reframe it, in order to ensure that the time leaders and others spend solving problems is well invested and that their efforts are highly leveraged. This reframing process turns inappropriate and potentially misleading problem definitions into clearer and more effective problem statements.

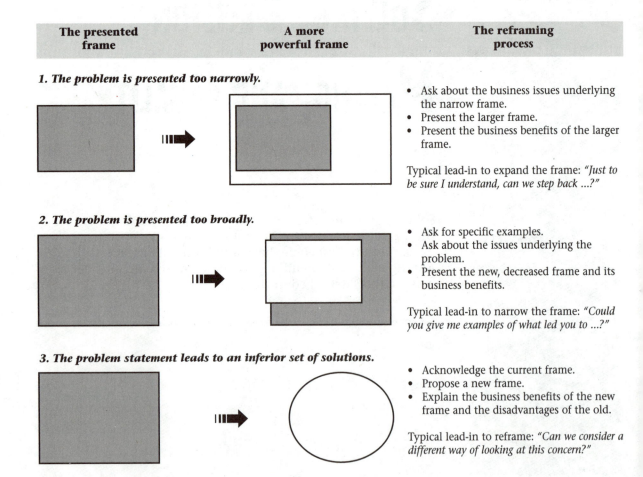

The presented frame	A more powerful frame	The reframing process

1. The problem is presented too narrowly.

- Ask about the business issues underlying the narrow frame.
- Present the larger frame.
- Present the business benefits of the larger frame.

Typical lead-in to expand the frame: *"Just to be sure I understand, can we step back ...?"*

2. The problem is presented too broadly.

- Ask for specific examples.
- Ask about the issues underlying the problem.
- Present the new, decreased frame and its business benefits.

Typical lead-in to narrow the frame: *"Could you give me examples of what led you to ...?"*

3. The problem statement leads to an inferior set of solutions.

- Acknowledge the current frame.
- Propose a new frame.
- Explain the business benefits of the new frame and the disadvantages of the old.

Typical lead-in to reframe: *"Can we consider a different way of looking at this concern?"*

SCOPING A PROBLEM

When thinking about the reframing process, remember that small words in a problem statement can dramatically change the view of a problem, and the number and range of solutions that are subsequently considered. For example: "I need to buy a new, midsize car" to "I need to buy a new car" to "I need to buy a vehicle" to "I need a vehicle" to "I need some form of transportation."

Leaders need to size up problems quickly and determine whether a problem definition is too narrow—often a disguised solution—and leads to an overly restricted range of options. Alternatively, a problem definition may be too broad and fuzzy—confusing and concealing underlying causes—and lead to ineffective solutions.

Use this continuum to assess the true nature of a presenting problem.

Very Narrow Problem Definition ← → **Very Broad Problem Definition**

Characteristics

• A solution	• Complex, fuzzy
• A symptom	• Multiple causes
• Assumes the cause is known.	• No one action will solve the issue.

Examples

Systems:
• "We need a new spreadsheet program."

Engineering:
• "How are we going to deal with the design problem?"

Human Resources:
• "We need to fire Mr. Doe."

Training:
• "Our problem is communication."

Public Affairs:
• "Let's redesign the brochure."

Financial:
• "Accounts receivable is in bad shape."

Impact

• Short-term, nonstrategic reputation as a leader	• Without further clarity of all contributing issues, the solution may fail.
• Solution may fail because it did not deal with underlying cause.	• Need to tolerate ambiguity and confusion on the way to clarifying a more specific problem definition.
• Suboptimal solutions	

Leadership Strategies

✔ Ask broadening questions that open up options.	✔ Ask for examples of the concern to make the concern more concrete.
✔ Ask questions that focus on end-results and underlying needs.	✔ Manage ambiguity and confusion by summarizing frequently.
✔ Avoid asking *why* questions, which tend to put the problem presenter on the defensive.	✔ You may wish to deal with the urgent or emergency aspects of the concern first, but be careful: You may never get to the underlying issues.

"People tend to see what they want to see. Out of the mass of detailed information, they tend to pick out and focus on those facts that confirm their prior perceptions and to disregard or misinterpret those that call their perceptions into question."

—Roger Fisher and William Ury, *GETTING TO YES*

Problem reframing is a powerful tool. The earlier a problem is reframed, the better. The longer a given problem definition is accepted, and the more people invest in a given way of understanding a problem, the harder it becomes to change perceptions and to challenge vested interests at a later date. Our message is clear: Challenge how problems are defined, and do this early in the problem-solving process. Here is an example of actual use of this reframing tool—the presentation, and the leader's questions to guide the reframing.

1. The problem is defined too narrowly or presented as a solution.

    Employee: *"I need a spreadsheet program installed on my computer."*

    Leader: *"Just to be sure I understand, what uses did you have in mind for the spreadsheet program?"*

2. The problem is defined too broadly or too ambiguously.

    Employee: *"We have a companywide communication problem."*

    Leader: *"Can you give me a few concrete examples of this problem?"*

3. The problem statement leads to an inferior set of solutions or it fails to consider the full range of critical concerns.

    Employee: *"We need to cut costs."*

    Leader: *"While costs need to be contained, can we also look at other possibilities that will increase revenue?"*

Focus on one problem that has recently been presented to you or that you have presented to others. Rather than taking the problem definition for granted, a trap we all fall into every now and then, use the workspace here to establish a more powerful frame for this problem. Referring to the previous example may help you formulate effective reframing questions.

Any frame will provide only a partial view of the problem.	**Once a problem frame is accepted, it is very difficult to change.**	**The frame chosen determines where you look for solutions.**

The problem as currently defined	Questions that will help develop a more powerful way of understanding this problem
This definition is (check one) ___ too narrow ___ too broad ___ inferior ___ appropriate	

RELATED LEADERSHIP TOOLS

6.2 Assumption Analysis	6.6 Six-Hat Thinking	7.3 Finding Cause
6.3 Complex Situations	6.7 Creativity and Innovation	10.6 Group Leader Skills

FOR FURTHER ASSISTANCE

Fisher, Roger, and William Ury. *Getting to Yes: Negotiating Agreement without Giving In.* Houghton Mifflin, 1981.

Hiebert, Murray. *Powerful Professionals: Getting Your Expertise Used Inside Organizations.* Recursion Press, 1999.

Russo, Edward, and Paul J.H. Schoemaker. *Decision Traps: Ten Barriers to Brilliant Decision Making and How to Overcome Them,* 2nd ed. Fireside, 1990.

Watzlawick, Paul, John H. Weakland, and Richard Fisch. *Change: Principles of Problem Formation and Problem Resolution.* W. W. Horton & Company, 1974.

7.2

A GENERAL PROBLEM-SOLVING MODEL FOR LEADERS

Inspired by the Xerox Problem-Solving Process, Charles Kepner, and Ben Tregoe.

Having a general problem-solving process or framework provides leaders with a way to begin understanding and managing a wide range of problems, decisions, or concerns. Here you will find just that—a general process that allows you to begin working a problem from a range of starting points (e.g., potential causes, potential solutions).

Problem-solving step	Key question to be answered	Pushing toward complexity	Keeping complexity under control	What is needed to proceed to the next step
1. Select and define the concern or problem.	Of all the things competing for your attention, which will you deal with at this time?	Many problems are likely pressing for your attention. People become vested in, and emotional about, their version of the concern.	Use a priority-setting process. Get agreement on the problem statement (i.e., how the problem is framed). [☞ 7.1 Problem Framing] [☞ 10.11 Priority Setting]	Develop a clear statement of the gap: What Is versus What Should Be. Personal interests must be dealt with sufficiently to proceed.
2. Analyze the problem for cause(s).	What is causing the shortfall between what is and what should be?	There is lots of data to consider, with many potential and unknown causes. People may be vested in a particular way of understanding the problem.	Use a systematic process for handling the data and for finding cause(s). [☞ 7.3 Finding Cause]	The most likely cause(s) are identified and verified.
3. Generate potential solutions.	What are the options for dealing with the cause(s) of the problem?	There may be many ideas about how to solve the problem. People may be vested in a particular solution.	Use a systematic way to list potential solutions, along with the benefits and risks of each solution. [☞ 7.5 Decision Making]	A list of agreed-to potential solutions.
4. Decide on a best solution.	What is the best alternative to solve the problem?	There may be a broad range of criteria for defining an effective solution. Each solution has corresponding benefits and risks.	Get agreement on the criteria for selecting a solution, along with a systematic method of applying these criteria.	The best solution is identified and agreed to. The potential benefits and risks of this solution are documented.

| 5. **Plan implementation of the change.** | Decide on the best way to implement the solution (i.e., the change). | You may need many people to buy into the change. The change may not fit well into the existing system. | Use a project management or change leadership model to implement the change. [☛ 5.1 Change Equation] | Develop a workable plan for implementing the change. [☛ 7.6 Potential Problems] |
| 6. **Follow through and evaluate implementation of the change.** | How do we make sure the solution is working? How do we refine the solution, if necessary? | Implementing difficulties always occurs in real life. If not dealt with, these difficulties will cause additional problems. [☛ 5.9 Resistance] | Have a follow-through process in place, and ensure that each step of the change is supported and realigned as conditions change. | Evaluate the change implementation, and complete a "lessons learned" review to continuously improve your change initiatives. |

The difficulty with a general model such as this one is that you may need a more powerful tool to deal with a highly unique problem. Here are other tools found elsewhere in this book that will help.

If your difficulty is:	Look at these tools:
Too few ideas or potential solutions	☛ 1.9 Paradigms, 5.10 Appreciative Inquiry, 6.6 Six-Hat Thinking, 6.7 Creativity and Innovation, 6.9 Brainstorming, 7.1 Problem Framing
People being vested in positions	☛ 6.2 Assumption Analysis, 8.5 Metacommunicating, 8.7 Active Listening, 9.5 Negotiation, 12.7 Dealing with Conflict
Handling data in a systematic way	☛ 5.1 Change Equation, 6.3 Complex Situations, 6.5 Force-Field Analysis, 7.3 Finding Cause, 7.5 Decision Making, 7.7 Quality Tools, 10.10 Closure, 10.11 Priority Setting

How to Use This Leadership Tool

"The most effective managers were also the best investigators. ... From the announcement of a problem until its resolution, they appeared to follow a clear formula in both orderly sequence and the quality of their questions and actions. In fact, when something went wrong, without a ready explanation, these managers asked remarkably similar questions to determine whether available information was relevant or irrelevant, important or trivial, critical or marginally useful. Since the same information, in the hands of equally experienced and intelligent managers, might result in distinctly different results, it was evident that successful problem solving involved more than the availability of information. Equally critical was the quality of logic applied to that information."

—Charles Kepner and Benjamin Tregoe, *THE NEW RATIONAL MANAGER*

General tools such at this one work best when adapted to your unique organizational needs (but not made more complicated). Adaptations might include:

❑ Use language that is currently being used in your organization.
❑ Integrate this tool with other accepted problem-solving, cause-finding, and decision-making processes (e.g., quality tools, project management, systematic troubleshooting).
❑ Integrate this tool with meeting planning processes [☛ 11.1 Process Cycle, and other meeting tools in Section 11]

Adapting this tool to your workgroup or team may involve any or all of these steps:

❑ Prepare a wall chart and other visuals to track the path of problem solving.

❑ Integrate with the workgroup or team's ground rules. [☛ 10.8 Ground Rules]
❑ Integrate with the people side of problem solving, including listening, dealing with conflict, and managing differences. (See tools matrix.)

WEB WORKSHEET

Select an upcoming situation in which this general problem-solving model will help you work a problem systematically.

> The gap: What Is versus What Should Be.

In preparation for meeting with your workgroup or team, list the data that you presently have regarding this problem.

1. Select and define the concern or problem.	[☛ 7.1 Problem Framing]
2. Analyze the problem for cause(s).	[☛ 7.3 Finding Cause]
3. Generate potential solutions.	[☛ 6.9 Brainstorming]
4. Decide on the best solution.	[☛ 7.5 Decision Making]
5. Plan implementation of the change.	[☛ 5.1 Change Equation, 10.12 RASCI Planning]
6. Follow through and evaluate implementation of the change.	

Related leadership tools

1.10 The GAS Model	7.1 Problem Framing	10.6 Group Leader Skills
6.3 Complex Situations	7.3 Finding Cause	11.1 Process Cycle

For further assistance

"Xerox Problem-Solving Process." *Harvard Business Review.* July–August 1993.

Kepner, Charles H., and Benjamin B. Tregoe. *The New Rational Manager.* Princeton Research Press, 1981.

7.3 PROBLEM SOLVING: A SYSTEMATIC APPROACH TO FINDING CAUSE

Inspired by Ben Tregoe and Chuck Kepner.

Problems seem to occupy the lion's share of a leader's day. Here are some examples.

➡ The new copiers jam a few times a day. People are saying it's because you purchased the low-bidding brand.

➡ The new valves seem to have higher maintenance costs than expected. It is being suggested that all maintenance people attend a costly training program so they can maintain the valves correctly.

➡ Absenteeism is much higher on certain days of the month than on others. The CEO says we need to send supervisors to a Progressive Discipline workshop.

➡ Purchasers of your product seem to be getting ill when they use it in a certain city. It has been suggested the product be withdrawn across the country.

Themes common to all these problems include:

• Performance expectations not being met.

• People are jumping to cause, blame, or expensive solutions.

This tool outlines a systematic process for getting at the most probable cause of problems like these *before* taking expensive and often misdirected action. Here is an outline of the process, with explanations in italics.

Step ❶ Clearly define the problem. Begin by specifying the expected performance, the actual performance, and the difference between the two.

Step ❷ Gather data about what *is* happening and what *is not* happening.

	Is happening	Is not Happening	What's unique?	Any changes?
What?	*What units or people are having the problem?*	*What units or people would you expect to have the problem but do not?*	*Anything distinctive about the units or people who have the problem and those that don't?*	*What changes might account for what is unique about this problem?*
Where?	*Where are the units or people having the problem?*	*Where are the units or people **not** having the problem?*	*Same question as above.*	*Same question as above.*
When?	*When are the units or people having the problem?*	*When are the units or people **not** having the problem?*	*Same question as above.*	*Same question as above.*
How much?	*What is the problem's fingerprint, the degree or pattern of the problem?*	*What could be the degree or pattern of the problem but is not?*	*What is distinctive about the degree or pattern that you are experiencing, compared to what it could be but is not?*	*Same question as above.*

Step ❸ Every problem leaves a distinctive fingerprint. Compare the Is Happening with the Is Not Happening. What is unique or distinctive about these two columns?

What changes, if any, have taken place related to these distinctions?

Step ❹ List the *potential* causes that could explain much, if not all, of the data.

Step ❺ Test each potential cause against the data, trying to rule out those causes that do not satisfactorily explain the data.

Step ❻ For the most probable cause(s), gather additional data that would confirm or disconfirm the cause before taking action.

Charles Kepner and Benjamin Tregoe, in their groundbreaking book, *The New Rational Manager,* summarized the process this way:

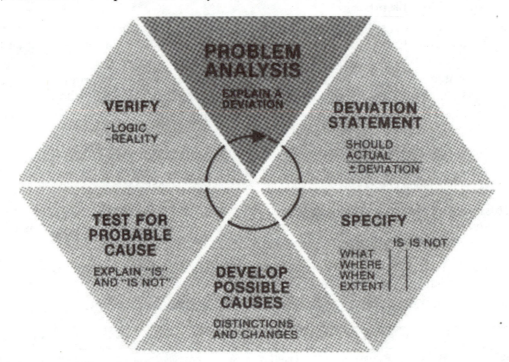

How to use this leadership tool

"One kind of problem that taxes our ability to ask the right questions is the problem that drifts in like fog, very gradually, until visibility has dropped to near zero. Some gradual change in conditions has occurred, and by the time the situation has become serious enough to gain everyone's attention its critical elements may be lost to view."

—Charles Kepner and Benjamin Tregoe, THE NEW RATIONAL MANAGER

By way of example, the leader of a Corporate Services group recently negotiated a new contract for photocopiers. People had liked the previous name-brand copiers, but the cost savings on the new copiers were just too attractive to pass up! Recently, more and more complaints have surfaced about the new copiers. The leader chalked up the first few as "just the usual complaints," but the complaints have kept coming. A series of technicians have adjusted the most seriously malfunctioning machines, and the adjusted copiers did seem to work better for a period of time thereafter. Nonetheless, people are blaming the leader for "buying inferior technology," an increase in paper jamming, the envelope handling features of the new photocopiers, and so on. The leader needs to get to the root of these concerns quickly.

Rather than simply blaming others (e.g., the new supplier), the leader sits down with the repair logs and makes a few telephone calls to assess the problem using this problem-solving template.

What should be happening: *The copiers should operate with very little jamming over long periods.*

What is actually happening: *At least some copiers are jamming more than they should.*

	Is happening	**Is not Happening**	**What's unique?**	**Any changes?**
What?	*Most jamming complaints from low-volume models*	*Very few jamming complaints from high-volume copiers*	*Low volume models are self-serve*	*No change*
Where?	*Most complaints from floors 3, 4, 9, 10, 12, and 21; most often 3 and 4*	*Very few jamming complaints from copiers on other floors*	*Marketing group on floors 3 and 4*	*Marketing moved from floors 9 and 10 during April and May*
When?	*Few jamming problems when new copiers installed in January*	*Problems start to escalate in May*		*New seasonal workers hired in May. New paper supplier in April.*
How much?	*Most complaints on Fridays*	*Other workdays*	*Many unique work processes occur on Fridays*	

Potential Causes and Testing:

1. *The new seasonal employees were not trained and are jamming the machines.*

   There are new employees throughout the building. Why mainly certain floors? Why mainly on Friday?

2. *The new copiers are needing more adjustment with use.*

   Why mainly some floors? Why mainly Friday? Why not the high-volume copiers that have higher use?

3. *The copiers are not adjusted for the new paper supplier.*

   Why only certain floors? Why mainly Fridays?

4. *Marketing group uses the copiers in a unique way on Fridays that jams copiers.*

Most Probable Cause:

4. *Marketing group uses the copiers in a unique way on Fridays that jams the copiers.*

   From a few phone calls and visits, the leader found that marketing representatives usually send out the week's *Product News* to new customers on Fridays. They are using the new addressable envelopes. For existing customers, these envelopes are addressed on the high-volume copiers. These new envelopes are being used in more and more parts of the organization, and seem to be the most probable cause of copier jamming.

A blank worksheet is provided for your use.

FINDING CAUSE WORKSHEET

Step ❶ Clearly define the problem, the difference between the Should and the Actual

Should:

Actual:

Steps ❷ and ❸ Gather Data about the Is and the Is Not, What's Unique, and Changes.

	Is happening	Is not Happening	What's unique?	Any changes?
What?				
Where?				
When?				
How much?				

Step ❹ List the *potential* causes that could explain much of the data above.

Step ❺ Test each potential cause against the data, trying to rule out those causes that do not satisfactorily explain the data.

Step ❻ For the most probable cause(s), gather additional data that would confirm or disconfirm the cause before taking action.

RELATED LEADERSHIP TOOLS

6.2 Assumption Analysis	6.5 Force-Field Analysis	7.1 Problem Framing
6.3 Complex Situations	6.6 Six-Hat Thinking	7.2 Problem Solving

FOR FURTHER ASSISTANCE

Kepner, Charles H., and Benjamin B. Tregoe. *The New Rational Manager.* Princeton Research Press, 1981.

7.4

POLARITIES: DEALING WITH INTRACTABLE PROBLEMS

Inspired by Barry Johnson.

Polarities are those dilemmas that won't go away, even if you throw more money and resources at them. Polarity refers to any situation in which two people or groups defend two ends of a spectrum in a mutually exclusive way. This does not include either–or decisions, like whether to change suppliers. Neither does it apply to continuums, like whether to use light or heavy cars. Examples of polarities that allow camps to form around an issue are:

- to centralize versus to decentralize;
- to use a top-down style of management versus a participative management style; or
- to use a team approach versus an individual approach to work.

Leaders need to consider two characteristics of polarities:

✔ Thinking either–or presents a clear view of only half the picture.

✔ In order to lead in polarizing situations, the emphasis has to shift from an either–or to a both–and approach.

To use the analogy of breathing, humans cannot have the benefit of one pole—oxygen—without tending to the other pole—carbon dioxide. (An ironic implication for organizations is that breathing, using both poles, is a life-sustaining process!)

How does this apply to leadership? Just as in breathing, the opposite camps in a polarized situation are paradoxically interdependent. Take the polarity example illustrated here: the question of organizing around individuals or teams.

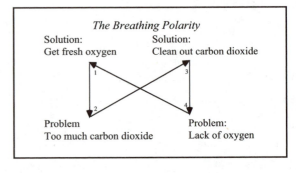

The Breathing Polarity

Solution: Get fresh oxygen

Solution: Clean out carbon dioxide

Problem Too much carbon dioxide

Problem: Lack of oxygen

The team pole may tend to praise its own upsides of teamwork, while pointing out the downsides of the individual pole. Yet, all leaders know that these poles are interdependent. You cannot have a strong team without strong individuals. However, if the individuals are too strong, they may undervalue the contribution of other members; then, in essence, you no longer have a real team. As a leader, how do you deal with this polarity?

Here is a diagram that illustrates the upsides and downsides (agreed upon by the group) of the individual versus team choice. Later, the group can design systems and policies to maximize the upsides and minimize the downsides. While going through this process, keep in mind that there will always be tension between the two poles. At times, the team will take precedence over the individual, and vice versa.

The Individual—Team Polarity

Individual		Team
Some Upsides: • quick action—no need to involve others • encourages individual initiative • efficient—no need for meetings • can work in idiosyncratic ways *Some Downsides:* • loss of team synergy • selfishness, small-mindedness • loneliness • loss of sharing and organizational learning		*Some Upsides:* • support and encouragement of others • can achieve things as a team that individual could not • a sense of belonging *Some Downsides:* • groupthink • time-consuming • need to deal with interpersonal conflicts

In managing polarities, watch for two dysfunctional camps, each with an either–or mind set (half the picture):

⟹ Crusaders see the status quo as a mistake, and want to move toward the upside of change (their solution).

⟹ Tradition-bearers approach change as a mistake, seeing only what might be lost and the downsides of change.

HOW TO USE THIS LEADERSHIP TOOL

"... in our organizations, there are often very serious and costly confrontations that take place because a 'both/and' polarity is treated like an 'either/or' problem to solve."

—Barry Johnson, *POLARITY MANAGEMENT*

Follow these steps to manage polarities:

1. Get those who have a stake in the issue together, and name the polarity or polarities that seem to be at the heart of the issue.

2. As in the diagram on the worksheet, discuss the upsides and downsides of the polarity or polarities that seem to be present (each of the four quadrants, as shown). Visibly record collective agreements.

3. Decide on action plans to maximize the benefits and minimize the downsides of the polarity. (Examples might be providing alternatives so that some work could be directed toward team goals, and some toward individual goals; the same could be done for rewards and recognition, roles and responsibilities, and so on.)

When dealing with two dysfunctional camps (crusaders and tradition-bearers), do the best you can to help both develop a more balanced perspective of the upsides and downsides in the change being proposed. Help crusaders find value in what others have built, and help tradition-bearers accept that a degree of risk accompanies any benefit of change.

POLARITY MAP WORKSHEET

Pole 1:			Pole 2:
Upsides:			*Upsides:*

```
        ↖               ↗
          ╲           ╱
            ╲       ╱
              ╲   ╱
               ╳
              ╱   ╲
            ╱       ╲
          ╱           ╲
        ↓               ↓
```

Downsides: *Downsides:*

RELATED LEADERSHIP TOOLS

6.6 Six-Hat Thinking	9.5 Negotiation	10.9 Visible Information
7.1 Problem Framing	10.6 Group Leader Skills	12.7 Dealing with Conflict

FOR FURTHER ASSISTANCE

Johnson, Barry. *Polarity Management: Identifying and Managing Unsolvable Problems.* HRD Press, 1992.

7.5

DECISION MAKING: MAKING DECISIONS LOGICAL AND DEFENSIBLE

Inspired by Ben Tregoe and Chuck Kepner.

Important decisions that leaders make are rarely without ambiguity or controversy. Yet, decide they must; it's part of the job. But this job becomes easier if leaders have access to a general-purpose decision-making tool that meets two criteria:

i.   It's logically defensible—the quality side of the decision.

ii. It's supported by key stakeholders—the commitment side of the decision.

Use this process to enhance the quality of your decisions. In addition, involving appropriate stakeholders in the process will lead to higher levels of commitment to these decisions.

❶ Define the goal of the decision: [☛ 2.7 Goal Statements, 7.1 Problem Framing]
   – Check the frame of the decision: "What's in the running, and what's out?"

❷ Brainstorm, then agree on decision criteria: [☛ 6.9 Brainstorming]
   – Clarify the criteria for making the decision.
   – Separate the "musts" (results that must be obtained), from the "wants" (desired but not essential).
   – Rank the "want" criteria in order of importance, or rate their importance on a scale of 1 to 10. [☛ 10.11 Priority Setting]

❸ Identify possible decision options.

❹ Rate these decision options against the decision criteria:
   – You may wish to rate how well an option meets a criterion on a scale of 1 to 10.

❺ Identify the risks and limitations for the highest-rated option(s).

❻ Using your decision criteria, select the option with the best rating and the most manageable risks.

❶ Decision Goal: *What do we want to accomplish as a result of this decision?*				
❷ Selection criteria: Results—desirable and undesirable		❸ Option 1	❸ Option 2	❸ Option 3
Brainstormed criteria	Criteria clarified and ranked			
List all conceivable decision criteria. (Be creative.)	*Next, organize and define each criterion as clearly as you can, then rank.*	❹ *Evaluate option against criteria (1–10).*	❹ *Evaluate option against criteria (1–10).*	❹ *Evaluate option against criteria (1–10).*
		Total =	Total =	Total =

❺ Assess the risks and the limitations of the highest rated option(s).

Highest-rated option:	
Risks and limitations: [☛ 7.6 Potential Problems]	How the risks can be minimized:

Second highest-rated option:	
Risks and limitations:	How the risks can be minimized:

❻ Select the option that best meets your decision criteria (provides the biggest benefits), and involves manageable risks.

[☛ 5.1 Change Equation]

Charles Kepner and Benjamin Tregoe, in their groundbreaking book, *The New Rational Manager,* summarized the process this way:

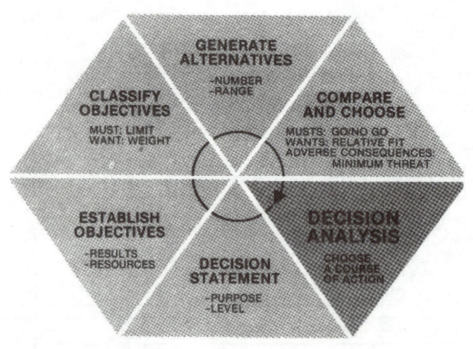

HOW TO USE THIS LEADERSHIP TOOL

"When people are provided with a common approach to decision making, they find they can indeed work as a team."

—Charles Kepner and Benjamin Tregoe, *THE NEW RATIONAL MANAGER*

Use this tool in a wide range of applications, from selecting the best person for a job to selecting complex technical equipment. For example, for selecting a new team member, start with the decision criteria, outlining skill requirements ranging from technical expertise to interpersonal skills to other decision criteria such as availability. Distinguish between "musts" and "wants." Having done this, you can rate employees from other departments, external contractors, and other job applicants against these decision criteria. Next, for those candidates who rate the highest against the decision criteria, assess the limitations that accompany each candidacy (e.g., training requirements, related staffing considerations). This process doesn't guarantee success, but it does help you minimize the risks associated with making challenging decisions.

Use the worksheet provided to organize and present decisions in a logical, defensible way. This not only helps minimize the risk and subjectivity in decision making; it also helps ensure commitment from the key stakeholders in the decision.

WEB WORKSHEET

DECISION-MAKING WORKSHEET

Decision Goal:				
Selection criteria: Results—desirable and undesirable		Option 1	Option 2	Option 3
Brainstormed criteria	Criteria clarified and ranked			

Assess risks and limitations for each of the highest-rated option(s)

Highest-rated option:		Second highest-rated option:	
Risks and limitations:	How the risks can be minimized:	Risks and limitations:	How the risks can be minimized:

Select the option that best meets your decision criteria (provides the biggest benefits), and involves manageable risks.

RELATED LEADERSHIP TOOLS

2.7 Goal Statements	6.9 Brainstorming	10.7 Getting Participation
6.6 Six-Hat Thinking	7.1 Problem Framing	10.11 Priority Setting

FOR FURTHER ASSISTANCE

Kepner, Charles H., and Benjamin B. Tregoe. *The New Rational Manager.* Princeton Research Press, 1981.

7.6 POTENTIAL PROBLEM ANALYSIS: DEALING WITH RISK TO A PLAN

Inspired by Ben Tregoe and Charles Kepner.

The purpose of Potential Problem Analysis is to protect a plan. By plan, we mean an established, methodical process for carrying out any project. Every plan involves some risk of unforeseen or unexpected roadblocks and the plan can be analyzed to anticipate them. This tool shows how to protect a plan in a systemic way. Before outlining the seven steps of Potential Problem Analysis, we describe some terms used therein.

Probability refers to the likelihood of a problem occurring. Using an airline example, the probability of an accident occurring is near takeoff and landing rather than in flight; therefore, more energy and planning would go into takeoff and landing stages of a flight plan.

Seriousness refers to the impact of the problem if and when it does occur. An incident may be highly probable, but not at all serious in its impact on the plan; or it could be highly improbable, but totally disastrous if it does occur.

Preventive actions are those actions you take to prevent problems from ever occurring. For an airline, for example, preventive actions include safety audits, regular maintenance of aircraft, and frequent use of pilot simulators for training.

Contingent actions involve minimizing the damage if, despite effort, problems occur anyway. Again, using the airline example, contingent actions include emergency exits, emergency landing procedures, and disaster planning.

The steps of Potential Problem Analysis are:

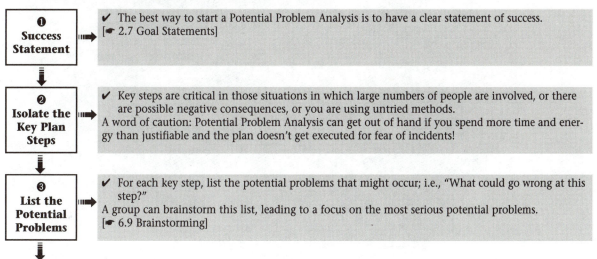

❶ Success Statement ⇒ ✔ The best way to start a Potential Problem Analysis is to have a clear statement of success. [☞ 2.7 Goal Statements]

❷ Isolate the Key Plan Steps ⇒ ✔ Key steps are critical in those situations in which large numbers of people are involved, or there are possible negative consequences, or you are using untried methods.
A word of caution: Potential Problem Analysis can get out of hand if you spend more time and energy than justifiable and the plan doesn't get executed for fear of incidents!

❸ List the Potential Problems ⇒ ✔ For each key step, list the potential problems that might occur; i.e., "What could go wrong at this step?"
A group can brainstorm this list, leading to a focus on the most serious potential problems. [☞ 6.9 Brainstorming]

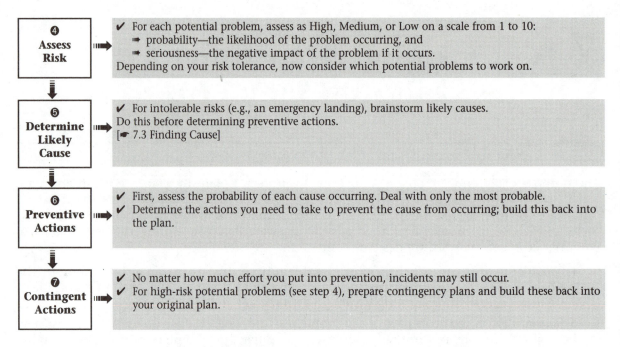

| ❹ Assess Risk | ✔ For each potential problem, assess as High, Medium, or Low on a scale from 1 to 10:
➡ probability—the likelihood of the problem occurring, and
➡ seriousness—the negative impact of the problem if it occurs.
Depending on your risk tolerance, now consider which potential problems to work on. |

| ❺ Determine Likely Cause | ✔ For intolerable risks (e.g., an emergency landing), brainstorm likely causes.
Do this before determining preventive actions.
[☛ 7.3 Finding Cause] |

| ❻ Preventive Actions | ✔ First, assess the probability of each cause occurring. Deal with only the most probable.
✔ Determine the actions you need to take to prevent the cause from occurring; build this back into the plan. |

| ❼ Contingent Actions | ✔ No matter how much effort you put into prevention, incidents may still occur.
✔ For high-risk potential problems (see step 4), prepare contingency plans and build these back into your original plan. |

Charles Kepner and Benjamin Tregoe, in their groundbreaking book, *The New Rational Manager,* summarized the process this way:

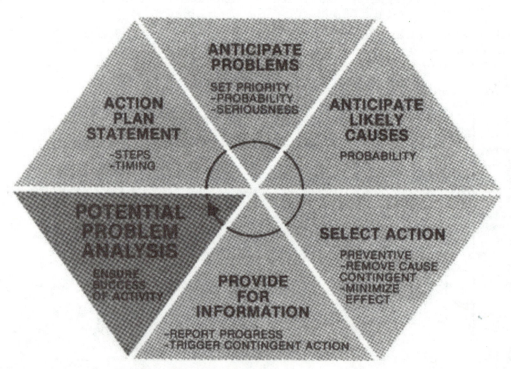

How to use this leadership tool

"Potential Problem Analysis is not a negative search for trouble. It is a positive search for ways to avoid and lessen trouble that is likely to come in the future. ... Merely being able to remember a thousand horror stories is of no use unless that body of information can be used to prevent more."

—Charles Kepner and Benjamin Tregoe, *THE NEW RATIONAL MANAGER*

This process is best used in a group setting when the project plan is nearly complete from a professional or technical perspective; use it with the project group as a whole, in order to get commitment to the results. Another typical use is in project review by a leader.

Use the worksheet provided to organize Potential Problem Analysis into a very brief form.

WEB WORKSHEET

POTENTIAL PROBLEM ANALYSIS WORKSHEET

Success Statement for the Plan:

Key Plan Steps	Potential Problems	Risk P and S	Likely Causes	Probability	Preventive Actions	Contingent Actions

RELATED LEADERSHIP TOOLS

6.2 Assumption Analysis	6.5 Force-Field Analysis	10.6 Group Leader Skills
6.3 Complex Situations	6.9 Brainstorming	10.11 Priority Setting

FOR FURTHER ASSISTANCE

Hiebert, Murray. *Powerful Professionals: Getting Your Expertise Used Inside Organizations.* Recursion Press, 1999.

Kepner, Charles H., and Benjamin B. Tregoe. *The New Rational Manager.* Princeton Research Press, 1981.

7.7   TOTAL QUALITY LEADERSHIP OVERVIEW

Inspired by William Deming, Joseph Juran, Peter Scholtes, William Conway, and Amoco Progress program designers.

The quality movement has had great impact on leadership and organizations. Arising out of programs that focused on keeping production processes within control limits (such as Statistical Quality Control or SQC), the movement has expanded. It now includes improving systems, as well as designing leadership processes, to support Total Quality organizations. Quality offshoots have included quality circles, the International Organization for Standardization (ISO), and benchmarking. The purpose of this tool is to provide an overview of some key elements of leadership in these quality areas.

A quality measure defines a critical measure of success. Examples are satisfied customers, shipments made within 24 hours, money saved, and calls answered within one minute. A quality measure can also define problems (e.g., errors, complaints, downtime, rejects), or it can define variables (e.g., time, cost, frequency, type, counts, response time). The creative piece of Statistical Quality leadership is deciding which quality measures to use to analyze a process.

Peter Scholtes has broadly summarized the key concepts of quality improvement.

KEY QUALITY IMPROVEMENT CONCEPTS

- **Processes and Systems**
- **Customers and Suppliers**
- **Quality**
  - of target values and features
  - of execution
- **Teams and Teamwork**
- **Scientific Approach**
- **Complexity**
  1. Mistakes or defects
  2. Breakdowns or delays
  3. Inefficiencies
  4. Excessive variation
- **Variation**
  - common causes
  - special causes
- **Statistically Designed Experiments**

Reprinted with permission from Scholtes, Peter. *The Team Handbook*. Joiner Associates, 1988, page 2-2.

The table that follows includes brief descriptions of commonly used specific quality measures. We caution against isolating use of these measures from the principles in the application section of this tool, because those principles form the underpinning for the measures. Please keep in mind that the principles need to come first!

The Quality Tool	What it is and what it is useful for:	What it looks like:
Run Chart	• Identifies trends by tracking a quality measure over a period of time. • Is usually tracked against a standard. • Makes it easier to visualize trends and detect problems.	 *Mears, p. 62*
Pareto Chart/ Diagram	• A straightforward bar graph that tracks a quality measure by cause(s), source, or type. • Highlights what to work on.	 *Mears, p. 36, "Purchasing Problems"*
Check Sheet	• A straightforward way to collect information in preparation for analysis. • Highlights what to work on.	 *Mears, p. 25, "Defective Item Check Sheet"*
Flowchart	• Maps a process in a common format. • Is used to identify trouble spots or non-value-adding steps and to plan improvement, particularly simplification.	*Mears, p. 20, "Burger Cooking Flowchart"*
Cause–Effect or Fishbone Diagram	• Clearly shows the relationships between effects and multiple causes. • Is particularly useful when the situation is messy and complex.	 *Mears, p. 55, "Quality Copies"*
Scatter Diagram or Correlation Chart	• Used to test how two quality measures are related. • Can help point out (rule out) cause–effect relationships.	 *Mears p. 58, "Scatter Diagram"*

The Quality Tool	What it is and what it is useful for:	What it looks like:
Histogram	• A straightforward way to illustrate the relative frequencies and variations in quality measure. • Helps analysis by making variations stand out.	 *Mears, p. 42, "Traffic Fines"*
Control Chart	• Whereas a histogram is a static snapshot in time, a control chart is a moving picture of a quality measure over time. • Two statistical measures are used, the average and the range, both bounded by upper and lower control limits. • It is used to measure the performance and stability of a process over time.	 *Mears, p. 71, "Points Outside"*

Diagrams reproduced with permission from Mears, Peter. *Quality Improvement Tools and Techniques.* McGraw-Hill, 1995.

How to Use This Leadership Tool

Leaders "... have learned that to move quality to the level of top priority is not a simple change. Certainly it is not just a matter of hoisting banners that proclaim that quality has top priority. Instead it has turned out to be a profound change."

—J. M. Juran, *JURAN ON LEADERSHIP FOR QUALITY*

Like all leadership tools, the quality leadership movement has had huge successes and proponents along with failures and detractors. Besides using the statistical quality tools, both quality gurus, Edwards Deming and Joseph Juran, were clear that a change of leadership style was required.

Loosely based on Deming's famous 14 Points, this is a checklist of principles upon which a total quality leadership program should be based. Rate yourself and write an action plan for those items needing action.

WEB WORKSHEET

Total quality principle	More information ☞	Your awareness	Your first steps to improve
✔ Leaders in the twenty-first century need to be trained in modern leadership philosophies and tools	1.1 Twenty-first Century Leader 1.2 Manage or Lead?		
✔ Leaders need to be aware of the possible need to redesign organizations in quantum, discontinuous breakthroughs, interspersed by periods of continuous improvement.	3.2 Sigmoid Curve 4.3 Reengineering 5.4 Change Scale		
✔ Leaders must be systems, change, and process improvement leaders for their organizations to thrive.	2.1 Systems Thinking 5.1 Change Equation		
✔ Leaders need to replace fear-based management with participative, team-based leadership.	4.4 Employee Involvement 4.6 Open-Book Leadership 10.6 Group Leader Skills		

✔ Leaders need to be aware that most organizational problems are caused by poor systems, not by unmotivated people. Quality comes from designing and improving processes and systems through which work gets done and results are achieved.	2.1 Systems Thinking 2.2 7S Model 4.1 Organizational Design 4.3 Reengineering		
✔ Leaders need to break down traditional barriers—stovepipes—between functions and departments. Any service or product should be a product of the whole, not of the sum of the parts.	4.3 Reengineering 4.9 Professional Expertise		
✔ Leaders need to break down the barriers between management and workers; salaried and hourly; union and nonunion; suppliers and supplied; organization and customers or clients. Leaders are needed at all levels.	4.4 Employee Involvement 4.6 Open-Book Leadership		
✔ Everyone should ensure quality before a product or service passes into another's hands. The success of the organization is everyone's responsibility.	2.5 Values 4.5 Culture 4.6 Open-Book Leadership		
✔ Because of rapid change, leaders need to provide constant and effective training and development for all employees.	14.3 Needs Analysis 14.4 Adult Learning		

RELATED LEADERSHIP TOOLS

1.1 Twenty-First-Century Leader	2.1 Systems Thinking	4.6 Open-Book Leadership
1.10 The GAS Model	4.3 Reengineering	7.8 Affinity Diagrams

FOR FURTHER ASSISTANCE

Deming, W. Edwards. *Quality, Productivity and Competitive Position.* MIT Press, 1982.

Hornor, Lawrence, and Curtis King. *Waste Chasers: A Pocket Companion to Quality and Productivity.* Conway Quality, Inc., 1993.

Juran, Joseph M. *Juran on Leadership for Quality: An Executive Handbook.* Free Press, 1989.

Mears, Peter. *Quality Improvement Tools and Techniques.* McGraw-Hill, 1995.

Scholtes, Peter R., Brian L. Joiner, and Barbara J. Streibel. *The Team Handbook,* 2nd ed. Oriel Inc, 1996.

QUALITY WEB SITES

The Association for Quality and Participation http://www.aqp.org/
   AQP is an international not-for-profit membership association dedicated to improving workplaces through quality and participation practices. This site has very helpful links to related sites.

American Productivity and Quality Center http://www.apqc.org/
   More than 500 members strong, APQC's International Benchmarking Clearinghouse offers a comprehensive package of products, services, knowledge, information, and opportunities with the flexibility to meet any organization's specific needs. See their Helpful Resources for a wide variety of links to other related resources.

American Society for Quality http://www.asq.org/
   ASQ site introduces you to many topics about quality. The Standards and Certification section provides information on the ISO 9000 and ISO 14000 standards, QS-9000 requirements, and ASQ certification programs.

7.8

AFFINITY DIAGRAMS: ORGANIZING MOUNTAINS OF DATA

Contributed by Diane MacDonald, and inspired Michael Brassard, Nancy Tague,
and by many quality gurus and quality organizations, such as Goal QPC.

Most of today's management tools are reductionist in nature, breaking problems into smaller parts to analyze and solve them. But what happens when you are faced with making sense of an overwhelming amount of information? Leaders have very few tools to help groups understand the big picture, seeing the larger context of current problems, as well as seeing relationships among the problems. The affinity diagram tool will help you organize a large number of ideas into logical groupings, ready for action. This tool is most useful when you:

✔ Have a large number of ideas to work with.

✔ Need to generate more ideas.

✔ Need to identify issues and themes prior to taking action.

✔ Are building consensus (especially when one person may dominate a discussion).

The affinity diagram is a quality management tool commonly used in planning and problem-solving sessions to help groups see new relationships and themes, and consequently new possibilities for action.

For example, a Community Leaders' Executive Committee had solicited community residents' feedback and ideas on a 10-year future community direction. Overwhelming data from more than 150 replies presented an organizational nightmare, with each member subjectively seeing certain data "jump out" at them for priority; for example, those with children saw "kids' programs" as a priority. Worried about the possibility that more forceful personalities would dominate discussion and outcome, the Community President proposed using the equalizing and silent affinity diagramming process outlined here. As a result:

• Participants experienced this process as affirming and inclusive, with all input having equal value.

• The process helped people develop their inductive thinking, learning how to move from the specific and particular to the general. (Being able to discriminate between these levels of thinking is an invaluable skill for effective planning and problem solving.)

Process steps

Step	Specifics
❶ **Materials**	❑ Lots of 4 × 6- inch Post-It® Notes; felt pens; flip chart sheets; a large, clear wall surface.
❷ **Develop and post a clear, focal question.**	❑ E.g., "What must we focus on over the next three years in order to be leaders in our field?" or, "What information do we include for customer use in our new handbook?" ❑ If you are experiencing difficulty formulating this frame question, see ☛ 7.1 Problem Framing.
❸ **Generate ideas** (if data is not already available).	To solicit data, here are two common ways to generate ideas for the affinity diagram. i. Ask participants to reflect privately, then write their thoughts on the Post-it® Notes. ii. Use the brainstorming process (ground rule: no judging or evaluating), with people calling out ideas that are immediately recorded on Post-It® Notes. [☛ 6.9 Brainstorming] ❑ When posting data, the rules are: One idea per Post-It® Note, each more than one word but no more than one sentence. Write with a felt pen, neatly enough for others to read it. Ensure that the sticky part of the Post-It® Note is at the top (upper horizontal) side.
❹ **Display and read Post-It® Notes.**	❑ When everyone's ideas are captured on Post-It® Notes, have people place all their Post-It® Notes in random fashion on the wall. ❑ Everyone moves along the wall, reading all the notes in silence.
❺ **Cluster the Post-It® Notes.**	❑ The task is for people to cluster or group Post-It® Notes, together with others they consider to have something in common—a natural affinity. Explain the rules. This process is done in complete silence. (Some claim that using the unpreferred hand physiologically forces one to think more consciously and less automatically!) ❑ If you see a Post-it® Note that you believe fits better in another grouping, remove it and place it in that other grouping, being conscious of your own reasoning for doing so. Another person who disagrees may move it again. ❑ When the activity stops (like popcorn popping stops), the group works with the leader to clarify how many clusters have been created. Create a vertical column out of each cluster, spacing them out to clearly identify the groupings. Leave the orphans—lone Post-It® Notes—alone.
❻ **Name that cluster!**	❑ Asking "What is the name that best describes this grouping?" read all the notes in the cluster aloud. Of the various suggestions, the group itself will usually acknowledge the best name with a loud "Yes!" ❑ Using a different colored pen, write the name of the cluster on another note and post it at the top of the vertical column. (Sometimes, the best name is actually one of the notes.) A verb + noun format will often better suggest action; e.g., Accelerate Skill Development instead of Training. ❑ Continue this process until all the groupings have been named. During this process, the group will often decide that a note fits better into a new grouping, or that two groupings belong together. Lone notes will also find a home.
❼ **Reflect on the names.**	❑ *Connect the focal question* to the names and the groupings. For instance, using our example focal question, you might say, "So, through this process, we are saying that if, for the next three years, we focus on (heading one, heading two, heading three, … etc.), we believe we will become leaders in our field."

The authors of this book had 150-plus tools to organize into readable form for you, the reader. Using the affinity diagramming process, this is how the table of contents emerged.

Leadership Development Competency Areas

Big-Picture Thinking	Strategic Thinking	Leading Change	Creativity/ Innovation

Systems Thinking	Sigmoid Curve	Change Readiness	Generating New Ideas
Preparing a Vision Statement	Environmental Scan	Getting Support for Change	Six-Hat Thinking
Values	Strategic Clients	The "People Side" of Change	Mind Mapping
Purpose		Systemic Change	Affinity Diagrams
		Dealing with Resistance	Brainstorming

HOW TO USE THIS LEADERSHIP TOOL

"The best way to have a good idea is to have a lot of ideas."

—Linus Pauling, Nobel Prize Winner

Some hints for successful use of this tool:

- Keep the size of the group small.
- As in brainstorming, it is okay to ask for clarification during idea generation, but it is not okay to critique the idea.
- Enforce the rule of silence during grouping, but discuss ideas before creating a heading.
- Don't agonize over the sorting. The point is not to achieve "truth," but workable categories.
- When one grouping becomes much longer than the others, think about subdividing the group.

WEB WORKSHEET

Now think of situations in which affinity diagramming would be a helpful tool. Fill in the matrix to get you started.

Description of the Situation:
[☛ 7.1 Problem Framing]
What would you suggest as the focal question?
Which group members would you need at the meeting?
[☛ 5.7 Stakeholder Groups]
How would you explain the need to use this tool?
[☛ 9.7 Selling Wheel]
What would you suggest as ground rules for this group and situation?
[☛ 10.8 Groundrules]

RELATED LEADERSHIP TOOLS

6.8 Mind Mapping	7.7 Quality Tools	10.7 Getting Participation
6.9 Brainstorming	10.6 Group Leader Skills	10.10 Closure

FOR FURTHER ASSISTANCE

Brassard, Michael. *The Memory Jogger Plus—Featuring the Seven Management and Planning Tools*. Goal/QPC, 1996.

Mears, Peter. *Quality Improvement Tools and Techniques*. McGraw-Hill, 1995.

Tague, Nancy R. *The Quality Toolbox*. American Society for Quality, 1995.

8

TOOLS FOR COMMUNICATION

Even in this electronic age, face-to-face conversations are still the most powerful and significant communications leaders have. Research shows that only 20 percent of communication is contained in a conversation's actual words, while 80 percent is in the tone of voice and other nonverbal cues. Further research shows that leaders believe they communicate three times more than do the people they are communicating with! These tools will help you examine your leadership communications, and provide concrete suggestions for dealing with typical communication concerns.

8.1 POWERFUL LEADERSHIP CONVERSATIONS

Inspired by Tor Norretranders, Jonathan Sydenham, Douglas Stone, Bruce Patton, Sheila Heen, Roger Fisher, and Deborah Tannen.

Even in this electronic age, face-to-face conversations are still the most powerful and significant communications leaders have. Research shows that only 20 percent of communication is contained in a conversation's actual words, while 80 percent is in the tone of voice and other nonverbal cues. Further research shows that leaders believe they communicate three times more than do the people they are communicating with! This tool helps you examine your leadership conversations and provides concrete suggestions for dealing with typical conversation problems.

THE FOUR LEVELS OF UNDERSTANDING

There are four levels of understanding to every conversation:

1. the data you hear,
2. information you glean from the data,
3. your interpretations of the information, and
4. your conclusions from the total conversation.

Level of understanding	What happens at this level	Issues with this level
1. Data (the data you hear during the conversation)	What you actually hear. Also what you sense, see, and feel as the other person is communicating.	Too much data is available during a conversation. The bandwidth of all sensory perception is over 10 million bits per second, while the bandwidth of consciousness is about 100 bits per second. Each individual tends to hear or focus on different data, all the while being unconscious of the entire field of data being communicated.
2. Information (the data you extract from what you hear)	Of all the data available in the conversation, this is the data that you actually attend to and take into consciousness.	The data you sense is filtered through very personal filters, like past life experiences, male or female conditioning, your personal values, how you feel about people in general, what is okay or not okay for you, and so on. As a leader, you need to be aware of your personal filters in order to check your interpretations of conversations.
3. Interpretations (how you make sense of the data you have extracted from the conversation)	You need to interpret the data that you have chosen to focus on. In this way you make sense of what is being discussed.	Now you try to make sense of the data. This, again, is filtered through your personal interpretation rules. As you get farther away from the actual conversation—with the passage of time, for example—the information you glean and the interpretations you make often become less accurate.
4. Conclusions/ evaluation (your evaluation of the total conversation)	After interpreting the data, you draw your own conclusions about the conversation as a whole.	Your conclusions typically reflect your self-interest. People tend to look for information and use interpretations that produce positive conclusions if they like the person or ideas, and negative conclusions if they don't.

YOU GET THREE CONVERSATIONS FOR THE PRICE OF ONE!

These three types of conversations are problematic, because they are seldom explicit or out in the open.

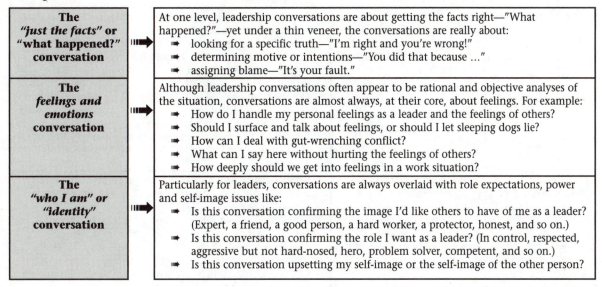

The *"just the facts"* or *"what happened?"* conversation	At one level, leadership conversations are about getting the facts right—"What happened?"—yet under a thin veneer, the conversations are really about: ➡ looking for a specific truth—"I'm right and you're wrong!" ➡ determining motive or intentions—"You did that because ..." ➡ assigning blame—"It's your fault."
The *feelings and emotions* conversation	Although leadership conversations often appear to be rational and objective analyses of the situation, conversations are almost always, at their core, about feelings. For example: ➡ How do I handle my personal feelings as a leader and the feelings of others? ➡ Should I surface and talk about feelings, or should I let sleeping dogs lie? ➡ How can I deal with gut-wrenching conflict? ➡ What can I say here without hurting the feelings of others? ➡ How deeply should we get into feelings in a work situation?
The *"who I am"* or *"identity"* conversation	Particularly for leaders, conversations are always overlaid with role expectations, power and self-image issues like: ➡ Is this conversation confirming the image I'd like others to have of me as a leader? (Expert, a friend, a good person, a hard worker, a protector, honest, and so on.) ➡ Is this conversation confirming the role I want as a leader? (In control, respected, aggressive but not hard-nosed, hero, problem solver, competent, and so on.) ➡ Is this conversation upsetting my self-image or the self-image of the other person?

HOW TO USE THIS LEADERSHIP TOOL

"When conversations go awry, we look for causes and usually find them by blaming others or ourselves. The most generous-minded blame the relationship. ... Much of this blame is misplaced. Bad feelings are often the result of misunderstandings that arise from the differences in conversational style."

—Deborah Tannen, *THAT'S NOT WHAT I MEANT*

Leaders need to be able to diagnose and read conversations. In this way they will be able to deal with typical conversation difficulties, and also coach others in handling communication problems. Keeping the four levels of understanding and the three types of conversations in mind, consider these two examples: a negative and then a positive communication exchange.

A NEGATIVE COMMUNICATION CYCLE

Level of understanding	Negative spiral characteristics	Suggested strategies for improving this conversational exchange
1. Data	You only hear, see, and feel the data that supports the conclusions you want to form (your preconceived notion of the truth).	❑ Get feedback on how well you listen, and pick up subtle cues from others. Leaders can be poor judges of their own behavior. [☛ 12.4 Feedback] ❑ Read and apply the self-awareness tools in this book. [For example ☛ 6.2 Assumption Analysis, 8.7 Active Listening]

2. Information (gleaned from data)	You are unaware of your picking and choosing from the available data, and of choosing data to fit your prior hypothesis.	❑ Be attentive beyond "just the words." Be aware of other people's nonverbals, and be aware of your own feelings. ❑ Work to increase your communication bandwidth. Be aware of only absorbing a small part of the data available in the conversation.
3. Interpretations (gleaned from the information)	Already off the mark by poor data selection, you jump to and respond to unfounded interpretations. You make bad assumptions.	❑ Become familiar with your criteria for picking and choosing from the available data. ❑ Check back using active listening techniques [☛ 8.7 Active Listening] to ensure that the information you're receiving is congruent with the information the sender intended. ❑ Be aware of criteria others may be using to pick and choose. Conflicts can be dealt with by having a metacommunication about what information you and the other person are taking in. [☛ 8.5 Metacommunicating] ❑ Be conscious of making interpretations and of whether or not they are based on good information. [☛ 13.6 Attribution Theory]
4. Conclusions/ Evaluations (gleaned from your interpretations)	In the worst case, you draw positive conclusions from people who support your power image and role as a leader, and negative conclusions from those who do not.	❑ Check back by using active listening techniques to ensure that your interpretations are congruent with the other person's intent. ❑ Examine your own interpretation rules by reading and applying the self-awareness tools in this book. [☛ 6.2 Assumption Analysis, 8.7 Active Listening, 14.7 Personal Preferences] ❑ Check back with others to see whether your conclusions are in sync with theirs. ❑ Get feedback from others on how well they think your conclusions match with what they expected. ❑ Learn about how you draw conclusions, and evaluate your skill by reading and applying the self-awareness tools in this book. [☛ See tool references above.]

A POSITIVE COMMUNICATION CYCLE

Note: Many characteristics of the positive communications spiral depend upon:

➡ Metathinking—being aware of how you are processing information as you listen,

➡ Metafeeling—being aware of your own feelings and the feelings of others, and

➡ Metacommunicating—being able to talk about how you are thinking, feeling, and communicating.

Level of understanding	Positive spiral criteria
1. Data	❑ In addition to what people are saying, you are sensitive to their tones of voice, to stress signs in their bodies, and so on. ❑ You observe yourself observing the other, noting when you resist taking in other people's words, your observations, and your own feelings. ❑ You are aware of your limited bandwidth of all sensory perception.

2. Information (gleaned from the data)	❏ You listen to find patterns; you are aware of your own filtering. ❏ You are aware of the tendency to formulate a response when you should be listening. ❏ Besides listening for data, you also listen for other people's feelings. [☛ 8.7 Active Listening]
3. Interpretations (gleaned from the information)	❏ You can separate the person from the issues. ❏ You are aware of your own interpretation rules. ❏ You are aware of choosing data to support your position. ❏ You ask for feedback to confirm your emerging interpretations.
4. Conclusions (gleaned from your interpretations)	❏ While recognizing your feelings, you remain objective about the issues. ❏ You listen at many levels, from "Please go on ..." to making empathetic responses. [☛ 8.8 Listening Techniques] ❏ You don't act on your conclusions until you have checked them out with the other person and discussed any differences. ❏ You consider your contribution to a problem without taking responsibility for the other person, and without blaming yourself or the other person.

RELATED LEADERSHIP TOOLS

8.4 Dialogue and Discussion	8.7 Active Listening	13.6 Attribution Theory
8.5 Metacommunicating	8.9 Cross-Cultural	14.7 Personal Preferences
8.6 Communication 101	12.6 Confrontation	15.2 Emotional Intelligence

FOR FURTHER ASSISTANCE

Norretranders, Tor, and Jonathan Sydenham (Translator). *The User Illusion: Cutting Consciousness Down to Size*. Viking Press, 1999.

Stone, Douglas, Bruce Patton, Sheila Heen, and Roger Fisher. *Difficult Conversations: How to Discuss What Matters Most*. Penguin USA, 2000.

Tannen, Deborah. *That's Not What I Meant: How Conversational Style Makes or Breaks Relationships*. Ballantine Books, 1991.

8.2

DIRECT LEADER-TO-EMPLOYEE COMMUNICATION STILL WORKS BEST

Contributed by Ursula Wohlfarth, inspired by research studies by the International Association of Business Communicators (IABC), the IABC Research Foundation, and Watson Wyatt Worldwide. Also inspired by Stephen Covey and Hendrie Weisinger.

Successful leaders communicate effectively and treat employees like adults. If presented properly, they know that employees typically handle bad or negative news well. What employees don't handle well is uncertainty and being kept in the dark. Studies support this view and show that companies emphasizing employee communications (e.g., viewing communication skills as a core leadership competency or as a key criterion when promoting employees) benefit from an 18 to 24 percent improvement in shareholder value (data from various Watson Wyatt Work USA studies). This tool will help you plan a successful large-scale, direct employee communications strategy.

COMMUNICATION WITH FRONTLINE EMPLOYEES

Frontline leaders are pivotal senders and receivers of information within organizations. They hold the lion's share of responsibility for communicating with frontline staff. Companies whose employees rank their immediate supervisors as their most desired source of information include AT&T, BHP, Cadbury, Schweppes, Commonwealth Bank of Australia, Forte, GE, GM, General Tire, Hewlett-Packard, and Telecom Australia. As a concrete example, 83 percent of General Motors employees in the United States rank their supervisors as their most trusted source of information.

GUIDELINES FOR EFFECTIVE COMMUNICATION

Frontline leaders must continually seek opportunities to share information with staff, and to reinforce and make available information that is provided from the top levels of the organization. Being fully understood requires that leaders open up two-way channels of communication to hear and deal with staff concerns. Thus, frontline leaders must be accessible to employees, and encourage regular feedback to ensure that communication is working. Corporate groups also have a role to play in developing integrated communications strategies that support business goals. Therefore, face-to-face contact between senior managers and frontline leaders is critically important.

Communication factors	How to's
❶ Use **CORE** to determine what to communicate to employees.	**C** – Changes taking place **O** – Objectives, business strategies **R** – Reasons behind decisions **E** – Effect on employees
❷ **DIRECT** shows you how to communicate information in a straight-forward and two-way manner.	**D** – Discuss details with employees. **I** – Invite questions. **R** – Recognize ideas, regardless of their source. **E** – Enable others to act. **C** – (Address) Changes openly. **T** – Translate difficult information into easily understood language.
❸ **TRUST** underlies all communication.	**T** – Trust comes from being candid and open with employees. **R** – Recognize employee communication needs. **U** – Usual behavior, predictable and consistent on your part, will gain you trust. **S** – "Sussing out values": Employees deduce your values from your behavior. **T** – Trust; don't break confidentiality.
❹ **HEAR** is a tool to improve listening skills.	**H** – Honor others and what they have to say. **E** – Echo what employees say to ensure you understand their intent. **A** – Ask questions to engage employees. **R** – Respond without becoming defensive.
❺ Keep the communication channels **OPEN**.	**O** – Open to feedback: Demonstrate a willingness to listen. **P** – Patience: Find time to meet with employees and hear their concerns. **E** – Empathy: Walk in others' shoes. **N** – Needs of your direct reports: Provide information employees need to do their jobs.

HOW TO USE THIS LEADERSHIP TOOL

"Resist the urge to stop communicating. Just because you have said it a million times doesn't mean it's been heard that many times. You can get tired of your voice long before you're understood or believed."

—Ron George, CEO, Suncor Energy

As a leader, you need to make it a high priority to communicate with your workgroup and direct reports, regardless of your level in the management structure. Think of a specific communication challenge you presently face or will need to handle in the near future. Use the worksheet provided to describe the situation; to plan the steps you will take to ensure your communication helps employees to fully understand the business needs; and to commit to meeting business goals.

WEB WORKSHEET

The communication challenge (the situation):

Communication factors	Your action plan
❶ Use **CORE** to determine what to communicate to employees. [☞ 5.1 Change Equation]	**C** – Changes taking place **O** – Objectives, business strategies **R** – Reasons behind decisions **E** – Effect on employees
❷ **DIRECT** shows you how to communicate information in a straight-forward and two-way manner. [☞ 10.6 Group Leader Skills]	**D** – Discuss details **I** – Invite questions **R** – Recognize ideas **E** – Enable others to act **C** – (Address) Changes openly **T** – Translate difficult information into easily understood language
❸ **TRUST** underlies all communication. [☞ 2.5 Values , 12.2 Trust]	**T** – Trust: Be candid and open **R** – Recognize needs **U** – Usual behavior **S** – "Sussing out values" **T** – Trust: confidentiality
❹ **HEAR** is a tool to improve listening skills. [☞ 8.7 Active Listening]	**H** – Honor others **E** – Echo **A** – Ask questions **R** – Respond
❺ Keep the communication channels **OPEN**. [☞ 10.7 Getting Participation]	**O** – Open to feedback **P** – Patience; find time **E** – Empathy **N** – Needs of your direct reports

RELATED LEADERSHIP TOOLS

8.1 Conversations	9.7 Selling Wheel	11.1 Process Cycle
8.3 Organizational Communication	10.6 Group Leader Skills	11.3 Meeting Checklist
8.7 Active Listening	10.7 Getting Participation	12.2 Trust

FOR FURTHER ASSISTANCE

Covey, Stephen. *The Seven Habits of Highly Effective People: Powerful Lessons in Personal Change.* Simon & Schuster, 1989.

Weisinger, Hendrie. *Emotional Intelligence at Work: The Untapped Edge for Success.* Jossey-Bass Publishers, 1998.

8.3

THE LEADER'S ROLE IN
ORGANIZATIONAL COMMUNICATION

Contributed by Ursula Wohlfarth and inspired by the International Association of Business Communicators (IABC) references. Also inspired by Stephen Covey and Hendrie Weisinger.

Communication is the tie that binds an organization together. This tool will help you, as a leader, to communicate openly with employees, and in doing so to contribute to the development of your organization as a whole. Effective communication practices make a difference in employees' attitudes toward the organization. The benefits of a well-informed staff include:

✔ increased commitment from employees, because they understand the organization's goals, and their own role in achieving those goals;

✔ greater cooperation across organizational business units and workgroups;

✔ elimination of rumors and incorrect assumptions that create misunderstanding or undermine employee morale;

✔ employees feeling recognized and motivated to take the initiative, such as offering new ideas.

Communication is a defining element of an organization's culture. Some organizations are described as open and forthright in their communication, while others are closed and highly controlled in their approach. Invariably, the organization's leaders set the tone for communications. If the CEO is sincere and up front in communicating with employees, then open communication becomes "the way we do business around here."

Frequently, communication is carried out on a formal and tactical level, and managed in a controlled way by a corporate communications department. The formal methods used in organizations include:

- employee forums,
- e-mail broadcasts,
- newsletters,
- intranet sites,
- voice mail broadcasts,
- memos and bulletins.

These formal methods work well to ensure that employees get the same information at the same time.

Although invaluable, these formal communication methods may not be effective in conveying the vital context for what employees want and need to know about their workplace and organization. Furthermore, employees often miss critical information that their organizations want them to have. That is, either they do not receive the information or they do not understand it. This may result from employees receiving too much information (e.g., e-mail proliferation) and not being able to differentiate between essential and nonessential information. Thus, leaders must use multiple methods of communication: formal (as already listed) and informal (e.g., one-on-one meetings, small group meetings, phone conversations, hallway chats). Leaders must repeat key information over time and in many different ways. This is especially critical during times of significant change within organizations, as employees often hear and interpret communications through their own anxieties, and even through their own worst fears.

An effective communication strategy is built on these five steps:

Step	What is needed	Key questions for leaders
❶ Outcome	Be clear on what is to be achieved.	*What do we want employees to do as a result of their receiving this information?*
❷ Messages	Put statements in easily understood language.	*What key information do employees need?*
❸ Context	Information is made relevant by connecting it to current organizational situations or goals.	*Why is it important for employees to understand and act on this information?*
❹ Reinforcement	Information is communicated more than once and in more than one way.	*What other methods should we use to ensure that employees understand essential information?*
❺ Feedback	Get input from employees on the outcome and the process of the communication.	*How was the information received and what impact did it have?*

HOW TO USE THIS LEADERSHIP TOOL

"Communications is not our core business, but a strategy to help us achieve our goals. It underlies everything we do, and is a skill that all leaders need for success."

—CEO, major oil and gas company

Leaders often need to communicate with large and geographically dispersed groups of employees. Here is an example of effective leadership communication that will help you think through how you might manage communications within your organization. The General Manager of a production facility announced a new health and safety program, with the objective of getting buy-in and active cooperation from all plant employees. The problem was that employees operated in round-the-clock shifts and were not available at one time, or in one place, to receive the information. The communication process the General Manager used proved to be successful. It demonstrates the effective use of multiple methods of communication, repeated over time.

⟹ The General Manager introduced the new health and safety program at an employee "town hall meeting," articulating the vision, context, and goals for the program.

⟹ The Health and Safety Manager reinforced this message, providing further information at many workgroup and team meetings.

⟹ The program was discussed at the monthly health and safety meeting of team leaders.

⟹ All employees received a memo about the new program, distributed through individual mail slots.

⟹ A notice was circulated to all shift supervisors, asking them to bring the new program to the attention of employees at the start of their shifts.

⟹ A supporting e-mail was distributed, and the same information was posted on bulletin boards.

⟹ The original information was reinforced with supporting messages for the next several months, to ensure that the new program was well understood.

WEB WORKSHEET

Use the template provided to plan your leadership communication strategy.

❶ **Outcome** (Be clear on what is to be achieved.)	*What do you want employees to do as a result of their receiving this information?* [☛ 2.4 Visioning, 2.6 Clarifying Purpose, 2.7 Goal Statements]
❷ **Messages** (Develop clear statements in easily understood language.)	*What key information do employees need?* [☛ 8.2 Direct Communication, 9.6 Presentations, 9.7 Selling Wheel]
❸ **Context** (Make the information relevant by connecting it to the current organizational situation or goals.)	*Why is it important for employees to understand and act on this information?* [☛ 5.1 Change Equation, 5.8 Human Transitions]
❹ **Reinforcement** (Ensure that information is communicated more than once and in more than one way.)	*What other methods should you use to ensure that employees understand essential information?* [☛ 10.7 Getting Participation]
❺ **Feedback** (Get feedback from employees on the effectiveness of your communications.)	*How did employees receive the information and what impact did it have on them?* [☛ 12.4 Feedback]

RELATED LEADERSHIP TOOLS

1.2 Manage or Lead?	5.1 Change Equation	9.1 Leadership Versatility
2.7 Goal Statements	5.2 Major Change	10.6 Group Leader Skills
4.4 Employee Involvement	8.2 Direct Communication	11.1 Process Cycle

FOR FURTHER ASSISTANCE

Covey, Stephen. *The Seven Habits of Highly Effective People: Powerful Lessons in Personal Change.* Simon & Schuster, 1989.

Weisinger, Hendrie. *Emotional Intelligence at Work: The Untapped Edge for Success.* Jossey-Bass Publishers, 1998.

8.4

LEVELS OF COMMUNICATING:
DEBATE, DIALOGUE, AND DISCUSSION

Inspired by Peter Senge, Richard Ross, Bryan Smith, Charlotte Roberts, and Art Kleiner.

It's important for a leader to differentiate among debate, discussion, and dialogue, all distinct processes with different communication purposes. One way to clarify them is to visualize all three along a continuum on which the communication purpose ranges from:

➡ winning—as in debate, to

➡ deciding—as in discussion, to

➡ gaining mutual understanding and shared commitment—as in dialogue.

| **Debate** *Beating down* | **Discussion** *Taking apart* | **Dialogue** *Building together* |

Debate is a contest with words. It's about winning or losing. Thus, people defend their views and avoid evidence that would weaken their positions. This communication process may have limited uses when an organization is faced with an either–or situation. In most cases, leaders do not want to produce winners and losers; thus the next two communication processes are more useful. [For more information on either–or situations see ☞ 7.4 Polarities.]

Discussion is about surfacing difficult issues, the data underlying these issues, and the reasoning that supports various positions. The communication purpose is to analyze, decide, and achieve closure (e.g., to make a decision, reach an agreement, or identify a set of priorities).

Successful discussion requires that the leader:

❑ Provide clarity about what you want in order to avoid misleading others about your intentions.

❑ Outline an agenda and context for the discussion to ensure a single focus and minimal distractions.

❑ Develop a meeting climate with a high level of openness and trust.

❑ Balance advocacy and inquiry during the discussion.

❑ Ensure understanding and agreement through summarizing.

❑ Stay conscious of and challenge your own awareness, thinking, and emotions, as well as the group's.

❑ Explore impasses and encourage new perspectives by asking questions such as, "What do we agree on?" or "What do we disagree on?" or "Can we pinpoint the source of disagreement (e.g., facts, methods, goals, values)?"

Dialogue is about thinking together. It involves balancing advocacy with inquiry and broadening the focus of conversations. In dialogue, people question the total process of thought and feeling that produced the issue or conflict. Elements of successful dialogue include:

✔ inviting or giving people the choice to participate;

✔ generative listening, whereby people quiet their inner voices and listen for deeper meaning in what others are expressing, saying, or feeling;

✔ self-awareness and ability to understand how you and group members see the world;

✔ a willingness to surface and inquire into the assumptions behind one's thinking, to refrain from imposing one's views on others, and yet not to hold back what one is thinking.

Successful dialogue requires that the leader:

❑ Use an external facilitator, or act as the group facilitator himself or herself. The process is initially unfamiliar to many and often surfaces challenging emotions and misunderstandings.

❑ Recognize that you can't force dialogue, but you can create an environment that promotes collective inquiry.

❑ Allow the process to work without a specific outcome in mind. (Dialogue will fail if it is rushed or directed toward decision making.)

❑ Maintain a high level of self- and group awareness. (Pay attention to what is happening within the group and within yourself, by taking time-outs to discuss how the dialogue process is going.)

❑ Explore all disagreements, even those that appear to be minor, using them as opportunities for improved understanding within the group.

How to use this leadership tool

"… the word 'dialogue' comes from the Greek dialogos. Dia *means through.* Logos *means the word, or more broadly, meaning. … The result is a free exploration that brings to the surface the full depth of people's experience and thought, and yet can move beyond their individual views."*

—Peter Senge et al, *THE FIFTH DISCIPLINE FIELDBOOK: STRATEGIES AND TOOLS FOR BUILDING A LEARNING ORGANIZATION*

When a challenging issue is raised in a workgroup or team (e.g., a new business strategy), emotions are raised, people can espouse polarized and mutually exclusive positions, and differences can seem irreconcilable. A leader or group facilitator, skilled in leading groups through dialogue, can help them reach a better understanding of each other's underlying values, assumptions, and perspectives. Through facilitated dialogue, entrenched and strongly held underlying assumptions can be surfaced, allowing the group to move to a new level of understanding, to develop new options for action, and to achieve a consensus that members might have thought impossible prior to participating in facilitated dialogue.

Use these charts as a checklist when preparing for a discussion or dialogue within your workgroup or team.

Discussion	Dialogue
Purpose __ to analyze and decide **Preparation** __ Pay attention to your intentions. __ Be clear about what you want. __ Plan the agenda and context for discussion. __ Create a safe haven (openness and trust are essential). __ Balance advocacy with inquiry. __ Build shared meaning (recognize that words are abstractions). __ Use self-awareness as a resource. (Ask yourself: "What am I feeling?" (Pause.) "What do I want at this moment?" (Pause.) __ Explore impasses and encourage new perspectives. (Ask, "What do we agree on?" and "What do we disagree on?") **Outcomes** __ Decisions are made. __ People leave with priorities and work assignments.	**Purpose** __ to balance advocacy with inquiry __ to discover the nature of choices and options **Elements** __ invitation (People are given the choice to participate.) __ generative listening (Listen for deeper meanings.) __ self-observation and introspection __ surfacing and inquiring into assumptions (Describe what's behind one's thinking; refrain from imposing views on others.) **Principles** __ Use a facilitator, as the process is initially unfamiliar and surfaces difficult misunderstandings. __ Start with techniques, then leave them behind. (You can't force understanding, but you can create conditions under which dialogue can occur.) __ Create a safe place to take a risk. __ Let things evolve. (Have a focus, but no specific outcome, in mind.) __ Be self- and group aware. (Pay attention to what is happening within the group and within yourself.) __ Use disagreement as an opportunity. (Explore differences, even though they may not be easily resolved.) **Outcomes** __ Deeper understanding __ Foundation for team decision making

RELATED LEADERSHIP TOOLS

1.6 Boards of Play	8.5 Metacommunicating	9.5 Negotiation
5.9 Resistance	8.6 Communication 101	12.6 Confrontation

FOR FURTHER ASSISTANCE

Senge, Peter M., Richard Ross, Bryan Smith, Charlotte Roberts, and Art Kleiner. *The Fifth Discipline Fieldbook: Strategies and Tools for Building a Learning Organization.* Currency Doubleday, 1994.

8.5 Metacommunicating: Talking about Talking

Inspired by Deborah Tannen.

On occasion, communication results in a deadlock such that neither party feels understood by the other. The most common response in these situations is more of the same communication, which isn't working. As a result, things can get even worse! When communication itself feels like part of the problem, invite the other person to talk about how you are both talking.

Talking about how you are talking is known as metacommunication, and can be an invaluable skill when misunderstandings are present and emotions are running high. For example, when a conversation is getting bogged down, you can intervene by simply saying, "I think this conversation is getting off track. How can we get it back on track?" Or, when negative emotions and conflict surface, you can say, "I don't want to butt heads with you. Can we talk about the impasse we seem to be heading into?" Note that these invitations to metacommunicate are best handled in direct and straightforward language. This is not the time to be metaphorical or philosophical. Your goal is to invite the others to talk about how you are all talking. Most people will respond at this meta level, and talk with you about the communication problem. You can then use this higher-level discussion (the metacommunication) to help solve the original problem.

An example of how metacommunication works

1. There is a disagreement or misunderstanding at the content level. That is, people are not agreeing on the issues, facts, data, essential features, promises that have been made, and so on.

    Example: You and the other person are disagreeing on the time it takes to complete a given phase of a project.

2. Move up a level to discuss the process of how you are discussing the content; that is, how you and the other person are dealing with this issue.

    Example: Ask something like, "Can we step back for a moment? We seem to be stuck on the project timeline, but the way we're talking about this is causing us to get dug into different positions. Can we talk for a minute about *how* we're talking about this problem?"

3. After discussing the difficulty at the process level and agreeing on principles for communicating, go back down to the content level and try again to resolve the issue, this time using the newly agreed-upon principles for communicating.

The exact wording is situational, but there are certain characteristics of an effective invitation to metacommunicate:

✔ A metacommunication starts by discontinuing communication at the current deadlock (the content level). Note that the behavior and frustration you are displaying yourself and seeing in the other person are only symptoms of something more fundamental.

✔ Be careful about ascribing negative motives to another person's behavior. People have habitual ways of dealing with situations, and they are probably not conscious of their own behavior or motives.

✔ Metacommunication invites the other to discuss the issue at a higher level (the process level). Discuss the communication difficulty, and establish some communication guidelines or principles for dealing with the disagreement at hand.

✔ The assumption behind metacommunication is that there is goodwill on both sides, that difficulties are due to unclear assumptions and lack of clarity of process, rather than to any planned or intentional attempt to trick the other person.

HOW TO USE THIS LEADERSHIP TOOL

"Conversational style isn't something extra, added on like frosting on a cake. It's the very stuff of which the communication cake is made."

—Deborah Tannen, *THAT'S NOT WHAT I MEANT*

Most leaders will have plenty of opportunity to use this tool. When communication starts to break down in a workgroup, for example, it can deteriorate quite quickly. It can begin to feel as if every conversation is tense and ends in frustration. This downward spiral can often be reversed if one of the parties to these conversations stands back and identifies what is happening in terms of the communication process itself. This is done by separating *what* is being discussed (the content level) from *how* it is being discussed (the process level).

WEB WORKSHEET

Metacommunication doesn't always work, but when it works, it works wonders! Use the worksheet provided to plan metacommunications to improve any difficult communication that you are currently or may soon be involved with. This might include:

1. situations in which you are expected to mediate disagreements within teams or workgroups;

2. situations in which you overhear others getting into communication difficulties; and

3. team-building sessions in which team members are having difficulty understanding each other or arriving at a team decision.

Situation	What specifically will you say to invite people to metacommunicate?

RELATED LEADERSHIP TOOLS

8.1 Conversations

8.2 Direct Communication

8.6 Communication 101

12.4 Feedback

12.6 Confrontation

12.7 Dealing with Conflict

FOR FURTHER ASSISTANCE

Argyris, Chris. *Flawed Advice and the Management Trap.* Oxford University Press, 2000.

Tannen, Deborah. *Talking from 9 to 5: Women and Men in the Workplace: Language, Sex, and Power.* Avon Books, 1995.

Tannen, Deborah. *That's Not What I Meant: How Conversational Style Makes or Breaks Relationships.* Ballantine Books, 1991.

Tannen, Deborah. *You Just Don't Understand: Women and Men in Conversation.* Ballantine Books, 1990.

8.6 COMMUNICATION 101: DEALING EFFECTIVELY WITH FEELINGS AT WORK

Inspired by Stephen Covey, Dave Irvine, Jon Katzenbach, Douglas Smith, and Deborah Tannen.

By the very nature of their work, leaders must help others to work through the conflicts and difficult emotions that inevitably arise in the course of working within groups, particularly groups that often have to struggle with time and other work pressures. This tool provides a range of approaches and how-to's for doing just that.

Proactive Skills:

❑ Establish ground rules early in your team's formation. Taking preventative action is nearly always easier than dealing with problems. [☞ 10.8 Ground Rules]

❑ Take time-outs to discuss how you are talking. From time to time, difficulties with communication require metacommunication. [☞ 8.5 Metacommunicating]

❑ Recognize your biases and assumptions; be cognizant of others' assumptions, interpersonal style, biases, perspectives, and cultural differences. [☞ 6.2 Assumption Analysis, 13.6 Attribution Theory]

Listening Skills:

❑ Rephrase or summarize before reacting. Most people handle critique of their ideas better if they feel that the other person has at least heard them. Listening is your ticket to talk.

❑ Listen at three levels: a) content—what is being said, b) process—how it is being dealt with, and c) emotion—the other person's feelings about the situation. [☞ 8.7 Active Listening, 8.8 Listening Techniques]

❑ Separate understanding from agreement. Understanding does not mean agreement.

Feedback Skills:

❑ Feedback is usually better received when it is a) factual (use concrete examples); b) specific; c) descriptive of your own feelings (not what you *think* the other person is feeling); and d) given soon after the feedback incident. [☞ 12.4 Feedback]

❑ Recognize people when they say or do something you appreciate. People will accept negative feedback better from a person who also gives positive feedback. [☞ 12.5 Negative Feedback]

❑ As a leader, model receiving feedback openly and nondefensively. Feedback is given in proportion to how well it is received. Rationalizing feedback or explaining away the behavior will usually be perceived as defensive. [☞ 15.6 Defenses]

❑ Praise in public; reprimand in private. Understandably, adults will defend their self-esteem and reputation beyond all else.

Empathy:

- ❑ Positions and expressed emotions can be better dealt with by trying to understand the other person's underlying needs. "Seek first to understand, then to be understood."
- ❑ Understand and honor the other person's point of view before you confront or state your differing point of view. [☞ 8.7 Active Listening]

Conflict:

- ❑ Recognize that conflict is inevitable, and that the ability to express, deal with, and resolve conflict is a good measure of an effective team.
- ❑ Deal with conflict when it is in the "pinch" stage (like a pain when it's starting to hurt). Conflict is much more difficult to handle in the "crunch" stage (when the pain gets out of control).
- ❑ Conflict is best dealt with by getting it out in the open. Suppressed conflict doesn't disappear; it is often felt and expressed in undesirable behavior. [☞ 12.6 Confrontation, 12.7 Dealing with Conflict]

And Some More:

- ❑ "You can fix things, but you can't fix people." Don't try to fix other people's feelings (especially with logic).
- ❑ Very often, leaders deal with problems in the way that created the problem in the first place. "More of the same" rarely works with feelings. Metacommunicate by stepping outside the problem. Focus on the problem, not on the persons.
- ❑ Get third-party help if you or your workgroup get stuck in conflict.

How to use this leadership tool

"Conflict … is a necessary part of becoming a real team. Seldom do we see a group of individuals forge their unique experiences, perspectives, values, and expectations into a common purpose, set of performance goals, and approach without encountering significant conflict. And the most challenging risks associated with conflict relate to making it constructive for the team instead of simply enduring it."

—J. Katzenbach and D. Smith, *THE WISDOM OF TEAMS*

Having a highly talented group of individuals in a work team sounds like a desirable situation, doesn't it? The tendency is to forge ahead and maximize the team's talent to get the job done. A leader is often shocked when the team starts to bicker, some actually sabotaging the success of others. Strangely enough, hiring the brightest people for innovative and groundbreaking work usually requires considerable time in building understanding and relationships within the team. Above all, the team members need to be able to see the advantage of doing their work as a team; that is, coordinating their activities and talents, rather than simply working as a group of individuals and pooling their output. [☞ 10.1 HiPo Teams]

Use the workspace provided to assess your workgroup or team's performance in dealing with feelings at work. If possible, involve your workgroup or team in this assessment.

WEB WORKSHEET

List strengths that your workgroup or team has shown in dealing with feelings at work.

Briefly summarize a couple of examples of these strengths.

Briefly summarize a couple of examples of weaknesses.

What steps can you, as a leader, take to encourage continued development of these strengths, and to address weaknesses?

What improvements are needed in how your workgroup or team deals with feelings at work?

Briefly summarize a couple of examples that illustrate this development need.

What two or three steps can you take, as a leader, to ensure that members are provided the opportunity to make needed improvements in how they handle feelings at work?

RELATED LEADERSHIP TOOLS

8.5 Metacommunicating	10.8 Ground Rules	12.6 Confrontation
8.7 Active Listening	12.4 Feedback	12.7 Dealing with Conflict

FOR FURTHER ASSISTANCE

Covey, Stephen. *The Seven Habits of Highly Effective People: Powerful Lessons in Personal Change.* Simon & Schuster, 1989.

Irvine, David. *Simple Living in a Complex World: Balancing Life's Achievements.* RedStone Ventures Inc, 1997.

Katzenbach, Jon, and Douglas Smith. *The Wisdom of Teams: Creating the High-Performance Organization.* HarperBusiness, 1993.

Tannen, Deborah. *Talking from 9 to 5: Women and Men in the Workplace: Language, Sex, and Power.* Avon Books, 1995.

Tannen, Deborah. *That's Not What I Meant: How Conversational Style Makes or Breaks Relationships.* Ballantine Books, 1991.

8.7

ACTIVELY LISTENING FOR CONTENT, FEELING, AND MEANING

Inspired by David Godfrey, Carl Rogers, and Stephen Covey.

Human nature being what it is, we tend to take rigid positions when emotions are running high. As such, stress and conflict can cause a leader's listening skills to wane. The steps listed here build on each other, and will help you develop an extra antenna for hearing others, even in stressful times.

1. *Set the physical and mental stage for good listening*. Physical: Arrange the physical aspects of a room for optimal listening. Mental: Clear your mind to allow room to focus on what the other person is saying.

2. *Prepare your ears and eyes for listening*. Research suggests that words represent only about 10 to 15 percent of people's communication. Most information is contained in the nonverbal aspects of the communication—tone of voice, rate of speech, eye contact, body posture, gestures, and so on.

3. *Keep appropriate silence*. Remaining quiet at appropriate times can yield surprisingly positive results. Given an extra few seconds, another person might just go a level deeper. Also, give people at least about 50 percent of the airtime. It's an excellent way of modeling how you would like to be heard.

4. *Ask good questions*. Ask questions that allow and encourage people to arrive at their own analyses and solutions. This is a particularly powerful form of communication known as the Socratic method. The ancient Greeks honed this method to perfection. Asking thoughtful questions also shows that you are listening deeply.

5. *Listen for content*. The content is the *what* of the problem; the process is the *how*. By content, we mean the technical or business part of a problem (i.e., the facts) as distinct from the process—how the problem is being solved. A bread-and-butter skill for leaders is actively listening at the content level.

6. *Listen for process*. Listening to process means listening to *how* a person is solving the problem—the steps being taken to reach a solution. Many leaders prefer to stay in the comfort zone of content, often jumping to causes, solutions, and action. Actively listening to process as well as to content, however, allows a leader to provide both good content advice and effective process suggestions. After all, effective process is the very essence of leadership, whether a planning process, an interpersonal process, or a problem-solving process.

7. *Listen for emotion*. No matter the concern—accounting problems, systems difficulties, maintenance issues—human emotions will be involved. Not infrequently, people have difficulty expressing their emotions during stressful moments (e.g., when disappointment or anger is expressed). This is a moment of truth for a leader, not a time to deny, downplay, or ignore the situation. Leaders can learn how to be comfortable when emotions are running high. Since you can process information at a faster rate than others

can speak, use the extra processing time to listen intently for the emotion in the situation. One way to encourage people to express their emotions is to name them: "It seems that you get frustrated when … ." It's difficult to solve problems rationally, and impossible to reach true consensus, if emotions are being disguised or not allowed honest expression.

How to use this leadership tool

"… a man hears what he wants to hear and disregards the rest."

—Simon and Garfunkel, "THE BOXER"

After you have completed this self-assessment, ask a few coworkers to rate you on your listening skills. Then compare their ratings with your own.

WEB WORKSHEET

Rate yourself from 1 = Needs a lot of improvement, to 5 = A definite strength.

1. Setting the physical and mental stage for good listening:
1 2 3 4 5   I do not allow the telephone to interfere with listening.
1 2 3 4 5   Before a meeting, I make notes about what I want to say, so during the meeting I can concentrate on what others are saying.
1 2 3 4 5   During a meeting, I make notes about how I want to respond, keeping my mind free during the meeting to hear the other person's words.
1 2 3 4 5   I seat myself in a way that encourages listening.
1 2 3 4 5   I realize most people can only keep about seven items in their short-term memory at any one time.

2. Listening with my eyes:
1 2 3 4 5   I make eye contact early and maintain an appropriate level of eye contact.
1 2 3 4 5   I am conscious of and sensitive to another person's nonverbal behaviors.
1 2 3 4 5   I use nonverbal clues to help me assess appropriate replies.
1 2 3 4 5   I am conscious of cultural differences in nonverbal behavior, particularly eye contact.

3. Appropriate silence:
1 2 3 4 5   I give others time to complete their thoughts.
1 2 3 4 5   I give others airtime.
1 2 3 4 5   I am conscious of and okay with periods of silence.
1 2 3 4 5   I can remain silent to help others formulate and state deeper thoughts and feelings.

4. Asking good questions:
1 2 3 4 5   I ask questions to show that I am listening.
1 2 3 4 5   I ask questions to help others talk through issues.
1 2 3 4 5   I am aware of the range of questions, from closed-ended to open-ended, and know when to use them.

5. Actively listening to content:

1 2 3 4 5   I consciously use summarizing and paraphrasing to clarify my understanding, before I give my point of view.

1 2 3 4 5   I am aware of the difference between stating an observation and making an evaluation.

1 2 3 4 5   I am able to name problems in a way that does not make them personal.

1 2 3 4 5   I am aware of the difference between listening to content and listening for process.

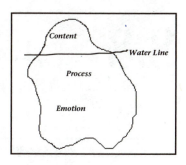

6. Listening for process:

1 2 3 4 5   I understand when to respond to process; that is, how we are dealing with the concern (as opposed to content).

1 2 3 4 5   I am able to metacommunicate; that is, talk about what we are talking about. [☞ 8.5 Metacommunicating]

1 2 3 4 5   I understand the power of framing and reframing, and can help others reframe issues or concerns when appropriate. [☞ 7.1 Problem Framing]

7. Listening for emotions:

1 2 3 4 5   I can hear the emotion in another person's words, voice, tone, and other nonverbals, and reflect that emotion back to the person.

1 2 3 4 5   I know when it is appropriate to make a listening response to other people's emotions.

1 2 3 4 5   I know I cannot fix emotions, I can only help people express them more clearly.

8. Listening overall:

1 2 3 4 5   I often ask for feedback on my listening skills.

RELATED LEADERSHIP TOOLS

1.8 Recursive Leadership	8.5 Metacommunicating	8.8 Listening Techniques
8.1 Conversations	8.6 Communication 101	12.4 Feedback

FOR FURTHER ASSISTANCE

Covey, Stephen. *The Seven Habits of Highly Effective People: Powerful Lessons in Personal Change.* Simon & Schuster, 1989.

8.8

LISTENING TECHNIQUES: TACTICS TO IMPROVE YOUR LISTENING

Inspired by Carl Rogers, Chris Argyris, Donald Schon, and numerous other sources.

Listening occurs at many levels, and thus leaders need a wide repertoire of listening responses. Adapt these examples to your unique situation.

Listening technique	Purposes	Typical listening lead-ins
Reassuring	• To show that you are interested • To encourage others to continue talking	➤ *"Mmm …" or "Uh-huh."* ➤ *"That's interesting."* ➤ *"I understand" or "I see."*
Restating & Paraphrasing	• To check your interpretation against that of the other person • To demonstrate that you are listening and that you understand what the other person is saying • To encourage others to analyze deeper aspects of the situation and discuss them with you.	➤ *"As I understand it, your plan is …"* ➤ *"You appear to have decided to …"* ➤ *"So, your reasons for favoring this option are …"*
Summarizing	• To bring the discussion into focus • To clarify priorities • To help you and the other person agree on major points	➤ *"In summary, the key ideas you have expressed are …"* ➤ *"If I understand how you see the situation, your major points are …"* ➤ *"As I see it, we have agreed to …"*
Clarifying Content	• To get at additional information • To help others explore a problem • To help others clarify their ideas • To make ideas more concrete	➤ *"I'm not sure I understand; could you clarify …?"* ➤ *"Do you mean …?"* ➤ *"I don't understand. Could you give me an example of …?"*
Clarifying Process	• To clarify how the situation will be dealt with • To formulate a method for dealing with the issue • To propose a method for dealing with the issue	➤ *"As I understand it, you are proposing xyz. Can we step back and …?"* ➤ *"You have proposed gathering information on the issue. Can we clarify the issue first?"* ➤ *"You have given me a lot of data about the problem. Can we talk for a moment about how we can proceed to solve the problem?"*
Showing Empathy	• To show that you understand how the other person feels about the situation • To help another express his or her feelings • To clarify feelings and commitment	➤ *"You appear to feel that …"* ➤ *"You seemed shocked when you heard…"* ➤ *"You seemed let down when …"*

How to use this leadership tool

Consider this example: You're leading a group of technical specialists. Although all are experts in their area, they have not had much direct experience with the organization's customers. Yet increasingly, they are being asked to work directly with customers. A crucial element of their success will be their ability to listen to the customer before suggesting solutions. This tool will help them develop their listening skills, resulting in more successful customer contact.

WEB WORKSHEET

Choose a couple of situations in which you or those you lead will be asked to listen deeply (e.g., in working with customers, within the workgroup, with a senior manager on an important project). Use the workspace provided to develop typical lead-in questions that will help ensure effective communication in these situations.

Typical listening situation	Best technique	Typical lead-in that you might use

Related leadership tools

8.1 Conversations	8.5 Metacommunicating	15.2 Emotional Intelligence
8.4 Dialogue and Discussion	8.7 Active Listening	15.4 Ladder of Inference

For further assistance

Argyris, Chris. *Freedom to Learn*. Merrill, 1969.

Argyris, Chris. "Good Communication That Blocks Learning." *Harvard Business Review*. July–August 1994, 77–85.

Argyris, Chris. "Teaching Smart People How to Learn." *Harvard Business Review*. May–June 1991, 99–109.

Argyris, Chris, and Donald A. Schon. *Organizational Learning: A Theory of Action Perspective*. Addison-Wesley, 1978.

Argyris, Chris, and Donald A. Schon. *Theory in Practice: Increasing Professional Effectiveness*. Jossey-Bass, 1992.

Rogers, Carl. *Freedom to Learn*. Merrill, 1969.

8.9 CROSS-CULTURAL COMMUNICATION

Inspired by John MacIonis, Nijole Benokraitis, Terri Morrison, Wayne Conaway, George Borden, and Hans Koehler.

With organizations becoming increasingly global and workforces becoming more culturally diverse, leaders often find themselves dealing with unfamiliar values, attitudes, and behaviors. These can prove hard to read, leaving a leader uncertain as to how to handle unfamiliar behavior and how to support and integrate much-needed cross-cultural contributions within a workgroup. This tool will help you recognize some subtle cultural cues. It will also encourage you to think about the cultural values that you assume to be natural and normal. Finally, suggestions are provided for dealing with cross-cultural differences within organizations.

Strange as it may seem, in order to understand your reactions to unfamiliar cultural behaviors, the first thing you need to do is examine your own givens, values, norms, and comfort zone—as well as what is *not* comfortable for you. In any part of the world, the workplace is rooted in a cultural context, whether it be the Confucian orderliness of Singapore or the extroverted expressiveness of Brazil. There are no exceptions to this: Every country, organization, and department has a culture that is expressed as "the way we do things around here." Thus, much of the way leaders conduct business is couched in a commonly accepted and assumed cultural context, in which they are comfortable, recognize the cultural signals, know how to behave, and can be confident that their colleagues share this context.

> *"All good people agree*
> *And all good people say*
> *All nice people like us, are WE*
> *And everyone else is THEY."*
>
> —Rudyard Kipling

Here are just a few examples of what leaders in the United States and Canada typically find acceptable and unacceptable.

Generally acceptable in the USA and Canada	Generally not acceptable in the USA and Canada	Other cultural norms
• Shake hands at first meeting. • Make eye contact with people.	• Any touching, other than shaking hands, might be considered improper (even by human rights legislation). • Public affection is generally taboo.	• In many cultures, bowing or kissing and touching are expected. • In others, direct eye contact may be considered disrespectful, even aggressive.
• Present ideas logically. Ask questions in a logical way, without emotion, and concentrating on facts. • Logical and organized dialogue is highly valued.	• Presenting ideas or asking emotionally. • Crying or expressing emotions demonstrably. • Demonstrating anger.	• In many Latin and African cultures, extroversion and emotion are highly valued and seen as powerful. People from the U.S. and Canada are often seen as being overly reserved and up-tight.

• Getting down to work immediately, without much personal talk. • Life and personal status are often defined by one's work.	• Spending a lot of time building rapport. Working long hours and producing results are highly valued. Talking to get to know the other person is not. • Using work time for personal purposes is not okay.	• Many cultures view daily greetings and meetings almost with reverence, as an opportunity to connect with a colleague or acquaintance and to relate how life is going for both of them.
• Being punctual for work, meetings, and back from lunch.	• Being late for anything at work is not okay, especially if new to a workgroup or in a junior position relative to other group members.	• In many cultures, the concept of time is flexible and not considered a big deal.
• Being organized; bringing paper, pen, and relevant materials to meetings.	• Looking disorganized. • Talking off the top of your head or speaking out of order at a meeting (especially if in a junior position).	• In many cultures, spontaneity is highly valued and is seen as a positive sign of immediate interest.
• Earning respect by working hard, contributing to business results, and showing personal integrity.	• Resting on your laurels, be this reputation, qualifications, breeding, inherited wealth, etc.	• Many societies are person-based, so qualifications, family, etc. lend credibility.

Hᴏᴡ ᴛᴏ ᴜsᴇ ᴛʜɪs ʟᴇᴀᴅᴇʀsʜɪᴘ ᴛᴏᴏʟ

"But if you cross over the sea,
Instead of over the way
You may end by looking on WE
As only a sort of THEY!"

—Rudyard Kipling

The most common reason why leaders make cross-cultural gaffes is that they are not aware of their own cultural or organizational norms. If you are faced with behavior that you find strange or that you or your workgroup find annoying, before talking to the individual, try to figure out where you yourself are coming from. What is it that you value in this situation, and that the offending person should be doing differently? Most commonly, this is expressed as annoyance, as in, "What is wrong with Pat? The meeting notice clearly stated that we begin at 3 p.m.!"

WEB WORKSHEET

Here is but one of many possible applications for this tool—as a process for coaching a new employee on the culture of your workgroup.

Step 1: With a specific situation and person in mind, complete all three columns.

Summarize the inappropriate or offensive behavior.	Describe which value of yours (or your workgroup) is being violated.	What cultural value might be guiding this individual's behavior?
(e.g., lowering eyes when spoken to)		

(e.g., speaking out of turn in meetings, acting superior)		
(e.g., boasting about past accomplishments and qualifications)		

Step 2: Coach the individual on culturally appropriate behavior. [☞ 13.1 Coaching]

Having completed this homework does not necessarily mean you should now confront the offending individual directly. In many cultures (including North America, in less obvious ways), directness or confrontation causes the offender to lose face. It might now be appropriate to set your homework aside, as coaching from a written text is seen in many parts of the world as serious, condemning, and permanent.

Next, follow these three tips:

a. **Where to say it:**   Take the person out for coffee or lunch in some private place.

b. **How to say it:**   Exchange pleasantries and show interest in learning about the other person's culture.

c. **What to say:**   Gently discuss the cultural differences at issue (i.e., the content of the three columns above). Do this verbally. Don't use written notes.

Related leadership tools

8.1 Conversations	12.4 Feedback	14.7 Personal Preferences
8.5 Metacommunicating	13.6 Attribution Theory	15.3 JoHari Window
8.7 Active Listening	14.6 Learning Styles	15.4 Ladder of Inference

For further assistance

MacIonis, John, and Nijole V. Benokraitis. *Seeing Ourselves: Classic, Contemporary, and Cross-Cultural Readings*. Prentice Hall, 1997.

Morrison, Terri, Wayne A. Conaway, George A. Borden, and Hans Koehler. *Kiss, Bow, or Shake Hands: How to Do Business in 60 Countries*. Adams Media Corporation, 1995.

Culture Shock: A Guide to Customs and Etiquette. This Graphic Arts Center Publishing Company series of books, one per country, is an excellent source of cross-cultural information.

8.10   MEDIA RELATIONS FOR LEADERS

Contributed by Eilis Hiebert and inspired by John Wade and numerous other sources.

Today's speed-of-light media can have a more powerful effect on an organization than at any time in history. Positive or negative, media look for newsworthy stories about environmental responsibility, chemical spills, human interest, downsizing, and especially crises. The media can make or break your organization's image. The way your organization is portrayed in the media can greatly influence public opinion, whether from a "good community citizen" point of view or from unfair reporting.

The media sometimes becomes the source of critical information for employees. Unfortunately, they may hear it first in mass media, rather than directly from their employer. Negative media coverage can have an impact on your employees. It can influence their morale and how they feel about the organization as an employer.

Ideally, your organization should have a media strategy and effective leadership for corporate and media communications. However, in reality, organizations have varying commitments to communication, from a separate communications department; to specific individuals responsible for public relations, communications, media, newsletter, and news items; to each department communicating its own message. Some organizations simply do not place a high value on developing positive media relationships.

Your organization needs to take charge of its portrayal in the media. This tool will provide basic tips on how to work effectively with the media, at both a planning level and a tactical one.

LONG-TERM MEDIA PLANNING

Media strategy should connect to business goals. Otherwise, why have a strategy? The connection could be to customer and community relations, to support investor relations, or to support fund-raising in the example of a nonprofit. Media relations means knowing the attributes of news, to *help the media get a story* and *help your organization get a story out*. Whatever your situation, as a leader, you need to be media-savvy. You need to be aware of your organization's media strategy and be able to get the right resources in place for an effective media relations program. This table presents a two-way symmetrical model for media planning.

What to do inside your organization	How to become media-savy
✔ Put in place a media strategy and media training, and identify spokespeople well in advance of when you need them. (Part of this is so you have a crisis plan in place, and your organization is ready to respond to any eventuality.) ✔ Most organizations prefer to have one consistent spokesperson deal with the media all the time, or it's the CEO's job. This should not stop you from hooking	❑ Help reporters cover your organization. Don't try to do it for them. Reporters strongly resist being told what to report. ❑ Establish direct contact with journalists, at both their initiative and yours. Call journalists when you think you have a story that may interest them. ❑ Set up interviews for journalists with management or specialists in your organization.

into the official system. Make communications a priority in your area. Don't wait until you *need* the media.

✔ Develop your *own* media awareness: Become media savvy, noticing the kinds of news items covered about businesses, organizations, and issues that might have relevance to your organization, and become familiar with the reporters who cover them. In this way, you will become aware of media possibilities and can communicate them to others.

✔ Build a mutually beneficial business relationship with the media. Reporters and writers, like most people, reciprocate care with care.

❑ Send the media a sheet of one-paragraph news tips that reporters can follow up themselves.

❑ Make sure that stories about your organization have a local angle or content, and are relevant to the reporter's publication.

❑ Be *available* to the media. Don't wait until you *need* the media; maintain contact.

❑ Keep media contact lists up to date.

❑ Set up an information storage and retrieval system in which you maintain fact sheets, complete articles, interviews, background information, photos, and stock video footage. Tell journalists what is in this system, and that they can have access to it whenever they wish. Update the information regularly.

❑ In the case of a crisis, have a designated spokesperson; brief that person immediately.

SOME TACTICS OF MEDIA RELATIONS

Four questions form the base of media thinking, or media savvy:

? *Who* to reach?
? *How* to reach them?
? *What* to say?
? *What* is in it for them?

There are many tactics to use when considering the answers to these questions, including:

❑ media conferences, for big news;
❑ media briefings, media availability sessions, and media conference calls;
❑ news releases or pitch letters, for items you want covered;
❑ interviews with relevant people;
❑ tours of your facility;
❑ public service announcements (PSAs), usually for nonprofits only;
❑ reaction to unfair reporting;
❑ feature stories to publicize what you want featured; and
❑ crisis communication.

If you have to write for any of the above, or approve them, or have them written:

1. Decide on the message.
2. Use short sentences and good paragraphs.
3. Use simple, familiar words.

See ☛ 8.2 Direct Communication tool for more information on large-scale communications.

HOW TO USE THIS LEADERSHIP TOOL

"… key to good media relations strategy is to make the newsperson's job easy. That is, give him [her] news of substance, with facts [s]he can rely on—all this conveniently packaged and delivered in good time."

—Richard Detweiler, Public Relations Consultant

The media tends to be thought of as an entity in itself, yet the media is made up of individuals trying their best to do a good job, just as you are. Remember that what makes news is events and situations that are newsworthy. Since you probably read at least one daily newspaper or magazine and watch or listen to electronic media, you yourself, as a leader, can be your own student of the media, observing how organizations are portrayed to readers.

WEB WORKSHEET

In this space, start your media plan:

Things to consider	Your plan
1. What is the explicit connection between your organization or group's strategy and the media?	[☛ 3.1 Strategy]
2. What steps do you need to take to make communications a strategic priority?	
3. List the things you can do to develop your own media awareness.	
4. What stories, events, angles, or issues would the public presently be interested in?	
5. Prepare a list of suggested topics for one-paragraph news tips the media can follow up.	
6. How or where can you find or generate an up-to-date media list? List journalists and publications that cover what your organization needs covered.	
7. List information that should be included in a storage and retrieval system.	
8. List the steps you can suggest to build a mutually beneficial business relationship with the media.	
9. List the priorities you would need to have in place if you had to respond to the media immediately in a crisis.	

Related leadership tools

1.11 Integrity	5.7 Stakeholder Groups	8.3 Organizational Communication
3.3 Environmental Scan	6.3 Complex Situations	9.10 Networking

For further assistance

Wade, John. *Dealing Effectively with the Media: What You Need to Know about Print, Radio and Television Interviews.* Reid Publishing, 1992.

(Note: This is a brief, easy-to-read book that could be given to prospective media spokespeople who want to educate themselves, along with formal media training.)

TOOLS FOR LEADING AND INFLUENCING OTHERS

Influence is at the heart of modern management practice. As one participant remarked in a leadership workshop, "The political leaders we remember as most successful are those who were great influencers and persuaders. Those we remember with mixed feelings (or worse) are those who had to resort to power and authority."

The tools in this chapter range from matching a leadership style with the situation, through delegation, to selling your good ideas, to the many facets of power.

9.1

LEADERSHIP VERSATILITY: MATCHING YOUR ROLE TO THE SITUATION

Inspired by Ronald and Gordon Lippitt, Paul Hersey, and Ken Blanchard.

Role versatility is a big part of what makes leaders effective. It's the ability to brainstorm with a group of colleagues one minute, and mandate the next; the ability to support a trusted employee in a time of crisis, then, in the next meeting, lead hard-nosed business negotiations with a competing organization. Thus, effective leaders adapt their approaches and roles to the needs of the situation. When a person comes into your office expecting to be heard, to "get something off my chest," you are able to listen; and when the next person who comes into your office suggests action that goes directly against organizational policy, you are able to say "No."

There is no best leadership style for every situation. Sometimes a participative style is best. Sometimes a directive style is required. Use the role continuum presented here to reflect on and match your role to the leadership requirements in each unique situation that you face as a leader.

RANGE OF LEADERSHIP ROLES

Nondirective	Directive
• coach/facilitator	• content expert
• helps others to help themselves	• directs others
• process helper/advisor	• controls the agenda
• participative leadership style	• authoritarian leadership style

Sounding Board or Process Facilitator	Clarifier	Problem-Solving Team Member	Process Resource	Educator or Trainer	Expert	Advocate	Regulator, Enforcer, or Governance
Often just listens; may give feedback, raise questions, and help clarify concerns.	Provides suggestions on how to deal with concerns, which helps others find their own answer.	As a team member, participates in the problem-solving process.	Helps choose optimal processes; frames issues and suggests new options.	Helps others develop new knowledge and skills.	Provides expert information and solutions to others.	Actively promotes and sells solutions to others.	Protects the integrity of the system or organization by ensuring compliance to standards.

WHEN TO USE

Nondirective	Directive
• when a person needs support	• when a person doesn't know how
• when developing skilled people	• when developing unskilled people
• if there are many ways of doing something	• when there's only one best way of doing something

HOW TO USE THIS LEADERSHIP TOOL

Give people a fish and you feed them for a day. Teach people how to fish and you help them to feed themselves. Teach people to sustain fish stocks and they feed many forever.

Before his promotion to a leadership role, Tom's favorite saying was, "Just tell me what to do, and I'll get it done." Shortly after his promotion, complaints started surfacing about Tom's style: "Tom treats us all like children. We do have heads on our shoulders, you know!" Another leader, Mary, preferred to be led by participative leaders who "Don't tell me what to do," but rather acted as a sounding board to help her determine the best action. She treated others the way she preferred to be treated. Soon, team members began complaining, "I wish Mary would just tell us what she wants. We spend far too much time trying to guess what is on her mind." Both of these leaders were well-intentioned, but lacked role flexibility.

Use this tool to assess your own leadership style and flexibility, or to coach others to do the same. In addition, when people approach you with a concern, be aware of the role embedded in their approach. In this way, you can make a conscious decision about how you wish to respond, as opposed to simply reacting and hoping for the best result. Use the questions in the worksheet to challenge and improve your versatility as a leader.

WEB WORKSHEET

Leadership Role Assessment	Improvement Actions
1. In a typical month, which role(s) would you use: • most often? • least often?	
2. In which role(s) do you feel: • most comfortable? • least comfortable?	
3. Which role(s) seem to be the best way to lead specific people in your group?	
4. Which role(s) are others asking you to fill? (You may wish to list people in your group.)	

5. If there is an inconsistency in your answers to questions 3 and 4, how might you resolve this difference?	

Related leadership tools

4.4 Employee Involvement
8.1 Conversations

9.2 Situational Leadership
12.1 The Relationship Bank

14.6 Learning Styles

For further assistance

Hersey, Paul, and Ken Blanchard. *Management of Organizational Behavior: Utilizing Human Resources.* Prentice Hall, 1982.

Lippitt, Gordon L., and Ronald Lippitt. *The Consulting Process in Action.* Pfeiffer & Co., 1986.

9.2 MATCHING YOUR LEADERSHIP STYLE TO THE SITUATION

Inspired by Paul Hersey, Ken Blanchard, Robert Tannenbaum, and Warren Schmidt.

Among the most successful leadership models is a group characterized as contingency or situational models. The common theme of these models is that there is not one best way to lead. That is, effective leaders adapt their behaviors to each unique situation. Thus, a leader will be very directive in one set of circumstances, yet delegate an entire project in another. Note that your success as a leader is not only dependent on matching your style to the situation, but is also related to developing and moving people along the continuum (from a closely supervised apprentice on the left, to a skilled, confident, and highly motivated leader on the right).

THE SITUATIONAL LEADERSHIP CONTINUUM

Leadership behavior	Makes decisions and provides directions on how to implement.	Makes decisions and "sells" to others.	Presents decisions and invites questions.	Presents decisions but remains open to refinements.	Presents problems and invites suggestions for solving them.	Works with others to frame problems and constraints; then delegates.	Clarifies issues and goals, turns job over to other person for action.

Directive Behavior ↕ ↕ ↕ ↕ **Participative Behavior**

Supervises closely and uses authority as a leader.					Delegates the whole job to others	

Situational Variables:

Nature of the job	Structured, one best way to do the job.			Job moderately complex.			Job highly complex.
Ability of people to do the work	Beginner; doesn't know how.	Person needs to know *why* to understand *how* to do the job.	Person beginning to build expertise.	Moderately expert; can complete the task within clear parameters.	Person is expert; may know job better than leader.	Person very expert; able to innovate if given the chance.	Person has expertise and good project management skills.
Willingness of people to do the work	Low maturity, very low confidence.			Wants freedom to do the job within constraints.			High maturity and confidence; able and self-starting.
Amount of coaching and follow-through required	Provide intensive coaching to help the person learn basic skills.		Provide coaching to help the person become capable of task analysis.		Provide coaching to help the person become capable and independent.		Provide coaching for goal congruence and continued learning.

One very popular situational leadership model was developed by Paul Hersey and Ken Blanchard. They define four leadership styles:

1. **Telling**—a leader provides detailed instruction and closely coaches the follower.
2. **Selling**—a leader provides explanations and principles, engages the follower in a discussion of the work, and coaches as needed.
3. **Facilitating**—the leader assists the follower with goal clarification and ideas, then coaches as needed
4. **Delegating**—the goal is clarified and the work turned over to the follower.

Any or all of these leadership styles can be used effectively, depending on the readiness of the follower as determined by:

- The *ability* of the person to do the job—has the necessary knowledge and skills to do the work.
- The *willingness* of the person to do the job—has the necessary confidence and commitment to do the work.

Hersey and Blanchard neatly summarized this into the model shown here:

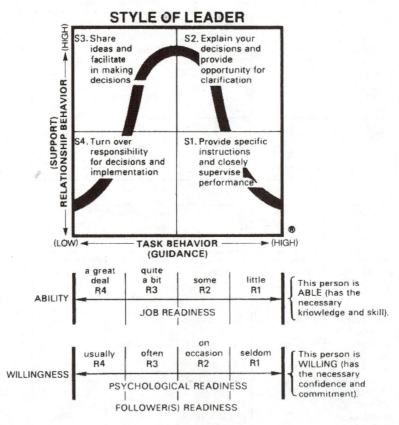

Reprinted with permission from Prentice Hall. Paul Hersey, and Ken Blanchard. *Management of Organizational Behavior: Utilizing Human Resources*, 7th ed., 1996, p. 215. All rights reserved.

How to use this leadership tool

"The successful leader is one who is able to behave appropriately. ... If direction is in order ... able to direct; if considerable participative freedom is called for ... able to provide such freedom."
—Robert Tannenbaum and Warren Schmidt, *HOW TO CHOOSE A LEADERSHIP PATTERN*

Contingency or situational leadership models demand that a leader analyze situations for critical variables, then use the leadership style that best fits the situation. Effective use of this tool means leaders have thought through a situation beforehand. Use this application matrix to assess and prepare for typical and specific situations you face as a leader.

WEB WORKSHEET

SITUATIONAL LEADERSHIP WORKSHEET

Leadership situation:

Person or team members:

Nature of the job:	Ability to do the work:	Willingness to do the work:
Structured Complex	Beginner Expert	Low maturity High maturity
Data:	Data:	Data:

Best leadership behavior:
Make decision yourself and provide clear directions.   Clarify issues and goals, then delegate.

Coaching and follow-through required:
[☛ 13.1 Coaching]

RELATED LEADERSHIP TOOLS

4.7 Job Satisfaction	10.1 HiPo Teams	13.1 Coaching
9.1 Leadership Versatility	10.7 Getting Participation	13.2 High-Performers

FOR FURTHER ASSISTANCE

Hersey, Paul, and Ken Blanchard. *Management of Organizational Behavior: Utilizing Human Resources.* Prentice Hall, 1996.

Tannenbaum, Robert, and Warren Schmidt. "How to Choose a Leadership Pattern." *Harvard Business Review.* May–June, 1973.

9.3 LEADERSHIP STRATEGIES FOR DELEGATING WORK

Inspired by Elliott Jaques, Paul Hersey, Ken Blanchard, Victor Vroom, Philip Yetton, and Wilf Hiebert.

As the complexity of work increases in modern organizations, effective delegation has become an essential leadership skill. Traditional delegation processes were of the one-size-fits-all variety. This tool combines the work of a number of experts to produce a situational model. It will help you delegate tasks and assign a portion of your accountability to others in a variety of organizational situations.

A SITUATIONAL MODEL OF DELEGATION

In this model, *task complexity* refers to the number, clarity, and rate of change of variables at play in a given situation; *risk* refers to the liability the organization faces if work is not completed to an acceptable standard; and *maturity* refers to the capability and commitment of the individual or team. Combining task complexity, risk, and the level of maturity of the individual or team, four delegation roles result—Developer, Coach, Partner, and Colleague.

THE DELEGATION PROCESS

	Delegator as **COACH**	Delegator as **PARTNER**
High	• Work as a coach. [☞ 13.1 Coaching] • Develop follower maturity. • Push the boundaries for growth.	• Ensure goal congruence. • Ensure clarity of expectations. • Stay involved as negotiated.
Task Complexity and/or Risk	Delegator as **DEVELOPER**	Delegator as **COLLEAGUE**
Low	• Simplify the task. • Teach the task. [☞ 14.5 On-job Training] • Push boundaries for growth.	• Ensure goal congruence. • Delegate whole task. • Define minimum constraints then trust and let go of need to manage.

| | Low | Individual or Team Maturity | High |

Step ❶ Predelegation thinking	❑ Clearly define the task in terms of the purpose of the task, the results you want, the key constraints, and your rationale for delegating. ❑ Determine the complexity of the task and assess the risk involved. ❑ Determine the maturity of the person or team you are expecting to delegate to. ❑ Use the delegating matrix to determine your need for involvement.

Step ❷ Delegation conversation	❑ Establish rapport and give rationale for delegating. ❑ Explain task parameters: *why*—the purpose; *what*—the goal; and *how*—the constraints or boundaries you are putting around this delegated task. ❑ Ask for and deal with any feelings, concerns, and suggestions. ❑ Ensure goal congruence and agreement on quality standards. (You and the delegatee need to have a common definition of success.)

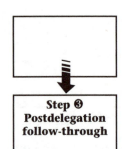

❑ Define an action plan, including roles, success measures, and next steps. Make this congruent with the situational model of delegation.
❑ Define accountabilities—yours and the delegatee's. [☛ 13.3 Accountability]
❑ Express your confidence, your availability for support, and your appreciation.

**Step ❸
Postdelegation
follow-through**

❑ Stay involved at the level you have agreed to (e.g., hold follow-through meetings).
❑ On occasion, step back with delgatee(s) and discuss roles and accountabilities. Assess experience gained, development and growth in maturity for those involved, and capacity and capability for future task delegation.

HOW TO USE THIS LEADERSHIP TOOL

"Effective delegation takes emotional courage as we allow, to one degree or another, others to make mistakes on our time, money and good name. ... Effective delgation must be two-way: responsibility given, responsibility received."

—Stephen Covey, *FIRST THINGS FIRST*

Leaders are reluctant to delegate for these reasons:

✗ "I don't have enough time to delegate properly."

✗ "I don't have the skills to delegate well."

✗ "It's easier to do it myself than to ask someone else."

✗ "The people to whom I could delegate are already too busy; don't have the knowledge, skills, or experience required; or aren't ready to accept this level of responsibility."

✗ "I've been let down in the past, and if they don't get the job done, I'll end up looking bad."

✗ "Risk taking is not encouraged in this organization, and delegation is risky."

SUGGESTIONS FOR EFFECTIVE DELEGATION

Pick and adapt the suggestions best suited to your situation.

❑ Learn the skills of coaching. [☛ 13.1 Coaching]

❑ Learn the skills of training and development; delegation is closely tied to your ability to develop others.

❑ Learn how to clearly state your role, your accountabilities, and the accountabilities of others. Delegation is tied to your perception of your role. [☛ 1.6 Boards of Play, 2.7 Goal Statements, 13.3 Accountability]

❑ Learn the skills of setting strategy, prioritizing, and managing time. Delegation is tied to leaders' defining strategies, priorities, and time management for themselves as well as others. [☛ 2.6 Clarifying Purpose, 3.1 Strategy, 13.5 Time Management]

❑ Have a meeting with your manager about issues related to delegation.

❑ Get feedback and coaching on your delegation skills. You need to know whether the cause of inadequate delegation is rooted in the inability or reluctance of others to accept delegated work, or in your inability or reluctance to delegate. [☛ 8.7 Active Listening, 12.4 Feedback]

❑ Learn about yourself as a leader, especially your needs for control and perfection. [☛ 1.2 Manage or Lead?]

- ❑ Delegate according to the unique circumstances of each situation. Different people and teams need a different level of delegation. [☛ 9.2 Situational Leadership]
- ❑ Think of delegation strategically—as part of your own growth and development, and as part of the growth and development of others. [☛13.10 Careers]
- ❑ Delegate the whole job whenever possible. Delegation is tied to work design. [☛ 4.7 Job Satisfaction]

WEB WORKSHEET

Use the workspace provided here to plan delegating work within your workgroup or team. Note which tasks and to whom you could delegate, using each of the four levels or strategies of delegation.

Delegator as COACH	Delegator as PARTNER
Delegator as DEVELOPER	**Delegator as COLLEAGUE**

RELATED LEADERSHIP TOOLS

4.4 Employee Involvement	9.1 Leadership Versatility	13.1 Coaching
4.7 Job Satisfaction	9.2 Situational Leadership	13.3 Accountability

FOR FURTHER ASSISTANCE

Hersey, Paul, and Ken Blanchard. *Management of Organizational Behavior: Utilizing Human Resources*. Prentice Hall, 1996.

Jaques, Elliot. *Requisite Organization: The CEO's Guide to Creative Structure and Leadership*.

Vroom, Victor, and Philip Yetton. *Leadership and Decision Making*. University of Pittsburgh Press, 1973.

9.4 INCREASING YOUR IMPACT: UNDERSTANDING CONTROL, INFLUENCE, AND INTEREST

Inspired by Stephen Covey.

This tool will help leaders make choices about how to focus their time and energy.

⟹ Some leaders lose focus by dabbling in or dwelling on interests over which they have no significant influence, or choose not to have an influence.

⟹ Some leaders confuse influence with control, and thus don't do either as well as they could.

⟹ Most leaders have the ability to expand their influence, but have gotten into habits or practices that have caused them to accept limitations as real and unassailable, rather than as imagined or self-imposed.

Interest: You can't act on every *interest* or concern you have in life. First, there simply isn't time; second, few leaders have the resources this would require. In the two diagrams here, the circles on the right show less time and energy being invested in the area of interest. This is a choice leaders make to free up resources and to improve their focus on the more leveraged areas of influence in business and in life.

Control: When it comes to managing and leading knowledge workers—and up to 80 percent of the North American workforce is made up of knowledge workers—at best leaders have the illusion of control. You simply cannot *command* commitment from highly skilled employees in a complex working environment. Most knowledge workers possess unique information about their profession and area of business that can be put to use only with their active cooperation and commitment. They reserve the right to make their own decisions about what they emphasize and where they provide their discretionary effort. As a result, leaders have lost much of their ability to fully control individual employee performance. Note in the diagrams that the area of control remains static and relatively small.

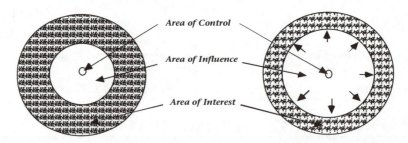

We're capable of influencing a great deal more in this world than we are comfortable admitting to ourselves.

Influence: Defined in the dictionary as "producing effects without exercising authority or control," leaders do have tremendous capacity to *influence*. There's not much that can't be influenced, if and when a capable person commits to making something happen. By strategically *influencing* those areas that provide the greatest leverage for success in organizations, leaders gain back control, not over daily employee activities, but rather at a higher level; that is, control over areas such as vision, work environment, goals, and morale. This requires that leaders develop and exercise a great deal of personal or informal power. That power is based on expertise and the commitment of followers, not on authority or on a leader's place in the hierarchy. The truth about a leader's area of influence is that much of your power is of your own making. Modeling the behavior that you expect of others is the most powerful form of influence in knowledge-based organizations. [☞ 1.8 Recursive Leadership, 15.2 Emotional Intelligence]

LEADER CHOICES

How big your area of influence becomes will depend upon the choices you make. History teaches us that when controlling or authoritative managers leave (temporarily or permanently), their control is greatly diminished; but when influential leaders leave, their influence remains, often indefinitely.

HOW TO USE THIS LEADERSHIP TOOL

"Anytime we think the problem is 'out there,' that thought is the problem."
—Stephen Covey

When changes are not being implemented as expected, there is a tendency for a leader to cast blame on outside forces (e.g., a lack of buy-in by senior management; stalling by group members). However, blaming doesn't usually work very well. A better alternative is for leaders to find ways to expand their influence and, when possible, take personal responsibility for implementing change. Use this tool to assess your area of personal *influence* as a leader, and to determine what decisions lie beyond your influence (i.e., in your area of interest). Use the workspace provided to begin this process.

WEB WORKSHEET

Area of Control
Which areas might you be trying to control, when influence would be a more powerful and lasting way to get the job done?

Area of Influence
Identify 2 or 3 areas of interest in your organization where you would like to have more influence.

What actions could you take if you committed to making something happen in these 2 or 3 areas of interest?

How might you be holding yourself back from taking these actions?

What first steps would help you begin to have more influence in these 2 or 3 areas of interest?

Area of Interest

List 2 or 3 areas of interest that you need to acknowledge, then make a conscious decision to let go of emotionally. (In this way, you can better focus on expanding your influence in other areas, rather than worrying about things that you either cannot influence or choose not to influence.)

RELATED LEADERSHIP TOOLS

1.2 Manage or Lead?	5.3 Change Readiness	13.10 Careers
1.6 Boards of Play	13.3 Accountability	15.1 Balance

FOR FURTHER ASSISTANCE

Covey, Stephen. *Principle-Centered Leadership.* Summit Books, 1991.

Covey, Stephen. *The Seven Habits of Highly Effective People: Powerful Lessons in Personal Change.* Simon & Schuster, 1989.

9.5 PRINCIPLED NEGOTIATION: CREATING LONG-TERM, WIN–WIN AGREEMENTS

Inspired by Roger Fisher, Elizabeth Kopelman, Andrea Kupfer Schneider, and William Ury.

In today's complex, rapidly changing work environments, leaders need a negotiating strategy to ensure that agreements are followed through and intended results are achieved. This tool summarizes some of the principles of a win–win negotiation process—often called the Harvard process—as distinct from hard-nosed strategies designed to get the most for one side, no matter the consequences (e.g., damaging working relationships). In this sense, negotiation is defined as the back-and-forth process to discover and optimally satisfy the wants and needs of both parties. The goal is to reach a consensual 50-50 agreement that will fulfill as many of the needs of each party as possible. This tool outlines the four principles of win–win negotiating that have become legendary for a) getting results, b) building working relationships, and c) ensuring a strong, mutual level of commitment to implementation.

1. SEPARATE THE PEOPLE FROM THE PROBLEM.

Assumptions	Difficulties	Some how-to's
• Relationships tend to become entangled with problems. • We tend to favor and like some people, and dislike others. • Negotiation nearly always involves the most human of all emotions: fear. [☛ 13.6 Attribution Theory]	• Whatever you say, others will often hear something different. • It is impossible to know exactly what the other(s) are thinking or feeling. • Perceptions are real, whether or not they are true. [☛ 8.1 Conversations]	✔ Be hard on the problem; be soft on people. ✔ Get to know the others as people. ✔ Acknowledge emotions as legitimate. ✔ Allow others to vent. ✔ Give others a stake in the outcome by involving them early in the process.

2. FOCUS ON INTERESTS RATHER THAN TAKING A POSITION.

A position is a predetermined outcome or conclusion (e.g., "Be here at seven a.m."). An interest is the need, want, or concern underlying the position (e.g., "We need an early start to get this job done.").

Assumptions	Difficulties	Some how-to's
• Taking a position locks people into a solution; focusing on interests opens up a range of new solutions. • There are numerous positions for every interest. [☛ 7.1 Problem Framing]	• Many people are so focused on a fixed position, they cannot see the underlying interest. • Leaping to conclusions (e.g., taking a position) is a common problem for most people.	✔ Explain the difference between interests and positions. ✔ Commit to your interests; be flexible regarding your positions. ✔ Realize that you and the others involved share many interests. ✔ Communicate your interests; ask others to communicate theirs; acknowledge their interests.

3. INVENT NEW ALTERNATIVES TO FULFILL THOSE INTERESTS.

Assumptions	Difficulties	Some how-to's
• The first alternatives or positions are almost certainly suboptimal for a win–win outcome. • Once underlying interests are clear, with goodwill, new alternatives are opened up that almost certainly will fulfill more interests of both parties. [☛ 6.7 Creativity and Innovation]	• This is creative work, often difficult during emotional negotiations. • Many people assume a fixed pie: "You can only gain when I lose." • Many people assume a single answer. • The negotiators in the room may represent others outside, who have fixed positions.	✔ Separate *inventing* options from *judging* options. ✔ Broaden the range of options on the table. ✔ Search for mutual gain options. ✔ Invent ways to make people's decision easy; point out benefits of new options. [☛ 9.7 Selling Wheel]

4. INSIST ON OBJECTIVE CRITERIA FOR EVALUATION.

Assumptions	Difficulties	Some how-to's
• In the emotional atmosphere of negotiations, objective criteria are needed to define win–win options. [☛ 7.5 Decision Making]	• People's emotions and fears often cloud rationality and objectivity.	✔ Frame each issue as a joint search for objective criteria. ✔ Reason, and be open to reason, as to which standards are most appropriate and how they should be applied. ✔ Never yield to pressure, only to principle.

HOW TO USE THIS LEADERSHIP TOOL

"Ultimately ... conflict lies not in objective reality, but in people's heads. Truth is simply one more argument ... for dealing with differences. The difference itself exists because it exists in (people's) thinking. Fears, even if ill-founded, are real fears and need to be dealt with. Hopes, even if unrealistic, may cause a war. Facts, even if established, may do nothing to solve the problem."

—Roger Fisher and William Ury, *GETTING TO YES*

A win–win approach to negotiations is important when a degree of interdependency will remain between the parties after an agreement has been reached. When you buy a used car, you have no further expectations of the other party. But agreements within and between organizations often involve ongoing relationships, in which long-term commitment and follow-through are essential. Examples include agreements on responsibilities within workgroups, agreements between departments that depend on each other for a product or service, and agreements between companies within a strategic alliance. Think about an agreement that you would like to conclude with another person or group. Use the workspace provided here to plan actions you can take to reach an agreement that both parties will be committed to following through with. List actions for all four principles.

1. SEPARATE THE PEOPLE FROM THE PROBLEM.

My assumptions about this situation:	Actions I can take:

2. FOCUS ON INTERESTS RATHER THAN TAKING A POSITION.

My assumptions about this situation:	Actions I can take:

3. INVENT NEW ALTERNATIVES TO FULFILL THOSE INTERESTS.

My assumptions about this situation:	Actions I can take:
	[☛6.7 Creativity and Innovation]

4. INSIST ON OBJECTIVE CRITERIA FOR EVALUATION.

My assumptions about this situation:	Actions I can take:
	[☛7.5 Decision Making]

RELATED LEADERSHIP TOOLS

1.6 Boards of Play	8.1 Conversations	12.6 Confrontation
2.7 Goal Statements	8.5 Metacommunicating	12.7 Dealing with Conflict
7.4 Polarities	12.1 The Relationship Bank	12.8 Difficult People

FOR FURTHER ASSISTANCE

Fisher, Roger, Elizabeth Kopelman, and Andrea Kupfer Schneider. *Beyond Machiavelli: Tools for Coping with Conflict,* 2nd ed. Penguin, 1996.

Fisher, Roger, and William Ury. *Getting to Yes: Negotiating Agreement without Giving In.* Houghton Mifflin, 1981.

Ury, William. *Getting Past No: Negotiating Your Way from Confrontation to Cooperation.* Bantam, 1993.

9.6 MAKING GREAT PRESENTATIONS

Inspired by Jean Illsley Clark and many other sources.

Making presentations involves a fear factor in the same league as mice, snakes, and death! Fear of public speaking causes sweaty palms, flushed face, heart thumping, and sleepless nights. Yet, of all the leadership competencies, this is one skill you certainly can learn, although not totally from a book. This tool will help you get started with the basics and planning. To become proficient, you need to practice, practice, practice—with feedback. If you are new to presentations, it's a good idea to take a workshop or join a Toastmasters International Club. If you are relatively experienced, find a coach. If you are an expert, you probably won't be reading this tool!

Step ❶ Know What You Want to Achieve

➡ Decide the goal of the presentation before the means: "If you don't know where you are going, any road will get you there."
➡ Write out the goal, objective, or desired result of the presentation in this form:
  At the end of my presentation, I want others to know and do these things … .
➡ If you can't write your goal clearly in a result form, you won't get results!

Step ❷ Know Your Audience

➡ Answer these questions about the audience (or participants, if you want participation):
  - Who are they? How many are there?
  - What do they know?
  - How supportive will they be of your goals?
  - Will they expect to participate?
➡ Answer the question, "What's in it for me?" *from the participants' viewpoint!*

Step ❸ Plan Your Presentation, Then Practice

Write out a plan for your presentation:
➡ Opening (Tell them what you are going to tell them.)
➡ Body (Tell them.)
➡ Close (Tell them what you told them.)
➡ If this is a selling or persuasive presentation, also see ☛ 9.7 Selling Wheel.
➡ What audiovisuals would support and enliven the presentation?
➡ What room arrangement would be most suitable?
➡ Finally, practice, get feedback, and practice; rehearse, do dry runs, and get coaching.

Step ❹ Presentation Opening

➡ Start with a hook to get attention, create relevance, establish the need:
  - relevant story or quote,
  - key point, bottom line,
  - your objective or goal, or
  - humor.
➡ Present an overview of your presentation.
➡ Ask for participation if you want it; state the form in which you want it.

Step ❺ Presentation Body

➡ Present using a framework of 3 to 5 main points with supporting points.
  (If you can't clearly see this framework with its main points, no one else will.)
➡ Ask for participation if needed.
➡ Deal with concerns and questions.

Step ❻ Presentation Close	➥ Summarize your key points.
	➥ Ask for action.
	➥ Get improvement feedback as soon as possible, while the presentation is fresh in your mind.

HOW TO USE THIS LEADERSHIP TOOL

"A retired four-star general used the following story when he began [his presentation].

'When I first began to give speeches, my wife would tell me to make it interesting. Later, when I was more experienced, she would tell me to ... keep it short. Now that I'm at the pinnacle of my career, she tells me to pull in my gut.'"

—Daria Price Bowman, *PRESENTATIONS*

Making presentations can be a challenge, but this is one skill anyone can learn to do well with some planning, coaching, and practice. Here is a presentation planner that will help you get started. If the presentation you are planning is important, get feedback on your plan and practice the presentation with a coach.

WEB WORKSHEET

Know What You Want to Achieve

Write out the goal, objective, or desired result of your presentation in this form:
At the end of my presentation, I want others to know and do these things ...

[☛ 2.7 Goal Statements]

Know Your Audience (or participants if you want participation).

Who are they? How many?

[☛ 5.7 Stakeholder Groups]
What do they already know?
How are they likely to receive your presentation? Can you anticipate their concerns and questions?
Are you expecting them to participate?

Answer this question from the participants' viewpoint: "What's in it for me?"

The Opening—The Hook

How will you open the presentation to capture interest?

The Body—The Framework

Main Point #1:
   subpoint:
   subpoint:

Main Point #2:
   subpoint:
   subpoint:

Main Point #3:
   subpoint:
   subpoint:

The Close—Action

How will you summarize your key messages? How will you ask for action?

RELATED LEADERSHIP TOOLS

9.7 Selling Wheel	10.7 Getting Participation	11.3 Meeting Checklist
10.6 Group Leader Skills	11.1 Process Cycle	11.7 Opening Remarks

FOR FURTHER ASSISTANCE

Clarke, Jean Illsley. *Who, Me Lead a Group?* Harper & Row, 1984.

Klatt, Bruce. *The Ultimate Training Workshop Handbook: A Comprehensive Guide to Leading Successful Workshops and Training Programs.* McGraw-Hill, 1999.

Toastmasters International http://www.toastmasters.org/
   Toastmasters provides a great way to improve your presentation and communication skills and lose the fear of public speaking.

3M's Meeting Network http://www.3m.com/meetingnetwork/presentations/
   A great site for links and resources for presentations, meeting leadership, and facilitation.

9.7 SELLING WHEEL: GETTING YOUR RECOMMENDATIONS ACCEPTED

Inspired by numerous sources.

Leaders may have great ideas, but nothing happens unless and until there is buy-in and commitment to change by those whose support is needed to turn those ideas into effective action (e.g., senior management, peers, workgroups, clients). To get people on board, leaders need to persuade others of the value and practicality of their recommendations. The tool for making this happen is the Selling Wheel.

❶ *Establish credibility and rapport.* People in business today are action-oriented and want you to get to the point quickly. While you're doing this, however, also work to establish rapport, using person-to-person conversation and eye contact. Know that decision making and commitment to follow-through are as much matters of the heart as of the head. Thus, both facts and relationships are important.

❷ *Establish the need.* We live in a results-oriented society. People often judge the success of your presentation by how well it answers their basic question, "Why?" Remind people of their needs and of the general benefits of your recommendations.

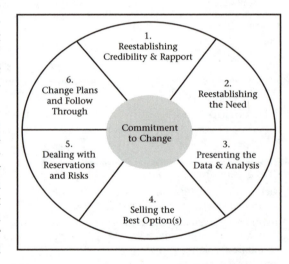

❸ *Present your data and analysis.* Too often, presenters fall in love with their data and analysis. Yet in our fast-paced, time-constrained world, most people want only the minimum of analysis. Presenting data is the most time-consuming part of most presentations. Give people only enough to understand the logic and value of your recommendations; don't frustrate them with an avalanche of data and analysis.

❹ *Sell your best option(s).* This is the heart of a persuasive presentation. Distinguish features (descriptors of solutions) from the benefits (why and how the features explicitly meet the client's needs). Too often, presenters overemphasize the features (the bells and whistles) as opposed to the benefits (why people should have these bells and whistles). It's the benefits that resonate with people. Benefits sell!

❺ *Deal with reservations and risks.* Having just described the benefits of your recommendation, it's now time to turn to the limitations and risks. Don't ignore or avoid discussing the risks. Doing so makes them conspicuous by their absence. Fearing conflict, many presenters don't allow people to voice their reservations. You can't do anything about what you don't know. It's better to hear reservations and have a chance to deal with them, than to have your recommendation scuttled outside the room, when you are not there to deal with the objections.

➏ *Plan follow-through as necessary.* Plan the next steps. Act quickly once you've begun the influencing process. It's rare to have all the decision makers and stakeholders in one room. Contact the key decision makers who were not at your initial presentation. Ask for their support. Listen to their concerns. Deputize as many people as possible to help you get your recommendations supported and approved.

HOW TO USE THIS LEADERSHIP TOOL

"One person with a belief is equal to a force of ninety-nine who only have an interest."
—John Stuart Mill

Often in organizations, great improvement ideas abound. Suppose an engineer wants to improve operations, for example. In presenting the idea, however, the engineer will often overwhelm management with analysis and technical detail, then become frustrated by lack of management support! The Selling Wheel can help shift the emphasis in such cases, pointing out the need to spend less time reviewing data and analysis, and more time clarifying the business need, outlining the benefits of the recommendations, and demonstrating to management how the risks they most fear can be minimized. This helps management focus on the benefits of the plan, tackle the risks, and connect the plan to the bottom line.

Use the worksheet provided to plan a persuasive presentation. All six steps are important, but step 4 is critical (sell your best option). People buy benefits. Plan how to present the benefits and deal with the reservations of each stakeholder group. [☞ 5.7 Stakeholder Groups]

Stakeholder group	Benefits this group will respond to	Risks that will concern this group
Senior Management	*Return on investment, fit with strategy*	*Difficulty getting support throughout the organization*

RELATED LEADERSHIP TOOLS

5.1 Change Equation   5.7 Stakeholder Groups   9.6 Presentations
5.5 Change Window   5.9 Resistance   9.8 Selling Large Projects

FOR FURTHER ASSISTANCE

Hiebert, Murray, *Powerful Professionals: Getting Your Expertise Used Inside Your Organization.* Recursion Press, 1999.
Rackham, Neil. *The Spin Selling Fieldbook: Practical Tools, Methods, Exercises, and Resources.* McGraw-Hill, 1996.

GETTING YOUR RECOMMENDATIONS ACCEPTED WORKSHEET

Step	Answer these participant questions:	Your presentation notes
❶ Establish rapport and trust.	❏ Why are we here? ❏ Why should we trust you?	
❷ Establish business need.	❏ What specific business need(s) are you addressing?	
❸ Present your data and analysis.	❏ What is the logical basis for your recommendation?	
❹ Sell your best option.	❏ Which option best fulfills the need? ❏ What are the key features of the option? ❏ What are the benefits (from the decision maker's perspective)?	[☛ 7.5 Decision Making]
❺ Deal with risks, reservations, and concerns.	❏ What concerns do we have about the recommendation? ❏ How can we deal with these concerns?	[☛ 5.9 Resistance]
❻ Adapt plans, follow through, and close.	❏ What are the next steps? ❏ Who else needs to be involved?	

9.8

SELLING LARGE PROJECTS:
A MUCH-VALUED LEADERSHIP SKILL

Inspired by Neil Rackham.

You may not have thought of selling as an important leadership skill, but leaders are expected to influence others, to move their ideas within their organizations, and to get support for plans, projects, and recommendations from a wide range of constituencies, including more senior leaders. But beware; selling techniques that are effective for small projects can be counterproductive when applied to selling large projects. This tool highlights the difference, and shows you how to adapt your selling efforts for both small and large projects, proposals, and recommendations.

Consider these contrasting demands when selling a small versus a large project or proposal.

Selling a Small Project or Recommendation	Selling a Large Project or Recommendation

• Value-adding is not a big issue:
  ➡ A manager can say "yes" on impulse without big risks.
  ➡ Not worth much management time.
	✔ Value-adding for stakeholders is a big issue:
	  ➡ Value must outweigh perceived risks.
	  ➡ Build value as the stakeholder perceives it.
	  ➡ Be clear about benefits and risks.

• State the key features and benefits.	✔ Ferret out the benefits and value added to your stakeholders by asking implication questions like, "If you don't do this, what will happen?"

• If leader makes a mistake, risk is low.	✔ In the case of a mistake, risk is high:
	  ➡ Ferret out risks and resistance, often hidden or indirect.
	  ➡ Deal with risks the change brings.
	  ➡ Others naturally become more cautious; therefore, you may need to make recommendations over a series of meetings.

• Building rapport and relationships is not a big issue. The manager typically doesn't want to spend much time with smaller proposals. Acceptance is often impulsive.	✔ Considerable building of rapport and relationships is needed:
	  ➡ Get to know the stakeholders informally.
	  ➡ Establish trust because of the risk factor.
	  ➡ Emphasize long-term support.

• It is easy to separate you, the leader, from the proposal or recommendation.	✔ The leader is harder to separate from the proposal or recommendation: ➡ Build trust in *you* and in your proposal.

• Single or simple stakeholder system; exposure is low.	✔ Multiple or complex stakeholder systems:
	  ➡ Personal exposure and identification with the project or recommendation should be high.
	  ➡ Deal with "hidden" stakeholders.

• Quick to close; key skill is to clearly plan for implementation.	✔ Being too quick to close can be dysfunctional: ➡ Pressuring leads to emotional, resistant behavior.

In his best-seller, *The Spin® Selling Fieldbook*, Neil Rackham describes the sequence used by high-performing, large-project salespeople.

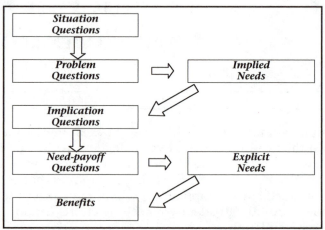

Extending Rackham's research to include leaders, here is an analysis of the questioning sequence used by persuasive leaders.

Reprinted with permission from McGraw-Hill. Neil Rackham, *The Spin Selling Fieldbook: Practical Tools, Methods, Exercises, and Resources*. McGraw-Hill, 1996, p. 49.

Type of question	What they are	Comments/tips
1. Situation Questions *"How many people are affected?"* *"What process do you currently use?"*	• Safe and easy questions to get background information about the client's situation. • Often begin with "What?", "Who?", "When?", and "How much?" • Helpful to start a conversation, but it's better to do your homework.	❑ Successful persuaders do ask these questions, but use them economically. ❑ These questions are not highly correlated with persuasiveness. ❑ The more senior the manager, the less he or she likes answering these questions.
2. Problem questions *"How satisfied are you with the current situation?"* *"What problems are you having?"*	• Questions about the problems, difficulties, dissatisfactions of a client that you can solve with your solutions. • More effective leaders ask more problem questions than situation questions, and they ask them sooner. • The best problem questions get at concrete needs.	❑ Problem questions are effective to the degree your products or services provide a solution to a client's problem. ❑ It is helpful to think less of solutions than the business problems that are solved by your solutions. ❑ For new leaders, these questions can help you become more effective quickly.
3. Implication questions *"How would that increase your costs?"* *"How does that impact your productivity?"* *"What effect does this problem have on your success?"*	• These are *"What will happen if you don't deal with this problem?"* questions. • The most powerful of all questions, these ask about the implications of not solving the problems identified. • These questions are about the effects or consequences of the client's problems. • Put bluntly, these questions induce pain by having the others themselves point out the negative consequences of not solving the problem, thus creating a strong need to solve the problem.	❑ The most persuasive leaders introduce solutions late in the discussion, after questions about the situation and problems.

Type of question	What they are	Comments/tips
4. Payoff questions *"How would an improved process help you?"* *"How much could you lower your costs by ...?"*	• These questions ask about the value of solving the problem and dealing with the implications. • These questions ask the clients to describe the benefits of a solution to themselves.	❑ Particularly in high-tech industries, leaders don't feel they are adding value unless they talk about solution. They are anxious to tell others about the new bells and whistles. ❑ These questions focus on solutions. ❑ These questions are used a great deal by effective leaders.

BOTTOM-LINE SKILLS FOR SELLING LARGE PROPOSALS, DECISIONS, AND RECOMMENDATIONS

✔ Put more effort into establishing relationships, because stakeholders put themselves on the line for large decisions.

✔ Show the value added and benefits to stakeholders by asking implication questions.

✔ Demonstrate how risks can be minimized and managed.

✔ Map the complex stakeholder system, and ferret out "hidden" stakeholders.

✔ Think long term; you can't establish a trusting relationship quickly.

✔ Move mentally from a *selling* process to a *change leadership* process.

HOW TO USE THIS LEADERSHIP TOOL

"Questions about the effects or consequences of a buyer's problem ... are the most powerful of all sales questions because they help the buyer see that the problem is serious enough to justify the hassle and cost of a solution."

—Neil Rackham, *THE SPIN SELLING FIELDBOOK*

Leaders need to shift into a change management role when selling a large project or program. This requires that they become more skilled at making the underlying needs explicit, relating with larger and more complex stakeholder groups, and ferreting out reservations about the project or program. Think of a large project, decision, or recommendation you are currently working on or will soon need to sell to others (e.g., in order to secure funding, support, follow-through, and so on). Use the workspace provided to plan how you will sell your ideas or recommendations to key stakeholder groups.

WEB WORKSHEET

Selling Principles for Large Projects	Action Planning
Value added for stakeholders is essential: ➡ Value must outweigh perceived risks. ➡ Build value as the *stakeholder perceives it*. ➡ Be clear about benefits and risks.	[☞ 3.1 Strategy, 5.7 Stakeholder Groups]

Ferret out the benefits and value added for your stake-holders by asking implication questions such as, "If you don't do this, what will happen?"	
In case of a mistake, risk is high: ➠ Ferret out resistance, which is not rational and is often hidden.	[☛5.9 Resistance]
Considerable building of rapport and relationships is required. ➠ Get to know the stakeholders informally. ➠ Establish trust, because risk is high. ➠ Emphasize long-term support.	[☛5.7 Stakeholder Groups]
It becomes difficult to see the leader as separate from the proposal or recommendation. ➠ Build trust in you and in your proposal.	[☛ 12.2 Trust]
There are multiple or complex stakeholder systems: ➠ Personal exposure and identification with the pro-ject or recommendation should be high. ➠ Ferret out and deal with "hidden" stakeholders.	[☛ 5.7 Stakeholder Groups]
Being too quick to close can be dysfunctional. ➠ Pressuring leads to emotional, resistant behavior.	[☛ 5.1 Change Equation, 5.2 Major Change]

RELATED LEADERSHIP TOOLS

5.1 Change Equation	5.3 Change Readiness	5.9 Resistance
5.2 Major Change	5.7 Stakeholder Groups	9.7 Selling Wheel

FOR FURTHER ASSISTANCE

Rackham, Neil. *Spin Selling*. McGraw-Hill, 1988.

Rackham, Neil. *The Spin Selling Fieldbook: Practical Tools, Methods, Exercises, and Resources*. McGraw-Hill, 1996.

9.9

POWER: A FUNDAMENTAL ELEMENT OF LEADERSHIP SUCCESS

Inspired by John French, Bertram Raven, Paul Hersey, Kenneth Blanchard, Jeffery Pfeiffer, Henry Mintzberg, and Bernie Novokowsky.

While management gurus recognize the use of power as integral to leadership success, they disagree on what power actually is! Thus, they debate endlessly as to how power differs from influence, coercion, control, and authority. Yet, as Henry Mintzberg notes, "Ordinary people ... know what it means to have power." Successful leaders combine seven sources of power in appropriate ways to achieve both short- and long-term goals.

Type of Power	Explanation
Formal or official power (organizational authority)	➡ This source of power is based on the authority of one's position within the organization. Managers expect that others, working under their authority within the organization, will act upon their requests or demands. Traditional organizational charts and job descriptions formalize this type of power.
Reward power	➡ This power is based in the leader's ability to provide rewards, real or intrinsic. In organizations, rewards are often positive incentives such as pay, promotion, or recognition.
Coercive or punishment power	➡ This power is based on fear of the leader, who controls potential punishments like undesirable work assignments, reprimands, or dismissal. Needless to say, the overuse of this type of power will damage a leader's ability to get results, especially if the leader is relying on others to use judgment and discretion on the job. There will always be times when a leader must exercise some form of coercive power in difficult situations.
Expert or information-based power	➡ This source of power stems from one's expertise, skill, and knowledge. Leaders of professional workgroups—engineering, finance, human resources, and so on—often rely heavily on this type of power.
Connection-based or associative power	➡ This source of power is based on the leader's connections and relationships with powerful others, be they inside or outside the organization. As organizational structures flatten and access to information improves, this type of power is becoming more important. In cultures that value loyalty to the family, tribe, or clan (e.g., in some Asian countries), this is a fundamental source of power.
Referent or charismatic power	➡ A leader high in this source of power is liked or admired by others based on personal traits. Often ephemeral, this power is based on belief in, admiration for, or identification with the leader.
Democratic or representative power	➡ These leaders have power based on democratic election. They represent others who have delegated power to them. They use their judgment and discretion on behalf of the group, and for the purpose of serving the group (e.g., a union representative, a mayor.) Unfortunately, this power source sometimes turns into other forms of power.

Power is a two-sided coin. One side is the power a leader perceives himself or herself to possess. The other side is the power followers desire from or are willing to concede to the leader. Modern leadership features the waning of more formal and coercive forms of power. This has occurred in knowledge-based, fast-moving, customer-focused organizations, where jobs with creativity, discretion, and judgment at their core cannot be clearly defined, and where commitment to results as opposed to compliance with activities or behaviors is fundamental to business success.

Most modern leadership models promote a concept of personal power—power with and power within.

	Leader As Boss	*Leader As Partner*	*Leader As Coach*
	←		→
Power characteristics	*Leader knows best; top-down (power over).*	*Share or delegate power (power with).*	*Encourage others to develop their own power (power within).*
Works best when	*Followers untrained or immature. Best used as temporary "tough love."*	*Followers are developing but are not able to take full accountability.*	*Others are expert, want to succeed, and are accountable; their goals are congruent with those of leader and organization.*

How to use this leadership tool

"There should never be any need for a leader to tell other people how powerful and influential he or she is. … Yes, leaders are power brokers. But they are power brokers on behalf of people they lead."

—Jim Kouze and Barry Posner, *THE LEADERSHIP CHALLENGE*

This application involves two aspects:

1. your personal conception and basis for power as a leader;
2. your conception and basis for developing power in others.

WEB WORKSHEET

Your personal basis for power

Source of Power	Your current use (if at all)	When best used (if at all)	Steps to improve this source of power
Official or formal power			
Reward power			
Coercive or punishment power			
Expert or information-based power			

Source of Power	Your current use (if at all)	When best used (if at all)	Steps to improve this source of power
Connection-based or associative power			
Referent or charismatic power			
Democratic or representative power			

Your basis for developing power in others

Now think of several individuals in your workgroup, how each of them create and use their own sources of power, and how each might consider improving the use of power within the organization.

Name of Person	Current Use of Power	A More Appropriate Use of Power

Related leadership tools

1.6 Boards of Play   9.2 Situational Leadership   12.1 The Relationship Bank
9.1 Leadership Versatility 9.4 Leader Impact   13.1 Coaching

For further assistance

Hersey, Paul, and Ken Blanchard. *Management of Organizational Behavior: Utilizing Human Resources*. Prentice Hall,1982.

Mintzberg, Henry. *The Rise and Fall of Strategic Planning: Reconceiving Roles for Planning, Plans, and Planners*. The Free Press, 1994.

Pfeffer, Jeffrey. *Managing with Power: Politics and Influence in Organizations*. Harvard Business School Press, 1992.

9.10 SUPPORT NETWORKS: THE SECRET OF ALL SUCCESSFUL LEADERS

Inspired by many, including Stephen Covey, Peter Drucker, Jeffrey Pfeiffer, and the Novations Group.

No one accomplishes anything of significance without the help of others. Leaders, in particular, need the support of many people to achieve their business, professional, and personal goals. A wide and well-developed support network:

✔ Provides guidance and assistance when needed. (Your support system needs to be in place *before you need it.*)

✔ Provides a sounding board and a place to test your thoughts. (A reality check can be very helpful in the complex world of modern organizations.)

✔ Provides emotional support. (Support networks are part of your stress-reduction system.)

✔ Helps you avoid pitfalls and minefields. (Relationships make organizations work, and thus politics within organizations is just a fact of life.)

✔ Provides much-needed feedback. (Leaders can be notoriously poor judges of their own behavior.)

✔ Challenges you to reach your potential. (We all need a nudge now and then to achieve our goals.)

Type of Support	Support Provided
Mentors/sponsors	➡ People at senior management levels in organizations who take a personal interest in your success and are willing to invest their time and energy to advise and coach you. They can also provide you with a range of opportunities, connect you with other influential leaders, and help you secure the resources you need to succeed.
Assistants, staff (those who report to you in the organization)	➡ These are the people to whom you can delegate tasks. They provide tangible services (e.g., policy development, project leadership). You want two kinds of loyalty from them. First, you want them to produce what you ask them to do. Second, you want them to help you avoid mistakes.
Professional service providers, expert advisors	➡ Leaders are increasingly dependent on professional advice in specialized areas such as information technology, human resource management, law, finance, environment, safety, and health. The era of the General Manager—the leader who generally knew everything about the job—is over. In today's complex world, leaders need to orchestrate up-to-date professional advice from many sources.
Formal coach(es)	➡ Leaders are increasingly engaging personal coaches, skilled in providing expert advice on business and leadership issues. In addition to providing confidential developmental feedback, coaches also help leaders develop meaningful development and business goals, and strategies for achieving those goals. They then challenge and support you to achieve these goals.
Informal coach(es), supporters, colleagues	➡ These supporters can be anywhere, at any level, inside or outside your organization. For example, the administrative assistant to a senior executive can be an effective informal coach to other leaders. Treating this person with dignity can make a difference in your access to the senior executive.

Type of Support	Support Provided
Challengers	➡ Lucy, of *Peanuts* fame, termed these people "the crabgrass in the lawn of life." You may find it strange that these people can be supporters! They will question your reasoning and force you to carefully examine your ideas and proposals. A natural reaction is to treat them like enemies and fight back. A better strategy is to meet with them, ask for their advice, and potentially get them on your side!
Family and friends	➡ These people know you in a wide range of settings and roles, and love you despite your faults. They understand how your approach to life and the decisions you have made have influenced who you have become.

HOW TO USE THIS LEADERSHIP TOOL

"It is easy to see the building of a network of suppport, either through the appointment and promotion process or through personal favors, as activities that are somehow illegitimate or inappropriate. Such a view would be incomplete at best. The development and exercise of power in organizations is about getting things accomplished. The very nature of organizations—interdependent, complex systems with many actors and many points of view—means that taking action is often problematic. Failures in implementation are almost invariably failures to build successful coalitions. Although networks of allies can obviously be misused, they are nevertheless essential in order to get things done. And, allies must be put in place through whatever practical means are at hand."

—Jeffrey Pfeffer, *MANAGING WITH POWER*

WEB WORKSHEET

Consider your current support network. What support is being provided? How might this network be improved? Are you relying on too few people? Are some categories of support missing or in need of strengthening (e.g., mentors, coaches)? Use the space provided to analyze and plan ways to expand and strengthen your support network. Consider people both inside and outside your organization.

Type of support	People who presently (or could potentially) provide this support	Description of support desired
Mentors/sponsors		
Assistants, staff		
Professional service providers, expert advisors	[☛ 4.9 Professional Expertise]	
Formal coach(es)	[☛ 13.1 Coaching]	

Type of support	People who presently (or could potentially) provide this support	Description of support desired
Informal coach(es), supporters, colleagues		
Challengers		
Family and friends		

RELATED LEADERSHIP TOOLS

1.8 Recursive Leadership   4.7 Job Satisfaction   9.2 Situational Leadership

4.4 Employee Involvement   5.7 Stakeholder Groups   12.1 The Relationship Bank

FOR FURTHER ASSISTANCE

Covey, Stephen. *Principle-Centered Leadership*. Summit Books, 1991.

Covey, Stephen. *The Seven Habits of Highly Effective People: Powerful Lessons in Personal Change*. Simon & Schuster, 1989.

Drucker, Peter. *The Frontiers of Management: Where Tomorrow's Decisions Are Being Shaped Today*. Harper & Row, 1986.

Drucker, Peter. *Managing in Turbulent Times*. Harper & Row, 1980.

Pfeiffer, Jeffrey. *Managing with Power: Politics and Influence in Organizations*. Harvard Business School Press, 1996.

10

TOOLS FOR LEADING TEAMS AND GROUPS

More and more work is being done in groups and teams, because:

✔ Organizations and technology are becoming more complex. Gone are the days when a General Manager could know everything about a work area. To get the job done today, leaders need to be skilled at marshaling complementary skills from a wide range of professions and professionals.

✔ Stakeholder systems are becoming more complex, and more people are requiring input into decisions in return for their support.

✔ Commitment, as opposed to compliance, is needed in knowledge-based organizations. Committed people generate higher-quality and more innovative products and services. However, commitment isn't automatic. It's an outcome of effective leadership, and is enhanced by involving, informing, and encouraging people to influence decisions within their workgroups or teams.

It is essential for a leader to be able to lead workgroups and teams.

10.1

HIGH-PERFORMING TEAMS:
ORGANIZING TO ACHIEVE RESULTS

Inspired by Jon Katzenbach and Douglas Smith.

Leaders are forever asking the question, "What's the best way to organize people to achieve business results?" Terms such as teamwork, team, and workgroup can be misleading, as they are often used in imprecise ways. This tool will clarify the different ways of organizing to optimize people's effort and contribution.

Four levels of organizing, each requiring successively greater interdependence and higher levels of teamwork, are defined and described:

Individual work ➡ Workgroup ➡ Team ➡ High-performing team

Even an individual working alone within an organization needs to relate and coordinate with others, however minimally. High-performing teams are based upon deeply shared values, goals, relationships, and processes; team members are highly involved with other team members. Workgroups, somewhere between individual work and high-performing teams, are sometimes preferred over team structures, as they require less interaction and coordination, and allow for individual accountability. A leader needs to weigh a number of factors in order to determine the best way to organize people to maximize business results, including the nature of the work; the need for joint accountability; and the time available for coordination, meetings, and information-sharing.

	How work gets done:	When it is best to use:
Individual Work	• The individual works alone, can do the whole job, needs little close support, and is solely accountable for producing a product or providing a service.	✔ Individual work is the best option when there are few shared goals with others, and very little synergy would be gained from other people's input and perspectives.
Workgroup	• Workgroups achieve shared goals by pooling individual work skills and knowledge to produce products and services. • Members consult with each other and then a workgroup leader makes the final decision, although some decisions may be made together. • Work is delegated to individuals who are solely accountable for that piece of work. • A workgroup does not need a separate identity.	✔ Workgroups are the best option when knowledge and skills need to be shared in order to get results, but the need for innovation or coordination is low. ✔ Workgroups are easier to form and disband than teams.
Team	• Teams are distinguished by interdependence. They achieve common goals by discussing, deciding, and doing work together. • A team has a vision of the team itself (e.g., working approach, team development).	✔ Teams are the best option when there is a need for coordination or innovation, and success or failure is not attributable to the sum of each individual's efforts, but rather to the aligned efforts of the team.

	How work gets done:	When it is best to use:
	• Due to coordination, communication, and relationship demands, teams are usually composed of a small number of members (12 or fewer), each with complementary skills. • Teams succeed, or fail, together. Members are individually *and* jointly accountable for a specific product or service that is unique to the team (i.e., a whole job).	✔ Teams are often distinguished from work-groups by synergy. The output of a work-group is basically the sum of individual efforts, while team output should be much greater than the sum of what a group of individuals could produce working alone.
High-Performing Team	• High-performing teams are distinguished by the production of exceptional and demanding results, with no expectation of rewards as individuals. • Members are deeply committed to results as well as to each other's growth and success. • High-performing teams are leaderful, as each member can speak for the team.	✔ High-performing teams are rare. This level of commitment, relationship, and caring for results, for team success, and for each others' individual development and success can be supported and encouraged, but cannot be commanded of people.

In their best-seller, *The Wisdom of Teams,* Jon Katzenbach and Douglas Smith summarized the continuum from a workgroup to a high-performing team on a "Team Performance Curve."

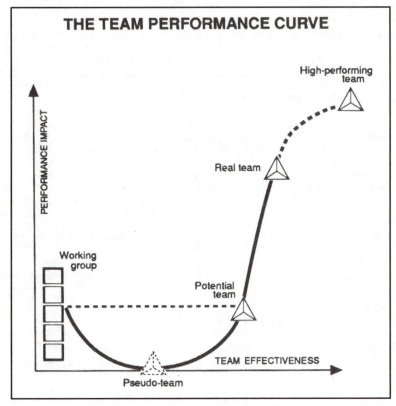

Reprinted by permission of Harvard Business School Press. From *The Wisdom of Teams: Creating the high-performance organization.* by Jon R. Katzenbach and Douglas K. Smith. Boston MA, 1993, p. 84. Copyright 1993 by the President and Fellows of Harvard College. All rights reserved.

How to use this leadership tool

"Effective team leaders realize they neither know all the answers, nor can they succeed without the members of the team. The wisdom of teams lies in recognizing that any person … who genuinely believes in the purpose of the team and the team itself can lead the team toward higher performance."

—Jon Katzenbach and Douglas Smith, THE WISDOM OF TEAMS

Should your group be organized as a workgroup or as a team? What level of teamwork should you expect from employees? The answer to these questions is, "It depends." Check (√) these statements to help you decide between a workgroup and a team structure. Keep in mind that workgroups require less coordination and meeting time than do teams, and unless the work demands joint accountability, a workgroup may be a more practical way to organize.

Workgroup requirements	Team requirements
___ Individual accountability is primary.	___ Requires both individual *and* joint accountability. [☛ 13.3 Accountability]
___ Work issues can be discussed, decided, then delegated to individuals in the group.	___ Work issues need to be discussed, decided, and completed as a team. (Thus, issue size is important.) [☛ 4.4 Employee Involvement]
___ There is likely a shared purpose within the workgroup.	___ There is clearly a shared purpose within the team. [☛ 2.6 Clarifying Purpose]
___ Individual work products are pooled to achieve overall workgroup results.	___ The team is working to achieve a specific result that is unique to the team (a whole job), and that is greater than the sum of the individual team members' contributions.
___ Challenge and support within the workgroup will enhance results, but individual performance is the key to workgroup success.	___ There is significant interdependence within the team. Individual success depends on the success of the whole team. The team will succeed or fail together.
___ Workgroup membership is a matter of practicing teamwork (e.g., relating well within the workgroup, working within organizational values).	___ Team membership is a matter of contribution. Those who contribute will be on the team. Those who don't won't be needed on the team.
___ Little attention needs to be paid to the workgroup itself, other than to group leadership skills.	___ There needs to be a vision of the team itself (e.g., working approach, team development). [☛ 2.4 Visioning, 2.5 Values, 4.5 Culture]
___ The group can be any size, depending on the skills of the group leader.	___ Team size should be fewer than 12.
___ Skill mix can vary considerably.	___ Skills must be complementary within the team.

Related leadership tools

4.4 Employee Involvement	10.3 Team Competencies	10.6 Group Leader Skills
8.6 Communications 101	10.4 Team Commitment	13.3 Accountability

For further assistance

Katzenbach, Jon, and Douglas Smith. *The Wisdom of Teams: Creating the High-Performance Organization.* HarperBusiness, 1993.

10.2   IMPROVING TEAM IQ

Contributed by George Campbell and inspired by William Dyer, Jon Katzenbach, Douglas Smith, Peter Scholtes, Phillip Hunsaker, Anthony Alessandra, and *Improving Team IQ* workshop participants.

Most leaders are acutely aware that teams are now central to the development and execution of corporate strategy. Sustainable competitive advantage is built on teams being smarter than competitors' teams. Smart teams are said to have high Team IQ. Strange as it may seem, Team IQ has little connection to the intrinsic IQ of individual team members. Teams composed of highly intelligent individuals can be dumb, while teams composed of average-intelligence members can be smart. This tool provides leaders with guidelines to facilitate members' working together in a way that engages the collective mind of the team, so the whole is greater than the sum of the parts. When this happens, high Team IQ is produced.

High team IQ	Low team IQ
✔ For an individual, to be a member of a team with high Team IQ is fun, energizing, and engaging.	✗ For an individual, it is frustrating and energy-draining to be a member of a low-IQ team, and many wish for more time alone in their offices to get some useful work done!
✔ A key component in their organization's competitive advantage, high-IQ teams make quality choices, use resources wisely, and produce creative, timely, and highly effective results.	✗ A drag to their organization's competitive advantage, low-IQ teams make poor decisions, absorbing large amounts of time and energy. For organizations, it is dangerous to have teams that are both inefficient and ineffective.
✔ Members feel stretched on these teams, as individual capacity is pushed to the limits. This stretching produces growth for the individuals, for the team, and for the organization.	

TEAM IQ SOURCES

By identifying the sources of increased or decreased IQ, you can actually choose the high Team IQ route for your teams. Although it is not difficult to produce, high Team IQ does require discipline. Two requisite factors are: i) getting the team off to a good start, and ii) ensuring that the team is committed to the work.

Sources of increased team IQ	Sources of decreased team IQ
Smart Work ➡ Teams need work that engages the intellectual capacity of members, the kind of work that requires the cumulative brainpower of the team. [☛ 3.1 Strategy]	*Dumb Work* ➡ Work could be done by an individual and is too narrow to engage the team's collective brain. Forcing a team into this kind of work leads to low Team IQ.
Focus on Success ➡ From success comes confidence, making more success likely! Set challenging targets, monitor progress, and celebrate success. This builds energy and capacity for more challenging work. [☛ 2.3 Directional Statements, 11.1 Process Cycle]	*Focus on Failure* ➡ Low-IQ teams are generally more focused on error and incomplete tasks than they are on their success. This tends to create a sense of being overwhelmed, decreasing capacity.

Sources of increased team IQ	Sources of decreased team IQ
Learn from Hard Times ➡ All teams have hard times, when the error rate is high and efficiency is low; when interpersonal stress is high, and organizational support is low. High-IQ team members recognize and talk about difficulties, take ownership, and take action to improve their situations. [☛ 8.1 Conversations]	*Make Hard Times Worse* ➡ When times are tough, things get worse, decreasing Team IQ. Inability to talk through difficulties causes individuals to complain, blame, and attack.
Build Trust by Delivering ➡ High-IQ teams build trust by underpromising and overdelivering; by consistently meeting commitments, especially when under pressure. [☛ 1.7 Results-Based Leaders, 12.2 Trust]	*Break Trust by Missing Deliveries* ➡ Failure to deliver reduces trust. In attempting to push their limits, low-IQ teams and members may commit to actions and timelines they cannot possibly deliver.
Find the Causes of Problems ➡ When things go wrong, high-IQ teams find the cause of the problem, then fix the cause so the problem does not recur. [☛ 7.2 Problem Solving, 7.3 Finding Cause]	*Find the Person to Blame* ➡ When things go wrong, low-IQ teams tend to identify a person to whom they can attach blame.
Engage in Conflict of Ideas ➡ Team synergy and high Team IQ come from differing ideas being discussed, challenged, combined, and transformed into new and improved thinking. [☛ 12.7 Dealing with Conflict]	*Engage in Personal Conflict* ➡ Attacking team members deflects the team from its real work, reduces listening, and produces the kind of emotions that hamper thinking.
Meet in the Meeting ➡ High-IQ teams get ideas and issues on the table in the meeting. The team is free enough that members can tell the truth in the meeting, about what is going well, problems, and real opinions about its work. [☛ 8.5 Metacommunicating, 10.8 Ground Rules]	*Meet after the Meeting to Discuss the Meeting* ➡ Subgroups, often people who did not speak up in the meeting, congregate afterward to criticize decisions made in the meeting.
Focus on High Priorities ➡ There are always too many things to do. High-IQ teams focus team energy and attention on high-value issues. They resolve these issues and move on. [☛ 3.5 Strategic Resourcing, 13.5 Time Management]	*Demonstrate Attention Deficit* ➡ Low-IQ teams tend to give equal weight to all issues, without prioritizing which issues to work on first.

HOW TO USE THIS LEADERSHIP TOOL

"How can a team of committed managers with individual IQs above 120 have a collective IQ of 63?"

—Peter Senge, *THE FIFTH DISCIPLINE*

Use this tool as a diagnostic to help a team assess its IQ and plan action. Here is a process to do that.

WEB WORKSHEET

A. Have everyone in the team independently complete the Team IQ questionnaire, using the Team IQ sources for ideas. It may help to have the questionnaires completed anonymously, for the purpose of compiling results for a collective diagnosis.

   1. Signs of low Team IQ: Identify specific behaviors and actions the team has taken that demonstrate low Team IQ.

2. Signs of high Team IQ: Identify specific behaviors and actions the team has taken that demonstrate high Team IQ.

3. Rate Team IQ, using the scale shown: IQ is rated in wattage, as Team IQ is a measure of the team's ability to do useful work.

4. Identify the rationale for your Team IQ rating: What has caused you to choose a particular rating?

5. Identify changes that could increase your Team's IQ: Identify specific action(s) your team could take to improve its Team IQ.

TEAM IQ QUESTIONNAIRE DATA

Signs of Low Team IQ

_____

_____

_____

_____

_____

_____

Signs of High Team IQ

_____

_____

_____

_____

_____

_____

YOUR RATING OF YOUR TEAM'S IQ

VERY LOW TEAM IQ		VERY HIGH TEAM IQ
	40 Watt 100 Watt 200 Watt	

RATIONALE FOR YOUR RATING

_____

_____

_____

_____

CHANGES THAT COULD INCREASE YOUR TEAM'S IQ

B. Assemble and debrief the team members' questionnaire answers in a group setting.

1. Collect the data, keeping information visible (a trust factor).

2. Ensure that people understand what is being said (a communications factor).

3. Prioritize the suggested changes for improving your Team's IQ.

4. Commit to implementing one to three of the changes.

5. Implement the changes.

6. Follow through and discuss whether the changes have improved Team IQ.

RELATED LEADERSHIP TOOLS

8.1 Conversations	10.3 Team Competencies	12.2 Trust
10.1 HiPo Teams	10.4 Team Commitment	12.7 Dealing with Conflict

FOR FURTHER ASSISTANCE

Dyer, William. *Team Building: Issues and Alternatives*. Addison-Wesley, 1987.

Hunsaker, Phillip, and Anthony Alessandra. *The Art of Managing People: Person-to-Person Skills, Guidelines, and Techniques Every Manager Needs to Guide, Direct, and Motivate the Team*. Prentice-Hall, 1986.

Katzenbach, Jon, and Douglas Smith. *The Wisdom of Teams: Creating the High-Performance Organization*. HarperBusiness, 1993.

Scholtes, Peter. *The Team Handbook: How to Use Teams to Improve Quality*. Joiner Associates, 1988.

TEAM COMPETENCIES:
THINKING, RELATING, AND ACTING

Inspired by Estela Bensimon and Anna Neumann.

Work teams need skills in three fundamental competency areas in order to operate effectively.

Get the Job Done and Produce Results:

- Plan well.
- Set and achieve goals.
- Share accountability.
- Measure task- and results-related behavior.
- Make decisions and recommendations.
- Monitor and control results.
- Coordinate and communicate well with stakeholders.
- Be efficient; do things right.
- Key statement: "We do these things to get results... ."

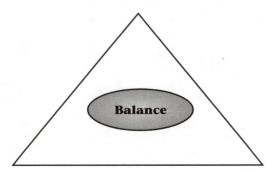

Use Quality Thinking:

- Strive for intellectual effectiveness.
- Use optimal process tools.
- See multiple perspectives and assumptions.
- Define perspective or frame for issues.
- Challenge and improve processes.
- Analyze, innovate, synthesize.
- Reach agreement and closure.
- Challenge each other.
- Promote project leadership literacy.
- Promote business and economic literacy.
- Think strategically and long-term.
- Take care of systemic issues.
- Do the right things.
- Involve the right people.
- Key statement: "We think ... ."

Take Care of Interpersonal Needs:

- Understand social needs of team.
- Give each other mutual support.
- See themselves as a team.
- Strive for synergy.
- Deal effectively with feelings.
- Honor differences.
- Challenge each other—open, honest debates.
- Honor and deal with conflict.
- Give and receive feedback.
- Be trusting and open.
- Search for win–win decisions.
- Have a joint commitment to success.
- Feel good about being part of the team.
- Key statement: "We feel ... ."

How to use this leadership tool

"We do not easily take responsibility for the performance of others, not lightly let them assume responsibility for us. Overcoming such resistance requires the rigorous application of 'team basics.'"

—Jon Katzenbach and Douglas Smith, *THE WISDOM OF TEAMS*

Some teams are great at analytical work and project management, yet become sidetracked by relationship problems and conflict. Other teams, seemingly supportive and happily working together, don't produce needed results on time.

WEB WORKSHEET

Whether you're a team leader, member, or coach, this tool will help you assess team strengths and development needs. Adapt and use this table with your team, to assess its strengths and problem areas. Then plan action to continually build on strengths, while also improving on or minimizing the team's limitations or development needs.

Competency area	As individuals: identify a few areas in each category to work on.	As a team: identify a few areas in each category to work on.	Improvement goals and action(s)
Get the job done and produce results: • Set and achieve goals. • Get the job done. • Make great recommendations and decisions. • Do the right things efficiently.			[☛ 1.7 Results-Based Leaders, 2.6 Clarifying Purpose]
Think effectively: • Analyze, innovate, synthesize. • Use optimal processes. • Think long-term and strategically. • Take care of systemic issues.			[☛ 2.1 Systems Thinking, 3.1 Strategy]
Take care of interpersonal needs: • Deal effectively with feelings. • Honor differences. • Give and receive feedback. • Have a joint commitment to success. • Feel good about being part of the team.			[☛ 4.5 Culture, 8.6 Communication 101]

RELATED LEADERSHIP TOOLS

1.7 Results-Based Leaders	4.1 Organizational Design	10.1 HiPo Teams
2.1 Systems Thinking	8.6 Communication 101	13.3 Accountability

FOR FURTHER ASSISTANCE

Bensimon, Estela Maria, and Anna Neumann. *Redesigning Collegiate Leadership: Teams and Teamwork in Higher Education.* Johns Hopkins University Press, 1994.

10.4 Inclusion, Control, and Affection: Developing Commitment and Teamwork

---

Inspired by Will Schutz.

Why do people commit, or fail to commit, to working cooperatively within organizations? What inspires people to become other-centered, as opposed to self-centered, within workgroups and organizations? These questions challenge leaders to create work environments that sustain motivation, teamwork, and accountability. Three interpersonal needs are especially central to securing peoples' commitment within workgroups and teams:

1. Inclusion—a sense of being recognized, involved, and accepted;
2. Control—a sense of having a responsible role and of being invited to influence; and
3. Affection—a sense of being respected, supported, and close to other members of the group.

Inclusion ("am i in or out?")

Behaviors	Feelings when included	Feelings when excluded
• associating with others • sharing information • joining in • having contact • participating	• recognized, respected • significant • involved • "in" (belonging) • a sense of status	• ignored • left out • forgotten • neglected

Control ("am i up or down?")

Behaviors	Feelings with sense of control	Feelings with no sense of control
• having a measure of control over your own work • having influence with group members, and over issues that affect you	• competent • confident • in control • a sense of personal and team power	• humiliated • powerless • inadequate • out of control

Affection ("am i close or distant?")

Behaviors	Feelings when liked	Feelings when disliked
• being able to disclose true thoughts and feelings to others in the group, without fear or punishment	• openhearted • accepted and accepting • honest • appreciated • liked • belonging	• rejected, put off • disliked, unlikable • distant • judged • alien

HOW TO USE THIS LEADERSHIP TOOL

"Most people don't care how much you know until they know how much you care."

—John Maxwell

Inclusion, control, and affection can be understood very simply. Consider a group of people going sailing on a Sunday afternoon. The inclusion issue is the decision to invite someone, and that person's decision to go or not go on the boat. The issue of control concerns who is navigating, operating the sails, watching for hazards, working the rudder, and so on. Affection concerns any close relationships that develop between people on the boat.

WEB WORKSHEET

Use or adapt this framework to improve the levels of inclusion, control, and affection within your workgroup or team. Ask each member to make a few notes in each row, and discuss these in the workgroup or team. Members can then plan improvements together, acknowledging and affirming what they are presently doing well, critiquing what they do least well and need to do better, and developing strategies for improving the overall functioning of the workgroup or team.

	What our group does best to ensure that each member has a sense of ... (Be as specific as possible.)	What we do least well (and need to do better) to ensure that each member has a sense of ... (Be as specific as possible.)
Inclusion		
Control		
Affection		

Specific action steps we will take to maintain and improve the dynamics in our workgroup or team:

RELATED LEADERSHIP TOOLS

8.1 Conversations	10.1 HiPo Teams	10.6 Group Leader Skills
8.5 Metacommunicating	10.3 Team Competencies	12.1 The Relationship Bank

FOR FURTHER ASSISTANCE

Schutz, Will. *The Human Element: Productivity, Self-Esteem, and the Bottom Line.* Jossey-Bass, 1994.

Schutz, Will. *The Truth Option.* Ten Speed Press, 1984.

10.5

DEALING WITH DISTURBANCES
IN WORKGROUPS AND TEAMS

Contributed by Layton Fisher and inspired by a conversation with George F. Harding.

Driven by increasing organizational complexity, leadership has come to mean group and team leadership. Yet it remains baffling to many leaders just how much individuals' behavior can change when they interact in a group setting. Perhaps you remember being part of a meeting or group and working on a task when the group couldn't seem to get focused: Some people were bickering, others were goofing off, others were quiet and withdrawn, and still others were plowing ahead, oblivious to the chaos or apathy around them. This tool will help you become more skilled in reading and managing group dynamics. It contains a powerful yet simple set of ideas designed to prevent problems, and to correct problems when they occur.

In any workgroup or team setting, human disturbances take precedence over teamwork and the task of the group. In addition, these disturbances take precedence in a particular order: *I*, then *We*, and finally *It*.

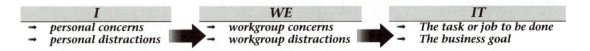

I	WE	IT
→ *personal concerns* → *personal distractions*	→ *workgroup concerns* → *workgroup distractions*	→ *The task or job to be done* → *The business goal*

THE I

This means that if *I* am disturbed—tired, had an argument at home before coming to the office, need to go to the washroom, am unclear about the purpose of the meeting, etc.—my disturbance will demand my attention. It will take precedence over giving my attention to *We*, the group. People will be distracted, thinking about what happened at home, looking at their watches and waiting for a break, or fumbling through their notes looking for the meeting notice so they can remember why they are here! People's energy and creativity, needed to produce superior results, will not be *present* to the group, to the *We*, until their *I* disturbances have been resolved.

THE WE

If there is a disturbance in the *We*, the workgroup or team—the agenda is unclear, there's confusion about who is in charge, there's leftover tension from a previous meeting, or unhealthy competition between members, etc.—this disturbance will take precedence over the work—the *It*. The *We* will demand people's attention and prevent focus from being directed toward *It*, the task (the purpose for coming together in the first place). People's energy and creativity, needed to produce superior results, will not be *present* to the group until their *We* issues have been resolved.

The need to deal with unresolved *I* and *We* issues is why people invest in informal and relationship time, like coffee discussions before morning meetings begin. This informal time gives space to vent and let go of a few *I* disturbances—heavy traffic, a fight with the kids, complaints about too many meetings. It's also a time for reconnecting with folks they haven't seen for awhile, meeting new members of the group, and so on.

THE IT

The ultimate purpose of a workgroup is to produce superior results in an efficient way. But superior and efficient performance cannot be accomplished without dealing with the *I* and the *We*. This is why opening rituals are so useful in workgroup and team meetings—introductions; reviewing the agenda; estimating meeting time; clarifying desired outcomes; reviewing roles for the meeting chairperson, timekeeper, scribe, and so on. Opening rituals help clarify some of the *We* issues and prevent these issues from becoming disturbances. It's also advisable to clarify the *It*, the group's task and goals (the reason the group came together in the first place).

Unleash the power of workgroups and teams by taking care of disturbances during meeting start-ups. Meetings with hurried starts—"Never mind the chitchat, let's get to work"—often get bogged down quickly. Disturbances take precedence if time is not allowed for clearing away *I* and *We* issues. This then draws individuals' and the group's attention away from the task at hand, the *It*. Always remember, at the beginning of a meeting or workgroup activity, to a) make time so that *I* disturbances can be aired and cleared away, b) review group or *We* issues, and c) clarify task or *It* outcomes. Doing so gives everyone in the group an opportunity to help ensure that their efforts produce superior results for the company.

HOW TO USE THIS LEADERSHIP TOOL

"Certain concerns almost always exist among the people entering a potential team situation. ... 'What are the real agendas here?' 'What is this going to mean for me?' ... 'How long is this going to last?'"
—Jon Katzenbach and Douglas Smith, *THE WISDOM OF TEAMS*

As a leader, you need a number of group models and tools. This diagnostic tool will help you anticipate and manage workgroups and teams. It's a simple approach for anticipating, noticing, and signaling problems: "I think we need to deal with some *We* issues now, before we move on," or "I think we have spent enough time on *I*, and need to start working on *It*, the task."

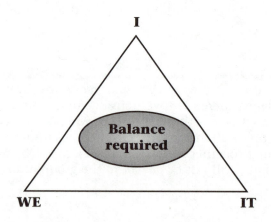

WEB WORKSHEET

Use the workspace provided to assess where you can use this tool and how you might go about introducing it to your workgroup or team.

Think back to a situation when your workgroup or team was not particularly effective. Which disturbances were likely not dealt with appropriately (*I, We,* or *It*)?

How could the *I, We, It* model have helped in this situation?

Think of an instance when your workgroup or team was particularly effective, producing superior results. How were *I, We,* and *It* dealt with and balanced?

How can you use the *I, We, It* model to improve your workgroup or team? (Note a couple of specific actions you will take.)

RELATED LEADERSHIP TOOLS

8.6 Communication 101	10.6 Group Leader Skills	12.3 Triangulation
10.3 Team Competencies	11.1 Process Cycle	12.7 Dealing with Conflict

FOR FURTHER ASSISTANCE

Berne, E. *Games People Play: The Psychology of Human Relationships.* Ballantine, 1964.

Cousins, Norman. *Human Options.* Berkley Books, 1981.

10.6 ASSESSING YOUR GROUP LEADERSHIP SKILLS

Inspired by William Dyer and numerous other sources.

More and more work is being done in groups and teams, because:

✔ Organizations and technology are becoming more complex. To get the job done today, leaders need to be skilled at marshaling complementary skills from a wide range of professions and professionals. [☛ 4.9 Professional Expertise]

✔ Stakeholder systems are becoming more complex, and more people require input into decisions in return for their support. [☛ 5.7 Stakeholder Groups]

✔ Commitment, as opposed to compliance, is needed in knowledge-based organizations. Committed people generate higher-quality, more innovative products and services. But commitment isn't automatic. It's an outcome of effective leadership, and is enhanced by involving and informing people and encouraging them to influence decisions within their workgroups or teams.

Rate your group leadership skills from 1 = Definitely needs improvement, to 5 = Very capable.

Helping a Group Get Established:

1 2 3 4 5   I can help a group establish its purpose and goals.
1 2 3 4 5   I can help a group establish its ground rules.
1 2 3 4 5   I can help a group clarify roles and individual accountabilities.
1 2 3 4 5   I can help a group deal with start-up difficulties.
[☛ 2.6 Clarifying Purpose, 2.7 Goal Statements, 10.8 Ground Rules, 11.1 Process Cycle]

Group Dynamics:

1 2 3 4 5   I understand the stages of group development.
1 2 3 4 5   In a group, I am simultaneously conscious of process (how issues are being dealt with) and content (what is being dealt with).
1 2 3 4 5   I can be helpful at either the content or the process level.
1 2 3 4 5   I can help a group deal with emotional issues and conflict.
1 2 3 4 5   I can give and receive feedback in a group setting.
[☛ 8.6 Communication 101, 10.1 HiPo Teams, 11.1 Process Cycle, 12.7 Dealing with Conflict]

Leading a Specific Group Session:

1 2 3 4 5   I can help a group clarify its purpose for a meeting.
1 2 3 4 5   I understand and can help a group establish the expected results of a meeting.
1 2 3 4 5   I can help a group establish suitable roles for a meeting.
1 2 3 4 5   I understand and can help a group with a process agenda for a meeting.
1 2 3 4 5   I can elicit participation at meetings.
1 2 3 4 5   I can make information visible.
1 2 3 4 5   I can use audiovisuals effectively.
1 2 3 4 5   I can keep a meeting on time and on track.
1 2 3 4 5   I can help a group close on decisions and plans.

1 2 3 4 5   I can deal with typical dysfunctional meeting behavior.
1 2 3 4 5   I know how to ensure both quality decisions and commitment in meetings.
[☛ 10.5 Group Disturbances, 10.7 Getting Participation, 11.1 Process Cycle, 11.3 Meeting Checklist]

Process Tools:

1 2 3 4 5   I understand the need for both developmental and evaluative thinking.
1 2 3 4 5   I have models and can use group problem-solving, decision-making, and planning tools.
1 2 3 4 5   I can lead a group in developing new ideas by using reframing and brainstorming processes.
1 2 3 4 5   I can help a group set priorities.
1 2 3 4 5   I can help a group sort out complex situations.
[☛ 6.3 Complex Situations, 6.9 Brainstorming, 7.2 Problem Solving, 7.5 Decision Making]

In General:

1 2 3 4 5   People see me as an effective group leader.
1 2 3 4 5   People see me as an effective meeting facilitator.

How to use this leadership tool

"In a well-functioning group, the behavior of the leader is not all that different from the behavior of other responsible group members. In fact, if it were not for the trappings of titles, private corner offices, desks with overhangs, a seat at the head of the table, and so on, it might be difficult to identify the leader in a group that is working well."

—Richard Farson, *MANAGEMENT OF THE ABSURD*

This tool will help you stand back and assess your effectiveness as a leader. Review your ratings. Highlight the skills that are currently strengths, and those that need improvement. Use the workspace provided here to plan how you will improve those leadership skills needing further development. Additionally, ask a couple of your trusted colleagues or members of your workgroup to complete the assessment, in order to give you feedback on your leadership skills.

WEB WORKSHEET

My group leadership strengths	How I will continue to develop my group leadership strengths

Group leadership development needs	Steps I will take to improve my group leadership deficits

RELATED LEADERSHIP TOOLS

1.2 Manage or Lead?	10.5 Group Disturbances	11.1 Process Cycle
10.3 Team Competencies	10.7 Getting Participation	11.3 Meeting Checklist

FOR FURTHER ASSISTANCE

Dyer, William. *Team Building: Issues and Alternatives*. Addison-Wesley, 1987.

10.7

GETTING PARTICIPATION

Inspired by Jean Illsley Clarke, Robert Jolles, and numerous other sources.

Eliciting group participation is a crucial skill for leaders, for many reasons:

✔ The best way to gain personal commitment and buy-in is through participation.

✔ Participation can lead to higher-quality, more innovative solutions.

✔ Two heads are better than one. Effective participation leads to synergy. Two or more people working together well can accomplish much more than the sum of the results of these same people working separately.

✔ Leaders need people's commitment, not their compliance. Ideally, you want the discretionary effort to support and advance the process, not impede it. The best way to get this discretionary effort is through involvement.

HOW TO SECURE PARTICIPATION IN A GROUP

There is no one best way to elicit participation from a group. Some suggestions are:

❑ *Ask for participation.* Making a direct and honest request for participation is very effective.

❑ *Build participation into project plans and meetings.* Plan when and how to elicit participation.

❑ *Do not dominate airtime yourself.* The most common reason for lack of participation is lack of opportunity provided by an overcontrolling or dominating leader.

❑ *The earlier you give people the opportunity to participate,* the more likely they are to participate.

❑ *People are more likely to participate in decisions and plans that they have opportunities to influence.* [☞ 9.2 Situational Leadership]

❑ *Express appreciation and thank people* who participate. Be careful of early implied evaluation of participant ideas: using a phrase like "Excellent idea" only when it supports your own viewpoint, for example. [☞ 12.1 The Relationship Bank]

❑ *Protect the first few ideas.* Participants often judge the safety of participation by how well the first couple of contributions are handled.

❑ *Ask open-ended questions to get participation going.*

❑ *Asking for examples is a powerful way of getting participation.* Participants often find it easier to tell a story than to state an abstract idea.

❑ *Always verbally summarize or visibly record key points,* so participants know you understand, before you make an evaluative or rebuttal response. [☞ 8.7 Active Listening]

How to handle participation in a group

✔ *Break the group into subgroups early;* ask a spokesperson to lead the reporting on an issue. People who may be reluctant to speak up in a large group will often participate readily in a small group.

✔ *Leave contentious issues until the group has warmed up to participation.* Put a safe agenda item at the beginning of the meeting.

✔ *Don't wait until you need participation to ask for it.* Consistently ask for and support participation.

✔ *Always summarize or paraphrase participants' contributions,* particularly if you have a differing view. [☛ 8.7 Active Listening]

✔ *Participants are much more likely to hear you if you demonstrate that you heard them.* If you hear something you disagree with, acknowledge or make the idea visible before commenting. [☛ 1.8 Recursive Leadership]

✔ *Be careful how you handle contentious contributions outside a meeting.* If you talk outside a meeting about how dumb the participants were inside the meeting, you can expect low participation at your next meeting. [☛ 10.5 Group Disturbances]

✔ *Call group members participants if you want them to be an active rather than a passive audience.* Call sessions where you want participation workshops, working sessions, or bull sessions rather than the more passive meetings, presentations, updates, or seminars.

✔ *How you arrange room seating can add to or detract from participation.* Arrange the room so participants can see and talk easily with each other. [☛ 11.3 Meeting Checklist]

✔ *Observe other group leaders.* What do they do that enhances or inhibits participation?

How to use this leadership tool

"The challenge is to make 'have-to's' into 'want-to's'."
—Geoff Bellman, *GETTING THINGS DONE WHEN YOU ARE NOT IN CHARGE*

Too much participation may cause as many problems as too little. *Too much:* Decisions will take too much time and some people will think you are abdicating your leadership role. *Too little:* People will feel that they have no ownership and that you are overcontrolling. The optimal amount of participation needs some thought and planning. Where do you need participation and how will you secure it?

WEB WORKSHEET

Think about specific situation(s) in which you need participation. Reread the checklists and make a specific action plan to secure participation

Participation technique	Your specific action

If you are serious about developing your participation skills, use this plan as a feedback and discussion agenda with others who have seen you lead. If you are coaching someone, use it as a coaching tool. [☛ 13.1 Coaching]

RELATED LEADERSHIP TOOLS

8.6 Communication 101	10.3 Team Competencies	11.1 Process Cycle
8.7 Active Listening	10.6 Group Leader Skills	12.2 Trust

FOR FURTHER ASSISTANCE

Clarke, Jean Illsley. *Who, Me Lead a Group?* Harper & Row, 1984.

Jolles, Robert L. *How to Run Seminars and Workshops: Presentation Skills for Consultants, Trainers, and Teachers.* John Wiley & Sons, 1993.

Klatt, Bruce. *The Ultimate Training Workshop Handbook: A Comprehensive Guide to Leading Successful Workshops and Training Programs.* McGraw-Hill, 1999.

10.8

GROUND RULES: HELPING GROUPS TO ACHIEVE BUSINESS RESULTS

Inspired by Peter Block and numerous other sources.

Clear and empowering ground rules help leaders achieve results through workgroups and teams. Thus, knowing how to establish and work with ground rules has become an essential leadership skill in modern, knowledge-based organizations.

WHAT ARE GROUND RULES?

Often part of a team charter, ground rules are explicit guidelines that support and demand healthy group process and member behavior. Similar terms include group norms, behavioral guidelines, group operating principles, and so on. Ground rules can cover such things as:

- ✔ how decisions will be made
- ✔ how information will be recorded
- ✔ how closure will be reached
- ✔ how conflict will be managed
- ✔ how meetings will operate
- ✔ what preparation is expected before a meeting

WHY ESTABLISH GROUND RULES?

Whether or not they are explicit, workgroups and even entire organizations have norms and established patterns of interacting (e.g., who supports whom, how sensitive information is handled). Over time, implicit norms and practices become embedded in the very fabric of a group or organization, and take on the mantle of dogma. Despite the difficulty these norms may cause, they come to be seen as normal, and as "how we do things around here." Thus, although some norms outlive their usefulness and become limitations on member satisfaction and group success, they are nonetheless self-perpetuating, and challenging them can seem like heresy. Explicit ground rules help to surface these norms, making them legitimate topics of discussion and challenge. In this way, ineffective norms and dysfunctional patterns of interacting are replaced. Over time, group satisfaction and achievement improve accordingly. [☞ 4.5 Culture]

HOW MANY GROUND RULES, AND HOW MUCH TIME WILL IT TAKE?

The nature, scope, and number of ground rules that are needed to facilitate group success will depend on a range of factors (e.g., the type of group interaction required, how much time the group is expected to spend together). For a short-term task force, a few minutes may be sufficient to establish a few key process and behavioral parameters. For long-term teams, a few hours may be needed over a few meetings. Generally, a short list of the most critical ground rules (six or seven) is more desirable than a long wish list.

A FIVE-STEP PROCESS FOR ESTABLISHING GROUND RULES

1. Explain the concept: What are ground rules? What are the benefits of making them explicit? Provide examples of typical group concerns and how ground rules support effective group functioning.

2. Brainstorm with the group: Visibly record a list of potential ground rules.

3. Clarify and organize: Go back over the list to ensure understanding, then organize the items into logical categories.

4. Prioritize: Give each participant 10 votes; ask them to assign votes to the ground rules they think are most important for group functioning. Use the highest-rated ground rules.

5. Monitor: Continually remind people of the ground rules. Keep them posted in the group's meeting room.

ADDITIONAL TIPS

✔ Consider generating ground rules over a number of meetings, especially with groups that are unfamiliar with this leadership tool. Even if you only elicit a few obvious ground rules at the first meeting, post these and refer to them at each successive group meeting. Also, at the start of each meeting, ask for additional ground rules that people may wish to add to the list.

✔ When group difficulties arise, use the existing ground rules, and add additional ground rules as needed to overcome the difficulties. If the list of ground rules becomes too long, prioritize and bring it back to a more manageable size. Finally, refer to the appropriate ground rule(s) when making an intervention in the group. For example, when a meeting is *not* starting on time, you might say something like, "As we agreed in our ground rules, now that we've waited five minutes, we need to begin."

HOW TO USE THIS LEADERSHIP TOOL

Eighty percent of conflict is due to unclear expectations.

Concerns about group meetings can range from participants coming late to groups failing to reach closure on decisions and plans. Posting a list of ground rules in the group's meeting room(s) can result in more effective meetings and sharply reduce frustrations. Here is a sample list of ground rules.

Ground Rules

- We will start meetings on time. Late participants will contribute $1 to the charity fund.
- Every meeting will have written Expected Results and an Agenda. We will rotate the responsibility for preparing these.
- Someone will summarize the decision or plan before we move on to a new topic.
- Group decisions and plans will be visibly posted in our meeting room.
- Only one person will talk at a time. No side conversations.
- It is always okay to disagree or to present another point of view.
- If someone becomes emotional over an issue, the next person must summarize before responding.
- If you don't agree, say so inside the meeting. Outside the meeting, everyone will support all decisions that were made in the meeting.
- As many decisions as possible will be made by consensus.

Develop a few critical ground rules at your next group meeting. Use voting, if necessary, to keep the list meaningful and brief.

Initial brainstormed list of ground rules	Votes	Revised short list of ground rules

RELATED LEADERSHIP TOOLS

10.3 Team Competencies   10.7 Getting Participation   10.10 Closure

10.6 Group Leader Skills   10.9 Visible Information   11.1 Process Cycle

FOR FURTHER ASSISTANCE

Block, Peter. *Flawless Consulting: A Guide to Getting Your Expertise Used*. University Associates, 1978.

Klatt, Bruce. *The Ultimate Training Workshop Handbook: A Comprehensive Guide to Leading Successful Workshops and Training Programs*. McGraw-Hill, 1999.

MAKING INFORMATION VISIBLE

Inspired by Robert Jolles, Peter Block, and numerous other sources.

If you are a leader, people will come to you with messy and complex problems, multiple and uncertain causes, and a range of possible solutions, each affecting a group of stakeholders in a different way. You want them to leave your office with the complex situation sorted out, *and* with a clear picture of what needs to be done.

In these situations, there are multiple benefits of making information visible (e.g., on a whiteboard or flip chart):

✔ It clarifies often unclear verbal communication.

✔ It cuts down on repetition. People know that you have grasped the key points.

✔ It demonstrates listening (i.e., you have written what you heard).

✔ Written words and pictures increase retention. They are aids to memory.

✔ Many people are visual learners. They much prefer to "see the problem."

✔ It aids innovation by helping people to put otherwise unrelated issues together.

✔ It serves as documentation of the meeting.

✔ It aids in priority setting and action planning by displaying the big picture.

Tips for making information visible:

❑ Use short phrases (three to five words) and use key points only.

❑ Write just enough to be able to reconstruct the idea. *Do not try to write long sentences.*

❑ Write the person's exact words and phrases whenever possible.

❑ Flip charts are ideal to use, because you can tear off the page and post it on the wall. In this way, you can display the full range of ideas being discussed.

❑ If you are brainstorming, write everyone's input first; discuss and clarify later.

❑ If spelling is a problem for you, abbreviate or put "sp?" next to the word.

❑ If you are sitting with one or two people, use a note pad to make information visible.

❑ Thank people for their contributions, but don't imply evaluation by using phrases like "Excellent idea."

TYPICAL CONCERNS ABOUT MAKING INFORMATION VISIBLE

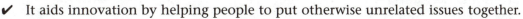

With practice, many of these concerns can be minimized:

• Only a few words or ideas can be captured for each idea expressed. This can actually be helpful, because it keeps the expression of ideas brief. It is challenging to distill a few key words from a complex idea, and still keep the tone and meaning of the speaker. On the other hand, the few chosen words can convey the heart of the idea and add to understanding.

- Recording information on a flip chart may at first appear to slow down a meeting. In fact, the investment of a few minutes up front to capture ideas and comments and make them visible to the entire group often yields substantial dividends later in a meeting.
- The leader needs to develop these skills:
  - Write large, legibly, and quickly.
  - Spell reasonably well.
  - Think about what to write, write clearly, and listen at the same time.
- The proper equipment must be available (e.g., whiteboard, flip chart, pens, tape, and so on).
- It takes practice for a leader to be able to record information on a flip chart or some other form of common text, contribute to the content of the discussion, and guide the process, all at the same time. Consider using another person as a recorder or scribe until you are comfortable handling these roles simultaneously.

How to use this leadership tool

A picture is worth a thousand words.

Signs of frustration in meetings include:

✗ wandering conversations,
✗ agenda items not concluded with clear decisions or plans,
✗ revisiting decisions from previous meetings,
✗ low creativity, and
✗ people feeling that they are not being heard.

Making information visible can help alleviate these frustrations. Keep a whiteboard or flip chart in your group's regular meeting room to capture brainstorming items, and visibly record decisions and plans. Your meetings will soon become more effective.

WEB WORKSHEET

1. Here are just a few of the opportunities you might have to make information visible. Check off those that fit, and add your own specific uses.

Opportunities for making information visible	What you will do to maximize these opportunities
❑ Working toward closure on decisions and action plans [☛ 10.10 Closure]	
❑ Brainstorming (e.g., recording data related to an issue) [☛ 6.9 Brainstorming]	

❑ Sorting out complex situations	[☛ 6.3 Complex Situations]
❑ Prioritizing items	[☛ 10.11 Priority Setting]
❑ Designing a new process	[☛ 11.1 Process Cycle]
❑ Organizing data for problem solving or decision making	[☛ 7.2 Problem Solving, 7.5 Decision Making]
❑ Planning	[☛ 10.12 RASCI Planning]

2. Make a list of equipment and supplies you need to have available for your meeting room. Examples:
   - ❑ flip chart and paper
   - ❑ colored marking pens appropriate for the media
   - ❑ whiteboard and proper pens
   - ❑ overhead projector, acetates, and proper pens

RELATED LEADERSHIP TOOLS

6.3 Complex Situations	6.9 Brainstorming	10.12 RASCI Planning
6.5 Force-Field Analysis	10.7 Getting Participation	11.3 Meeting Checklist

FOR FURTHER ASSISTANCE

Block, Peter. *Flawless Consulting: A Guide to Getting Your Expertise Used.* University Associates, 1978.

Hiebert, Murray. *Powerful Professionals: Getting Your Expertise Used Inside Organizations.* Recursion Press, 1999.

Jolles, Robert L. *How to Run Seminars and Workshops: Presentation Skills for Consultants, Trainers, and Teachers.* John Wiley & Sons, 1993.

Klatt, Bruce. *The Ultimate Training Workshop Handbook: A Comprehensive Guide to Leading Successful Workshops and Training Programs.* McGraw-Hill, 1999.

10.10 CLOSURE: HELPING GROUPS MAKE DECISIONS AND PLANS EFFICIENTLY

Inspired by John Cleese, Victor Vroom, Philip Yetton, and John E. Jones.

Have you ever been to a meeting at which the discussion went on and on? Or a decision was just about to be made, and the topic switched to a new issue? Or much of the meeting was spent deciding what was decided at the last meeting? Closure skills improve the efficiency of group meetings. They do this by ensuring that decisions are made, plans are understood, and people are committed to taking appropriate action.

Using clear terminology helps:

✔ Terms such as consensus and consultation are often misunderstood. *Consensus* means most agree, and everybody can live with the decision. *Consultation*, on the other hand, is a process of gathering input from others, but then making the decision yourself. Thus, when you're consulting with someone, it's important to let the person know that, while you will be listening carefully to what he or she has to say, *you* alone will ultimately be making the decision.

✔ The distinction between consensus and voting can be explained this way: With voting, 50 percent or more of the people in the group need to agree; with consensus, 50 percent or more of *each person* needs to agree. Thus, with consensus, the decision reached may not be your preferred option, but you can live with it and support it.

Use this matrix to ensure that you are clear on terminology.

CLOSURE MATRIX

Method of deciding	Typical question or statement	Pros	Cons
Unanimity	*"Do we all agree?"*	High degree of ownership and commitment.	Can take a lot of time, and may prove to be impossible.
Consensus	*"Can you live with this?"* or, *"Can you go along with this?"*	Everyone has a minimum level of acceptance.	Can appear wishy-washy. At its worst, consensus might result only in compliance.
Voting	*"How many agree?"* or, *"Are most of us agreed?"*	Fits with our democratic culture; relatively fast.	May create losers and winners.
Consultation	*"I need to make this decision myself, but I want your input. Can you tell me …?"*	Encourages input and involvement, even though the leader will ultimately make the decision.	Some people may think that the leader never really heard them out or took their perspective seriously.
Directive	*"I'll make the final decision."*	Fast. Can break deadlocks. Useful in emergencies.	People may think that their views were not considered. May result in implementation problems.

TIPS FOR HELPING GROUPS REACH CLOSURE

❑ Signs that closure may be needed include: People repeat themselves; the topic is switched away from the concern at hand; group members seem to be tuning out.

❑ Float trial balloons. If you think an issue has been discussed enough, ask, *"It seems from the discussion that _____ is the way to go. Do you agree?"*

❑ When you hear consensus being reached in the group, make it visible on a whiteboard, overhead projector, or flip chart. Ask whether your visible notes represent the consensus. Sometimes wordsmithing is all that's needed.

❑ A somewhat risky but effective method is to ask a group member to summarize the closing statement. You might say: *"We seem to be ready for closure. Would someone summarize the decision? I'll write it on the white board."*

❑ If closure is expected to be difficult, first lead a discussion about the criteria for closure.

❑ Note the importance of closure in the group's ground rules.

HOW TO USE THIS LEADERSHIP TOOL

"A great deal of a manager's work has to do with allocating resources: manpower, money, and capital. But the single most important resource we allocate ... is our own time."

—Andy Grove, *ONLY THE PARANOID SURVIVE*

Evidence that meetings are in need of this tool:

✗ Your meetings are getting longer and longer.

✗ The group gets 90 percent of the way to a decision, then the discussion drifts back to background information.

✗ The unwritten question, "Have we got consensus?" has gradually become, "Have we got unanimity?"

✗ Any concern or risk associated with the decision seems to prevent closure.

WEB WORKSHEET

Use this closure matrix to improve an upcoming meeting. Clarify what methods of closure you and your group will use, and when they will be used.

A decision that will need to be made at this meeting	Possible closure question(s)
How the group might reach closure (√ one): __ Unanimity __ Consensus __ Voting __ Consultation __ Directive	

A decision that will need to be made at this meeting	Possible closure question(s)
How the group might reach closure (√ one): __ Unanimity __ Consensus __ Voting __ Consultation __ Directive	
How the group might reach closure (√ one): __ Unanimity __ Consensus __ Voting __ Consultation __ Directive	

RELATED LEADERSHIP TOOLS

8.7 Active Listening   10.7 Getting Participation   10.11 Priority Setting

10.6 Group Leader Skills   10.9 Visible Information   11.3 Meeting Checklist

FOR FURTHER ASSISTANCE

Vroom, Victor, and Philip Yetton. *Leadership and Decision Making*. University of Pittsburgh Press, 1973.

10.11

PRIORITY SETTING IN A WORKGROUP OR TEAM

Inspired by Todd Jick, William Dyer, Peter Senge, and numerous other sources.

It's easy and all too common to become bogged down in details or attend to urgent work while more important or strategic work is left undone. The methods presented here will help you set work priorities within a workgroup or team.

Each of the methods assumes that the workgroup will be using a visible list of distinct items (e.g., a list on a flip chart), and that this list will be relatively complete. That is, it will cover the full range of action items that the workgroup or team is currently facing. In addition, the first step in each of the approaches is to read through the list of items within the workgroup and clarify the meaning of each item as you go. If new items are generated, add them to the list. If two or more items are found to be similar, rewrite them into one item. The goal is to have an accurate list of distinct items with as few gaps and overlaps as possible before you begin to determine priorities.

The next steps common to each of the methods is to explain why you are proposing a particular method for setting priorities, and to get agreement that only the top few items will be considered as priorities for action planning. Finally, don't get bogged down in attempting to rank every item. More often than not, the workgroup only needs to agree to clusters of priorities (e.g., the top four priorities, the next six, and so on). The goal, regardless of which method is used, is a small number of high-priority items that will focus the workgroup or team's energy.

METHODS OF PRIORITY SETTING

Method	Best used when	How to
Quick & Dirty	• The group has a good track record of quickly coalescing around work priorities. • There is little risk associated with picking the wrong priority. • The situation is relatively conflict-free (e.g., no one has a vested interest). • The workgroup is relatively small (e.g., up to 12 members).	1. Ask each member of the workgroup or team to take turns putting checkmarks beside their top 2 or 3 priority items. 2. Typically, a short list of 4 to 8 priority items is generated. 3. If necessary, the group can use this same approach to reprioritize the newly generated short list of items. (Note: If 2 or 3 items do not receive clear priority, use one of the other methods.)
Points Method	• The workgroup will coalesce around a set of priorities if a straw vote is taken. • Commitment to follow through is at least as important as a technically correct solution.	1. Give each member of the workgroup or team a number of points (e.g., 25) that he or she can distribute among the items listed. 2. Tally the votes to determine the top few (e.g., 5 to 7) priorities. (Note: Instead of allotting a number of points, allot each member a number of self-sticking dots to place alongside the items listed.)

Method	Best used when	How to

Logical Method	• The situation requires a technically correct answer.
	• Workgroup or team members will commit to a logically correct answer.
		1. Discuss various methods for assembling data logically; for example, consider these tools:
		  ☛ 7.2 Problem Solving
		  ☛ 7.5 Decision Making
		  ☛ 7.7 Quality Tools
		2. Select and apply the method most appropriate to your situation.

Criteria Method	• Getting agreement on priorities may be difficult, because:
	  - There is a high potential for disagreement and conflict around priorities.
	  - Vested interests exist within the workgroup or team.
	
	[☛ 12.7 Dealing with Conflict]
		When the potential for conflict is high, it's important to explain the process and clearly state *why* it is being used.
		1. Ask the workgroup to step back from the list of items for a moment.
		2. Ask members to spend time discussing the criteria or principles they will use to set priorities. For example:
		  - priorities as your customers would see them, or
		  - priorities based on some higher-level principles, or
		  - considerations such as corporate strategy.
		3. Generate an agreed-to set of criteria that will be used to help the workgroup or team determine priorities.
		4. Set priorities based on the agreed criteria.

How to use this leadership tool

"Priority is a function of context, or the 'bigger picture' in which something occurs. ... It's big-picture renewal that puts us in touch with the purposes and patterns of life."

—Stephen Covey, *FIRST THINGS FIRST*

Priority setting focuses the workgroup's energy and commitment on the critical few, high-impact items. A counterpoint to brainstorming, it is the most common form of evaluative thinking. While brainstorming increases the number of options under consideration and raises the level of ambiguity, priority setting guides workgroups toward closure and decision making, and lowers the level of ambiguity.

Type of Thinking	Techniques	Ground Rules
Developmental • Used to generate and surface many ideas.	*Developmental* • Brainstorming • Lateral thinking	*Developmental* • No evaluation, clarification only. • Build on others' ideas. • Creative thinking is encouraged. • Quantity is more important than quality.
Evaluative • Used to narrow in on the best plan of action.	*Evaluative* • Priority setting • Decision making	*Evaluative* • Challenging and questioning are okay. • Debate is okay. • Closure is sought on the best ideas or actions.

WEB WORKSHEET

Think of situations in which you would use each of the priority-setting methods described here. In addition, design an approach to priority setting that is tailored to the unique circumstances of your work situation.

Priority-setting method	When you would use it
Quick & Dirty	
Points Method	
Logical Method	
Criteria Method	
Your own customized method	

RELATED LEADERSHIP TOOLS

6.9 Brainstorming   10.8 Ground Rules   10.10 Closure
10.7 Getting Participation   10.9 Visible Information   10.12 RASCI Planning

FOR FURTHER ASSISTANCE

Dyer, William. *Team Building: Issues and Alternatives*. Addison-Wesley, 1987.

Jick, Todd D. *Managing Change: Cases and Concepts*. Irwin, 1993.

Senge, Peter M., Richard Ross, Bryan Smith, Charlotte Roberts, and Art Kleiner. *The Fifth Discipline Fieldbook: Strategies and Tools for Building a Learning Organization*. Currency Doubleday, 1994.

10.12 RASCI: A Planning Tool for Workgroups and Teams

Inspired by Richard Beckhard and Reubin Harris.

A RASCI chart helps leaders organize and manage complex projects involving a range of stakeholders. It provides a clear picture of what will be done, by whom, by when, and with what support. Look at the words in the RASCI acronym and their meanings. Then, tailor this type of control or communications chart by adding, deleting, or modifying terms to fit the unique circumstances of your project or team situation.

R = Responsible (Who is ultimately responsible for this action or result?)

A = Approval or Authority (Who needs to make the final decision?)

S = Support or Stakeholder (Whose commitment is needed for success?)

C = Consult (Who needs to be consulted for their knowledge, ideas, or input? Note that this is different from obtaining approval or support).

I = Inform (Who needs to be informed before action is taken?)

These partial examples will help you understand how a RASCI chart is used.

Goal: To provide training to all users of the new XYZ system.

Actions	By when	R	A	S	C	I
Identify all the users needing training.	June 30	Pat		Training vendor	HR training	Steering committee
Identify the general training objectives.	June 30	Chris	Kelly	Training vendor	Software vendor	
Identify specific users needing specialized training.	July 31	Pat	Lee	Training vendor		
[additional steps]						
Set up training schedules.	September 31	Pat	Kelly	Training vendor	Corporate services	Steering committee

An alternative is to list the key people or groups and their RASCI, as shown in this example.

Actions	By when	Pat	Chris	Kelly	Lee	Training vendor	Steering committee	Others
Identify all the users needing training.	June 30	R				S	I	HR Training-**C**
Identify the general training objectives.	June 30		R	A		S		
Identify specific users needing specialized training.	July 31					S		Software Vendor-**C**
[additional steps]								
Set up training schedules.	Sept. 31					S	I	Corporate Service-**C**

TIPS

✔ Assign responsibilities only to individuals or true teams (i.e., teams with clear joint accountabilities). [☛ 13.3 Accountability]
✔ Place responsibility at the lowest feasible level. (Senior management is always ultimately responsible.) [☛ 9.2 Situational Leadership]
✔ It may be helpful to use this tool in conjunction with tool ☛ 5.7 Stakeholder Groups.

HOW TO USE THIS LEADERSHIP TOOL

"Responsibility charting clarifies behavior that is required to implement change tasks, actions, or decisions. It helps reduce ambiguity, wasted energy, and adverse emotional reactions between individuals or groups whose interrelationships are affected by change."

—Richard Beckhard and Reubin Harris, *ORGANIZATIONAL TRANSITIONS: MANAGING COMPLEX CHANGE*

A common frustration and cause of inefficiency in workgroups and teams is a lack of clear roles and responsibilities. A RASCI chart can be a huge help in these situations.

The RASCI chart is best used when:

✔ A new workgroup or a new project is being started.
✔ Many people are involved in any project.
✔ A number of new people have joined a project, or the roles of people have changed.
✔ A plan is complex.
✔ There is conflict or confusion in an existing team or workgroup (e.g., "Who has the ball?").

Follow these steps to use the RASCI chart:

1. Get commitment for using the RASCI charting process by showing group members a relevant example (perhaps the example provided here).
2. Define or clarify how the RASCI chart will be used. (Needless to say, this is only possible if the goal of the overall project is clear.) [☛ 11.1 Process Cycle]

3. Decide on a format and complete the matrix by:
   - brainstorming the action steps that need clarity;
   - refining, clarifying, and ordering the action steps; and
   - agreeing who has the R (responsibility for the goal).

WEB WORKSHEET

Goal: _____

Actions	By when						Specific others

RELATED LEADERSHIP TOOLS

2.7 Goal Statements	5.7 Stakeholder Groups	9.2 Situational Leadership
5.1 Change Equation	5.8 Human Transitions	13.3 Accountability

FOR FURTHER ASSISTANCE

Beckhard, Richard, and Rueben Harris. *Organizational Transitions: Managing Complex Change.* Addison-Wesley, 1987.

Tools for Leading Meetings

The most universal complaints of leaders and employees alike revolve around meetings: too many, too long, no results, no follow-through. This section contains all the tools leaders require to hold successful meetings.

11.1

PROCESS CYCLE: PLANNING EFFECTIVE MEETINGS AND EVENTS

The tool described here has been in use for so long that we could not trace it back to its original creator.

When planning a business meeting or an event such as a workshop, management retreat, or conference, leaders usually plan *content* (e.g., topic areas), but often overlook or inadequately plan *process* (e.g., meeting purpose, outcomes being sought). This oversight can result in inefficient, costly meetings that fail to live up to their potential. People's time is expensive, so it's essential that meetings be carefully planned. The payoff is better decisions and greater commitment to implementing and following through on those decisions. The process cycle is a tool for ensuring that these payoffs are realized.

THE PROCESS CYCLE

Use this tool to plan and communicate an event of any duration (e.g., a couple of hours, a day, a week). For ease of reading, the word *meeting* is used here, but could be replaced by *seminar* or the name for whatever event you are planning.

Process cycle step	What you need to do
❶ **Purpose** (Answers the question, *"Why are we having this meeting?"*)	❑ Brainstorm the meeting purposes. Agree on what the purposes are and are not. (Reaching agreement on what the purpose *is not* helps dispel false expectations and keeps the meeting focused. For example, someone might assume that a decision on a new product line should be made at the meeting, when, in reality, the leader or group only wants to focus on a marketing strategy for existing products.) ❑ Agree on the top two or three purposes for the meeting.
❷ **Outcomes** (Answers the question, *"What will we take away from this meeting?"*)	❑ Develop clear (measurable or observable) outcome statements. Outcome statements describe the benefits that participants and other stakeholders will gain as a result of the meeting. Outcome statements provide focus and a basis for evaluating the meeting.
❸ **Steps** (Answers the question, *"What steps do we need to take to achieve our outcomes?"*)	❑ Brainstorm what needs to happen before, during, and after the meeting to achieve the desired outcomes. Don't worry about sequence at this point. ❑ Determine premeeting assignments based on the outcomes being sought, and agree on responsibilities for ensuring that prework is completed. ❑ Next, put these steps in sequence. A little fine-tuning, and you now have the event agenda.
❹ **Capabilities** (Answers the question, *"Who needs to be at the meeting and what ground rules can we use to guide our actions?"*)	❑ Who needs to participate in this meeting? Who should *not* be present? Whose presence is not essential? ❑ What attitudes and behaviors do they need to exhibit (e.g., willingness to share information, maintain confidences, take reasonable risks)? ❑ What ground rules are needed to ensure effective participation and to discourage unacceptable behaviors, such as belittling others' ideas? ❑ What resources are required to prepare for and conduct this meeting? Who will arrange for these resources? What administrative requirements need to be looked after (e.g., facility setup)?
❺ **Feedback** (Answers the question, *"What evaluation and follow-through are needed after the meeting?"*)	❑ How will this meeting be evaluated? ❑ Who needs to be informed of meeting outcomes? ❑ How do we capture our learning as a group? ❑ What will we do to continually improve our meetings?

How to use this tool

"…If leaders specify too much about purpose, goals and approach … they may gain compliance to 'their' purpose. But they are likely to lose commitment to a team purpose."

—John Katzenbach and Douglas Smith, *THE WISDOM OF TEAMS*

Use this tool often, because events are expensive, and this time needs to be well-invested. Just think about the cost of five to a dozen or more people sitting around for an hour, a day, or even longer. This is valuable time, and you need to ensure that your meetings are focused and that people show up prepared.

For a meeting of a half day or longer, it's more powerful to involve others in planning. Use this tool with a small group (e.g., a cross-section of four to six people, possibly including a senior manager who might not be attending but is sponsoring the upcoming meeting). It will take about an hour. For a larger group of a dozen or so people, this planning usually requires a couple of hours. Hold the planning session two or three weeks prior to the scheduled meeting date, so group members will have time to complete the prework assignments that inevitably result when using this tool (e.g., preparing a report for the meeting).

For a short meeting of one or two hours, we recommend this tool for preparing a draft meeting plan. Send it to all participants for their input prior to the meeting. In addition, check with the group at the start of the meeting, in case they want to make any last-minute amendments.

WEB WORKSHEET

Process Cycle Worksheet

Use this template to plan an upcoming meeting, workshop, or event.

❶ **Purpose** (Brainstorm what the purpose is and is not, then prioritize.)	*Why are we having this meeting?*
❷ **Outcomes** (Develop observable and measurable outcomes for each high-priority purpose.)	*What will we take away from this meeting?*

❸ **Steps** (Brainstorm steps, then put them in sequence and assign prework.)	*What steps do we need to take to achieve our outcomes?*
❹ **Capabilities** (Who needs to participate, and what specifically is needed from each person?)	*Who needs to be at this meeting, and what ground rules can we use to guide our actions?*
❺ **Feedback** (Evaluate, inform others, and follow through on decisions.)	*What evaluation and follow-through will be needed after this meeting?*

Related leadership tools

2.6 Clarifying Purpose	10.6 Group Leader Skills	10.8 Ground Rules
2.7 Goal Statements	10.7 Getting Participation	11.2 Meeting Purpose

11.2

MEETINGS: PURPOSE AND FUNCTION IN WORKGROUPS AND TEAMS

Inspired by Antony Jay, M.M. Milstein, and Owen Edwards.

"Meetings fulfill a deep human need. Man is a social species. In every organization and every human culture of which we have record, people come together in small groups at regular and frequent intervals, and in larger tribal gatherings from time to time. If there were no meetings in places where people work, their attachment to their work would be less, and people would meet in societies, clubs, or pubs when work was over."

—Antony Jay, "HOW TO RUN A MEETING"

Attending meetings is a fundamental and essential process for workgroups and teams. No matter how well electronic and other communication methods are used, people are social beings and need face-to-face contact. Meetings can be effective or they can be a waste of time; they can be the best or the worst experience in a workgroup or a team. In addition, meetings are costly: A meeting of a few people can easily cost from $600 to $1,200 per hour in salaries alone.

For the benefits of a meeting to outweigh the costs, the meeting must be guided by basic rules of planning, leading, and follow-up.

When meetings are well-managed, people:	When meetings are not well-managed, people complain that meetings are:
➢ Come prepared.	➢ Too long
➢ Work hard.	➢ Called too often or not often enough
➢ Make important decisions.	➢ Poorly organized and poorly led
➢ Leave with a sense of accomplishment.	➢ Unfocused, or not focused on the most important issues
➢ Produce results.	➢ Easily diverted by members with other agendas

This tool will help you lead results-oriented meetings while also connecting with human needs for interacting and communicating. This table describes the range of purposes and functions that workgroup or team meetings serve when they are managed and led well.

Typical purposes of workgroup and team meetings
✔ sharing information and issues
✔ defining priorities and direction
✔ generating new options and making decisions
✔ generating and gathering data, and sorting out complex situations
✔ developing understanding and commitment to plans and action
✔ reminding participants that they share a common purpose despite their individual jobs and roles
✔ identifying participants to be accountable for and to perform certain tasks

Typical functions of workgroup and team meetings

- **Meetings define workgroups and teams.** Those present belong; those absent do not. Indeed, meetings are often the only occasions when a workgroup or team seems to exist. At other times, it may seem as if people are focusing more on their individual roles and projects than on group goals and teamwork.

- **Meetings germinate group culture and enable group learning.** Knowledge and experience are shared, work habits nurtured, influence and power exercised, and ways of understanding and working are established in the workgroup or team.

- **Meetings clarify collective purpose and focus.** In this way, the workgroup gains and maintains power to achieve business results. Meetings also help members understand how their work aligns with the work of others in the group and with the group's overall success.

- **Meetings support commitment to the group's purpose** and to specific decisions and action plans. Membership implies an obligation to support group decisions.

- **Meetings demonstrate status.** Human nature being what it is, we are often concerned with our status relative to others in a group. One's standing and degree of influence are often displayed in the interactions and decision-making processes that take place in meetings.

- **Meetings meet a very human need,** to be part of a group and communicate with other human beings.

HOW TO USE THIS LEADERSHIP TOOL

"Sometimes the meeting is the message, and accountable results are simply by-products. It is the entirely human inclination of…managers to want a tribal assembly from time to time—the frequency usually varying according to the level of managerial anxiety—not only to communicate ideas and problems, but to see the expressions around the table, (and) to gauge the mood. …"

—Owen Edwards, *UPWARD NOBILITY: HOW TO SUCCEED IN BUSINESS WITHOUT LOSING YOUR SOUL*

How would you summarize or briefly describe the purposes and functions served by your workgroup or team meetings? Consider having the members of your workgroup or team respond independently to the two questions posed here. After they have done so, discuss their answers within the workgroup or team, as a way of gaining clarity on meeting purposes and functions. After members' responses have been discussed in the group, prioritize them for the group as a whole. This will be a learning experience for the group, as the purposes and functions served by workgroup or team meetings are redefined and perhaps even significantly reframed. [☞ 7.1 Problem Framing]

WEB WORKSHEET

What purposes are served by our workgroup or team meetings?

[☞ 2.6 Clarifying Purpose]

What key functions are served by our workgroup or team meetings?

RELATED LEADERSHIP TOOLS

1.3 Leadership	10.1 HiPo teams	11.3 Meeting Checklist
2.6 Clarifying Purpose	11.1 Process Cycle	11.6 Agenda

FOR FURTHER ASSISTANCE

Edwards, Owen. *Upward Nobility: How to Succeed in Business without Losing Your Soul.* 1991.

Jay, Antony. "How to Run a Meeting." *Harvard Business Review.* 1976.

Milstein, M. M. *Toward More Effective Meetings: The 1983 Annual for Facilitators, Trainers, and Consultants.* University Associates, 1983.

11.3
MEETING CHECKLIST: FROM PLANNING TO FOLLOW-UP

Inspired by Andy Grove, Antony Jay, and M.M. Milstein.

Meetings have an earned reputation for inefficiency. This tool provides five steps and checklists to help leaders prepare, operate, and follow through on the meetings they sponsor. Although meetings come in many stripes and colors, all will require some version of these five steps. Adapt the steps to suit your own meeting and leadership needs.

"One possible reason why things aren't going according to plan is that there never was a plan."

—Ashleigh Brilliant

1. Preparing for the meeting

❑ Use a planning tool [☛ 11.1 Process Cycle] to plan the meeting. (While doing this, keep in mind the cost and benefit of the meeting compared to other ways of communicating—memo, e-mail, conference calls, one-on-one meetings, or smaller group meetings.)

❑ Decide who will be the key people at the meeting, then involve a cross-section of them in drafting the purpose and outcomes for the meeting. (Note that these should be active participants, not passive attendees.)

❑ Develop and sequence the agenda so the most important topics are dealt with near the beginning of the meeting. [☛ 11.6 Agenda, 13.5 Time Management]

❑ Distribute the draft statement of purpose and outcomes and the proposed agenda prior to the meeting. Advise participants as to what prework or meeting preparation is required.

❑ Manage workgroup and team meeting size (4 to 7 people is ideal, 10 is tolerable, 12 is the upper limit). If having difficulty getting the meeting down to size, you might decide:
   a. whether smaller groups can work through some of the topics in advance;
   b. whether everyone has to be present for every item; and
   c. whether two or more meetings are needed.

❑ Discuss any special roles you want people to play at the meeting (e.g., recorder, process facilitator).

❑ Prepare the chairperson's opening remarks, and produce meeting materials.

❑ Determine administrative and resource requirements (e.g., room setup, equipment, refreshments).

2. Starting the meeting

"A meeting convened to make specific decisions is hard to keep moving if more than six or seven people attend."

—Andy Grove, *HOW (AND WHY) TO RUN A MEETING*

❑ Arrive early to ensure that the room and other administrative arrangements are in order.

❑ Start on time. This sets a precedent and rewards those who arrived on time.

- ❑ Quickly refine the purpose, goals, and agenda that were distributed prior to the meeting. Add, delete, combine, or reorder items as necessary. This helps to ensure that the group takes responsibility for the meeting's success.
- ❑ Orient the group to the task at hand—purpose, outcomes, process, constraints, and so on. [☞ 11.7 Opening Remarks] Don't invite comments until you have completed your opening remarks.
- ❑ Set a positive, hardworking, and open meeting environment.
- ❑ Ask for active participation:
  - ➠ Don't evaluate or put down participant contributions.
  - ➠ Some silence is okay.
  - ➠ Listen actively to what people say, summarizing their contributions.
- ❑ Quickly review any meeting ground rules. [☞ 10.8 Ground Rules]
- ❑ Quickly review appropriate information from the previous meeting.

3. Advancing the meeting

- ❑ Stick to the agenda once it's agreed to, unless something significant develops. Meeting participants may dislike this constraint. However, they will be even more dissatisfied if agenda items are not dealt with. [☞ 11.5 Chair Accountabilities]
- ❑ Manage the meeting process: Introduce each agenda item, explaining what is to be accomplished and why it is important. Encourage discussion, summarize and review decisions, establish target dates for completion, and so on. [☞ 10.6 Group Leader Skills]
- ❑ If the meeting gets sidetracked: [☞ 12.7 Dealing with Conflict, 12.8 Difficult People]
  - ➠ Never try to one-up a meeting participant; don't evaluate the participant.
  - ➠ Use listening responses (summarizing, paraphrasing).
  - ➠ Remind the group of the purpose of the meeting and of time constraints.
  - ➠ Ask that discussion of side topics take place after the meeting.
- ❑ Get closure on each agenda item—if not a decision or plan, then how the item will be moved forward. Summarize and record (visibly, if possible) agreements reached. This provides a sense of completion for meeting participants. In addition, knowing that actions will be followed up on and that things will happen as a result of the meeting is very motivating for all concerned. [☞ 10.10 Closure]
- ❑ The most common complaints about meetings have to do with the length of meetings:
  - ➠ Frequently remind the group of meeting purpose and of results expected.
  - ➠ Ask for closure on discussions and decisions.
  - ➠ Make information visible (use a flip chart or a whiteboard). [☞ 10.9 Visible Information]
  - ➠ Remind the group of time constraints.
  - ➠ Make meeting process refinements, as required.
  - ➠ Maintain a balance between tight control and innovative discussions.

4. Ending the meeting

- ❑ Have your meetings end on time or sooner. (Items near the end of the agenda should be of a lower priority anyway, and thus easier to reschedule.)
- ❑ Ask participants for commitment to the decisions made and actions proposed during the meeting.
- ❑ If appropriate, set the date for the next meeting and build a draft of the agenda. Include unfinished business from this meeting.
- ❑ Keep minutes of decisions reached, actions assigned, and deadlines for fulfillment. This motivates action and minimizes misinterpretations. [☞ 10.12 RASCI Planning]

❑ Evaluate the meeting to ensure your meetings keep improving. Ask, "What went well?" and "What could we have done differently?"

❑ Thank meeting participants for their contributions.

5. Following up on action plans

❑ Distribute minutes within a day or two following the meeting. [☛ 11.8 Minutes]

❑ Follow up on assigned tasks and publicize progress. This is where the rubber meets the road. Without follow-though on action plans, your meetings will lose power.

HOW TO USE THIS LEADERSHIP TOOL

"Meetings are the fulcrum…the central nervous system of an information society, the center stage for personal performance."

—George David Kieffer, *THE STRATEGY OF MEETINGS*

Use the workspace provided here to develop a plan for managing a meeting that you will be chairing or leading in the near future. Summarize specific actions you will take to ensure that all five steps are well-managed.

WEB WORKSHEET

1. Preparing for the meeting
[☛ 2.6 Clarifying Purpose, 2.7 Goal Statements, 10.7 Getting Participation, 11.1 Process Cycle, 11.6 Agenda]

2. Starting the meeting
[☛ 8.4 Dialogue and Discussion, 10.8 Ground Rules, 11.7 Opening Remarks]

3. Advancing the meeting
[☛ 10.9 Visible Information, 10.10 Closure, 10.11 Priority Setting]

4. Ending the meeting
[☛ 10.12 RASCI Planning]

5. Following up on action plans developed in the meeting

AN ASSESSMENT FOR MEETING LEADER SKILLS

Use this table to assess your skills as a meeting leader. If you are serious about your development, you will ask others to assess your skills as well.

Assessing your success as meeting leader

Organizing the meeting
❑ yes ❑ no Did you involve key participants in defining the purpose and outcomes for the meeting?
❑ yes ❑ no Was the meeting plan distributed well in advance of the meeting?
❑ yes ❑ no Did you ensure that people came to the meeting prepared?

Starting up the meeting
❑ yes ❑ no Did your opening remarks clarify the purpose, process, and boundaries for the meeting?
❑ yes ❑ no Did you clarify your role as chairperson, and how it relates to the outcomes being sought from the meeting?

Relating with meeting participants
❑ yes ❑ no Did you relate personally with each meeting participant?
❑ yes ❑ no Were you positive and enthusiastic?
❑ yes ❑ no Did you provide a comfortable setting for the meeting?
❑ yes ❑ no Did you negotiate, clarify, and adhere to ground rules with the group?
❑ yes ❑ no Did you create a protective climate in which it was safe for people to speak up?
❑ yes ❑ no Did you invite and support people's contributions to the meeting?
❑ yes ❑ no Did you keep a comfortable pace?
❑ yes ❑ no Did you start on time and end on time?

Facilitating the meeting
❑ yes ❑ no Did you divide the meeting into orderly steps?
❑ yes ❑ no Were discussions thought-provoking?
❑ yes ❑ no Did you invite and challenge meeting participants to think and innovate?
❑ yes ❑ no Did you offer your opinions?
❑ yes ❑ no Did you enable meeting participants to tap the resources of the group as a whole?
❑ yes ❑ no Did the discussion relate directly to the outcomes being sought from the meeting?
❑ yes ❑ no Did you provide opportunities for meeting participants to share information with each other?

Evaluating the meeting
❑ yes ❑ no Did you ask meeting participants what they achieved?
❑ yes ❑ no Did you work with meeting participants to evaluate the meeting?

Reflecting on your success as chairperson
❑ yes ❑ no Did you take care of yourself by being well prepared for your role as meeting chairperson?
❑ yes ❑ no Did you specifically state to meeting participants your responsibility to them?
❑ yes ❑ no Have you considered how to build on your achievements as a meeting chairperson, as well as improving where needed?

RELATED LEADERSHIP TOOLS

11.1 Process Cycle	11.3 Meeting Checklist	11.7 Opening Remarks
11.2 Meeting Purpose	11.6 Agenda	13.5 Time Management

FOR FURTHER ASSISTANCE

Grove, Andy. *High Output Management.* Vintage Books, 1983.

Grove, Andy. *Only the Paranoid Survive: How to Exploit the Crisis Points That Challenge Every Company and Career.* Currency Doubleday, 1996.

Jay, Antony. "How to Run a Meeting." *Harvard Business Review.* 1976.

Milstein, M. M. *Toward More Effective Meetings: The 1983 Annual for Facilitators, Trainers, and Consultants.* University Associates, 1983.

11.4

MEETING ROLES

Inspired by Richard Dunsing.

"Each meeting is a miniature management cycle."

—Richard Dunsing, *YOU AND I HAVE SIMPLY GOT
TO STOP MEETING THIS WAY*

Each of the meeting roles presented here is unique, although you may not require all of them at any given meeting. For example, not all meetings will benefit equally from having a timekeeper or a process advisor. Nonetheless, consider the usefulness of these roles as you plan the various meetings you lead within organizations.

Role	Responsibilities
Chairperson (meeting leader)	❑ Provide overall leadership for the meeting. ❑ Ensure that participants understand; also, promote commitment to the purpose, goals, agenda, roles, process, and ground rules [☛ 2.6 Clarifying Purpose, 2.7 Goal Statements, 11.1 Process Cycle, 11.6 Agenda] ❑ Orient the group to the meeting (e.g., introduce the meeting, restate purpose), and to each topic (e.g., why the topic is important, how participants are expected to contribute). [☛ 11.7 Opening Remarks] ❑ Focus the process of the meeting (e.g., keep the group on track, challenge the group to tackle issues, summarize decisions reached and plans made, summarize the entire meeting). [☛ 10.6 Group Leader Skills, 10.10 Closure] ❑ Draw out the best thinking of the group (i.e., ensure that all members contribute, protect minority opinion, test for consensus). [☛ 10.7 Getting Participation] ❑ Share leadership with meeting participants, and build a climate for dialogue (e.g., open, encouraging, appreciative, nondefensive). [☛ 8.4 Dialogue and Discussion] ❑ Work within the meeting ground rules and model the behavior you expect of others in the meeting (e.g., minimize off-topic discussion, demonstrate commitment to the process, be open to other peoples' methods of communicating). [☛10.8 Ground Rules]
Meeting Participants (all involved)	❑ Prepare for the meeting as requested, using the agenda as a guide. ❑ Place items of concern on the agenda. ❑ Arrive on time. ❑ Support those who are filling other roles (e.g., meeting timekeeper). ❑ Work within the meeting ground rules (e.g., minimize off-topic discussion, demonstrate commitment to the process, be open to other peoples' methods of communicating). ❑ Participate (e.g., share views, respond to questions, provide input). ❑ Listen carefully, constantly check perception of what was heard, and express differences positively. ❑ Be alert to process (how things are discussed), to content (what is being discussed), and to outcomes (why you are meeting). ❑ Organize input by speaking clearly when a contribution is relevant, and making only one point at a time:

	– State the idea you want the group to consider. – Relate your idea to the discussion at hand. – Support your idea with evidence. – Ask meeting participants to respond to your idea. ❑ Follow through on decisions and action plans agreed to at the meeting.
Recorder (scribe, minute taker)	❑ Capture participants' thinking, preferably visibly on a flip chart, whiteboard, or other visible medium. [☛ 10.9 Visible Information] ❑ Clarify vague statements and unclear conclusions. ❑ Record, preferably visibly, all decisions, the rationale, and actions agreed upon. ❑ Prepare and distribute meeting minutes promptly (within a day or two after the meeting at the most).
Process Advisor (facilitator)	❑ Be skilled in applying the principles and techniques of group process (e.g., organizing, goal setting, conflict management, brainstorming, problem solving, action planning, assigning responsibilities, questioning). ❑ Observe group process during the meeting and intervene with suggestions for improvement. [☛ 10.6 Group Leader Skills]
Timekeeper	❑ Keep track of time, and assist the group with time management during the meeting. ❑ Help the group to start and end on time.
Administrator	❑ Distribute the agenda and prework well in advance of the meeting. ❑ Ensure that the meeting facility and equipment are booked, set up, and ready to go. ❑ Ensure that meeting equipment and materials are available and ready. ❑ Ensure that refreshments are available.

HOW TO USE THIS LEADERSHIP TOOL

"The meeting must have goals, priorities, timeframes, task assignments, and evaluation to be effective. It will have agendas, internal procedures, and rules to guide members toward their goals. Without these, any meeting energy generated will be unfocused."

—Richard Dunsing, *YOU AND I HAVE SIMPLY GOT TO STOP MEETING THIS WAY*

Would your meetings benefit by having responsibilities more clearly assigned and roles more clearly defined? Adapt and, if necessary, add to this list of meeting roles for your workgroup or team. Use the workspace provided here to outline the roles and duties most needed for your meetings.

WEB WORKSHEET

Organizer (administrator)	*Chairperson* (meeting leader)

Timekeeper	Process Advisor (meeting enabler)
Meeting Participants (all involved)	Recorder (scribe)
Other (specify) _____	Other (specify) _____

RELATED LEADERSHIP TOOLS

9.1 Leadership Versatility	10.7 Getting Participation	11.1 Process Cycle
10.6 Group Leader Skills	10.8 Ground Rules	11.5 Chair Accountabilities

FOR FURTHER ASSISTANCE

Dunsing, Richard J. *You and I Have Simply Got to Stop Meeting This Way.* Amacom, 1978.

11.5

THE CHAIRPERSON'S ROLE:
DUTIES AND ACCOUNTABILITIES

Inspired by Antony Jay and M.M. Milstein.

The chairperson is the meeting leader, and is accountable for the success of the meeting. As meeting leader, you need to be committed to the meeting's purpose, prepare thoroughly, ensure that others come to the meeting prepared, and guide the meeting toward achieving defined results. Here is an outline of the chairperson's accountabilities and duties.

Chairperson accountabilities
(what the chairperson is expected to **achieve**)
✔ Ensure that meetings are well planned, with a clear purpose and clearly defined outcomes.
✔ Ensure that the right people are invited to participate in the meeting.
✔ Ensure that participants come to the meeting prepared.
✔ Hold all meeting participants responsible for contributing to the success of the meeting.
✔ Ensure that meetings achieve their defined purpose and outcomes.
✔ Ensure that meeting minutes are accurate and are sent to meeting participants promptly.

Chairperson duties
(what the chairperson is expected to **do**)

Planning the meeting:
❏ Send the agenda to invited participants well in advance of the meeting. (The agenda should contain meeting purpose, outcomes, topics, and preparation required.)
❏ Contract premeeting assignments with invited participants.
❏ Assign meeting roles. [☛ 11.4 Meeting Roles]

Starting the meeting:
❏ Organize, open, and facilitate the meeting. [☛ 11.7 Opening Remarks]
❏ Clarify ground rules (e.g., expected participation, and how closure on items will be achieved) [☛10.8 Ground Rules]
❏ Contract with meeting participants to finish on time, if they come prepared and on time.
❏ Let meeting participants know the game plan (e.g., meeting purpose, outcomes being sought, the process to be used, exactly what will and will not be covered, time available).

Facilitating discussion:
❏ Provide structure to facilitate meeting discussion, and keep the meeting directed toward defined outcomes (e.g., interpret and clarify discussion in order to keep the meeting moving forward). [☛ 10.6 Group Leader Skills]
❏ Start discussion of each agenda item by clarifying why the item is on the agenda and what the group needs to accomplish (e.g., make a decision, preliminary discussion only, assign responsibilities).

Managing participation:
❏ Prevent misunderstanding by clarifying and summarizing the discussion whenever you or another meeting participant is not clear on what has been said. [☛ 8.1 Conversations]
❏ Listen carefully; encourage meeting participants to speak up; handle digressions promptly. [☛ 8.7 Active Listening]

Keeping the meeting on track:

❑ Get clear closure by summarizing decisions when ending discussion on an agenda item; confirm action plans, responsibilities, and timelines that have been agreed to. [☛ 10.10 Closure]
❑ Check periodically to ensure that you are on schedule.
❑ Keep tight time limits for discussions, and let participants know how long each topic is expected to take (e.g., have times on the agenda, announce how much time is left on a given topic area).
❑ Keep a flip chart titled Parking Lot, and park issues that you don't have time to handle. (Get agreement with meeting participants as to how and when Parking Lot issues will be handled.) [☛ 10.9 Visible Information]

How to use this leadership tool

"Just as the driver of a car has two tasks, to follow his route and to manage his vehicle, so the chairperson's job can be divided into two corresponding tasks, dealing with the agenda items and dealing with the people."

—Antony Jay, "HOW TO RUN A MEETING"

Think of one or two specific meetings that you currently lead or anticipate leading in the near future. Use the space provided here to plan and tailor your accountabilities and duties as chairperson.

WEB WORKSHEET

Your unique accountabilities as chairperson
(what you will hold yourself accountable for achieving as the meeting chairperson)
[☛ 13.3 Accountability]

Your unique duties as chairperson
(how you want to operate and what you want to do in your role as the meeting chairperson)

RELATED LEADERSHIP TOOLS

10.6 Group Leader Skills	11.4 Meeting Roles	13.3 Accountability
10.7 Getting Participation	11.7 Opening Remarks	13.5 Time Management

FOR FURTHER ASSISTANCE

Milstein, M. M. *Toward More Effective Meetings: The 1983 Annual for Facilitators, Trainers, and Consultants.* University Associates, 1983.

Jay, Antony. "How to Run a Meeting." *Harvard Business Review.* 1976.

11.6

THE MEETING AGENDA: WHY, WHAT, AND HOW

Inspired by Antony Jay and M.M. Milstein.

A well-planned agenda speeds up meetings and helps ensure that meaningful results are achieved. This tool provides useful tips and an application framework for preparing effective meeting agendas.

The purpose of the meeting agenda
✔ to define the purpose of the meeting ✔ to plan meeting content and flow ✔ to define results expected and assign responsibilities for each agenda item ✔ to keep the meeting on track ✔ to organize meeting minutes

The elements of the meeting agenda

The meeting agenda:
  ➡ Clarifies the purpose and the outcomes expected from the meeting. [☛ 2.6 Clarifying Purpose, 2.7 Goal Statements]
  ➡ Lists the meeting date, start and end times, and location.
  ➡ Lists the meeting participants and roles (e.g., chairperson, recorder).
  ➡ For each item on the agenda, notes the outcome being sought, who has responsibility for the item, and the time allotted for each item.
  ➡ Clarifies premeeting requirements and responsibilities. (Attach background reading as appropriate.)

Guidelines for working with the meeting agenda
❑ Note the reason for each topic on the agenda (e.g., information sharing, information gathering, decision making, problem solving). ❑ Order agenda items by importance, and place in logical sequence (e.g., don't discuss the timetable for moving offices until it's agreed that budget funds are available to make the move this year). [☛ 13.5 Time Management] ❑ Don't allow the group to waste time on an urgent but unimportant or trivial agenda item, to the exclusion of a non-urgent but important item. This is when it really pays to put times on the agenda and stick to them. ❑ Organize the agenda so items that ought to be kept brief are introduced 10 or 15 minutes prior to lunch or some such break. ❑ Don't list a category called Other Business. This is little more than an invitation to waste time. This doesn't mean that, in an emergency, an extra agenda item cannot be added, nor does it prevent your including time for unstructured discussion after the meeting has ended. ❑ Aim for 1-hour meetings, 2 hours at the most. Effectiveness usually decreases after 2 hours. ❑ Pay attention to which items tend to unite or divide the group. Sequence these items appropriately. For example, you may want to start and end the meeting on a positive note. [☛ 8.3 Organizational Communication, 8.6 Communication 101, 10.5 Group Disturbances]

- ❑ Consider placing agenda items of high interest to the group near the end of the agenda. Then the group may be keen to work its way through the agenda quickly. At any rate, they'll get some useful work completed while energy levels are high. When they finally do reach these high-interest agenda items, energy levels will be reinvigorated.
- ❑ The chairperson is responsible for distributing the agenda well in advance of the meeting, in order to allow meeting participants time to prepare.
- ❑ Title the predistributed the agenda the Proposed Agenda, then finalize the agenda with the group at the beginning of the meeting.

How to use this leadership tool

"The usual mistake is to make the agenda unnecessarily brief and vague. For example, the phrase 'development budget' doesn't communicate much, whereas the longer explanation 'to discuss the proposal for reduction of the [next year's] development budget now that the introduction of our new product has been postponed,' guides members to form views or even look up facts and figures in advance."

—Antony Jay, "HOW TO RUN A MEETING"

Here is a suggested format for writing meeting agendas. Adapt this to suit your specific meeting requirements, then practice the discipline needed to ensure that your meeting agendas are planned and organized well, and directed toward clearly defined, agreed-upon, and meaningful business results.

WEB WORKSHEET

Meeting agenda format

Workgroup/team	Meeting purpose

Meeting date _____   Chairperson _____   People required

Start/finish times
_____
_____   Recorder   _____

Facilitator   _____

Location   _____

Other roles and person's name:
_____
_____

Agenda item	Person responsible	Time allocated	Measurable/observable outcomes expected

Premeeting requirements and responsibilities (e.g., prereading materials, preparatory work)

RELATED LEADERSHIP TOOLS

2.7 Goal Statements	11.3 Meeting Checklist	11.8 Minutes
11.1 Process Cycle	11.7 Opening Remarks	13.5 Time Management

FOR FURTHER ASSISTANCE

Jay, Antony. "How to Run a Meeting." *Harvard Business Review.* 1976.

Milstein, M. M. *Toward More Effective Meetings: The 1983 Annual for Facilitators, Trainers, and Consultants.* University Associates, 1983.

11.7 THE CHAIRPERSON'S OPENING REMARKS

Inspired by Roger Mosvick and Robert Nelson.

Meeting leaders often rush directly into discussing content or topic items, leaving participants vague as to why an item is being discussed and what outcome is expected from the discussion. Making a brief introduction—3 or 4 minutes at the beginning of a meeting—is one of a leader's most important responsibilities. Done well, the introduction yields a number of positive results:

✔ It orients the group to the purpose of the meeting, and clarifies the context for the meeting.

✔ It enables meeting participants to sharpen their focus, and thus helps shorten meeting time.

✔ It provides an information base for the meeting.

✔ It clarifies meeting process and minimizes unrelated discussion during the meeting.

The chairperson's orientation can be prepared in five steps.

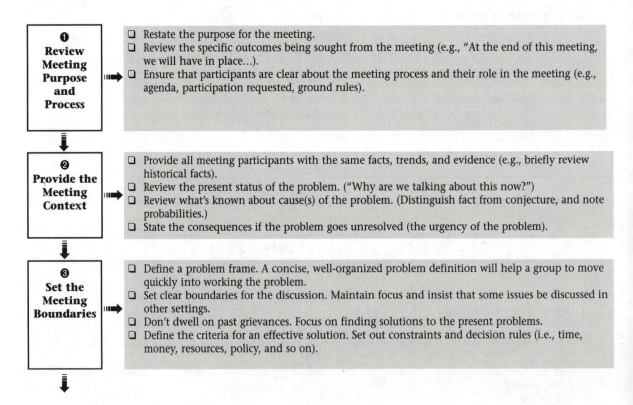

❶ Review Meeting Purpose and Process
- ❏ Restate the purpose for the meeting.
- ❏ Review the specific outcomes being sought from the meeting (e.g., "At the end of this meeting, we will have in place...).
- ❏ Ensure that participants are clear about the meeting process and their role in the meeting (e.g., agenda, participation requested, ground rules).

❷ Provide the Meeting Context
- ❏ Provide all meeting participants with the same facts, trends, and evidence (e.g., briefly review historical facts).
- ❏ Review the present status of the problem. ("Why are we talking about this now?")
- ❏ Review what's known about cause(s) of the problem. (Distinguish fact from conjecture, and note probabilities.)
- ❏ State the consequences if the problem goes unresolved (the urgency of the problem).

❸ Set the Meeting Boundaries
- ❏ Define a problem frame. A concise, well-organized problem definition will help a group to move quickly into working the problem.
- ❏ Set clear boundaries for the discussion. Maintain focus and insist that some issues be discussed in other settings.
- ❏ Don't dwell on past grievances. Focus on finding solutions to the present problems.
- ❏ Define the criteria for an effective solution. Set out constraints and decision rules (i.e., time, money, resources, policy, and so on).

❹ **Agree on** **the Agenda**	❑ Distribute the agenda well ahead of the meeting; label as Proposed Agenda. ❑ Obtain the group's commitment to the meeting plan. (This prevents needless discussion.) ❑ Finalize the agenda with the group at the beginning of the meeting. Reaching consensus can be relatively easy at this early stage, before disagreements begin or positions become polarized.
❺ **Appoint a** **Recorder**	❑ Handle this step before or at the beginning of the meeting. ❑ Inform the meeting participants as to how the recorder will be interacting with the group. (E.g., he or she will contribute a point of view, check the group's progress on each point, summarize decisions before moving on to other agenda items, and so on.) ❑ Any differences over the recorder's summary need to be clarified immediately, before moving on in the meeting. ❑ The recorder is also charged with writing the meeting minutes.

How to use this leadership tool

"If there is a single vital skill the successful manager must have, it is the skill to manage a meeting effectively."
—Roger Mosvick and Robert Nelson, *WE'VE GOT TO STOP MEETING LIKE THIS*

WEB WORKSHEET

Use the space provided here to plan your opening remarks for the next meeting you will be chairing.

Step ❶: Summarize how you will review the meeting's purpose and process.

[☛ 2.6 Clarifying Purpose, 11.1 Process Cycle]

Step ❷: Outline what meeting participants will need by way of a common information base, and provide a context for the meeting.

Step ❸: Set the meeting boundaries. Define the outcomes being sought from the meeting.

[☞ 2.7 Goal Statements, 10.8 Ground Rules]

Step ❹: Ensure that the meeting agenda is sent to invited participants well in advance of the meeting. Label this a Proposed Agenda; note that it will be finalized during the meeting start-up.

Step ❺: Briefly summarize who will be the recorder or scribe, and what role that person will play in the meeting.

[☞ 10.9 Visible Information]

RELATED LEADERSHIP TOOLS

10.6 Group Leader Skills	10.9 Visible Information	11.5 Chair Accountabilities
10.8 Ground Rules	11.3 Meeting Checklist	11.6 Agenda

FOR FURTHER ASSISTANCE

Mosvick, Roger K., and Robert B. Nelson. *We've Got to Stop Meeting Like This: A Guide to Successful Meeting Management.* Scott, Foresman and Company, 1996.

11.8

THE MEETING MINUTES: WHY, WHAT, AND HOW

Inspired by Antony Jay, George David Kieffer, M.M. Milstein, Roger Mosvick, and Robert Nelson.

Anyone at a meeting can record the minutes. However, the chairperson needs to be accountable for ensuring that the minutes are accurate and are distributed promptly after the meeting (i.e., within a day or two following the meeting). This tool reviews the purpose and elements of minutes, and provides guidelines for writing them. Adapt these to the needs of your own workgroup or team.

The purpose of meeting minutes
✔ to encourage action and results and serve as a record for follow-up
✔ to avoid reworking old issues (as John Cleese put it, "deciding what was decided at the last meeting")
✔ to provide a record of the items discussed and decisions made
✔ to provide input for subsequent meeting agendas

Elements of meeting minutes
➡ Focus the minutes on meeting results or outcomes—decisions and agreed actions—rather than on summarizing and recording meeting process and dialogue.
➡ Clearly list the meeting decisions and follow-up actions to be taken, including who is responsible and by when. [☛ 10.12 RASCI Planning]
➡ Indicate the disposition of each agenda item.
➡ List the names of the chairperson, any others who played a special role (e.g., recorder, process facilitator), and all meeting participants.
➡ Note meeting date, location, duration, and the times the meeting commenced and adjourned.
➡ Note date, time, and place of the next meeting.

Guidelines for writing meeting minutes
❑ The recorder should be able to write the minutes in near final form as the meeting progresses. If the chairperson summarizes the discussion around each agenda item prior to moving on the next agenda item, the recorder should be able to use these summaries as confirmation for the minutes.
❑ In project teams, minutes are often recorded on a flip chart, whiteboard, or electronic media so decisions and action planning are clear at the time. [☛ 10.9 Visible Information]
❑ The minutes should focus on results and agreed-on actions. [☛ 10.12 RASCI Planning]
❑ The minute recorder can be very helpful in enhancing clarity and action, by summarizing the results of each agenda item in real time during the meeting. For example, "So, what I'm recording is that we decided XYZ, and that Chris will review this decision with Bryan and Jeff by April 5th."
❑ The minutes should be highly summarized, not a burden to read. Be brief; summarize outcomes and points of agreement or disagreement; don't record detailed input.

- ❏ Avoid writing minutes for the purpose of informing those who were not at the meeting. Doing so is not only an onerous task, it also encourages people not to attend meetings. In addition, it results in long-winded minutes that people won't read.
- ❏ Be open to amending the minutes if meeting participants argue that something different was agreed upon; however, do not revise them for a minority view. Amendments are best handled by preventative actions: summarizing the decisions and actions during the meeting, and visibly recording the minutes using a common medium such as a flip chart or whiteboard.
- ❏ Write the minutes soon after the meeting and distribute them promptly (within a day or two).

How to use this leadership tool

"Once approved at the next meeting, the minutes become a record that can help resolve differing interpretations and remind the leader and others of commitments made."

—M.M. Milstein, *TOWARD MORE EFFECTIVE MEETINGS*

Adapt this worksheet to suit your workgroup or team, then practice the discipline of keeping succinct and accurate meeting minutes.

WEB WORKSHEET

Meeting minutes worksheet

Workgroup/team	Meeting purpose

Meeting date _____

Start/finish times

_____

_____

Location _____

Chairperson _____

Recorder _____

Facilitator _____

Meeting participants

Agenda item	Meeting decision and/or action agreed to	Responsibility	Deadline

RELATED LEADERSHIP TOOLS

10.10 Closure   10.12 RASCI Planning   11.6 Agenda
10.11 Priority Setting   11.1 Process Cycle   13.5 Time Management

FOR FURTHER ASSISTANCE

Jay, Antony. "How to Run a Meeting." *Harvard Business Review.* 1976.

Kieffer, George David. *The Strategy of Meetings: How to Make Your Next Business Meeting a Win for Your Company and Your Career.* Warner Books, 1988.

Milstein, M. M. *Toward More Effective Meetings: The 1983 Annual for Facilitators, Trainers, and Consultants.* University Associates, 1983.

Mosvick, Roger K., and Robert B. Nelson. *We've Got to Stop Meeting Like This: A Guide to Successful Meeting Management.* Scott, Foresman and Company, 1996.

12

TOOLS FOR LEADING RELATIONSHIPS

"If it weren't for the people, the g-- d------ people, earth would be an engineer's paradise." That was Kurt Vonnegut's skeptical version of this key leadership issue. Leading real, imperfect people is no doubt a challenge for leaders. These tools will help you do that.

12.1

THE RELATIONSHIP BANK: MAINTAINING WORKING RELATIONSHIPS

Inspired by Stephen Covey and Roger and Rebecca Merrill.

Like it or not, organizations are inherently political systems, and the all-powerful informal organization is a product of many networks of relationships. While it's essential to treat all coworkers and customers with dignity and respect, you won't have time to invest heavily in every possible relationship within your organization. That's why it is important that you maintain and develop your working relationships strategically—with individuals and groups that you must rely on to get your work done. However, without ongoing effort, relationships tend to go stale over time. Thus, if you ignore your key relationships, sooner or later you may find that everything you do takes longer, requires more effort, and yields lower results. This is just a basic fact of organizational life!

The metaphor of a relationship bank gives new meaning to the terms *trust account* and *balance sheet.* For example, if you make a few deposits in a relationship by being understanding, flexible, open, supportive, reliable, considerate, listening, and so on, then it won't hurt quite as much when you make a withdrawal. A withdrawal could be deliberate, for example, challenging or confronting; or it could be inadvertent, such as forgetting to follow through on a promise. But without having a balance on deposit, a withdrawal puts the relationship into the red (i.e., a negative balance).

Examples of relationship deposits	Examples of relationship withdrawals (Like deposits, you will notice that withdrawals also come in various sizes.)
✔ Seeking to understand others ✔ Keeping your promises ✔ Clarifying and meeting another person's expectations ✔ Demonstrating loyalty to someone even when the person is not present ✔ Apologizing for a mistake ✔ Being open to receiving and acting on feedback	✗ Demanding to be understood ✗ Failing to follow through on a promise ✗ Unkindnesses, discourtesies ✗ Failing to meet someone's expectations ✗ Dishonesty, conceit, arrogance ✗ Rejecting feedback or failing to thank someone for feedback

How use this leadership tool

"When the trust account is high, communication is easy, instant and effective."

—Stephen Covey, *THE SEVEN HABITS OF HIGHLY EFFECTIVE PEOPLE*

Strategic relationships within an organization are like oil in a machine. They lubricate and facilitate effort and decision making. They multiply your power, and your ability to get things done, by creating the goodwill necessary for others to trust in your judgment.

Having a positive balance in the relationship bank doesn't guarantee that the other person won't get irritated or angry when you make a withdrawal. However, having a positive balance does mean that others are more likely to listen to what you have to say and give you the benefit of the doubt when things don't go as planned.

WEB WORKSHEET

This could be one of the most important tools in this book for leaders to understand and practice. Using the workspace provided here, take a few minutes to plan how you will maintain, and continuously develop, your strategic relationships within your workgroup and organization.

Column 1:   List your five most strategic working relationships within your workgroup and organization. [☞ 5.7 Stakeholder Groups, 9.10 Networking]

Column 2:   Summarize why this relationship is important.

Column 3:   Summarize what actions you can take to maintain a high level of trust and goodwill with this person or group. [☞ 12.2 Trust]

Person or group	Why this relationship is strategic/important	Actions needed to maintain your trust account with this person or group
1.		
2.		

3.		
4.		
5.		

RELATED LEADERSHIP TOOLS

4.5 Culture	8.6 Communication 101	12.2 Trust
8.4 Dialogue and Discussion	8.7 Active Listening	12.4 Feedback
8.5 Metacommunicating	10.4 Team Commitment	15.2 Emotional Intelligence

FOR FURTHER ASSISTANCE

Covey, Stephen. *Principle-Centered Leadership.* Summit Books, 1991.

Covey, Stephen. *The Seven Habits of Highly Effective People: Powerful Lessons in Personal Change.* Simon & Schuster, 1989.

Covey, Stephen, Roger Merrill, and Rebecca Merrill. *First Things First: To Live, to Love, to Learn, to Leave a Legacy.* Simon & Schuster, 1994.

12.2

BUILDING TRUST INTO WORKING RELATIONSHIPS

Inspired by Stephen Covey, James Kouzes, Barry Posner, Earnie Larson, Harriet Lerner, and Fernando Bartolomé.

"If only we had more trust," leaders say, as if it somehow depends on fate. It doesn't. Although trust cannot be controlled, it can be built within workgroups. Low trust has a devastating effect on communication and teamwork, often manifested in withholding of information, rejecting others' information, or withholding discretionary effort. These behaviors reinforce low trust, eliciting similar behavior from others, to confirm their suspicions.

Trust presents a paradox in that it needs to be earned, but in order to be earned, it first has to be given. This tool provides essential how-to's for developing trust within organizations.

In some organizational cultures, it is easy to be trusting because of the general atmosphere of trust. In dog-eat-dog cultures, trusting a little is an act of courage. In these low-trust atmospheres, you may wish to become what Alan Wilkins calls a "border guard," creating an enclave of trusting behavior within your leadership group. Although trust is measured by what you actually do, trust does not require that you be naive and regularly be taken advantage of. Neither should you fall into the trap of writing people off on the basis of personal chemistry or personality, dismissing them into a category unworthy of trust. To obtain trust, remember that "the best way to get model behavior is to model the behavior." [☛ 1.8 Recursive Leadership]

GUIDELINES FOR UNDERSTANDING TRUST

Here are ten guidelines that will help you understand the nature of trust.

Element of trust	What this means in leadership practice
Trust is delicate.	If trust is broken, it's hard to repair. That's not to say that, given the right circumstances, it's impossible to win back. Given a basic respect and goodwill between people and willingness to work on their relationship, trust can be regained. But it takes a lot of work.
It takes courage and vulnerability to trust.	Courage and vulnerability are especially difficult if you've experienced strong betrayal in your life. Surprisingly, leaders who have never experienced strong betrayal may not have learned to trust wisely. Trust means having given others the benefit of the doubt—"I will trust these people until there is clear evidence that they cannot be trusted."
Trust is based on what you do.	If you want to be trusted as a leader, you must first give evidence that you're trustworthy. Trust isn't based on your credentials (i.e., your experience or education). It's based on your relationships and what you do, particularly in difficult situations. Doing includes demonstrating competence and being sincere and reliable.
Trust cannot be controlled.	Trust cannot be controlled, legislated, or forced. That doesn't mean that leaders cannot influence trust. What it does mean is that you need to do your best, but be prepared to let go if your best isn't good enough. Nobody is trusted by everyone, and some people aren't capable of trusting anyone.
Trust has to be constantly earned.	Like relationships and communication, trust either grows or stagnates; it cannot be held constant. You simply can't put trust on autopilot. Trust needs to be demonstrated and reinforced regularly or it slowly loses strength.

Trusting others predisposes them to trusting you.	Behavior begets behavior; trusting others predisposes them to trust you. Thus, listening to others helps ready them to listen to you. If you want others to share information with you, start by sharing your information with them. Where people are involved, nothing works all of the time, but this *is* a useful guideline.
Trusting only flourishes in a respectful environment.	Trust can only grow in an environment of goodwill, respect, and willingness to work on your relationship with another person. Without these elements in place, trust atrophies. Conflict resolution strategies either make things worse or have only minimal impact.
Trust is based on integrity and honesty.	People trust people who are loyal to their espoused values. Integrity and honesty sometimes demand frustrating compromise among loyalties—to your values, to a relationship, to an organization, and so on. Manage these compromises carefully, not denying your own perceptions, nor taking the burden of someone else's problem on your own shoulders.
Trust does not mean perfection.	Leaders don't have to be perfect to be trustworthy. All leaders sometimes fall short of other people's expectations, and even of their own expectations. See your mistakes as learning opportunities or as temporary and isolated events, rather than as proof that there's an inherent flaw in your character.
Trust is built on long-term goodwill.	People tend to trust people who have a positive goodwill balance in the relationship bank with them. [☛ 12.1 The Relationship Bank] That is, if you make deposits in your working relationship by being supportive, reliable, and so on, then it won't be quite as damaging when you make a withdrawal (e.g., make a mistake). Without a balance in the bank, however, a withdrawal damages the relationship. Having a lot of positives on deposit doesn't mean that people won't get upset with you, but that they will likely listen more objectively, and will give you the benefit of the doubt.

How to use this leadership tool

"You demonstrate your trust in others through your actions—how much you check and control their work, how much you delegate and allow people to participate. Individuals who are unable to trust other people often fail to become leaders. … Conversely, [leaders] who trust others too much may also fail, because they can lose touch and a sense of connectedness to their team. Delegation becomes abdication."

—James Kouzes and Barry Posner, THE LEADERSHIP CHALLENGE

Here is a self-assessment of some behavioral measures of trust. It is easy to delude oneself about one's own behavior; this assessment is best reviewed with a coach or others who will give you feedback.

WEB WORKSHEET

A Leader's Trust Self-Assessment

Trust behavior	My self-assessment (0 = poor to 10 = great)	Improvement actions
I am open with information and rarely withhold it.	0 | | | | 5 | | | | 10	[☛ 8.1 Conversations]
I give new people the benefit of the doubt, and trust them until given reason not to.	0 | | | | 5 | | | | 10	[☛ 15.2 Emotional Intelligence]

I am honest and forthright with people.	0 | | | | 5 | | | | 10	[☛ 8.5 Metacommunicating]
I am clear about my values and act in accordance with them.	0 | | | | 5 | | | | 10	[☛ 2.5 Values]
I regard people by and large as trustworthy.	0 | | | | 5 | | | | 10	[☛ 15.3 JoHari Window]
I am collaborative in my personal style.	0 | | | | 5 | | | | 10	[☛ 9.1 Leadership Versatility]
I work hard at creating and maintaining an atmosphere of trust.	0 | | | | 5 | | | | 10	[☛ 4.5 Culture]
I confront apparent breaches of trust rather than have them fester.	0 | | | | 5 | | | | 10	[☛ 12.6 Confrontation]
I am willing to forgive the admitted breaches of trust of others.	0 | | | | 5 | | | | 10	
I am willing to accept and ask for forgiveness for my breaches of trust.	0 | | | | 5 | | | | 10	[☛ 12.4 Feedback]

Related leadership tools

1.8 Recursive Leadership	4.5 Culture	8.5 Metacommunicating
1.11 Integrity	4.6 Open-Book Leadership	15.2 Emotional Intelligence

For further assistance

Bartolomé, Fernando. "Nobody Trusts the Boss Completely—Now What?" *Harvard Business Review.* March-April 1989. 135–142.

Covey, Stephen. *The Seven Habits of Highly Effective People: Powerful Lessons in Personal Change.* Simon & Schuster, 1989.

Kouzes, James, and Barry Posner. *The Leadership Challenge.* Jossey-Bass Inc., 1987.

Larson, Earnie, and C. Larson-Hegarty. *From Anger to Forgiveness: A Practical Guide to Breaking the Negative Power of Anger and Achieving Reconciliation.* Ballantine Books, 1992.

Lerner, Harriet G. *The Dance of Anger: A Woman's Guide to Changing the Patterns of Intimate Relationships.* Harper & Row, 1985.

Lerner, Harriet G. *The Dance of Intimacy: A Woman's Guide to Courageous Acts of Change in Key Relationships.* Harper & Row, 1989.

12.3

TRIANGULATION: THE SUREST WAY
TO DAMAGE A RELATIONSHIP

Inspired by Harriet Lerner.

"I'm just more comfortable talking about people behind their backs."

—the character of George Costanza as played
by Jason Alexander on *Seinfeld*

The term *triangulation* refers to talking with a third person to complain or to put down another person with whom you are having a disagreement. We all triangulate a little every now and then; it's only human. In some organizations, however, people "recreationally bitch" about others as a matter of habit! Healthy work environments have less triangulation than do organizations in which people are feeling worthless, unappreciated, powerless, and frustrated. It's not that triangulation causes these feelings, although it ensures that they fester and spread; rather, it is that we tend to triangulate when we're feeling overcontrolled, unproductive, and undervalued. Leaders, above all people, can ill afford to triangulate! Doing so destroys workgroups and teams and sets a poor example for others to follow.

Here's an illustration of triangulation: Person *A* (in the diagram) has problems with Person *B*. Person *A* then talks with Person *C*. Person *A* might say something like, "You won't believe what *B* is up to now!" or, "This has got to be one of *B*'s biggest screw-ups yet!" Person C has become engaged, often unwittingly, in the triangle, with A trying to get C to confirm a position about B.

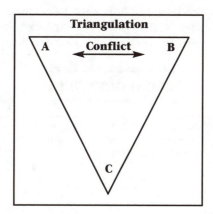

It takes courage and skill to confront people directly, particularly when trust is low or you're engaged emotionally (e.g., angry, hurt, frustrated). Thus, in this example, it's easier for Person *A* to complain to Person *C,* rather than to deal directly with Person *B*.

Triangulating damages relationships.	Constructive alternatives to triangulating:
✗ Triangulation doesn't resolve the issue. Rather, it often prolongs and amplifies disagreements and misunderstandings.	✔ Talk with an outsider (e.g., a coach, a friend outside of work, your spouse) with the clear intention of seeking help in dealing with the issue. This can be done without damaging work relationships.
✗ When people triangulate, open secrets thrive in organizations. Eventually, most employees hear through the grapevine about others' conflicts or problems, but no one is able to openly admit this knowledge for fear of exposing their source or their role in triangulating.	✔ Talk with an insider (e.g., your boss, a person who knows both you and the person you are having a disagreement with). Your intent and actions in this conversation are critical. It must be an attempt to resolve the issue with the other person's help. Empathize and speak of the other person with respect. You must also be willing to look at your part in the disagreement, as opposed to just blaming the other person.
✗ Triangulation contaminates the work environment. It does this by drawing other people into disputes, often unnecessarily.	✔ Develop your conflict management skills via training, reading, or coaching. Practice what you learn. Take care to ensure that your communication remains balanced and constructive and focuses on finding solutions rather than catching the other person doing something wrong.

How to use this leadership tool

"Triangles take countless forms, but we can count on the fact that when tensions rise between two parties, a third will be triangled in, lowering anxiety in the original pair."

—Harriet Lerner, *THE DANCE OF INTIMACY*

Triangulation is deadly in teams, and in organizations generally. Use this tool to become more self-aware and to observe your own communication habits. Also, listen for triangulation within your workgroup or team. Discuss this concept with peers and team members. Use the space provided to reflect on triangulation within your workplace. You're bound to improve your communication habits if you're willing to struggle honestly with these questions.

WEB WORKSHEET

Self-awareness is an essential attribute of leadership. Reflect briefly on your own communication over the past months. What one or two indirect communications (i.e., triangulating) have you been participating in that could potentially damage your or other people's relationships within the organization?

[☛ 15.3 JoHari Window, 15.4 Ladder of Inference]

Note a couple of ways you can you handle these situations more directly.

[☛ 8.1 Conversations, 8.5 Metacommunicating, 8.6 Communication 101]

Have you noticed any indirect communication within your workgroup?

Specify a couple of steps you can take to ensure that more direct, honest, and relationship-enhancing confrontation occurs within your workgroup or team.

[☛12.4 Feedback, 12.6 Confrontation]

RELATED LEADERSHIP TOOLS

8.6 Communication 101	12.5 Negative Feedback	13.1 Coaching
12.4 Feedback	12.7 Dealing with Conflict	13.6 Attribution Theory

FOR FURTHER ASSISTANCE

Lerner, Harriet. *The Dance of Anger: A Woman's Guide to Changing the Patterns of Intimate Relationships.* Harper & Row, 1985.

Lerner, Harriet. *The Dance of Intimacy: A Woman's Guide to Courageous Acts of Change in Key Relationships.* Harper & Row, 1989.

12.4

GIVING AND RECEIVING FEEDBACK: THE DOS AND DON'TS

Inspired by Carl Rogers, Shaun Murphy, David Irvine, and numerous other sources.

Feedback is fundamental to effective leadership, and a leader must be willing to take personal responsibility for both giving and receiving difficult feedback. If you're *not* getting a lot of feedback from others, it may be because of how you have received feedback in the past, rather than because others don't have information that would be valuable to you. Conversely, if people don't want feedback from you, it may be related to how you have provided feedback to them in the past, rather than because they wouldn't find value in your perspective. [☛ 1.8 Recursive Leadership]

GUIDELINES FOR FEEDBACK

Helping others to receive your feedback	Helping others to give you feedback
Steps 1. Check to see if the other person is willing to hear your feedback (e.g., an appropriate time, place). 2. Focus on: – your specific observations (what you saw the other person say or do, without interpreting or evaluating); – the consequences of this behavior; – your reactions to this behavior; – things that are within the other person's control to change (e.g., arrive on time for the weekly meetings). 3. State what you want. 4. Thank the other person for listening.	**Steps** 1. Listen, even if it hurts. – Make eye contact. – Show you're listening by summarizing the feedback into your own words. – Clarify by asking for examples. 2. Find at least one part of the feedback that's useful. Even if the feedback feels incorrect, find a *kernel of truth*. 3. Thank the giver for the feedback, even if it was given poorly. 4. Say what you will do with the feedback, even if it's only to think about it for awhile.
Dos and Don'ts ➤ Describe, don't evaluate. ➤ Avoid inferences, labels, and judgments. ➤ Avoid hearsay. Speak from your own experience. ➤ Don't triangulate. If a third party is to be involved, arrange for that person to be present. ➤ Don't repeat yourself. Say it once; then listen. ➤ Don't give advice unless it's asked for. ➤ Avoid raising nonrelated issues from the past. ➤ Don't let things build. Give feedback as soon as possible. ➤ Don't ignore the importance of timing. There are bad times to raise certain issues. ➤ Be careful about pursuing *why*. Doing so questions other people's motives, and usually results in their becoming defensive.	**Dos and Don'ts** ➤ It's natural and okay to feel defensive; just don't act it. ➤ Be careful about assuming motive, but if you are convinced that the other person's intentions are not honorable, then walk away. Don't subject yourself to *cheap shots*. ➤ Don't discount, downplay, or deny. These actions decrease the likelihood of getting more feedback. ➤ Don't do other activities while receiving feedback. (Even if you're hearing every word, your actions will be misinterpreted.) ➤ Avoid overloading yourself. When you have received all the feedback that you can handle at the moment, let the giver know. ➤ Don't expect to be given feedback in a thoughtful, polite, or helpful way. Expecting this limits your learning. The most helpful information sometimes comes from people who give feedback awkwardly.

How to use this leadership tool

"Criticism is a by-product of significant action. … And the more valid the criticism, the more difficult it is to receive."

—Warren Bennis, *AN INVENTED LIFE*

If people don't give you feedback, rather than complaining or wondering why this isn't happening, be proactive. Decide whose feedback you would value, then go out and seek their perspective. Similarly, think of people who might benefit from receiving your feedback, and then take the initiative to provide feedback to them.

WEB WORKSHEET

We learn best from our successes. As a first step in preparing a feedback improvement plan, use the space provided to review a past success that you had when giving and receiving difficult feedback.

Briefly outline a situation in which you did a particularly good job of providing difficult feedback to another person.	Briefly outline a situation in which you received difficult feedback particularly well.
What specifically did *you* do that made this process go so well?	What specifically did *you* do that made this process go so well?

The skill of giving and receiving feedback is too important for a leader to take for granted. Reread the do's and don'ts provided and, thinking about your past successes with giving and receiving feedback, use the space provided to plan improvements in how you carry out this essential leadership behavior.

Improvements in how you give feedback to others	Improvements in how you receive feedback from others
Areas where I can be providing more feedback to others:	Areas where I need to seek out more feedback from others: [☛15.2 Emotional Intelligence, 15.3 JoHari Window]
Specific steps I want to do better and more regularly when giving feedback to others: [☛ 8.1 Conversations]	Steps I can take to request this feedback: Steps I can take while receiving this feedback:
Things to avoid when providing this feedback:	Things to avoid when receiving this feedback: [☛ 15.6 Defenses]

RELATED LEADERSHIP TOOLS

8.4 Dialogue and Discussion	8.7 Active Listening	12.7 Dealing with Conflict
8.5 Metacommunicating	12.5 Negative Feedback	15.3 JoHari Window

FOR FURTHER ASSISTANCE

Klatt, Bruce, Shaun Murphy, and David Irvine. *Accountability: Getting a Grip on Results,* 2nd ed. Stoddart, 1998.

Rogers, Carl. *Freedom to Learn.* Merrill, 1969.

12.5

PREPARING YOURSELF TO GIVE NEGATIVE FEEDBACK

Inspired by Sidney Simon and Dave Irvine.

Giving negative feedback is demanding work, yet something leaders must do on a regular basis. It requires that you:

✔ Be able to tolerate the discomfort that comes with confronting others directly.

✔ Be able to do without approval from others.

✔ Be aware of your own personal power, and of how your behavior affects others.

✔ Understand and start within the other person's frame of reference or perspective.

✔ Approach the other person in terms of the present problem, rather than in terms of anger or past problems.

✔ Challenge the other person to improved performance or behavior.

✔ Provide the supports necessary (e.g., time, a level of trust) for the other person to make needed improvements, even though doing so may require a degree of risk.

Leaders need to ask themselves these questions prior to confronting others:

? Are you in an appropriate mood or attitude to give direct, honest, empathetic feedback? Leaders who are angry or feeling a low sense of self-esteem frequently fail to give appropriate feedback.

– Their feedback tends to be evaluative and judgmental, rather than data-based.

– They tend to feel and act defensively and take other people's behavior personally, even though this behavior was not intended personally.

– They tend to discount or overlook the interests of others.

– They may have unrealistically high expectations of others.

[☛12.1 The Relationship Bank, 13.6 Attribution Theory, 15.4 Ladder of Inference]

? Is the other person in the right mood to hear what you have to say?

– Timing is important. Ensure that this is a good time and place for the other person to hear your feedback and to discuss the issues that concern you.

? Can the person receiving your feedback do anything about it?

- Confronting someone who has no ability to correct the situation is irresponsible. In addition to damaging your relationship with this person, such an action could damage that person's self-confidence and self-respect.

? Will this increase your respect for yourself and for the other person?

- Mutual respect is critical to maintaining a sense of teamwork and community in the workplace. Confrontation works best when you have a basic level of respect and goodwill for the other person and a desire to improve your working relationship with this person.

? Are you willing to work with and support the other person?

- You must be willing to own your part of the problem, do your part to improve the situation, and provide support to the other person as he or she takes the necessary steps to improve the situation. [☞ 13.1 Coaching]

? Are you sure that none of your own hang-ups are in this feedback? Ensure that:

- Your feedback is as objective and sincere as possible.
- You are not bringing in baggage from the past that is no longer applicable.
- Your own biases and beliefs are not being inappropriately imposed on the other person.

[☞ 8.1 Conversations]

? Is it possible that instead of, or in addition to, your feedback, this person needs more guidance, support, understanding, encouragement, or recognition?

How to use this leadership tool

"There is risk you cannot afford to take (and) there is risk you cannot afford not to take."
—Peter Drucker, *THE FRONTIERS OF MANAGEMENT*

Prepare yourself for giving difficult feedback to others by answering the questions presented here. Be as specific and honest with yourself as possible. You might find it helpful to have a friend, coach, or trusted colleague assist you with your preparation. In addition, if the consequences of giving feedback poorly are significant, you might even role-play giving feedback with a colleague prior to the actual event.

WEB WORKSHEET

1. What one or two things can you do to prepare yourself to give direct and honest feedback? (Be as specific as possible.)

2. What specifically do you want the person who will be receiving your feedback to do differently as a result of this feedback?
3. What steps will you take to prepare the other person to hear your feedback?
4. How will you work with and support the other person as he or she attempts to make the needed improvements? [☛ 13.1 Coaching]
5. How can you provide this feedback so that it builds on, and improves, the working relationship you have with the person who will be receiving this feedback?
6. How can you be sure that none of your own personal hang-ups are in this feedback? [☛ 13.6 Attribution Theory, 15.6 Defenses]

RELATED LEADERSHIP TOOLS

8.1 Conversations	12.4 Feedback	13.1 Coaching
8.5 Metacommunicating	12.6 Confrontation	13.6 Attribution Theory
8.7 Active Listening	12.7 Dealing with Conflict	15.4 Ladder of Inference

FOR FURTHER ASSISTANCE

Irvine, David. *Simple Living in a Complex World: Balancing Life's Achievements.* RedStone Ventures Inc, 1997.

Simon, Sidney B. *Getting Unstuck: Breaking through Your Barriers to Change.* Warner Books, 1989.

Simon, Sidney B. *Vulture: A Modern Allegory on the Art of Putting Oneself Down,* 2nd ed. Values Press, 1991.

12.6

THE 5 CS: ESCALATING CONFRONTATION JUDICIOUSLY

Inspired by David Irvine, William Purkey, and Abe Wagner.

Leaders continually find themselves having to resolve people or performance problems, whether the person is taking inappropriate action or failing to take action. When facing people problems, you can choose to confront those involved; stop dealing with them, or at least minimize your dealings with them; or accept their behavior. This is easier said than done, however. This tool provides you with a number of logical, easy-to-follow steps for carrying out these alternatives. The five steps are:

| Concern | ➡ | Confer | ➡ | Consult | ➡ | Confront | ➡ | Conclude |

These steps are incremental in nature, providing you with guidance for upping the ante with each successive step if the previous step failed to achieve the desired results. Depending on the importance and urgency of the situation, the strength of your relationship with the other person, and how strongly you feel about the other person's behavior, you may choose to skip some of these steps.

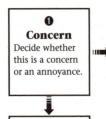

❶ Concern
Decide whether this is a concern or an annoyance.

Decide whether the other person's behavior is a *concern* that needs to be dealt with, or an annoyance that should be overlooked. If you feel you need to deal with the person's behavior, ask yourself, "Is there some action I can take to change or improve the situation?" If your answer is "no," then make the choice to let go emotionally. If you can't emotionally let go, then disengage, or in some way minimize your interdependency with this person. If the answer is "yes," move to step 2, *confer.*

❷ Confer
Raise concern directly with other person.

Raise the concern directly with the other person, using these guidelines.
- Pay attention to the importance of timing; choose a time when you think the other person will be willing and able to hear your perspective. Get the other's permission to raise the issue: "Would you be willing to hear some constructive feedback about how you handled that situation?"
- Do this in private. Be clear and direct.
- Describe, don't evaluate. Describe what you saw or heard; do not judge or label the behavior.
- Don't assume motive. Don't assume that you know the motive behind the behavior.
- If you honestly can, give three positives and a request: "You're always on time for meetings, you contribute openly, and you add a lot of fun to our meetings. My concern, however, is with how you ... ."

❸ Consult
Raise the stakes.

If you still haven't achieved the desired result, it's time to raise the stakes one level. You are now discussing two issues. One is the original problem that still exists; the other is that your request (made when conferring) has been ignored.

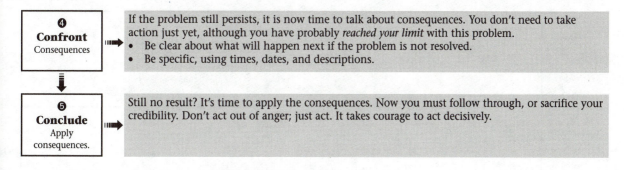

	If the problem still persists, it is now time to talk about consequences. You don't need to take action just yet, although you have probably *reached your limit* with this problem.
❹ **Confront** Consequences	• Be clear about what will happen next if the problem is not resolved. • Be specific, using times, dates, and descriptions.
❺ **Conclude** Apply consequences.	Still no result? It's time to apply the consequences. Now you must follow through, or sacrifice your credibility. Don't act out of anger; just act. It takes courage to act decisively.

Hᴏᴡ ᴛᴏ ᴜsᴇ ᴛʜɪs ᴛᴏᴏʟ

"If I decided to accept all behaviors without comment, I would discount myself and deny those close to me the opportunity to learn about my thoughts and feelings concerning their behavior, and perhaps to change what they are doing. If I chose to stop transacting with everyone who is engaging in uncomfortable behaviors, I would soon run out of friends and associates."

—Abe Wagner, *THE TRANSATIONAL MANAGER*

Use the space provided to prepare for a challenging disagreement or disciplinary situation that you need to handle in the near future. Plan your approach objectively, noting each step that you might take as it becomes necessary.

Most leaders would use this process infrequently. If you tried to confront every little bit of ineffective behavior you came across, you would probably get very little else accomplished, and you certainly wouldn't have much fun.

WEB WORKSHEET

Step	Actions to take
❶ **Concern**	
❷ **Confer**	
❸ **Consult**	

❹ **Confront**	
❺ **Conclude**	

RELATED LEADERSHIP TOOLS

8.1 Conversations	9.5 Negotiation	13.1 Coaching
8.5 Metacommunicating	12.4 Feedback	13.6 Attribution Theory
8.7 Active Listening	12.7 Dealing with Conflict	15.4 Ladder of Inference

FOR FURTHER ASSISTANCE

Irvine, David. *Simple Living in a Complex World: Balancing Life's Achievements.* RedStone Ventures Inc, 1997.

Purkey, William. *Inviting School Success: A Self-Concept Approach to Teaching and Learning.* Wadsworth, 1984.

Purkey, William. *Self-Concept and School Achievement.* Prentice Hall, 1970.

Wagner, Abe. *The Transactional Manager: How to Solve People Problems with Transactional Analysis.* Prentice Hall, 1981.

12.7

CONFLICT: FIVE LEVELS FOR DEALING WITH CONFLICT

Inspired by Thomas Crum, Roger Fisher, Elizabeth Kopelman, Andrea Kupfer Schneider, David Irvine, and Bernie Novokowsky.

Expecting all conflict to end in complete resolution is a good way to stay frustrated as a leader. Conflict can be dealt with at many levels, starting with the most idealistic (complete and joint resolution) to the least effective (suffering in silence).

Resolution strategies	Expectation & goals	What is needed?	Steps required	Challenges
Level ❶ **Complete and Joint Resolution** "Forgive and let go emotionally."	• Complete resolution. • You and others come to an emotional, practical, and satisfying long-term resolution.	• People willing to work the resolution process and to forgive and forget. • Often, a highly emotional process impacting core values and beliefs.	• Clarify expectations of the process. • Explore needs, assumptions, values, emotions, and style differences. • Focus on joint interests and new options. • Agree on new behaviors. [☞ 2.5 Values]	• Often talked about, but rarely achieved and practiced. (Many religions propose this level of forgiveness.) • Need to be tolerant of accidental slippage in agreements. [☞ 15.2 Emotional Intelligence]
Level ❷ **Joint Management of the Conflict** "We agree to disagree, and will jointly live with our differences."	• A working relationship. • "I'm okay, you're okay—with warts." • Reduce the conflict to an acceptable level and work around it. • Understand where the other person is at.	• Willingness to continue talking. • Willingness to maintain working relationship. • Willingness to agree to just letting the issue be. • Reconcile differences.	• Compromise and find neutral ground. • Agreements are made at the level of behavioral and business outcomes. • Often helpful to have a third-party facilitator. [☞ 13.3 Accountability]	• Sometimes, communication is the problem. When this is so, it is difficult to resolve communication problems by having more communication. • Being accepting of other person's behavior without compromising personal values. [☞ 8.5 Metacommunicating]

Level ❸ **Personal Management of the Conflict** "I'll just live with it."	• You change your behavior. • You refuse to be drawn into the conflict. • You unilaterally change your response to red flags.	• Willingness to change one's behavior unilaterally. • Ability to control one's own behavior ("No one can make me angry").	• Often, counseling or a workshop is helpful to improve perspective or develop skills. [☛ 15.2 Emotional Intelligence]	• People may not be able to live with the fact that their antagonists do not have to change also.
Level ❹ **Separation or Distancing** "You go your way, and I'll go mine."	• If the conflict cannot be managed, an option is separating or distancing the persons involved in the conflict.	• Be able to work independently from each other.	• Often, management needs to be involved to approve the separation of roles and eliminate interdependence.	• By virtue of their roles, people may be required to work together. In this case, one person may have to leave the organization.
Level ❺ **Suffering** "I'll play the martyr."	• Obtain satisfaction by complaining or by passively resisting.	• A stoical or easy-going philosophy. • Willingness to live in an atmosphere of suppressed anger and tension.	• Ability to supplement emotions with productive work and other distractions.	• Can be a depressing option in the long run.

Hᴏᴡ ᴛᴏ ᴜsᴇ ᴛʜɪs ʟᴇᴀᴅᴇʀsʜɪᴘ ᴛᴏᴏʟ

"I was angry with my friend.
I told my wrath; my wrath did end.
I was angry with my foe.
I told it not; my wrath did grow."

—William Blake

If you're not careful, as a leader you might find yourself going home at night worn out from dealing with conflicts, whether petty annoyances or deep-seated differences of opinion. Most of us are personally uneasy with conflict. This tool can lift a load from your shoulders by providing you with a wider range of options than simply demanding complete resolution or living in anger.

Think of two or three conflict situations in your workgroup or organization. What level of resolution might be most appropriate given the unique circumstances of each situation? Use the workspace provided to plan how you might work toward closure in each of these conflict situations.

WEB WORKSHEET

Conflict description	Best resolution strategy	Action plan

RELATED LEADERSHIP TOOLS

2.5 Values   8.5 Metacommunicating   12.4 Feedback

8.1 Conversations   9.5 Negotiation   14.1 Scarcity and Abundance

FOR FURTHER ASSISTANCE

Crum, Thomas. F. *The Magic of Conflict: Turning a Life of Work into a Work of Art*. Simon & Schuster, 1987.

Fisher, Roger, Elizabeth Kopelman, and Andrea Kupfer Schneider. *Beyond Machiavelli: Tools for Coping with Conflict*, 2nd ed. Penguin, 1996.

Irvine, David. *Simple Living in a Complex World: Balancing Life's Achievements*. RedStone Ventures Inc, 1997.

12.8 DEALING WITH DIFFICULT PEOPLE: A TIMELESS LEADERSHIP CHALLENGE

Inspired by Albert Bernstein, Sydney Craft Rozen, Robert Bramson, and Roberta Cava.

No matter how skilled you become as a leader, difficult people will challenge you. Books about difficult people identify these people by colorful names like Ogres, Machiavellis, Fence-Sitters, Corporate Grouches, Dinosaurs, Bulldozers, Blowhards, and Stones. This tool will help you understand these difficult people, whether they are employees, bosses, or customers, and suggest ways of dealing with them. But first, a general word of caution: Most people, like yourself, are struggling to do the best they can. If you continually find people in your life difficult while other people don't find them so, you may need some feedback and coaching on your personal style.

Principles for dealing with difficult people (whatever their organizational position):

➡ Every person lives by a set of values, principles, and rules. Just as a fish takes water for granted, most people are unaware of the basis of their thoughts and actions. Self-awareness is an essential leadership attribute. Learn about yourself and how others may be different from you. [☛ 14.7 Personal Preferences]

➡ Rarely does it work to deal with the problem behavior at the level that it was expressed. Don't get drawn into the problem person's logic. Rather, step outside the person's frame of reference to deal with the behavior. [☛ 8.5 Metacommunicating]

➡ Don't take it personally. Although on occasion you would like to throttle the culprit, keep your professional cool. Our innate reptilian responses—fight, flight, or freeze—are rarely effective with difficult people. (This tool provides alternative strategies.) [☛ 15.2 Emotional Intelligence]

➡ All difficult people genuinely believe that their behavior is logical and realistic. Bizarre as it may seem, difficult people may be trying to help you!

➡ Not much works with the most difficult of difficult people. If a difficult person's behavior is a result of deep-seated insecurity, challenging the behavior, even indirectly, will push the difficult person into an even more defensive position.

Here are some common types of difficult people and how you can understand them. A checklist of suggestions for dealing with each type of difficult person is presented in the next section.

Type	How to recognize them	What drives their behavior
Aggressors	Most people describe difficult people as Aggressors—easy to recognize by their bullying, bombarding, pushiness, emotional arrogance, and use of anger. Some references distinguish between Aggressors. With Secure Aggressors, you need to stand up and fight a word battle to become one of	For Aggressors, the world is a win–lose place. Power means being able to control people, resources, and space. Being vulnerable is anathema to them. They believe people must fear and respect them. Aggressors need to continually

	the gang. Challenge Insecure Aggressors, however, and they will fight harder. A better strategy here is to assume that the tougher the outer shell, the softer the inside.	prove themselves and defend themselves against others. They are the archetypal warriors.
Know-It-Alls	Know-It-Alls like to upstage everyone with data. They come in two variants: Spocks, who are indeed experts, and Windbags, who are not.	Know-It-Alls believe they are superior intellectually. They defeat dreaded ambiguity with expertise, data, logic, and analysis. They will follow their logic, even into bizarre disasters.
Negativists	Favorite Negativist phrases are, "It won't work because..." or, "They won't let us do that." As natural devil's advocates, Negativists find fault with any idea. It's important to separate Negativist behavior from legitimate risk analysis. In discussing risks with a true Negativist, you will get more doom and gloom.	Negativists gain power by tapping into general feelings of helplessness in organizations. They may feel that people—managers in particular—are conspiring to thwart their personal efforts.
Sticklers	Sticklers or bureaucrats go by the rules—real or imagined. Means are more important than ends. No matter how productive or beneficial your idea, they want to do it by the book, often quoting authority figures and policies to support what they consider okay or not okay. They will know and quote policies to be followed and forms to be filled.	Sticklers seek security by pleasing superiors. They gain power by controlling access to organizational power. [☛ 9.9 Power]
Indecisives	Indecisives won't give a clear "yes" or "no" answer to anything. They use a wide range of runarounds and stalls to keep you dangling on a string.	Indecisives want to please everyone. They don't handle conflict well. They avoid risk at all costs.

HOW TO USE THIS LEADERSHIP TOOL

"The secret to dealing with irrational people lies in knowing their rules. Everything people do, no matter how crazy it seems, follows some system of rules."

—Albert Bernstein and Sydney Craft Rozen, *DINOSAUR BRAINS*

Dealing with difficult people is challenging, and simple recipes won't work in all cases. The best long-term strategy is to learn more, first about yourself and about human behavior in general, and next about tools and techniques for dealing with difficult people. Before you use any of the techniques provided here, collaborate with a trusted colleague or coach—one who handles difficult behaviors particularly well. You may even want to role-play your responses with a coach to ensure that you're ready to deal with the difficult person.

Aggressors	❑ Stay cool and don't take it personally. Give them time to let off steam.
	❑ Butt in if you have to; many Aggressors fill airtime as a form of dominance.
	❑ Differentiate between secure and insecure Aggressors.
	❑ If *Secure* type, stand up to the Aggressors. Call their bluff. State your counter opinion clearly and forcefully. They respect those who push back. Practice with a coach.
	❑ If *Insecure* type, pushing back can make things worse. Avoid a head-on fight. Don't challenge their control. Use metacommunication to tactfully challenge them at a process level.
	In either case, be ready to back off when a truce is signaled.
Know-It-Alls	❑ The basic approach with Know-It-Alls is to have them look at new options without directly challenging their expertise. They will see direct challenges as attacks.
	❑ Do your homework. Be prepared. Marshal your facts into a logical progression.
	❑ Acknowledge an expert's legitimate knowledge.
	❑ Summarize, and then ask extensional questions like, "As you said, the processes were designed for head office. How could they be modified for the field?"
	❑ Ask for analytical detours: "Based on what you said, if we hypothesized...."
	❑ Don't expect credit; expect that *your* good ideas may be owned by the expert at the next meeting.
Negativists	❑ Help them distinguish between helpful potential problem analysis, and analysis based on their worst fears (sometimes called "inaction by despair").
	❑ Avoid getting sucked in to their negativism.
	❑ Except for the inexhaustible pessimists, set a Horror Floor. Exhaust the Negativist by asking for the worst possible scenario. Don't argue, agree, or propose solutions. Listen and summarize.
	❑ Don't confront negativism at the same level it is expressed. Use metacommunication to challenge at a process level.
	❑ Be prepared to go it alone or to get support from others.
Sticklers	❑ Do your homework. Show that your ideas are safe. Thoroughly prepare your plans and do a potential problem analysis, showing that you've covered all the bases.
	❑ Ferret out any policies or procedures and show that your proposal does not violate these. Remember, the deeper issues for Sticklers are safety and looking good in the eyes of superiors.
	❑ Help Sticklers to plan and rehearse meetings with their leaders. You may offer to accompany them or, even better, offer to take the heat by accepting full responsibility yourself.
Indecisives	❑ Help Indecisives by surfacing concerns. Make it very safe for them to state reservations about your proposal.
	❑ When you can, support them with their concerns.
	❑ Help them problem-solve their concerns.
	❑ If you suspect that one of their concerns is a lack of confidence in you, make it supersafe for them to be at least partially direct.
	❑ It may be possible to take the risk away from the Indecisive by visibly taking full responsibility for any problems with your proposal or recommendation.

Related leadership tools

8.1 Conversations	9.9 Power	12.7 Dealing with Conflict
8.5 Metacommunicating	12.4 Feedback	14.7 Personal Preferences
8.7 Active Listening	12.6 Confrontation	15.2 Emotional Intelligence

For further assistance

Bernstein, Albert, and Sydney Craft Rozen. *Dinosaur Brains: Dealing with All Those Impossible People at Work.* Ballantine Books, 1996.

Bramson, Robert. *Coping with Difficult People.* Dell Publishing Company, 1988.

Cava, Roberta. *Difficult People: How to Deal with Impossible Clients, Bosses, and Employees.* Firefly Books, 1997.

12.9 THE ESSENTIALS OF CUSTOMER SERVICE

Inspired by many authors, including William Davidow and Bro Uttal.

Understanding and satisfying customers' needs should be a top priority for leaders. Just consider:

✔ Customers are more likely to switch service providers because of poor service rather than price.

✔ A dissatisfied customer will inform seven or eight other potential customers of poor service.

✔ The majority of customers will do business with you again if you resolve their complaints.

✔ It costs five times as much to gain a new customer as it does to keep a current customer.

Two pitfalls for customer providers are:

✘ for a physical product, overrelying on its technical attributes to sell the product;

✘ for less tangible human services, realizing these cannot be standardized; each service delivery is a unique experience, dependent upon the service provider's skills, knowledge, and motivation.

This tool will acquaint you with some essentials of customer service, and provide suggestions on customer service delivery.

Determine who are your best customers.	✔ Stretching to satisfy every market segment may result in providing low-quality service to all customers. Group your customers in a logical way for your business (e.g., demographics, age). Rank customer groups by their value to your business, and determine the cost and benefit of customer service to each type of customer. Probably, 20 percent of your customers or customer groups produce 80 percent of your results. [☛ 3.1 Strategy, 3.6 Strategic Relationships, 5.7 Stakeholder Groups]

Understand your customer's point of view.	✔ Good service is defined from the customer's point of view. Take steps to:
	  – Understand your customers' long-term goals (think from their point of view).
	  – Develop long-term relationships (favor customer needs over your product or service).
	  – Do the little things for your customers (strive to do things right the first time).
	  – Invest in processes to determine the level of customer satisfaction.

Manage customer expectations.	✔ Not all customers need the same service, but you need to deliver what was promised. ✔ Keep customer expectations slightly below the level of service that you intend to provide (underpromise and overdeliver). ✔ Provide too little service (or the wrong kind), and your customer may leave; provide too much service, and your company will price itself out of the market.
Manage customer impressions.	✔ Impressions rise and fall based upon how customers see service providers working with them. Provide tangible evidence that a service has been performed (e.g., a service report). ✔ Manage the climate for service, including such seemingly minor factors as uniforms, brochures, employees' appearance, and condition of lobby, office, grounds, vehicles, and so on.

Develop easy-to-use services.	✔ Make it easy for customers to know where to go for help. Eliminate red tape. Develop unique, flexible, and customized solutions for customers. ✔ Don't force customers to run organizational mazes. The first person to talk with the customer needs to take responsibility for helping that customer contact the right person in the organization. ✔ Provide follow-up contact for major customers. [☛ 2.1 Systems Thinking]
Make your guarantee simple.	✔ Don't force your customers to jump through hoops to complain. Evasion antagonizes people more than simply saying, "We can't do it." ✔ Provide a small reward of some kind to the customer, to make up for the hassle factor (e.g., offering a free dessert if the service has been inadequate in a restaurant).
Train and empower service employees.	✔ Set high expectations for this service, and train employees to meet these expectations. ✔ Reward employees for meeting or exceeding customer service standards. ✔ Treat employees the way you want them to treat customers. In a way, they are your customers! ✔ Ensure that employees know their authority and how to use it. ✔ Define clear service processes, like how to deal with a complaint, and remove organizational barriers (e.g., cumbersome approvals) so employees can respond quickly to customer needs. ✔ A key service factor is the personal relationship between a customer and an individual service provider. Consider assigning specific employees to handle major customers. [☛ 14.3 Needs Analysis, 14.4 Adult Learning, 14.5 On-Job Training]

HOW TO USE THIS LEADERSHIP TOOL

"Good is not good where better is expected."

—Thomas Fuller

Consider having each member of your workgroup or team complete this assessment independently, then come together to review and discuss the ratings. Develop action plans to improve upon your current level of customer service.

WEB WORKSHEET

Service dimensions	Rate from 0 to 10 (0 = poor to 10 = great)
Responsiveness ("We are available when customers want us.")	0 | | | | 5 | | | | 10
Service Processes and Equipment (e.g., billing, inventory control, training)	0 | | | | 5 | | | | 10
Assurance ("Our actions inspire trust and confidence.")	0 | | | | 5 | | | | 10
Empathy ("We provide individualized attention.")	0 | | | | 5 | | | | 10
Reliability ("We perform as promised.")	0 | | | | 5 | | | | 10

As you set improvement targets, remember this: Measurable criteria that are common to a production orientation (e.g., inventory turnover), although useful, may be insufficient measures of customer service. [☛ 2.8 Balanced Scorecard]

Given the customer service ratings you have provided, use this worksheet to describe how well your workgroup or team is doing on each of the essentials of customer service. Use the third column to plan future improvement.

	Current description (as of date: _____)	Service improvement plans
Who are your best customers?		[☛ 3.6 Strategic Relationships]
Describe the range of your customers' needs.		[☛ 3.3 Environmental Scan]
How are you managing your customers' expectations?		
What customer impressions are made by your organization?		
In what ways are your services easy to use?		[☛ 2.1 Systems Thinking]
What is your guarantee to customers?		
How have you empowered employees to provide exemplary customer service?		[☛ 9.2 Situational Leadership]

RELATED LEADERSHIP TOOLS

2.1 Systems Thinking	3.6 Strategic Relationships	5.6 Aligning Systems
2.6 Clarifying Purpose	4.4 Employee Involvement	12.1 The Relationship Bank

FOR FURTHER ASSISTANCE

Davidow, William H., and Bro Uttal. *Total Customer Service: The Ultimate Weapon.* HarperCollins, 1990.

13

TOOLS FOR LEADING PERFORMANCE

Successful leaders are not only high-performers themselves; they also can elicit high performance from others. Beginning with the crucial skill of coaching, this section contains many performance leadership tools.

13.1

COACHING AND SUPPORTING
THE SUCCESS OF OTHERS

Inspired by Shaun Murphy and Robert Lucas.

"The hottest thing in management is the executive coach," trumpets Fortune magazine. Hype aside, recent organizational emphasis on coaching makes explicit what was often only informally expected of leaders—to develop others. This tool:

- Describes the conditions necessary to a successful coaching relationship.
- Explains the seven elements of the coaching process.
- Provides a comprehensive discussion guideline for coaching others.

CONDITIONS FOR A SUCCESSFUL COACHING RELATIONSHIP

An enduring and successful coaching partnership is:

✔ Voluntary—Many mentoring programs failed when pairings were not voluntary.

✔ Based upon growth, not on creating dependencies. (Ironically, the ultimate success of a coaching relationship is achieved when the coachee doesn't need you as a coach!)

✔ Directed at improving the coachee's job performance and career potential (not at pleasing or appeasing).

THE ELEMENTS OF COACHING

Each of these seven elements is essential to coaching success. These are not stages, since most are iterative and ongoing and provide a range of strategies for the coach and coachee to work on simultaneously.

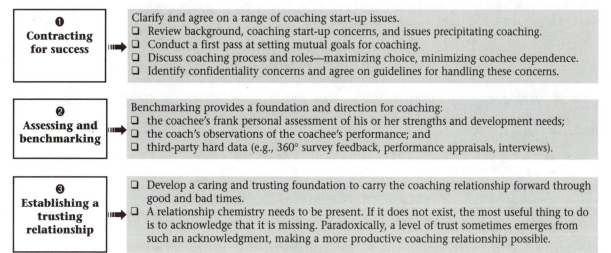

❶ Contracting for success ⇒	Clarify and agree on a range of coaching start-up issues. ❑ Review background, coaching start-up concerns, and issues precipitating coaching. ❑ Conduct a first pass at setting mutual goals for coaching. ❑ Discuss coaching process and roles—maximizing choice, minimizing coachee dependence. ❑ Identify confidentiality concerns and agree on guidelines for handling these concerns.
❷ Assessing and benchmarking ⇒	Benchmarking provides a foundation and direction for coaching: ❑ the coachee's frank personal assessment of his or her strengths and development needs; ❑ the coach's observations of the coachee's performance; and ❑ third-party hard data (e.g., 360° survey feedback, performance appraisals, interviews).
❸ Establishing a trusting relationship ⇒	❑ Develop a caring and trusting foundation to carry the coaching relationship forward through good and bad times. ❑ A relationship chemistry needs to be present. If it does not exist, the most useful thing to do is to acknowledge that it is missing. Paradoxically, a level of trust sometimes emerges from such an acknowledgment, making a more productive coaching relationship possible.

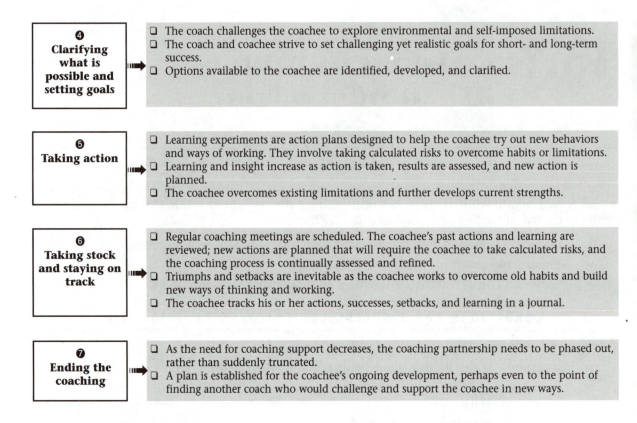

	④ Clarifying what is possible and setting goals	❏ The coach challenges the coachee to explore environmental and self-imposed limitations.
		❏ The coach and coachee strive to set challenging yet realistic goals for short- and long-term success.
		❏ Options available to the coachee are identified, developed, and clarified.

	⑤ Taking action	❏ Learning experiments are action plans designed to help the coachee try out new behaviors and ways of working. They involve taking calculated risks to overcome habits or limitations.
		❏ Learning and insight increase as action is taken, results are assessed, and new action is planned.
		❏ The coachee overcomes existing limitations and further develops current strengths.

	⑥ Taking stock and staying on track	❏ Regular coaching meetings are scheduled. The coachee's past actions and learning are reviewed; new actions are planned that will require the coachee to take calculated risks, and the coaching process is continually assessed and refined.
		❏ Triumphs and setbacks are inevitable as the coachee works to overcome old habits and build new ways of thinking and working.
		❏ The coachee tracks his or her actions, successes, setbacks, and learning in a journal.

| | **⑦ Ending the coaching** | ❏ As the need for coaching support decreases, the coaching partnership needs to be phased out, rather than suddenly truncated. |
| | | ❏ A plan is established for the coachee's ongoing development, perhaps even to the point of finding another coach who would challenge and support the coachee in new ways. |

How to use this leadership tool

"Coaching is a human function, not a management function."

—Peter Block, *STEWARDSHIP*

Almost every tool in this book could potentially be of value when coaching individuals or groups. Use the workspace provided to think through the questions you might ask while coaching, the leadership tools that might be of value in the coaching process, and what actions you might take to excel at coaching others.

WEB WORKSHEET

Elements	Questions to consider	☛ Resources for coaching	Your action plan
❶ Contracting for success	➡ What start-up concerns do we each have? ➡ What is important to you at this time? ➡ What overall process are we going to use? ➡ What are our initial goals for coaching?	2.7 Goal Statements 9.4 Leader Impact 11.1 Process Cycle 13.3 Accountability 13.8 Competencies	

❷ **Assessing and benchmarking**	➡ What data do we have to assess the current situation (e.g., perceptions, observations, assessments, surveys)? ➡ What data or information would we like to have, and how would this be helpful?	1.2 Manage or Lead? 1.6 Boards of Play 13.5 Time Management 13.10 Careers 15.2 Emotional Intelligence	
❸ **Establishing a trusting relationship**	➡ Are we on the same wavelength? ➡ How easy or difficult do we find it to discuss our genuine concerns? ➡ What could we do differently to enhance our ability to work together? ➡ Do I, as your coach, clearly understand you and your issues? ➡ Do we trust each other?	8.1 Conversations 8.5 Metacommunicating 12.1 The Relationship Bank 12.2 Trust 12.4 Feedback 14.4 Adult Learning 14.7 Personal Preferences 15.4 Ladder of Inference	
❹ **Clarifying what is possible and setting goals**	➡ What does success look like for you now and in the future? ➡ What do you want to be remembered for? ➡ Who are your heroes? ➡ Tell me about a time when you were at your very best. What was it like for you? What made it possible? ➡ What accomplishments are just beyond your grasp?	1.5 Seven Habits 1.7 Results-Based Leaders 3.1 Strategy 3.2 Sigmoid Curve 7.1 Problem Framing 13.10 Careers 15.5 Habits	
❺ **Taking action**	➡ How much risk are you willing to tolerate? ➡ What results and learning are expected from each learning experiment (action plans designed to challenge the coachee)? ➡ What support is needed between coaching meetings?	1.6 Boards of Play 5.1 Change Equation 5.3 Change Readiness 5.8 Human Transitions 7.4 Polarities 14.6 Learning Styles	
❻ **Taking stock and staying on track**	➡ What progress has been made since coaching began? ➡ What actions have resulted in the most useful learning? ➡ What risks have seemed reasonable? Which have seemed too demanding? ➡ Is the coachee being both supported and challenged? ➡ In what ways has the coaching relationship developed?	1.6 Boards of Play 3.2 Sigmoid Curve 12.7 Dealing with Conflict 14.2 Rethinking Your Thinking 14.3 Needs Analysis 14.6 Learning Styles 15.3 JoHari window 15.6 Defenses	
❼ **Ending coaching**	➡ How will we wind down and eventually end the coaching relationship? ➡ What support will be needed? ➡ Where can the coachee continue to get support and challenge in the future?	9.10 Networking 13.2 High-Performers 14.1 Scarcity and Abundance 15.2 Emotional Intelligence	

RELATED LEADERSHIP TOOLS

2.3 Directional Statements	9.1 Leadership Versatility	13.3 Accountability
3.2 Sigmoid Curve	13.2 High Performers	13.5 Time Management

FOR FURTHER ASSISTANCE

Lucas, Robert W. *Coaching Skills: A Guide for Supervisors.* Irwin, 1994.

13.2

COACHING HIGH-PERFORMERS: AN OVERLOOKED ELEMENT OF SUCCESS

Contributed by George Campbell and inspired by Chris Argyris, Geoff Bellman, John O'Neil, Lyle Sussman, and Richard Finnegan.

Coaching high-performers, an obvious yet powerful source of organizational improvement, is a neglected area. The very fact that they *are* high-performers somehow seems to negate their need for coaching. Leaders frequently misdirect their coaching efforts to poor or mediocre performers, leaving high-performers to find their own way. This tool clarifies the difference between problem-based coaching and high-performance coaching, and provides steps to developing a style for coaching high-performers.

The leverage achieved from helping high-performers is extraordinary. When high-performers grasp new concepts or new ways of working, their drive for accomplishment and ability to implement create powerful momentum. Their success draws the rest of the organization in the same positive direction—an example of a rising tide raising all boats. High-performers reject coaching from the traditional, problem-based mode. It doesn't meet their needs. Coaching needs to feed their appetites and expectations. Like elite athletes and master musicians, high-performers embrace coaching that fits their fast-moving, success-filled world. Coaching needs to support their optimistic and forward-thinking attitudes, and challenge them to set and attain lofty goals.

Problem-based coaching	High-performer coaching
Follow the squeaky wheel theory. ✔ Offer coaching to people who are causing trouble; help bring their performance up to standard.	*Follow the springboard theory.* ✔ Work with people who are already successful; help accelerate their already stellar progress. [☛ 3.2 Sigmoid Curve]
Work with the known. ✔ Help poor and mid-level performers bring their work up to an expected level of achievement.	*Work toward the unknown.* ✔ Help the high-performer become a lamplight for new ideas, new ways of performing. Help them discover new capacities, new ways of applying knowledge and skills. [☛ 1.6 Boards of Play]
Work toward solving a problem. ✔ Coaching starts with the definition of a problem or identification of a performance gap.	*Work toward achieving a vision.* ✔ Coaching starts with the definition of a vision. Current performance is not really the issue; defining the vision and finding a route to its achievement is the key. [☛ 2.4 Visioning]
Think short-term. ✔ Focus on the steps needed to close the performance gap.	*Think long-term.* ✔ Focus on career, business breakthrough, and life ambitions. [☛ 14.2 Rethinking Your Thinking]
Construct a linear process. ✔ Agree on a logical, step-by-step process for closing the performance gap.	*Build a nonlinear, quantum-leap process.* ✔ Encourage leaps, keeping the long-term map in mind. High-performers will fill in the spaces between the leaps. [☛ 1.9 Paradigms]

End with goal achievement.	End when vision is achieved.
✔ Coaching ends when the performance gap is closed or the short-term goals are achieved.	✔ Coaching ends when significant movement is achieved in the direction of the long-term goal.

BLINKING AND HIGH PERFORMANCE

The most effective time to offer coaching to high-performers is at significant change points—in their careers, their organization, or the business environment. Find or create a situation that causes the high-performer to blink. This has to be a situation that presents a serious challenge to the high-performer's ability to continue stellar performance, and also presents an opportunity to achieve significant returns to the business. The blink point may be the performer's need to overcome a performance plateau or to reach a higher skill level. As one high-performer observed at such a career point, "The skills that got me here will now get in the way of my success."

Blink-causing situations vary from person to person, but the opportunities abound:

→ Changes in job scope, when it is no longer possible to rely on the same old ways of doing things (e.g., the high-performer who used to have 8 people reporting to him or her and now has 150).

→ Change in responsibility (e.g., a move from responsibility for cost or revenue to accountability for profit).

→ Change in exposure level (e.g., the boss used to protect the high-performer from the consequences of error, whereas he or she now has true decision-making responsibility).

→ Change in organizational philosophy (e.g., the high-performer used to compete with other departments but is now expected to work in partnership internally and compete with other companies).

→ Change in the market (e.g., customers now think your product is a commodity, whereas it used to be unique).

→ Change in career progress (e.g., disappointment at being passed up for a key promotion).

Odd as it may seem, smart and successful people are often not good at learning outside their areas of competence. While they are being successful and getting all kinds of positive feedback, it is very hard to talk with them about another career path or new ways of doing things. Taking a novel path requires the ability to see the path, awareness of the need for taking the new path, and the courage to risk failure. Successful people don't have much experience with failure. Consequently, they are at times unsure of their ability to cope if they fail at something important. [☞ 15.2 Emotional Intelligence]

HOW TO USE THIS LEADERSHIP TOOL

"The literature on employee coaching represents a consistent theme: coach the employee who fails to meet standards, reward and praise the employee who meets or exceeds standards."

—Lyle Sussman and Richard Finnegan: "COACHING THE STAR"

Coaches can help high-performers make use of challenging situations in a way that forges new capabilities and a deeper level of confidence. Coaches do this by helping the high-performer reflect on his or her life goals and purpose, choose which challenges to engage, identify new paths to success, solidify old skills and tools, and focus on building success in the new situation. Here is a series of steps for coaching high-performers, with space to make action notes. You may wish to complete this action matrix with the high-performer.

WEB WORKSHEET

Coaching steps	Action notes
1. Identify or create the growth opportunity, when the high-performer's old set of skills and old ways of performing will be inadequate to produce real success.	[☞ 3.2 Sigmoid Curve]
2. Agree on coaching as a tool. Coaching must be seen as a reward for good performance and an aid to success in a very challenging but worthwhile situation.	
3. Agree on the coach. The credibility of the coach is critical. High-performers will not accept help from just anyone. If you are the right person, proceed. If not, find an acceptable and resourceful coach.	
4. The coach and high-performer build their relationship together. The personal chemistry has to work, and the relationship needs to be built on trust and mutual respect.	[☞ 12.2 Trust]
5. The high-performer articulates a vision for both career and life ambition. Successful people are often not self-reflective. The organizations in which they work may not encourage reflection. Rather, the organizations want immediate action and business success. As a result, successful people can gain a great deal by thinking about their life's direction. It is here that their passions reside.	[☞ 2.4 Visioning]
6. Identify and design learning experiments: action to take in the direction of the vision; resolving some challenges of the new situation; using new skills or a new approach. Plan small but important steps. Focus on achieving success when planning. Debrief actions taken to extract learning.	
7. Design new learning experiments, keeping the vision in mind.	
8. Develop momentum and a feedback process, then get out of the way. Once the new path or the new skills are established, the high-performer's need for coaching diminishes quickly. Recognize this. End the formal coaching relationship, and provide ongoing informal support over time.	[☞ 9.1 Leadership Versatility]

No high-performers to coach? Perhaps you should look in the mirror. If your people seem to be only B-level performers, you are likely hindering your own performance and that of your group. Consider getting some coaching for your own development.

Related leadership tools

1.7 Results-Based Leaders	3.2 Sigmoid Curve	13.1 Coaching
3.1 Strategy	8.1 Conversations	13.10 Careers

For further assistance

Argyris, Chris. "Teaching Smart People How to Learn." *Harvard Business Review.* May-June 1991, 99–109.

Bellman, Geoff. *Your Signature Path.* Berrett-Koehler, 1996.

Campbell, George. *Facilitation Skills Workshop.* Vector Consulting Associates, 1991.

O'Neil, John. *The Paradox of Success.* Putnam, 1993.

Sussman, Lyle, and Richard Finnegan. "Coaching the Star: Rationale and Strategies." *Business Horizons.* March-April 1998.

13.3 ACCOUNTABILITY AGREEMENTS: DEFINING ACCOUNTABILITY WITHIN ORGANIZATIONS

Inspired by Bruce Klatt, Shaun Murphy, David Irvine, and Paula Martin.

The Accountability Agreement helps leaders transform often unspoken and misunderstood jobs, roles, and employment contracts into explicit expectations, personal promises, and business results. It also defines a fair exchange of results and rewards among employers and employees. To be accountable is to be subject to giving an account, answer, or explanation to someone, even if only to yourself. Simple as it may sound, the concept of accountability is a challenge to apply in today's fast-paced organizations. This tool will help you do that.

THE KEY PRINCIPLES OF ACCOUNTABILITY

Six principles provide a foundation for accountability within organizations. Each is essential, and together they form the practical theory that underlies an Accountability Agreement.

- ✔ Accountability is a statement of personal promise.
- ✔ To be accountable means you are answerable for results, not just activities.
- ✔ To be accountable for results, you must have the opportunity for judgment and decision making.
- ✔ Your accountability is yours alone, without qualification. It is neither shared nor conditional.
- ✔ Accountability is meaningless without significant consequences.
- ✔ Finally and very importantly, every member of the organization is accountable for the organization as a whole.

THE ACCOUNTABILITY AGREEMENT

Establishing Accountability Agreements involves sitting down with those to whom you are accountable (e.g., employees, supervisors, clients) and negotiating a simple, practical, one- to two-page agreement consisting of seven elements.

❶ **Business focus statement**	✔ Start by writing your highest-level accountability and clarifying your business-within-the-business. This statement answers questions such as, "What products and services do you provide to customers?" and "What is your unique contribution within the organization?" [☛ 3.1 Strategy]
❷ **Accountabilities**	✔ Include a dozen or more specific statements of *results* (not activities!) that you are promising to achieve within your organizational role. It is helpful to separate these into operational and leadership accountabilities.
❸ **Support statement**	✔ Describe the resources and support that you require from others (e.g., your boss, your peers, employees who report to you) in order to fulfill your accountabilities. In this way, the notion of accountability becomes distributed; it flows downward and sideways, as well as upward, in organizations.
❹ **Measures**	✔ List ways that you will measure success as to each of your accountabilities. This list then serves as a reference while setting operational and leadership goals. [☛ 2.7 Goal Statements]

❺ *Goal statements*	✔ Flowing out of your accountabilities, write specific and measurable or observable goals for a given time period.
❻ *Consequences*	✔ Summarize an agreement on the positive consequences that you will receive (i.e., rewards, recognition, compensation) for fulfilling your accountabilities and reaching your goals.
❼ *Evergreen plan*	✔ Prepare a plan to keep your Accountability Agreement up to date so that the business bargain between you and your employer remains clear, vibrant, and mutually rewarding.

HOW TO USE THIS LEADERSHIP TOOL

"All commerce, both social and economic, is based on the principal of exchange—giving something and getting something else."

—Susan Campbell, *FROM CHAOS TO CONFIDENCE*

These *selected* elements are taken from the Accountability Agreement of a manager of a natural gas processing facility. They are provided as examples of the type of information typically contained in an Accountability Agreement.

❶ *Business Statement:* My business is producing and processing raw natural gas to marketable products in a way that is safe, is environmentally responsible, maximizes long-term profit, and enhances XYZ's image as a positive contributor in the state.

❷ *Accountabilities:* I am personally accountable for:
Operational accountabilities: A safe operation. The long-term protection of the asset; achieving production, quality standards, and targets.
Leadership accountabilities: The success of my direct reports; my own learning as a leader.

❸ *Support Statement:* Three additional engineers on project XYZ. A LAN hookup within the department during the first quarter. Funding for consulting help during project XYZ start-up.

❹ *Measures:* Lost time accidents, volume throughputs, new contracts, improvements to services.

❺ *Goals:* A 9% return on capital during the 3rd quarter. Complete plant turnaround by May 1st.

❻ *Consequences:* I will be funded to attend the international petroleum show in Houston next year.
I will receive a salary increase equivalent to those of the top 5% of employees.

❼ *Evergreen Plan:* I will review my Accountability Agreement quarterly within the workgroup and make changes, as appropriate, within one week of each review meeting.

WEB WORKSHEET

Write a first draft of your Accountability Agreement, or coach an employee to do the same. [☛ 1.10 The GAS Model]

Business focus statement

Accountabilities

I am personally accountable for:

Operational accountabilities –

Leadership accountabilities –

Support statement

Measures

Goals

[☛ 2.7 Goal Statements]

Consequences

Evergreen plan

Related leadership tools

1.7 Results-Based Leaders	2.7 Goal Statements	4.7 Job Satisfaction
2.1 Systems Thinking	3.1 Strategy	13.4 MBO

For further assistance

Klatt, Bruce, Shaun Murphy, and David Irvine. *Accountability: Getting a Grip on Results,* 2nd ed. Stoddart, 1998.

Martin, Paula K. *Discovering the WHAT of Management.* Renaissance Educational Services, 1990.

13.4 MANAGEMENT BY OBJECTIVES

Inspired by Peter Drucker, Paul Hersey, Ken Blanchard, and George Odiorne.

Management by Objectives (MBO) is a timeless and venerable leadership tool. Although its heyday (the 1960s through the 1980s) has now past, the basic principles of MBO remain relevant. At the time of its introduction, MBO was a reaction to the micromanagement practice of controlling the activities of others, while paying only indirect attention to the actual business results an individual or workgroup was achieving. Nonetheless, adapted to present-day organizational reality, this tool is useful for helping leaders set goals, then plan and manage toward achieving those goals.

MBO comes in many variants, but these principles are common:

- Effective leaders lead by clarifying goals, then determining and managing activities to achieve them.

- The clearer the goal—what you are trying to accomplish—the better the chance of achieving it.

- Goal setting is a collaborative activity. (In the original organizational milieu of MBO, this goal-setting process started at the top and cascaded down. In much faster-moving, modern organizations, goals are clarified at all levels and in real time.)

- Success is measured by how well goals are achieved—"What gets noticed is what gets measured," and "What gets measured gets done."

One typical variant of MBO viewed the process as a funnel with business results as the end target.

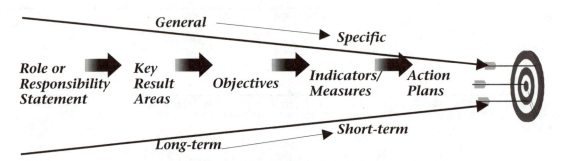

A typical MBO set of statements would include:

❶ **Role or Responsibility Statement**

This statement describes the general reason for the job or workgroup. It answers questions like:

"What is the reason this job exists?" or *"What is the basic function of this workgroup?"*

❷ Key Result Areas (KRAs)

This list of phrases describes the key areas in which the person or workgroup needs to produce results: *"What overall results are you expected to produce within your role area?"*

❸ Objectives

These are specific result- or achievement-oriented statements. They clearly describe, as quantitatively as possible, what the person or workgroup will achieve within a period of time. (For more information on writing goal statements, see ☛ 2.7 Goal Statements).

❹ Indicators or Measures for Each Objective

If objectives were not clearly and quantitatively measurable (e.g., "increased employee satisfaction"), a leader would list agreed-to indicators of success.

❺ Action Plans

The plans listed critical actions a person would take to achieve objectives.

How to use this leadership tool

*"The design of the ideal business sets the direction. It also makes it possible to set targets—
for efforts as well as results."*

—Peter Drucker, *MANAGING FOR RESULTS*

Most leaders and organizations fine-tune or redesign the MBO process to suit their organizational context. For example:

- Role statements are replaced by personal or workgroup mission statements.
- Since modern organizations are complex and knowledge-work is highly interdependent, key stakeholders or support networks are identified in individual work plans.
- Rewards and consequences are identified for meeting and not meeting objectives.
- The process is often renamed (e.g., Management of Results) to reflect a results orientation.

One reason MBO waned as a common management practice was that large binders of MBO agreements were generated with considerable effort. People thought that if a little goal setting was valuable, then more would be even better. The result was that the MBO process became a massive paper chase, and became bogged down under its own weight. Remember, when it comes to setting goals, less is often more. That is, fewer goals provide better focus and are more actionable than many goals. Thus, setting fewer goals often leads to a better results. [☛ 1.10 The GAS Model]

MBO is a recursive process. As such, ask yourself, "What is my goal for the goal-setting process?" Design a process that will be congruent with the results you expect! [☛ 1.8 Recursive Leadership]

WEB WORKSHEET

Steps for introducing an MBO-type process into your workgroup or team:

Design step	Things to consider	Your design of an MBO-type process for your workgroup or organization
1. Clarify the goal for the process.	What do you want to achieve as a result of this process? How would this process fit with other initiatives in the organization? [☛ 2.7 Goal Statements]	
2. Clarify whose support is needed for the process to succeed.	Who are the key people who must buy in to using this process? What benefits would these key people want, and what reservations might they have? [☛ 3.6 Strategic Relationships]	
3. Outline the framework of the process to be used.	What would be the key elements of an MBO-type process in your workgroup or organization? [☛ 11.1 Process Cycle]	
4. Meet with key stakeholders to gain support and process improvements.	Be clear on your goals for this process, but don't overdetermine the process. Give people lots of opportunity to influence the design of the process so it becomes their process. [☛ 9.7 Selling Wheel]	

Now, write some preliminary MBO statements:

❶ **Role or Responsibility Statement**

❷ **Key Result Areas (KRAs)**

❸ **Objectives**

❹ **Indicators or Measures for Each Objective**

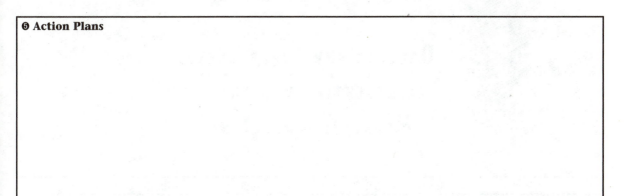

❺ Action Plans

RELATED LEADERSHIP TOOLS

1.7 Results-Based Leaders	2.8 Balanced Scorecard	13.3 Accountability
2.3 Directional Statements	3.1 Strategy	13.5 Time Management

FOR FURTHER ASSISTANCE

Drucker, Peter. *The Practice of Management,* 2nd ed. Harperbusiness, 1993.

Hersey, Paul, and Ken Blanchard. *Management of Organizational Behavior: Utilizing Human Resources.* Prentice Hall, 1982.

Odiorne, George. *Management by Objectives.* Pitman, 1965.

13.5

URGENCY AND IMPORTANCE: THE ESSENTIAL ELEMENTS OF MANAGING YOUR TIME

Inspired by Stephen Covey and Roger and Rebecca R. Merrill.

This tool concerns the use of a leader's most scarce resource—his or her time. How you spend your time has a great bearing on your long-term success as a leader. One of the paradoxes of time is that the busier you are, the more you need to take time to step back and examine how you are using your time! Yet few of us are able to do this, as we get caught in what Stephen Covey calls the Urgency Addiction. Daily planning often misses the most important issues, whereas when you step back from day-to-day activities and prioritize on a weekly, monthly, or annual basis, your activities are tied into a much broader and more strategic perspective.

This tool will allow you to examine and reprioritize how you use your time. Two criteria—importance and urgency—provide an organizing framework for understanding the long-term implications of time management on your success as a leader.

	Urgent	Not urgent
Important	❶	❷
	Activities • emergencies, pressing problems • deadline-driven tasks, crises • business necessity work • crisis meetings • rushing to meet important deadlines • some (most?) administrative work *Implications* • essential things done • short-term focus • crisis management, putting out fires • stress, burnout • working hard but with unsatisfactory long-term results	*Activities* • preventing problems • important relationship-building • production capacity activities • recognizing strategic opportunities • visioning, planning, preparing • renewal and thoughtfulness *Implications* • on top of things • vision, perspective, strategic • disciplined, in true control • improved control, fewer crises • new opportunities captured • self-confidence and balance

Not Important	❸	❹
	Activities	*Activities*
	<ul><li>interruptions</li><li>some calls, mail, reports, meetings</li><li>many (most?) deadline activities</li><li>many requests from others</li><li>reacting to other peoples' problems</li></ul>	<ul><li>look busy or comfortable work</li><li>much e-mail and paper mail</li><li>distractions or trivia</li><li>some phone calls, idle chitchat</li><li>pleasant or escape activities</li></ul>
	Implications:	*Implications:*
	<ul><li>distracted from important work</li><li>broken promises, goals, accountabilities</li><li>feeling victimized and out of control</li><li>addiction to action, adrenaline high</li><li>shallow and broken relationships</li><li>working hard with little to show for your effort</li></ul>	<ul><li>blaming busy-ness for not getting the important things done</li><li>addiction to detail</li><li>loss of career and business opportunities</li><li>becoming dependent on others or on institutions for the basics of life</li><li>loss of self-confidence and self-esteem</li></ul>

The heart of effective leadership is focusing on box ❷, important but not urgent activities. Nevertheless, because no one is yelling at the moment or no deadline is pressing, and because these activities demand creative thinking and discipline, they are often overlooked or given only minimum attention. Yet these are highly leveraged activities. They are the core of leadership success, and the essence of a successful life.

Examine box ❸, urgent but not important, and box ❶, urgent and important. These activities tend to be visible and rewarding, in the short term. As a result, leaders are caught up in them, often losing sight of what is important in the long haul. Box ❹, part of all of our lives, speaks for itself.

How to use this leadership tool

"Time management is really a misnomer—the challenge is not to manage time, but to manage ourselves."
—Stephen Covey, *THE SEVEN HABITS OF HIGHLY EFFECTIVE PEOPLE*

The key to leadership success is accepting responsibility for your own development, staying on top of your important and urgent work (thereby ensuring short-term success), while also practicing the discipline to accomplish meaningful results in the long term (i.e., important but not urgent work).

This tool assumes you are already *aware* of what is important in your career as a leader. If you are not sure, you may wish to use some of the Strategic or Systemic tools listed at the end of this section. Using the template provided, plan a few specific, serious, and powerful changes in how you use your most scarce resource—your time. Alternatively, use this template in coaching others to look seriously at their own time management practices, and to make a few meaningful changes in their thinking, habits, and goals.

WEB WORKSHEET

	Urgent	Not urgent
Important	List activities that you feel are essential to short-term success and cannot be avoided. What one or two steps can you take to minimize these demands on your time, while also ensuring that these activities are completed appropriately?	Setting aside the time pressures you are currently experiencing, list three important short-term goals that will guide you toward your long-term goals as a leader. [☞ 3.1 Strategy] List three or four steps you might take if you were really serious about achieving these goals.
Not Important	List three or four activities in this area that you could delegate to others or stop doing completely, if you really tried. [☞ 9.2 Situational Leadership]	List one or two habits you need to break so that activities in this area don't eat up your valuable time. [☞ 15.5 Habits]

RELATED LEADERSHIP TOOLS

1.6 Boards of Play	2.7 Goal Statements	13.3 Accountability
2.6 Clarifying Purpose	3.2 Sigmoid Curve	13.10 Careers

FOR FURTHER ASSISTANCE

Covey, Stephen, Roger Merrill, and Rebecca R. Merrill. *First Things First: To Live, to Love, to Learn, to Leave a Legacy.* Fireside, 1996.

13.6

ATTRIBUTION THEORY: ASSESSING PERFORMANCE AND BEHAVIOR

Inspired by Harriet Lerner, and Martin Seligman.

However well-intended leaders might be, treating people fairly and impartially is not always a simple task. Some types of work are more quantifiable than others, and thus easier to evaluate objectively; for example, product sales volumes, billable hours, product return rates, customers served, and so on. When outcomes are measured primarily in terms of quality as opposed to quantity, however, performance is not as easily evaluated. For example, how do you objectively evaluate the quality of a presentation, the contribution of an individual to team output, or the usefulness of a report or a book? In cases like these, subjectivity is a necessary part of the evaluation. Attribution is the name given to this subjective process, in that we attribute causes, results, problems, and so on, to others, often with less than adequate information on which to base our judgment. Although it's unfortunate, assigning attributes to another person's performance is often necessary. It simply isn't possible, or where possible, it would not be cost-effective, to gather the kind of detailed information that would be needed to make a completely objective evaluation. The legal system does require this level of detail, but organizations would slow to a crawl if this level of investigation and proof were required prior to making every people-related decision.

Attribution theory is best understood through an example. If you relate well with someone, you're more likely to evaluate that person's performance through rose-colored glasses; if someone else constantly rubs you the wrong way, you may be more inclined to evaluate that person's performance harshly.

Not surprisingly, attributions are very much at play in all organizations, in processes such as annual performance reviews and 360° feedback. This is because the performance of an individual knowledge-worker is notoriously difficult to evaluate objectively. Boundaries are fuzzy, as people work interdependently; and output is not easily measured or quantified, as this work involves adding value as opposed to completing a whole product. Nevertheless, feedback is required by both the organization and the employee.

AN EXAMPLE OF HOW ATTRIBUTION CAN AFFECT YOUR EVALUATION OF ANOTHER PERSON'S PERFORMANCE

	If you *like* the person	If you *dislike* the person
If the person *succeeds*	This person: • is deserving. • has earned success. • is dedicated and works hard. • is smart. Only he or she could have pulled this off.	This person: • was just lucky (e.g., was in the right place at the right time). • is just a show-off. Anyone could have done it. We all contributed; this person simply got the credit.

If the person *fails*	This person: • faced uncontrollable or impossible circumstances (e.g., economic downturn, bad boss, inadequate resources). Nobody could have done the job under those conditions. In view of the situation, it's amazing that it went as well as it did. No one is perfect. No one could have pulled this off.	This person: • has an inherent character flaw. • is not very bright. It was just a matter of time before bad habits caught up with the person. Only a loser could have made such a mess of things.

HOW TO USE THIS LEADERSHIP TOOL

"We rarely find that people have good sense unless they agree with us."

—Duc de la Rochefoucald

Keep in mind that others will surely attribute motives, causes, results, and failures to your performance and behavior as a leader! Thus, this tool will also challenge you to develop and maintain strategic relationships. You need to be aware of what is being attributed to you. You also need to take the opportunity to influence these assessments by others.

Use the workspace provided to challenge your own thinking and arrive at a more objective assessment of other people's performance and behavior. It can be difficult to see your own biases, so you may want to review your responses to these questions with a trusted coworker or coach.

WEB WORKSHEET

Your attributions of others

Given your interests, expertise, preferences, and relationships, whose performance or behavior are you likely to *over*appreciate?

Whose performance or behavior are you likely to *under*appreciate?

[☛ 15.2 Emotional Intelligence]
What steps can you take to ensure that your evaluation of others is more balanced and more firmly based on facts as opposed to attributions?

[☛ 15.3 JoHari Window]

The attributions others might make of you

Which people or groups are important to your success within the organization?

[☛ 3.6 Strategic Relationships]
How will you develop and maintain these relationships so appropriate credit is given for your achievements, and appropriate understanding is provided when circumstances limit the results that you are able to achieve?

[☛ 12.1 The Relationship Bank]
Strategies to help you: Observe performance on a regular basis—make note of achievements weekly or at least monthly, and avoid making judgments on individual items. When doing a performance review, bring forward all your notes for reminders and a look at the big picture.

[☛ 8.1 Conversations]

RELATED LEADERSHIP TOOLS

8.1 Conversations	12.4 Feedback	15.3 JoHari Window
12.1 The Relationship Bank	13.1 Coaching	15.4 Ladder of Inference

FOR FURTHER ASSISTANCE

Lerner, Harriet G. *The Dance of Anger: A Woman's Guide to Changing the Patterns of Intimate Relationships*. Harper & Row, 1985.

Seligman, Martin E.P. *Learned Optimism,* 2nd ed. Pocket Books, 1998.

13.7 DOCUMENTING EMPLOYEE PERFORMANCE AND BEHAVIOR

Inspired by Connie Quinn.

Leaders often recoil at the idea of having to complete annual performance reviews, or having to document performance or behavior problems as part of disciplinary action. Keeping specific, accurate, and current records on significant employee performance and on-the-job behavior can make these chores a lot easier.

The obvious benefits of documenting	*The less-obvious benefits of documenting*
✔ Completing a specific, objective, and balanced performance review becomes considerably easier if these notes are maintained regularly. ✔ This level of documentation is essential for disciplinary action within most organizations.	✔ It is a structured way to ensure that you are providing regular and balanced feedback to your employees. ✔ Reviewing this documentation provides data for assessing and improving your *own* communication and leadership performance.

SAMPLE FORMAT FOR DOCUMENTING PERFORMANCE AND ON-THE-JOB BEHAVIOR

Employee Name: _____

Date	Positive performance/behavior	Date	Negative performance/behavior

GUIDELINES FOR USING THIS FORMAT

Although this is simply an organized way of keeping up-to-date records, it is a surprisingly powerful leadership tool *if* these guidelines are followed:

   ✔ One absolute requirement for using this form is that you make entries only after you have first reviewed the relevant information directly with the employee concerned. In this way, you can be assured that you have provided timely feedback to the employee and that your notes are accurate and reliable. Only if this step is followed will this form prove to be a powerful leadership tool.

   ✔ Use this form regularly (at least weekly). Although it takes only a few minutes to make these notes, it does take ongoing discipline to regularly provide feedback to employees. Although providing feedback does take time, research shows that regular feedback is required for high performance, regardless of whether you use the form of documentation outlined here.

✔ Be specific when completing this form. When possible, use numbers, measures, observations, exact words and phrases, and so on. Feedback is much better received when it is based on factual data.

✔ Aim for more positives than negatives. For a normal workgroup, a ratio of at least seven positives per negative is recommended. High performance results from building on strengths. Negative feedback is better received from a leader who also gives deserved positive feedback.

✔ Keep this form in a secure location (e.g., locked file cabinet or password-protected computer file). It is your private property.

✔ Although these forms are really notes to yourself, write clearly and objectively. This will aid your ability to recall the particulars of each notation. In addition, in the rare and unusual event that these notes are discovered and subpoenaed by a court of law (e.g., in a suit for unlawful dismissal), you will most likely find that this clarity works to your considerable advantage.

✔ It is not necessary to inform employees that you are using this form; but if you are asked, we recommend being honest about the form's existence and its purpose. An appropriate response would be something like: "I keep these notes only so that I'm better able to provide specific information on annual performance reviews. In addition, nothing here would surprise an employee, as I make these notes only after I have first discussed a matter with the employee in question."

✔ Not every positive or negative behavior should be documented using this form. Documenting everything would be far too time-consuming. The purpose is to have data for individual performance improvement and team results, not to amass a quantity of words.

How to use this leadership tool

"Feedback is the breakfast of champions."

—Ken Blanchard, *THE ONE-MINUTE MANAGER*

Prepare a form like the one shown here and maintain performance and on-the-job behavior documentation for every person in the organization who reports directly to you. Set a goal to provide regular feedback to people, and provide a suitable ratio of positive to negative (i.e., constructive) feedback. Discipline yourself to keep these forms current. Over a few months, this will become a positive work habit, reinforced by the benefits of improved communication with employees and by a new sense of comfort in preparing and reviewing performance reviews with staff.

Take a few minutes every couple of months to review the information you have noted for each employee. Have you provided balanced feedback? Are your comments objective and specific? Taken as a whole, what does this information say about each employee? About the group as a whole? About your leadership? Struggling with questions such as these and staying open to feedback from others will help you remain conscious of your leadership strengths and development needs, promoting not only group performance, but continuous improvement for you as a leader. Use only direct observations of behavior by you; don't use others' observations unless you can verify them. Ensure that your comments concern only behaviors that are related to job performance requirements.

WEB WORKSHEET

Employee Name: _____

Date	Positive performance/behavior	Date	Negative performance/behavior

RELATED LEADERSHIP TOOLS

8.1 Conversations	12.5 Negative Feedback	13.3 Accountability
12.4 Feedback	12.6 Confrontation	13.6 Attribution Theory

JOB COMPETENCIES: MEASURING AND PREDICTING PERFORMANCE

Contributed by Wilf Hiebert, and inspired Lyle and Signe Spencer.

Leaders need objective measures for recruiting, training, and rewarding employees. Yet in modern knowledge-based organizations, the attributes that matter most are difficult to measure or observe (e.g., initiative, creativity, confidence, political acuity, and so on). Clearly defined job competencies help leaders to assess attributes related to job performance that are difficult to measure or observe. Once defined and validated, job competencies can be used for a range of practical purposes: as recruiting tools that detail specific, hard-to-define qualifications for a job; in developing job-related training programs; and in tailoring performance evaluation tools to specific jobs.

WHAT IS A COMPETENCY?

A competency is an enduring, underlying characteristic of an individual, indicating ways of behaving and thinking that are directly related to an objective measure of effective job performance.

➡ *Underlying characteristic* refers to an enduring part of a person's personality that predicts behavior across job situations.

➡ *Directly related* means that the competency predicts performance.

➡ *Objective* means the competency can predict something being done well or poorly as measured by specific criteria.

WRITING A COMPETENCY DEFINITION

Competency definitions begin with *intent:* the motive or trait that underlies action toward a business result.

Intent	➡	Action	➡	Result
motives, traits, self-concept		behaviors (knowledge, skills)		on-job performance

UNDERLYING CHARACTERISTICS

The characteristics levels in this table can be thought of as being on a continuum, with the first level (motives) being the most difficult to assess and develop, and the last level (skills) being the easiest to observe and develop.

Underlying characteristics	Definition	A leadership example
1. Motives	What people consistently think about or desire. Motives direct behavior toward or away from certain actions and goals.	Achievement-motivated leaders consistently set challenging goals for themselves, take personal responsibility for results, and use feedback to improve. [☞ 1.7 Results-Based Leaders]
2. Traits	Emotional characteristics that are the building blocks of personality. They result in predictable responses to situations.	Rather than acting defensively or blowing up under stress, confident leaders approach and solve problems constructively, building relationships in the process. [☞ 15.2 Emotional Intelligence]
3. Self-concept	The mental image of one's self, including attitudes, values, and self-image.	Confident of their worth, effective leaders believe most people can be effective in most situations. [☞ 14.1 Scarcity and Abundance, 15.3 JoHari Window]
4. Knowledge	Knowledge a person has in specific content areas, that can be used to produce results.	Knowledge of a wide range of leadership tools helps leaders select and tailor the tools to their unique circumstances.
5. Skills	The ability to perform specific physical or mental tasks in order to produce results.	Effective leaders use analytic skills (processing knowledge, determining cause and effect) and conceptual skills (recognizing patterns in complex data). [☞ 7.2 Problem Solving, 7.5 Decision Making, 7.7 Quality Tools]

HOW TO USE THIS LEADERSHIP TOOL

"In complex jobs, competencies are relatively more important in predicting superior performance than are task-related skills, intelligence, or credentials."

—Lyle and Signe Spencer, *COMPETENCE AT WORK*

Data for developing job competencies can be gathered by observing a job being performed effectively (e.g., observing critical job-related incidents), or through behavior-based interviewing. As complexity and informed judgment are required, this work is best done by a small task force of internal stakeholders, along with assistance from a professional who is skilled in developing job competencies. [☞ 1.10 The GAS Model]

Use the workspace provided to begin the process of identifying competencies for a particular job. Distinguish between behaviors required for satisfactory performance and those that differentiate a superior level of performance. You are likely to find that the difference is more related to *how* a job is performed than to *what* is being performed (i.e., most people typically follow the same basic procedures, practices, and policies).

WEB WORKSHEET

Job: _____

Underlying characteristics	Basic behaviors and actions required to perform the job satisfactorily	Advanced behaviors and actions that differentiate superior job performance
1. Motives		
2. Traits		
3. Self-concept		
4. Knowledge		
5. Skills		

RELATED LEADERSHIP TOOLS

1.7 Results-Based Leaders   10.3 Team Competencies   13.3 Accountability

1.8 Recursive Leadership   13.2 High-Performers   15.2 Emotional Intelligence

FOR FURTHER ASSISTANCE

Spencer, Lyle M. Jr., and Signe Spencer. *Competence at Work: Models for Superior Performance*. John Wiley & Sons, 1993.

HUMAN CAPITAL: TRULY THE
MOST VALUABLE ASSET

Contributed by Clem Blakeslee and inspired by Brian Friedman, James Hatch, David Walker, Riel Millar, Ikujuro Nonaka, Hirotaka Takeuchi, David Ulrich, Jack Zenger, and Norman Smallwood.

Human capital is people—the human beings who keep an organization humming, vibrant, and innovating. Modern industrial societies have generally lost the recognition that human talent and human intellect, as well as human sweat, represent wealth. Writings about the development of the New World recognized the capital infusion that immigrants represented. Robert Reich, former U.S. Secretary of Labor and a Harvard economist, has argued that the industrial societies that are most competitive are those that truly respect the concept of human capital and consistently pursue the enhancement of human capital. Recent attempts to focus attention on human capital speak of intellectual capital, knowledge management, and learning organizations.

Yet an ambivalence exists in modern organizations. On one hand, the value of human assets in organizations is often talked about as a capital investment: "our greatest resource." On the other hand, people are often treated like overhead, "G&A," an expense. In national and corporate terms, we squander human capital by treating it as though it were merely an expense. Contrast this indifference with the successful emphasis of Singapore on human capital and human resource development.

HUMAN KNOWLEDGE AND SKILLS AS COMPETITIVE ADVANTAGES

Defining human capital is more challenging than using the traditional economic measures. The traditional capitalization based in bricks and mortar seems to be changing. Witness the present stock market performance, applying a much larger premium to the intangible, softer assets like innovative capability, strategic position, leadership, human resource capabilities, systems, first-to-market responses, and so on.

Ulrich, Zenger, and Smallwood define human capital as:

> **Human Capital = Employee Capability × Employee Commitment**

Nonaka and Takeuchi don't speak of human capital, but of a related concept, knowledge creation, with the sequence:

Knowledge Creation ➞ **Continuous Improvement** ➞ **Competitive Advantage**

The Organisation for Economic Cooperation and Development (OECD) based in Europe published a book that states: "Spurred by the emerging knowledge economy, government policy makers, human resource managers, financial accountants, and educators are developing methods for systematically evaluating and recording knowledge assets acquired through experience, education, and training." This book [subtitled *Human Capital Accounting for the Knowledge Economy*] explains why it is possible, in terms of economic theory and accounting practices, "to implement new human capital information and decision-making systems."

How to use this leadership tool

"All organizations now say routinely, 'People are our greatest asset.' Yet few practice what they preach, let alone truly believe it."

—Peter Drucker, *THE NEW SOCIETY OF ORGANIZATIONS*

Effective understanding and use of human capital is closely aligned with creating an effective organization. Every organization needs to understand and realize a return on its human capital. Yet, just as with bricks and mortar investments, no one strategy will work for every organization. The big-picture model presented here was inspired by the work of Friedman, Hatch, and Walker in their book, *Delivering on the Promise*.

WEB WORKSHEET

	Some things to do	**Your action plans**
1. Balanced Strategy Clarification	❑ Clarify your overall direction, goals, and strategy. Include and integrate human capital requirements. ❑ Consider using a balanced scorecard. ❑ Highlight the values underlying the human capital strategy. ❑ Use systems thinking to integrate and highlight trade-offs. [☛2.1 Systems Thinking, 2.5 Values, 2.8 Balanced Scorecard, 3.1 Strategy]	
2. Human Capital Impact Appraisal	❑ Appraise the current human asset base; assess investment needed to support the human capital strategy. ❑ Use impact measures like the cost of replacing a person: impact of loss of intellectual and skill assets. ❑ Involve stakeholders (have the process mirror your values as well as expected outcomes). [☛ 2.8 Balanced Scorecard, 5.7 Stakeholder Groups]	
3. Design/ Redesign of Human Systems	❑ Design systems and programs that support the human capital strategy (e.g., recruitment, development, training, succession, incentives). ❑ Use systems thinking to integrate and highlight trade-offs. ❑ Involve and communicate with stakeholders. [☛ 2.1 Systems Thinking, 4.1 Organizational Design, 8.3 Organizational Communication]	

4. Implementation of Changes	❑ Particularly in traditional organizations, change will not be easy and needs to carefully planned. ❑ Integrate appropriate accountabilities into the change. [☛ 5.1 Change Equation, 5.2 Major Change, 5.8 Human Transitions]	
5. Follow-Through	❑ In light of the fact that more is said than done about human capital recognition, ensure that follow-through and assessment are carried out. [☛ 13.3 Accountability]	

Related leadership tools

1.7 Results-Based Leaders	4.1 Organizational Design	4.5 Culture
3.1 Strategy	4.3 Reengineering	4.7 Job Satisfaction

For further assistance

Friedman, Brian, James A. Hatch, and David M. Walker. *Delivering on the Promise: How to Attract, Manage, and Retain Human Capital.* Free Press, 1998.

Millar, Riel. *Measuring What People Know: Human Capital Accounting for the Knowledge Economy.* The Organisation for Economic Cooperation and Development, 1996.

Nonaka, Ikujiro, and Hirotaka Takeuchi. *The Knowledge-Creating Company: How Japanese Companies Create the Dynamics of Innovation.* Oxford University Press, 1995.

Slemko, Janet K. *Mind Wealth: Turning Knowledge into Assets.* BookPartners, Inc., 1999.

Ulrich, David, Jack Zenger, and Norman Smallwood. *Results-Based Leadership.* Harvard Business School Press, 1999.

13.10

THE FOUR STAGES® MODEL: UNDERSTANDING CAREER STRATEGIES

Inspired by Gene Dalton and Paul Thompson.

The Four Stages® model is a powerful tool for guiding career planning, particularly improving one's leadership potential. To be a true leader, one must be at Stage 3 or above, according to this model. You can't reach these stages without first succeeding at the earlier stages (apprentice and professional expert). So, how do you know if a person is performing at Stage 3 or higher? One good indicator is that at Stage 3, an individual stops competing as a functional expert, and instead gets results by encouraging excellence in others.

THE FOUR STAGES® CAREER MODEL

	Stage 1 Apprentice professional	Stage 2 Professional expert	Stage 3 Group/team leader	Stage 4 Organizational leader
Characteristics of each career stage	❑ Works dependently. ❑ Works under supervision. ❑ Lacks experience. ❑ Learns the business. ❑ Helps, follows. ❑ Works on part of a larger project. ❑ Accepts coaching and supervision. ❑ Completes directed activity, routine and detailed work. ❑ Accomplishes tasks on time.	❑ Works independently. ❑ Develops depth in own area. ❑ Is assigned own projects and clients. ❑ Relies more on self and peers, and less on supervisor, for answers. ❑ Develops credibility and reputation. ❑ Responsible for significant results. ❑ Develops own resources. ❑ Develops judgment, confidence, and intuition.	❑ Works interdependently. ❑ Understands the business. ❑ Gets results through others. ❑ Coaches, mentors, develops others. ❑ Works in several areas at once. ❑ Deals with a range of stakeholders. ❑ Leads groups. ❑ Offers ideas, someone else implements them. ❑ Has breadth of technical and process skills.	❑ Works systemwide. ❑ Integrates others' work with business. ❑ Leads through vision and strategy. ❑ Influences organizational direction. ❑ Assures excellence. ❑ Exercises power by policy formation, new directions and roles. ❑ Has mental toughness, makes tough decisions. ❑ Represents the organization. ❑ Assesses trends in the environment. ❑ Sponsors key people.
Barriers at each stage that can prevent movement to the next stage	❑ Inability to accept feedback ❑ Expecting others to structure work ❑ Not accepting responsibility for professional work	❑ Lack of professional competence ❑ Lack of confidence, initiative, or focus ❑ Lack of commitment to the work or the organization	❑ Unwillingness to assume responsibility for others ❑ Lacking people and leadership skills ❑ Unwillingness to let go of details	❑ Inability to provide long-term organizational direction ❑ Inability to identify and sponsor the best people

	Not finding a coach or mentor Indecision about career Not finding the right fit or job Not settling into a profession	Lack of interpersonal skills Getting stuck in a role versus a results mind-set Lack of people skills Inability to deal with ambiguity	Scarcity mind-set (not sharing information, the need to be right, competing for recognition)	Lack of influence with key stakeholders and significant industry leaders Unwillingness or inability to use power

HOW TO USE THIS LEADERSHIP TOOL

"To move from one stage to the next, individuals must demonstrate competence in performing the functions inherent in the next stage. In this sense, career development is an individual responsibility. However, organizations can do a great deal to either aid or hinder individual development efforts. Company policies and practices have the potential to substantially affect an employee's ability to work out a satisfying career."

—Gene Dalton and Paul Thompson, *NOVATIONS*

Too often, people think of careers in terms of specific jobs or levels of responsibility within an organization. However, career success is ultimately about the level of one's own development (technical, interpersonal, intellectual, emotional, and so on), not about a specific job or a given level of management responsibility.

Use this tool to rethink the traditional approach to career planning, and to develop new insights into planning your career or coaching others to do the same. Pay particular attention to Stage 3 (Group/team leader). This is the most basic leadership stage and includes a mind-set of achieving satisfaction *through* helping others to achieve results, and *through* seeing others develop and succeed as professionals.

WEB WORKSHEET

Think of your own career or the career of another person and answer these questions.

1. Looking at the stage checklists, at what career stage is the person primarily working at the present time?

2. What career stage would you like the person to achieve within the next _____ years?

[☞ 3.2 Sigmoid Curve]
3. What characteristics does the person already exhibit for succeeding at the next career stage? (Be as specific as possible.)

4. What barriers does this person need to overcome in order to progress to the next career stage? (Be as specific as possible.)

[☛ 5.8 Human Transitions]

5. What steps will you take, or coach the other person to take, in order to overcome these career barriers and to provide opportunities to develop the skills needed at the next career stage?

[☛ 13.1 Coaching]

RELATED LEADERSHIP TOOLS

1.2 Manage or Lead?	5.8 Human Transitions	13.1 Coaching
1.6 Boards of Play	9.9 Power	13.3 Accountability

FOR FURTHER ASSISTANCE

Dalton, Gene, and Paul Thompson. *Novations: Strategies for Career Management.* Scott, Foresman and Company, 1986.

13.11 PROFESSIONAL LEADERSHIP: DELIVERING EXPERTISE

Inspired by Peter Block, Geoff Bellman, and thousands of consulting skills workshop participants.

Organizations are increasingly dependent on accurate, innovative, and timely professional expertise from a wide variety of sources—engineering, systems, public affairs, human resources, legal, environmental, finance—the list goes on. This tool is addressed to leaders in such professional areas, providing them with a simple five-step model to better deliver their expertise in a timely, appropriate way, so they are perceived as valued members who contribute to the bottom line of the organization.

Organizations today offer and expect a great deal more of internal professionals working in staff support roles. As described by one staff professional, "It seems to me that in the past,

the professional's role started with someone else assigning and framing the technical problem to be solved. That is, the support professional picked up gift-wrapped problems. The professional's job ended with the presentation of his or her recommendations. It was up to the line manager whether the recommendation was accepted and implemented. This is no longer the case! What organizations need now are 'full cycle' professionals who can take responsibility for the entire expertise delivery cycle, from clearly defining the business issue, to selling their recommendations, through to sustaining the change once their recommendations have been implemented."

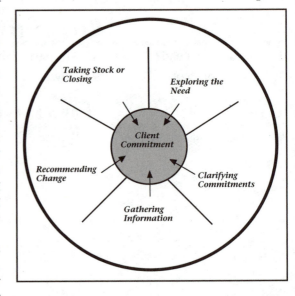

Thus, to be effective today, professionals need to possess more than technical expertise. They also need a process for delivering their expertise, like the internal consulting model or framework illustrated here. Although rarely applied in a linear fashion, an internal consulting model provides staff professionals with a purpose and strategy for their work. When challenged, they can confidently explain their consulting process to clients.

THE EXPERTISE DELIVERY MODEL

This is a field-tested, effective, five-stage model designed to deliver professional expertise inside an organization. Thousands of professionals presently use, adapt, customize, and internalize this model, confident that their consultations are following a proven process that leads to success.

Expertise delivery stage	Key logical issues	Key relationship issues	Typical problems at this stage
Exploring the Need	Getting at cause Getting at the underlying need Distinguishing what is wanted from what is needed Scoping the problem	Establishing rapport Establishing trust Assessing readiness for change	Jumping to cause or action Accepting presented cause at face value Unclear problem leading to ill-defined projects Not thinking ahead to key issues of client change
Clarifying Expectations/ Commitments	Clarifying outcomes Clarifying roles Clarifying process and next steps	Clarifying roles Clarifying stakeholders Clarifying commitments	Unclear expectations leading to conflict One-way expectations Scope creep Unclear/inappropriate roles
Gathering Information	Data gathering and diagnosis Mapping the system	Building ownership Mapping the stakeholder system	Dealing with ambiguity Dealing with complexity Overlooking important stakeholders
Recommending Change	Understanding that making recommendations means change Selling the change	Dealing with natural reservations and resistance	Presenting features but not benefits Suppressing reservations and resistance Not explaining *why*
Taking Stock or Closing	Wrapping up the consultation Improvement planning	Transfer of ownership Determining roles in change	No follow-through No closure

HOW TO USE THIS LEADERSHIP TOOL

"You do not merely want to be considered just the best of the best. You want to be considered the only ones who do what you do."

—Jerry Garcia

Besides having an effective expertise delivery model, powerful professionals need to begin by stepping back and looking at their roles strategically. They need to ask—and answer—lots of searching questions about how they deliver expertise inside their organizations:

✔ What are the external pressures on, and strategic direction of, our organization?

✔ What can we offer that is more strategic to the organization?

✔ Where do we currently spend our time? With which internal clients? External customers?

✔ How do we help our clients with strategic changes in our domain of expertise?

✔ Who *are* our major clients? Who *should* be our clients? What services do we offer them?

✔ How do we market value-added services inside our organization to our clients?

✔ To which requests should we say "No," because they are low in value; which do we outsource?

Note that all of these questions are asked in the plural. Although individual professionals need to think through their individual strategies, it is much more powerful for an entire professional group, rather than just its individuals, to clarify these strategic issues. The benefits of having a clear professional group strategy are immense. When professionals complain about the inadequacies of their clients and organization, they often don't realize that they have not looked at themselves with the same critical eye. Professional strategies and internal marketing are covered in other tools. [☛ 3.5 Strategic Resourcing, 3.9 Marketing Services]

After clarifying a business strategy for their specialty, professionals need a *professional services delivery model*. Modify the five-step process shown below to tailor a *professional services delivery model* to the unique needs of your individual consulting practice or of your professional service group.

WEB WORKSHEET

Expertise delivery stage	Purpose	Your customized delivery model	Key activities and results for this stage
1. **Exploring the Need**	Clarify the client's underlying needs before proceeding.		[☛ 7.1 Problem Framing]
2. **Clarifying Commitments**	Ensure that all parties are clear on results and processes before action is launched.		[☛ 2.7 Goal Statements]
3. **Gathering Information**	Gather further information on the defined problem.		[☛ 7.2 Problem Solving, 7.5 Decision Making, 7.7 Quality Tools]
4. **Recommending Change**	Recommend what and how clients should change.		[☛ 5.1 Change Equation, 9.7 Selling Wheel]
5. **Taking Stock or Closing**	Effectively wrap up the project or planning improvements.		[☛ 10.12 RASCI Planning]

Related leadership tools

1.7 Results-Based Leaders	3.9 Marketing Services	7.1 Problem Framing
3.5 Strategic Resourcing	4.9 Professional Expertise	13.10 Careers

For further assistance

Bellman, Geoff. *The Consultant's Calling: Bring Who You Are to What You Do.* Jossey-Bass, 1990.

Bellman, Geoff. *Getting Things Done When You Are Not in Charge.* Simon & Schuster, 1992.

Block, Peter. *Flawless Consulting: A Guide to Getting Your Expertise Used.* University Associates, 1978.

Hiebert, Murray. *Powerful Professionals: Getting Your Expertise Used Inside Organizations.* Recursion Press, 1999.

14

TOOLS FOR LEARNING

Change is taking place at the speed of electronics. Learning, the basis of directed human change, is taking place at the speed of human minds. These tools help ground leaders to help themselves and others to continue learning in a fast-paced world.

14.1

SCARCITY AND ABUNDANCE: THE IMPORTANCE OF ATTITUDE

Inspired by Viktor Frankl, Roger Harrison, Gay Hendricks, Kate Ludeman, Peter Senge, and Abe Wagner.

Leaders' underlying attitudes have profound and far-reaching effects within their workgroups and organizations. Usually formed in early life and from previous work experience, attitudes often don't reside at a conscious level. For purposes of this tool, we define attitude, also known as frame of reference, as the way you understand yourself, others, and your relationships with others. Leaders need to understand the impact of their own frames of reference on their ability to get things done through other people within organizations.

	Scarcity	Abundance
Basis	Assumes scarce resources: • Fixed pie or zero-sum perspective (if you give someone a piece of your pie, you have less). • Only so much interesting work and recognition are available. • Leads to we–they thinking.	Assumes a synergy: ✔ With people, 1 + 1 can be more than 2 (by cooperating, we enlarge the pie and everyone can have more). ✔ It is a world of plenty if we share what we have. ✔ There's ample recognition for all. ✔ Is community-oriented. ✔ Leads to a willingness to give away your hard-earned expertise.
Features	• Continuous struggle • Competition • Win–lose	✔ Sharing, cooperating ✔ Listening ✔ Concern for mutual success ✔ Realistically cautious
Position	• Need to be right and convince others of your position. • Making others look good diminishes your own success. • The expert, aggressive, or know-it-all leader.	✔ My leadership success comes through the success of others. ✔ Willingness to hear contrary points of view. ✔ Desire to learn from others. ✔ Build success on success over time.
Actions	• Defending and defensive • Turf protection • Selling, advocating • Arguing to win	✔ Mentor, coach, and lead others. ✔ Find value in and share in other people's successes. ✔ Share your work and rewards so that others can also benefit.

	Scarcity	**Abundance**
Appropriate Uses	Scarcity mind-set is more appropriate: • You have no expectations of other people after the deal is finalized (e.g., buying a used car from a stranger in as-is condition). • You know the other person(s) is willing to work or negotiate only in a win–lose way.	An abundance mind-set will serve leaders better in the long run: ✔ In dynamic, knowledge-based organizations, success requires working interdependently. ✔ In real teams, people win or fail together.

This tool outlines two extremes: a Scarcity frame of reference and an Abundance frame of reference. Use the distinctions listed here to begin examining your own leadership attitude or frame of reference.

How to use this tool

> *"The experiences of [concentration] camp life show that people do have a choice of action. There are enough examples, often of a heroic nature, which prove that apathy can be overcome, irritability suppressed, and people can preserve a vestige of spiritual freedom, of independence of mind, even when under severe psychic and physical stress. We who lived in concentration camps can remember those people who walked through the huts to comfort others, giving away their last piece of bread. They may have been few in number, but they offer sufficient evidence that everything can be taken from a person except one thing: the last of the most wondrous of human freedoms, the freedom to choose one's own attitude in any given set of circumstances, to choose one's own way."*
>
> —Viktor Frankl, *MAN'S SEARCH FOR MEANING*

Two points must be emphasized.

1. Having the right attitude does not replace the necessity for clear agreements or legal contracts.
2. Sometimes a scarcity attitude or mind-set is appropriate (e.g., when you are involved in negotiations in which you don't care about the relationship, about the level of goodwill, or about follow-through by the other person).

WEB WORKSHEET

Think of situations you are currently involved in or soon likely to become involved in (e.g., an upcoming decision, a negotiation with a peer in your organization, a presentation to senior management). Use the space provided here to reflect on the benefits and potential pitfalls of approaching each situation with a scarcity or an abundance mind-set.

The situation	A scarcity mind-set	An abundance mind-set
	Potential benefits	Potential benefits
	Potential pitfalls	Potential pitfalls

RELATED LEADERSHIP TOOLS

5.8 Human Transitions	6.7 Creativity and Innovation	7.4 Polarities
6.6 Six-Hat Thinking	7.1 Problem Framing	13.6 Attribution Theory

FOR FURTHER ASSISTANCE

Frankl, Victor E. *Man's Search for Meaning: An Introduction to Logotherapy,* 2nd ed. Beacon Press, 2000.

Harrison, Roger. "Strategies for a New Age." *Human Resources Management.* 22(3), Fall 1983, 209–235.

Hendricks, Gay, and Kate Ludeman. *The Corporate Mystic: A Guidebook for Visionaries with Their Feet on the Ground.* Bantam, 1996.

Senge, Peter M., Richard Ross, Bryan Smith, Charlotte Roberts, and Art Kleiner. *The Fifth Discipline Fieldbook: Strategies and Tools for Building a Learning Organization.* Currency Doubleday, 1994.

Wagner, Abe. *The Transactional Manager: How to Solve People Problems with Transactional Analysis.* Prentice Hall, 1981.

14.2 SINGLE-LOOP AND DOUBLE-LOOP LEARNING: WHEN TO STAY THE COURSE AND WHEN TO REEVALUATE

Inspired by Chris Argyris, Donald Schon, and Peter Senge.

There are times when a leader has to make a decision to stick with a prearranged goal, regardless of feedback. Alternately, there are times when a goal has to be reassessed in the light of unanticipated feedback. Knowing when to hold the course and when to readjust goals is a highly sophisticated leadership skill. Among other things, it involves a leader's intuition, logic, self-awareness, courage, and openness to feedback from others. These decisions challenge leaders to think outside the assumptions and limitations they may have unconsciously imposed upon themselves. This tool provides insight into these difficult decision-making and goal-setting processes.

Single-loop learning assumes that established goals are correct, and aims to optimize the system (i.e., the focus is on efficiency). *Double-loop learning,* also called generative learning, assumes that established goals can and should be challenged. It aims to ensure that the right goals are in place (i.e., the focus is on effectiveness). While neither method of learning is necessarily superior, each is applicable in different situations. Single-loop learning works well when conditions are stable and predictable, whereas double-loop learning is a wise practice in times of rapid and continuous change.

In the diagram, both single- and double-loop learning start with step ❶, setting goals. Thereafter, single-loop learning assumes that established goals are correct, and cycles within steps ❷, ❸, and ❹ in order to achieve those goals. Double-loop learning, on the other hand, assumes that established goals can be challenged and changed. It cycles back to step ❶ and reassesses goals in light of new information (i.e., feedback). Based on revised goals, new action plans are made, and different actions are taken.

Double-loop learning reassesses goals.

❷ **Plan Action**

❶ **Set Goals**

Single-loop learning only checks for goal attainment.

❸ **Take Action**

❹ **Assess Feedback**

EXAMPLES OF SINGLE- AND DOUBLE-LOOP LEARNING

	Cruise control example	Leadership example
Single-loop learning	• *A given speed is set: the goal.* • *A feedback loop connects actual speed with the control of fuel flow into the engine.* • *Speed oscillates near a fixed point.* • *The cruise control blindly controls the speed.*	• *Goals are set.* • *The goals are accepted as given, and performance management processes assess work done toward these established goals.* • *Effort oscillates near the goals.*
Double-loop learning	• *A starting speed is set.* • *If conditions do not change, the cruise control blindly controls the speed.* • *But the goal is not static: As driving conditions change, the speed setting is adjusted to reflect a new goal (e.g., an increased emphasis on safety).*	• *Starting goals are set.* • *The environment is continually scanned. If conditions do not change, the initial goals remain.* • *As conditions change, goals are adjusted or changed entirely to reflect the new conditions.*

HOW TO USE THIS LEADERSHIP TOOL

"You gotta know when to hold 'em, and know when to fold 'em…"
—Kenny Rogers' song, "THE GAMBLER"

Double-loop learning challenges work habits, assumptions, and ways of understanding the world. This does not mean, however, that single-loop learning is not more valuable in certain situations. For example, Thomas Edison's struggle to invent the light bulb and the Wright brothers' persistence in creating a heavier-than-air flying machine both required staying the course (i.e., single-loop learning). At other times, however, double-loop learning is more appropriate and takes more courage. For example, a leader publicly admits that due to changing circumstances, a much-valued goal has proven to be unfeasible, or that a deadline cannot be achieved without an increased risk to employee safety.

WEB WORKSHEET

Use the space provided to make notes on which learning process—single- or double-loop—best applies to the specific goals you are presently working to achieve. In addition to challenging you to think through your existing learning process, this exercise will help you hone your skills for working with future goals and decision processes.

> List one or two goals that you intend to stick with over the next few months, regardless of the feedback you have been receiving.

List one or two key reasons why you intend to stick with these goals.

List one or two goals that you will reassess and adjust, in light of the feedback you have been receiving.

List one or two key reasons why you intend to reassess these goals.

Note: After you have listed the goals you intend to stick with and those you intend to reassess and your reasons for each, test your decisions by running these by a trusted colleague, a coach, or your workgroup. Doing so makes your decisions visible and your decision-making process open to challenge. Effective leaders are not afraid to test their thinking in public.

RELATED LEADERSHIP TOOLS

1.6 Boards of Play	3.2 Sigmoid Curve	6.5 Force-Field Analysis
1.9 Paradigms	6.2 Assumption Analysis	8.4 Dialogue and Discussion

FOR FURTHER ASSISTANCE

Argyris, Chris. "Good Communication That Blocks Learning." *Harvard Business Review*. July-August 1994, 77–85.

Argyris, Chris. "Teaching Smart People How to Learn." *Harvard Business Review*. May-June 1991, 99–109.

Argyris, Chris, and Donald A. Schon. *Organizational Learning: A Theory of Action Perspective*. Addison-Wesley, 1978.

Senge, Peter M., Richard Ross, Bryan Smith, Charlotte Roberts, and Art Kleiner. *The Fifth Discipline Fieldbook: Strategies and Tools for Building a Learning Organization*. Currency Doubleday, 1994.

14.3 NEEDS ANALYSIS: MEASURING RETURN ON TRAINING INVESTMENTS

Inspired by Donald Kirkpatrick, Robert Mager, and Trisha Wilcox.

A leader's success in developing people is a key competitive advantage in knowledge-based work environments. Yet training is costly: Participants' time away from work, course design, and travel all cost money, not to mention your time as a coach to ensure that employees' new knowledge and skills are being used effectively on the job. In addition, investments in training are all too often poorly selected and ineffective. This tool will help you measure training ROI (return on investment).

You can measure the success of a training event on four levels, from the most commonly used but least helpful measure (participant reaction) through to the most complex but most helpful measure (actual results).

The four levels of measurement	What is measured and its value as a measurement	Typical measuring process
1. Reaction	Measures how a participant feels about a training event. Least helpful, but easiest to measure.	Ask participants to complete a training course evaluation form. Ask: "How do you feel about what you learned at the training event?"
2. Learning	Measures how much the participant learned during the training event. Most helpful in technical training, when there is one best way to do the job.	Standardized testing. Pre- and post-learning-event measures are required.
3. Performance	Measures how well participants are using their learning on the job. Most helpful when training is skill-based and there is one best way to do the job.	Usually measured by observing on-the-job performance. Pre- and post-learning-event measures are required.
4. Results	Measures return on investment for a training event. The most definitive measure, yet least used, as measurement is complex and costly.	Often it's impossible to directly connect the acquisition of new knowledge and skills in a given learning event to bottom-line business goals.

Post-learning-event measures are rarely helpful without pre-event measures. The needs analysis and return on investment process shown here is based on the four levels of measurement already outlined.

Level of valuation	A. Preparation	B. The learning event	C. Follow-through
Results	❶ Identify the organizational goal, and the gap between present and desired goal achievement.		❽ Measure business results, and estimate the contribution training has made to these results.
Performance	❷ Identify performance targets (behaviors) required to meet the business goal, and assess the gap between present and desired employee behavior.		❼ Support, coach, and measure performance against targets. Remove barriers; reward performance.
Learning	❸ Identify the knowledge and skills (K&S) needed to meet performance targets, and identify the gap between present and desired K&S.		❻ If practical, test to assess the level of post-learning-event K&S. Compare with pre-learning-event findings.
Reaction		❹ Select and develop a learning event that will build the required K&S.	❺ Gather participant reactions at the end of the learning event.

HOW TO USE THIS LEADERSHIP TOOL

"No one knows how much time [leaders] in future organizations will spend reflecting, modeling, and designing learner processes. But it will be a great deal more than was spent in the past."

—Peter Senge, *THE FIFTH DISCIPLINE*

Research shows that your continued involvement as a leader is crucial in translating participants' learned ideas and skills into organizational results. Critical elements for getting results from training investments include:

✔ Link training to organizational or business needs. [☛ 3.1 Strategy]

✔ Meet with participants *before* the training event to clarify why the training is needed, what results are expected, and what follow-through coaching and support will be provided. [☛ 13.1 Coaching]

✔ Meet with participants *after* the training event to discuss their learning, their concerns, and how they will be applying their new knowledge and skills on the job.

✔ Set goals and plan follow-through, both for training participants and for yourself (as their leader). [☛ 2.7 Goal Statements, 10.12 RASCI Planning, 13.3 Accountability]

✔ Remove barriers to performance. [☛ 2.1 Systems Thinking]

✔ Give feedback on performance—both positive feedback when goals and standards are met, and improvement feedback when performance falls short of desired targets. [☛ 12.4 Feedback]

✔ Model desired performance and behavior yourself (always a critical element of developing people and guiding their performance). [☛ 1.8 Recursive Leadership]

Checklist to help a leader get value from training

Provide one-on-one coaching. [☛ 9.2 Situational Leadership, 13.1 Coaching]

The quickest and easiest results can usually be obtained through one-on-one coaching. Select items that apply to your participants.

❑ Meet with each training participant to discuss reactions, learning, concerns, and on-job applications.

❑ Participants will have planned action in the workshop. Coach them with new ideas, reality checks, and follow-through.

❑ Review participant materials and on-job applications.

❑ Set goals and specific performance standards with participants. Plan follow-through, including your own.

❑ Celebrate and build on the positive. Some participants may already be using some workshop practices.

❑ End the coaching meeting by clarifying and documenting expectations.

Involve the group. [☛ 4.4 Employee Involvement, 10.7 Getting Participation]

Often, you can obtain more leveraged results through group participation and group action. Select items that apply to your group.

❑ Set goals and specific performance standards with participants as a group. Plan follow-through, including your own.

❑ Work with the group to design job aids that will expedite work without adding bureaucratic overhead.

❑ Organize group support and follow-through; for example, no-fault project debriefing sessions, mentoring groups to share wisdom and skills, or simulated group practice sessions with peer coaching.

Align systems. [☛ 2.1 Systems Thinking]

While employees are often blamed for performance problems, research consistently shows that barriers that have been inadvertently built into organizational systems are most often the underlying cause of performance problems. Examples are lack of clear accountabilities and misunderstanding of strategic direction. Ensure, to the degree possible, that organizational systems are aligned with your training initiative (e.g., compensation systems, career development programs, performance management systems, methods of assigning work, and so on).

Improve your own leadership practices. [☛ 1.8 Recursive Leadership]

What you do speaks louder than what you say. Model the behavior you expect in others.

- ❑ Learn more about the skills of coaching.
- ❑ Learn more about employee performance and career development. [☛ 13.10 Careers]
- ❑ See your success as the success of others. Do not compete with your people; your reward comes from their success.

RELATED LEADERSHIP TOOLS

2.1 Systems Thinking	9.2 Situational Leadership	13.3 Accountability
9.1 Leadership Versatility	13.1 Coaching	14.6 Learning Styles

FOR FURTHER ASSISTANCE

Kirkpatrick, Donald. *Evaluating Training Programs.* American Society for Training and Development, 1975.

Klatt, Bruce. *The Ultimate Training Workshop Handbook: A Comprehensive Guide to Leading Successful Workshops and Training Programs.* McGraw-Hill, 1999.

Mager, Roger, and Peter Pipe. *Analyzing Performance Problems: Or, You Really Oughta Wanna,* 2nd ed. David S. Lake Publishers, 1984.

14.4

ADULT LEARNING: PRINCIPLES FOR HELPING ADULTS LEARN

Inspired by Malcolm Knowles.

Knowing how to apply adult learning principles improves a leader's ability to influence and help others learn, whether on the job or within group meetings. Adult learning principles are almost the opposite of traditional teaching assumptions and methods. Understanding the logic behind these principles will help you facilitate and lead in a way that is in tune with and supports the needs of adults.

To enhance adult learning, leaders need to build upon adults' experiences; create relevance for the learning; and keep learning practical by making it concrete and by actively involving the learners in a variety of ways.

ADULT LEARNING PRINCIPLES

Principle	Rationale	Practices
Adults have a lot of experience and are protective of their learning from this experience.	• Adults have a lot invested in their experience. They have something to contribute and something to protect. • Every adult learns at his or her own pace and in his or her own way. • Few adults want or expect to change their self-concepts. It's not a leader's role to force personal change.	✓ Adults want to test new learning against what they already know; they won't buy your answer unless they understand *why*. Leaders need to encourage questioning and value different perspectives. ✓ Adults don't want to risk looking stupid or being shown up in any way. It's critical that leaders maintain adults' self-esteem at all times. ✓ Feedback, encouragement, and empathy are keys when adults first try out a new skill.
Adults want to focus on real-life, here-and-now problems and tasks, rather than on academic or philosophical situations.	• Adults see learning as a means to an end, not as an end in itself. • Adult learning is voluntary. Adults will only learn what they want to learn, in order to do what they want to do.	✓ As busy people, adults want to focus on immediate and current issues, not on learning that may be useful in the distant future. ✓ Leaders need to create relevance by using concrete examples of how the learning will be helpful to adults. ✓ Adults become restless if they feel their time is being wasted. They must know what there is to gain and what is in it for them.
Most adults are accustomed to being active and self-directed in their learning.	• The best adult learning is a consequence of experience. Experience alone is clumsy and evolutionary, and makes for a slow and painful teacher. But experience combined with coaching and other methods of learning (e.g., reading, on-the-job instruction, participating in a workshop) is a powerful developmental combination.	✓ For learning to occur, adults have to get involved in their own learning. ✓ Leaders need to help adults connect learning activities with business and personal results. ✓ Adults want to be consulted and listened to. They become engaged and focused when challenged and supported. They resist and defend themselves when they feel threatened.

How to Use This Leadership Tool

"Men must be taught as if you taught them not, and things unknown posed as things forgot."

—Alexander Pope

The wisdom embedded in these adult learning principles applies whether you are supervising, coaching, or teaching adults. Think of a specific situation in which you will be supervising, teaching, coaching, or leading an individual or group. Use the space provided to plan how you will apply adult learning principles in this situation.

WEB WORKSHEET

Adult learning principle: Adults have a lot of experience, and are protective of their learning from this experience.

What experiences will the individual or group bring to this learning situation?

[☛ 14.7 Personal Preferences]

How I will use these experiences in the learning process?

Adult learning principle: Adults want to focus on real-life, here-and-now problems and tasks, rather than on academic or philosophical situations.

What connections can I make between the learning objectives and here-and-now payoffs?

[☛ 4.4 Employee Involvement, 10.7 Getting Participation]

How can I build examples and practical experiences (e.g., simulations, discussions) into this learning?

Adult learning principle: Adults are accustomed to being active and self-directing in their learning.

What steps can I take to ensure that people feel a sense of ownership in this learning?

How can I empower the group (or a specific individual, as the case may be) to tailor the learning objectives to their own specific work and development needs and to set their own pace for learning?

Related leadership tools

8.7 Active Listening	10.7 Getting Participation	14.6 Learning Styles
10.6 Group Leader Skills	14.5 Teaching a Job	14.7 Personal Preferences

For further assistance

Klatt, Bruce. *The Ultimate Training Workshop Handbook: A Comprehensive Guide to Leading Successful Workshops and Training Programs.* McGraw-Hill, 1999.

Knowles, Malcolm, and Associates. *Andragogy in Action.* Jossey Boss, 1980.

14.5 TEACHING A JOB: AN ESSENTIAL SKILL FOR FRONTLINE LEADERS

Inspired by the people who designed the on-job training process as part of the Second World War training effort.

Frontline leaders are expected to provide basic training in procedures and processes ranging from dealing with customer complaints to using applications software. Here is a time-honored process for teaching a specific job or task to an individual or small group (e.g., two or three employees). Follow these steps (prepare, instruct, practice, follow up) to ensure that people learn and to enable the job performance your organization requires from its employees.

PREPARE

Plan what you will teach.

- ❏ Write out the goal or performance standard in behavioral terms: what you want the learner (person being trained) to be able to do. [☞ 2.7 Goal Statements]
- ❏ Assess the background of the learner: related job experience, current skills, knowledge level, and preferred style of learning. [☞ 14.6 Learning Styles]
- ❏ Break down the training into digestible steps. Thus, if the job is large or complex, break training into a number of learning segments of 30 minutes or less. (Note: Distinguish the teaching sequence—the best way for the learner to learn the job—from the actual working sequence.)
- ❏ Prepare training checklists and visual learning aids. People learn better with visuals.
- ❏ Make a list of typical job-related problems and safety concerns.

Prepare the training site.

- ❏ Find a place for training where it's safe to practice and distractions can be kept to a minimum.
- ❏ Organize the site, and assemble learning aids and equipment.

INSTRUCT

Prepare the learner.

- ❏ Create relevance for the learning by explaining *why* it is needed and *how* it will benefit the learner. [☞ 9.7 Selling Wheel]
- ❏ Put the learner at ease by giving permission to make mistakes and providing opportunities to express concerns.
- ❏ Describe the goal of the training in simple and practical terms.
- ❏ Ask the learner what he or she already knows related to the job; then build on that.

Teach the job.

- ❏ Present the context for the job or task: how it fits into the bigger picture at the work site.
- ❏ Demonstrate the job or task to the learner. Do this in simple, digestible steps.
- ❏ For each step, explain *what* you are doing, *why* it needs to be done, and *how* to do it.

- ❑ Next, reverse roles and have the learner explain each step to you.
- ❑ As appropriate, point out any errors and safety concerns.
- ❑ When the instruction is complete, ask the learner to demonstrate the complete job or task.

PRACTICE

- ❑ Practice is essential. Success is not what the learner knows, but what the learner can do.
- ❑ Encourage the learner by pointing out successes and reminding him or her of the benefits of knowing the job.
- ❑ Correct any errors immediately in a supportive and understanding way. [☛ 12.4 Feedback]
- ❑ Congratulate the learner when he or she performs the job or task to a reasonable standard.
- ❑ Inform learners where they can get help on an ongoing basis.

FOLLOW UP [☛ 13.1 Coaching]

- ❑ Check on-the-job progress frequently and regularly for a period after training. Try to catch performance errors before they become performance habits.
- ❑ If possible, pair the learner with an experienced employee to ensure ongoing support.
- ❑ Reward and celebrate success when demonstrated results are being achieved.

HOW TO USE THIS LEADERSHIP TOOL

"More and more (leaders) are being asked to teach some aspect of their expertise or 'know-how.'
Too often, these people are taught 'what' to instruct, but not 'how' to instruct ... ."

—Bruce Klatt, *THE ULTIMATE TRAINING WORKSHOP HANDBOOK*

WEB WORKSHEET

Preparation is the key to successful on-job training. Use the workspace provided to plan how you will organize to teach a job or task. Note the major learning steps involved. For example, if you're teaching an individual how to operate a new heavy-lift crane, major learning steps might include safety, maintenance, calculating loads, and so on. Next, major learning steps need to be broken down into bite-size learning chunks. Take crane safety, for example; this could be broken down into safety procedures when working around power lines, when working in windy conditions, when working at night, when refueling, and so on. Finally, for each of the bite-size learning chunks, consider the critical teaching points that need to be covered in your instruction; for example, why a given safety procedure is important, or common errors to avoid when operating a crane at night, and so on.

The **job or task** that is being taught: _____
The **goal** you want to achieve as a result of teaching this job or task *(what the learner will be able to do at the end of this instruction):*

[☛ 2.7 Goal Statements]

Major learning steps	Bite-size learning chunks	Critical teaching points

RELATED LEADERSHIP TOOLS

2.7 Goal Statements	5.9 Resistance	12.4 Feedback
4.4 Employee Involvement	9.2 Situational Leadership	14.4 Adult Learning
5.1 Change Equation	9.7 Selling Wheel	14.6 Learning Styles

FOR FURTHER ASSISTANCE

Klatt, Bruce. *The Ultimate Training Workshop Handbook: A Comprehensive Guide to Leading Successful Workshops and Training Programs.* McGraw-Hill, 1999.

14.6 LEADERS AND LEARNING STYLES

Inspired by David Kolb, Anthony Alexander, and Phillip Hunsuker.

"Different strokes for different folks" is a useful adage for a leader. People simply do not all think and learn in the same ways. (Ironically, treating people fairly can mean treating them quite differently!) One important aspect of these differences is how people learn. This tool will help you understand your own learning preferences, the learning preferences of others, and how you can turn these differences—often sources of conflict—into sources of enrichment, strength, team diversity, and improved business results.

THE FOUR LEARNING STYLES

The central point of this tool is that different people, including leaders, learn in different ways. There is no right or wrong learning style, and most people can use at least a couple of learning styles if necessary. Nonetheless, a person will learn more willingly and easily when allowed to use his or her preferred learning approach.

Learning style	Learning preferences
Sensors (Kolb's *concrete experience*)	➡ Tend to rely on feelings, values, and empathy to make conclusions. ➡ Like to learn by talking it out, interacting, and discussing with others. ➡ Dislike a lot of theory. "Sit still and be quiet" doesn't work well with this style.
Assessors (Kolb's *reflective observation*)	➡ Tend to observe, listen, and carefully assess information. ➡ Like to learn by listening and watching. ➡ Dislike sharing, role-playing, and interaction-based learning approaches.
Thinkers (Kolb's *abstract conceptualization*)	➡ Tend to rely on logic and rational evidence to make conclusions. ➡ Like to learn from impersonal models and systematic analysis. ➡ Dislike unstructured, open-ended exercises and discussions.
Doers (Kolb's *active experimentation*)	➡ Tend to learn by trying it out and doing. ➡ Like to learn from practical simulations, projects, and small-group discussions. ➡ Dislike lectures and passive learning.

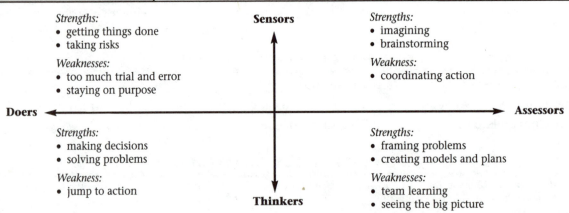

What are the practical implications of differences in learning styles for you, the leader?

➡ Don't assume others like to learn in the same way you do.

➡ Don't assume failure is due to ignorance; with a different learning design, a person may excel.

➡ Help people to see that differing learning styles are a benefit, not a curse. Successful projects need to employ a range of learning styles to capitalize on the strengths and minimize the weaknesses of each style.

➡ Use a variety of approaches when designing a communication or a learning event, thus appealing to the different learning styles.

How to use this leadership tool

"Zorba scratched his head. 'I've got a thick skull, boss, I don't grasp these things easily. Ah, if only you could dance all that you have just said, then I'd understand. … Or if you would tell me all that in a story, boss.'"

—Nikos Kazantzakis, *ZORBA THE GREEK*

This tool has many applications for a leader:

✔ Learn about your own learning style.
✔ Understand the learning preferences of others.
✔ Diagnose communication difficulties based on differences in learning styles.
✔ Minimize conflict by valuing different learning approaches.
✔ Help assign people to appropriate jobs or tasks.
✔ Design a job to increase the chances of success by accommodating individual learning preferences.
✔ Build a team by recognizing learning styles and capitalizing on the learning strengths of the members.
✔ Help to design a communication or learning event.
✔ Coach, teach, and facilitate the learning of others in a way that capitalizes on their strengths.
✔ Assess training and development packages to determine how they accommodate differing learning styles.
✔ Help to set up a coaching relationship.

WEB WORKSHEET

Your personal learning style assessment and application

Use the workspace provided to assess your learning and instructional style as a leader.

1. What are your personal learning preferences?
2. When and how are these personal learning preferences a strength?

3. When and how are these personal learning preferences a *problem, weakness, or limitation?*

4. What insights do the answers to items 2 and 3 give you about clicking with some people and experiencing bad chemistry with others?

5. Think of a practical application (e.g., on-the-job training, a meeting, a communication, coaching others, a learning event, a team-building session) and use this model to help plan the event in a way that will accommodate the learning styles of the participants.

Describe the goal of the event or situation:

What methods will you use to accommodate the various learning styles?

How can you help capitalize on the various strengths and overcome or minimize the limitations of each learning style?

RELATED LEADERSHIP TOOLS

6.6 Six-Hat Thinking	9.2 Situational Leadership	13.6 Attribution Theory
8.1 Conversations	10.7 Getting Participation	14.5 On-Job Training
9.1 Leadership Versatility	13.1 Coaching	14.7 Personal Preferences

FOR FURTHER ASSISTANCE

Hunsaker, Phillip L., and Anthony J. Alessandra. *The Art of Managing People: Person-to-Person Skills, Guidelines, and Techniques Every Manager Needs to Guide, Direct, and Motivate the Team.* Prentice Hall, 1986.

Klatt, Bruce. *The Ultimate Training Workshop Handbook: A Comprehensive Guide to Leading Successful Workshops and Training Programs.* McGraw-Hill, 1999.

Kolb, David. *Experiential Learning: Experience As the Source of Learning and Development.* Prentice Hall, 1984.

14.7 PERSONAL PREFERENCES: CAPITALIZING ON INDIVIDUAL DIFFERENCES

Inspired by Isabel Briggs-Myers, David Keirsey, Otto Kroeger, Janet Thuesen, Marilyn Bates, and Carl Jung.

You may have wondered why your leadership approach works well in some situations and fails miserably in others; why you click with some people, yet find others impossible to work with; why some relationships seem so easy and comfortable, while others are a continual struggle. Throughout the ages, people have wondered about their similarities and differences. The goal of this tool is not psychological analysis; rather, it's to help you deal more effectively with human differences. This tool will help you gain a better understanding of yourself and your own preferences, as well as those of other people, leading to more effective leadership interactions.

A century ago, philosopher and psychologist Carl Jung devised a way of grouping human similarities and differences into four categories of pairs, thereby describing the built-in, and natural preferences of individual ways of being in the world. These four categories of pairs or preferences are:

Introversion (I) or Extroversion (E)
Intuitive (N) or Sensing (S)
Thinking (T) or Feeling (F)
Perceiving (P) or Judging (J)

To help you understand and use these sets of preferences, the descriptions in this table accentuate the extremes of each set of preferences. There is no right or wrong set of preferences, and it is okay *not* to have a strong personal inclination toward either pole in any pair.

Comparison of Introversion and Extroversion

I _____ E

Introversion	Extroversion
Drained by people	Charged up by people
Thinks alone	Thinks by talking
One-on-one or a few	Groups
Small, close network	Broad network
Depth of contact	Breadth of contacts
Act after thinking	Act first, think after

Comparison of Intuitive and Sensing

N _____ S

Intuitive	Sensing
What could be	The actual, what is
Innovation, change	Practicality
Big picture	Stick to facts
Options, more options	Make it work
Strategic	Worked in the past
Patient with complexity	Patient with details

Comparison of Thinking and Feeling

T _____ F

Thinking	Feeling
Rationally correct	Feels right
Weight of evidence	Impact on people
Based on logic	Based on commitment
Critique	Appreciate
Consistent with principles	Consistent with values
Find rules, laws, models	Find and build commitment

Comparison of Perceiving and Judging

P _____ J

Perceiving	Judging
Open to possibilities	Keeping on track
Open to more data	Deciding
Flexible	Planned
Spontaneous	Order
Adapt	Anticipate
Open-ended	Concluded, closed

Some Implications of Personal Preferences

✔ You, as a leader, have preferences on each of the four scales. Their combined effect greatly influences how you like to work. Use the application tool to gain insights into your own preferences.

✔ Each person with whom you interact also has personal preferences. How much these preferences coincide with or differ from your own can be a source of clicking, of seeing things the same way, or of conflict.

✔ These conflicts can actually be beneficial. For example, if you are a strong T and depend on thinking to draw conclusions, you can benefit greatly from hearing an F perspective, if you can work together.

✔ Any strength on one side of a preference pair corresponds to a flat spot on the other side for which you could use assistance.

How to use this leadership tool

"It's strange, but wherever I take my eyes, they always see things from my point of view."

—Ashleigh Brilliant

As a leader, you have a natural inclination to do things in a particular way, and also to assume that others should do things in the same way. Your personal approach is assumed to be right. Yet what seems rational and natural to one person can seem bizarre and counterproductive to another! The twofold trick to using the preferences approach is:

• First, understand your own strengths and blind spots as a leader.

• Second, appreciate the differing perspectives of others, not as sources of affliction or conflict, but as sources for complementing (rounding out) your own personal preferences.

Step 1: Assess your own personal preferences: Read the description lists for each pair of preferences. In the space provided here, rate how strongly you identify with these descriptors, with +5 representing a strong preference for a given pole, and 0 representing no particular preference for either pole.

I E	N S	T F	P J
+5 | | | | 0 | | | | +5	+5 | | | | 0 | | | | +5	+5 | | | | 0 | | | | +5	+5 | | | | 0 | | | | +5

Step 2: Assess the personal preferences of another person: Next, assess the personal preferences of another person (perhaps a person you are having difficulty understanding or working with). Note that these assessments are provisional in nature; they represent a static and descriptive snapshot at a given point in time. They should not be used to pysch out another person's behavior. Use this tool to help you deal more effectively with others, but never use it to force-fit other people into rigid stereotypes or categories.

Step 3: Assess how you might improve your working relationship with the other person: To get you started, here are some common differences and their impacts.

Leader	Direct report	Issues that might arise given your differences in personal preferences	Strategies the leader might pursue to work with the direct report (the person reporting to the leader)
NT	ST	The leader prefers to be innovative and look at the big picture, while the direct report prefers to work with the tried and true and may see the leader as a head-in-the-clouds type.	Find common ground in the T. Present your innovative ideas in a logical format. Honor your limitations and ask for help to ground your ideas in the real world. Find value in the direct report's ability to organize data, facts, and information logically.
P	J	The leader is okay with ambiguity and is willing to deal with issues as they arise. The direct report would prefer more clarity and a plan.	Be aware that raising the level of ambiguity may be stressful to the direct report. Respond to the direct report's need for clarity, before opening the conversation up to include other issues. The direct report can help you by documenting and working toward making a decision.
NF	ST	The leader may appear to be too idealistic and subjective, while the direct report is concerned with the nuts and bolts, or basic issues.	In a noncondescending way, help the direct report express his or her thinking and facts—known as feelings and ideas to you! Remind yourself of the contribution of ST's: If they buy in, they will make your innovative ideas work!

Think of several people you need to work with. Clarify issues and strategies for working with them effectively.

Leader	Other person	Issues that might arise given your differences in personal preferences	Strategies you might employ to work well with this person

RELATED LEADERSHIP TOOLS

1.9 Paradigms	8.7 Active Listening	12.8 Difficult People
6.2 Assumption Analysis	8.9 Cross-Cultural	13.6 Attribution Theory
8.5 Metacommunicating	12.7 Dealing with Conflict	14.6 Learning Styles

FOR FURTHER ASSISTANCE

Keirsey, David, and Marilyn Bates. *Please Understand Me: Character and Temperament Types.* Prometheus Nemesis Book Company, 1984.

Kroeger, Otto, and Janet M. Thuesen. *Type Talk at Work: How the 16 Personality Types Determine Your Success on the Job.* Dell Publishing Company, 1993.

15

Tools for Taking Care of Yourself

Stephen Covey uses the analogy of "sharpening the saw." Ancient tales speak of "killing the goose that lays the golden eggs." No matter what metaphor you use or how you think about it, you will not be a great leader over the long haul if you don't take care of yourself.

15.1 BALANCE: TAKE CARE OF YOURSELF!

Inspired by Kevin Cashman, Stephen Covey, David Irvine,
Harold Kushner, Robin Skynner, John Cleese, and Robert Pirsig.

If you want to be around for a long time as a leader, you need to find balance in your own life, and help others find balance in theirs. *Fast Company* says it all about the corporate culture of the new millennium. "Sleep Is the New Status Symbol for Successful Entrepreneurs," says a *Wall Street Journal* article. The refrain is the same: faster, smarter, creative destruction; shorter cycle times; the customer is always right; business at the speed of light. Alongside this frenetic organizational culture are disturbing societal problems: rising divorce rates, rise of depression, increasing use of violence, overuse of mood-altering drugs, downsizing and early retirements creating an underemployed class.

This tool will help you navigate the maze of external influences toward finding, establishing, and maintaining your own balance. Suggestions to start an exercise regime and schedule quality time with the family are merely platitudes if you don't first answer the fundamental questions outlined here.

1. *Understand who you are.* If you do not regularly step back to ask and act on some fundamental questions about who you are, your purpose and your priorities, you are condemned to live at the mercy of external influences. Blaming others for your circumstances provides only temporary venting and relief. You need to take control of your own life.

2. *Distinguish what is urgent from what is important.* This fast-moving world encourages high-energy fire fighting—dealing with urgent matters. Being busy, amassing tons of airline points, receiving hundreds of e-mails, and making big bucks are the hallmarks of success. But as Stephen Covey points out, the truly important things in one's life are rarely urgent, yet they get shuffled behind the ever-increasing urgent items demanding our immediate attention.

3. *Nurture your close relationships.* Close relationships are not business acquaintances or people in your net**work**. (Note the word *work* hiding there!) Human beings are social beings. You need people in your life who make time for you, with whom you can discuss any issue, on whom you can depend in times of stress, and vice versa.

4. *Simplify your life.* Advertising and the urge to keep up create many false "oughtta haves." Separate what you really *need* from a) what others may think you need, and b) what you want. Every one of those unnecessary wants complicates your life. Like monkeys on your back, they demand to be fed, they defecate, and they tend to procreate.

5. *Integrate more reflection and renewal into your life.* A good leader needs to think. A great leader needs to think at much higher and broader levels, and in a much longer time frame. Find a time and place for reflection. Many leaders find reading reflective books a source of insight and inspiration. Listen to your body. Take your vacations! Reserve your weekends. Take responsibility for taking care of yourself.

6. *Manage stress more effectively.* Yes, studies show that many leaders can handle stressful situations better than most—in fact, they may thrive on stress. Yet, human beings have limitations. Separate what you need to *control* from what you need to *influence* and what you need to *let go.* As a leader, be aware of producing undue stress in others. What you can handle with ease may be stressful for them.

7. *Deal with damaging habits.* No one sets out to abuse himself or herself. Often, short-term fixes become long-term problems. Habits are often very difficult to change. Get help if you are abusing alcohol, abusing loved ones, or abusing stimulants. If you are out of shape, start exercising.

8. *Stop taking yourself so seriously.* Lighten up. Engage in some frivolous activities.

How to use this leadership tool

"Technology brings us powerful tools and incredible capabilities. It also sets a brutal pace for us to follow."
—Dave Irvine, *SIMPLE LIVING IN A COMPLEX WORLD*

Take the time right now to reflect on yourself and your own life. Examine your life using the eight suggestions listed, asking yourself:

1. What are you happy about in this area that you would like to continue?
2. What are you concerned about in your life?
3. Most importantly, what are you going to do about it?

WEB WORKSHEET

---

1. Understanding who I am:
What is important in my life right now as evidenced by what I do versus what I say?

[☞ 1.4 Leadership Principles, 1.8 Recursive Leadership]
What should be important in my life?

[☞ 2.5 Values]

---

2. Distinguishing what is urgent from what is important:
Items that are important in my life, but that I never get around to.

[☞ 13.5 Time Management]

---

3. Nurturing my close relationships:
Which close relationships have suffered because I am so caught up in busy-ness?

[☛ 9.10 Networking. 12.1 The Relationship Bank]

4. Simplifying my life:
In what ways have I complicated my life with things I do not really need?

5. Integrating more reflection and renewal into my life:
What steps can I take to get away and keep my life in perspective?

[☛ 9.4 Leader Impact]
What kinds of things can I do to renew myself at a deep level?

6. Managing stress more effectively:
How do I handle stress in my life?
What do I need to do to reduce the stress in my life?

[☛ 15.7 Stress]

7. Dealing with damaging habits:
What damaging habits do I have in my life?
Where should I get help to deal with changing these habits?

[☛ 15.5 Habits, 15.6 Defenses]

8. Not taking myself so seriously:
What kinds of things can I do to balance the serious and the fun parts of my life?

Related leadership tools

1.5 Seven Habits	13.5 Time Management	15.5 Habits
4.7 Job Satisfaction	15.2 Emotional Intelligence	15.7 Stress

For further assistance

Cashman, Kevin. *Leadership from the Inside Out: Becoming a Leader for Life*. Executive Excellence Publishing, 1999.

Covey, Stephen. *The Seven Habits of Highly Effective People: Powerful Lessons in Personal Change*. Simon & Schuster, 1989.

Irvine, David. *Simple Living in a Complex World: Balancing Life's Achievements*. RedStone Ventures Inc, 1997.

Kushner, Harold. *How Good Do We Have to Be? A New Understanding of Guilt and Forgiveness*. Little, Brown and Company, 1996.

Kushner, Harold. *When All You've Ever Wanted Isn't Enough: The Search for a Life That Matters*. Simon and Schuster, 1986.

Pirsig, Robert. *Lila: An Inquiry into Morals*. Bantam, 1991.

Pirsig, Robert. *Zen and the Art of Motorcycle Maintenance*. Bantam, 1974.

Skynner, A. C. Robin, and John Cleese. *Life and How to Survive It*. W. W. Norton & Co., 1996.

15.2

LEQ: THE LEADERSHIP
EMOTIONAL QUOTIENT

Inspired by Daniel Goleman, Stephen Pinker, Peter Senge, David McClelland, and June Donaldson.

You are bright, hardworking, and technically skilled. Although these qualities probably got you into a leadership role, they are not enough for leadership success! Lyle Spencer, author of a standard reference on leadership competencies, says, "What you learned in school distinguishes superior performers in only a handful of the five or six hundred jobs for which we've done competence studies. It's just a threshold competence; you need it to get in the field, but it does not make you a star. It's emotional intelligence abilities that matter more for superior performance." In a *Time* magazine article on emotional intelligence, Nancy Gibbs says, "Researchers found that ... executives failed most often because of 'an interpersonal flaw' rather than a technical ability."

The purpose of this leadership tool is to provide an overview of a leadership competence area variously known as emotional intelligence (EI), emotional quotient (EQ), emotional literacy, emotional smarts, and emotional competence.

Emotional intelligence, greatly valued in some societies, is the ability to "read" and understand your own emotional competence, as well as to interact and operate effectively with people and personalities, individually and collectively. Many leaders pride themselves on their technical and cognitive abilities; emotional smarts also need to be recognized, practiced, and developed, so it becomes second nature to consider the people aspect an integral part of all business dealings.

This table illustrates the differences between the cognitive and the emotional; the second table separates emotional competencies into two categories, one inside yourself and the other outside, interacting with others.

Cognitive and skills competence	Emotional competence
• Baseline competence—you need it to get in the race	• Comparative advantage—what it takes to succeed as a leader and a human being
• What you know and what you can do, technically and professionally	• How well you handle yourself and others
• Your expertise: knowledge and skills	• Interpersonal, intrapersonal, and team skills
• Your intellectual and skills capital	• Your personal and social capital
• Measured by degrees, diplomas, IQ tests, certifications	• Measured by empathy, adaptability, compassion, influence, charisma, balance
• Get results through ideas, rational processes, and skills	• Gets results through people

Your *inside* or personal emotional competencies	Your *outside* or social emotional competencies

• *Knowing who you are* (warts and all!)
   ➡ self-awareness of own feelings
   ➡ getting feedback to align your self-perception with that of others
   ➡ having sufficient self-esteem to be able to take risks
 • *Personal self-mastery* (dealing with your own feelings)
   ➡ taking responsibility for yourself; not blaming others for your shortcomings
   ➡ handling yourself well in emotional and changing situations
   ➡ not being threatened by others' expertise or aggressiveness
   ➡ integrity and trust
   ➡ balance between big picture (vision, creativity, innovation) and detail (structures, priorities, \getting things done)
   ➡ consciously modeling the behavior you expect in others
 • *Motivation and drive* (having a results orientation)
   ➡ formulating and holding yourself accountable for your goals
   ➡ a balance between becoming (wanting and leading change) and being (getting things done)
   ➡ able to get personal results, but not at the expense of your colleagues
	• *Awareness of others' emotions and needs*
	   ➡ empathic and understanding; able to walk in another's shoes
	   ➡ taking a personal interest in others and what others have to say
	   ➡ active listening skills
	   ➡ knowing and, if appropriate, adapting to the maturity, styles, and preferences of others.
	 • *Social skills*
	   ➡ helping others succeed; seeing your success as the success of others
	   ➡ teamwork: knowing when to collaborate and when to compete
	   ➡ networking: building a win–win support system
	   ➡ basic counseling skills: being able to help people express their concerns, needs, and feelings
	   ➡ communication skills
	   ➡ roles and power relationships: reading and working within the inevitable organizational power structures

HOW TO USE THIS LEADERSHIP TOOL

"...feelings are at the heart of what's going on, they are the business at hand and ignoring them is nearly impossible. ... Framing the feelings out of the conversation is likely to result in outcomes that are unsatisfying for both people. ... Emotions have an uncanny knack for finding their way back into the conversation, usually in not very helpful ways.

—Douglas Stone et al., *DIFFICULT CONVERSATIONS*

Emotional competence is not something you can assess on your own. As human beings, we are notoriously poor judges of ourselves!

WEB WORKSHEET

We suggest you use this assessment first on your own; then, sit down with a coach—ideally, someone who knows you very well—to get feedback and examples and prepare an action plan.

Emotional competency	My assessment	Coach's assessment
Knowing who you are (warts and all!) ➡ self-awareness of own feelings ➡ getting feedback to align your self-perception with that of others ➡ having sufficient self-esteem to be able to take risks [☞ 15.1 Balance, 15.3 JoHari Window]		
Personal self-mastery (dealing with your own feelings) ➡ taking responsibility for yourself; not blaming others for your shortcomings ➡ handling yourself well in emotional and changing situations ➡ not being threatened by others' expertise or aggressiveness ➡ integrity and trust ➡ balance between big picture (vision, creativity, innovation) and detail (structures, priorities, getting things done) ➡ consciously modeling the behavior you expect in others [☞ 1.8 Recursive Leadership, 15.5 Habits]		
Motivation and drive (having a results orientation) ➡ formulating and holding yourself accountable for your goals ➡ a balance between becoming (wanting and leading change) and being (getting things done) ➡ able to get personal results, but not at the expense of your colleagues [☞ 1.7 Results-Based Leaders, 13.3 Accountability]		
Awareness of others' emotions and needs ➡ empathic and understanding; able to walk in another's shoes ➡ taking a personal interest in others and what others have to say ➡ active listening skills ➡ knowing and, if appropriate, adapting to the maturity, styles, and preferences of others. [☞ 8.7 Active Listening, 14.7 Personal Preferences]		
Social skills ➡ helping others succeed; seeing your success as the success of others; crucial to leader success ➡ teamwork: knowing when to collaborate and when to compete ➡ networking: building a win–win support system ➡ basic counseling skills: being able to help people express their concerns, needs, and feelings ➡ communication skills ➡ roles and power relationships: reading and working within the inevitable organizational power structures [☞ 8.1 Conversations, 9.1 Leadership Versatility, 13.10 Careers]		

RELATED LEADERSHIP TOOLS

1.5 Seven Habits	8.1 Conversations	13.10 Careers
5.8 Human Transitions	8.7 Active Listening	14.7 Personal Preferences

FOR FURTHER ASSISTANCE

Goleman, Daniel. *Working with Emotional Intelligence.* Bantam Doubleday Dell Publishing, 2000.

Pinker, Stephen. *How the Mind Works.* W.W. Norton & Company, 1997.

Senge, Peter M. *The Fifth Discipline: The Art and Practice of the Learning Organization.* Doubleday, 1990.

15.3

THE JOHARI WINDOW: WHAT YOU DON'T KNOW CAN HURT YOU

Inspired by Phillip Hanson, Joe Luft, and Harry Ingham.

As human beings, we play very different roles with different people. This makes two bedrock aspects of effective leadership very difficult—self-awareness and asking for feedback. The JoHari window, so named after its founders, Joe Luft and Harry Ingham, illustrates aspects of personality (interests, values, views), and is aimed at helping people think about how they relate with others, and about their need to know themselves and be open to feedback from others. The four panes of the window are:

⟹ *Known* or *Open* area, characterized by a leader's free and open communication with others.

⟹ *Facade* or *Hidden* area, the area where a leader feels vulnerable and hides from others.

⟹ *Blind Spot,* the area where a leader doesn't know how his or her behavior affects others, but others know.

⟹ *Unknown* area, encompassing such indistinct or inexpressible areas as deep fears, early childhood memories, latent potentials, and unrecognized resources.

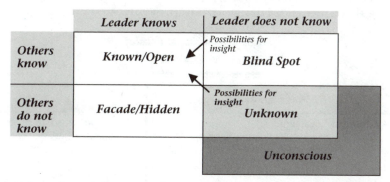

The JoHari model can be used to describe a number of leadership stances, four of which are illustrated here.

The Ideal Window. With a large Known/Open pane, these leaders are open, nondefensive, self-aware, and willing to sharing information, thoughts, and feelings. This can be overdone, however, and casual acquaintances may see too much sharing as threatening or naive. [☞ 15.2 Emotional Intelligence]

The Interviewer. With a large Facade/Hidden pane, these leaders' fears don't allow for testing views or information in public. A large Facade area causes leaders to ask questions but withhold their own views, interests, and needs, leaving others to wonder where they are coming from. Without exposure and challenge, however, a leader's assumptions become outdated and, over time, limit his or her effectiveness. [☞ 15.6 Defenses]

The Bull in the China Shop. With a large Blind Spot, these leaders lack awareness of their own motivations and impact; ironically, others may see these only too clearly. In this area, leaders appear evasive and out of touch with others. For example, you may give feedback to others, but not solicit or welcome feedback from others, or ignore or discount feedback that others offer to you. [☞ 13.6 Attribution Theory]

The Turtle. With a large Unknown pane, these leaders are unaware of their motivations, leaving others to speculate why they do what they do. These leaders don't give out information about themselves that people can react to. They appear to have a shell around them. Although feedback in this area is very valuable, it would need to come from a trusting and patient coach, because maturity and emotional growth are lacking and badly needed in these leaders. [☞ 13.1 Coaching]

HOW TO USE THIS TOOL

"It is through feedback that we implement the poet's words, 'to see ourselves as others see us.' It is also through feedback that other people know how we see them."

—Phillip Hanson, *THE 1973 ANNUAL HANDBOOK FOR GROUP FACILITATORS*

Complete the window provided here, describing the behavior and motivation you use within the workgroup or team you currently lead. Write examples of your behavior that correspond to each quadrant. You will need the help of a coach or trusted colleague to examine your Blind Spot and Unknown quadrants.

Another application is to review these categories with a person you are currently coaching. Note areas where the person you are coaching would most like to improve. Write a brief action plan for beginning this process of change and improvement.

WEB WORKSHEET

	Things I know	Things I don't know
Things They Know	**Known** (the ideal window) An example of my behavior in this area is: My motivation for behaving this way was:	**Blind Spot** (the bull in the china shop) An example of my behavior in this area is: My motivation for behaving this way was:

	Things I know	Things I don't know
Things They Don't Know	**Facade** (the interviewer) An example of my behavior in this area is: My motivation for behaving this way was:	**Unknown** (the turtle) An example of my behavior in this area is: How will I get help to understand my motivations?

Action plan for changing or improving my leadership effectiveness within my workgroup or team:

RELATED LEADERSHIP TOOLS

8.1 Conversations	9.1 Leadership Versatility	14.7 Personal Preferences
8.5 Metacommunicating	12.4 Feedback	15.1 Balance
8.7 Active Listening	13.1 Coaching	15.2 Emotional Intelligence

FOR FURTHER ASSISTANCE

Hanson, Phillip. "The JoHari Window: A Model for Soliciting and Giving Feedback." In John E. Jones, and William J. Pfeiffer, eds. *The 1973 Annual Handbook for Group Facilitators*. University Associates Inc., 1973.

15.4 UNDERSTANDING OUR ASSUMPTIONS AND BIASES

Inspired by Chris Argyris, Peter Senge, Douglas Stone, Bruce Patton, Sheila Heen, and Roger Fisher.

Leaders need to understand what makes themselves, as well as those around them, tick. This includes understanding the beliefs, assumptions, and mental models that human beings hold about the people and the world around them. This tool enables you to inquire into, challenge, and check your own assumptions, conclusions, and beliefs. It also gives you the opportunity to examine and possibly modify some of your own mental models. The ladder shows how we focus, assimilate data, and draw conclusions. It describes a linear process, the Ladder of Inference, to aid our understanding of our complex mental processes—even though these processes are not linear in nature! The ladder is best understood by reading it in ascending order, from ❶, an initial experience, to ❻, taking action based on conclusions about this experience.

THE LADDER OF INFERENCE

❻ You act on your conclusions.

❺ You draw conclusions.
Your conclusions based on your assumptions

❹ You make assumptions.
Your assumptions about what the person meant

❸ You make sense and add meaning.
How you make sense of the selected data

❷ You select data from this experience.
From all the data available, what you chose to take into consideration or consciousness

❶ You have an experience.
What you see, hear, and feel in a given situation

Chris Argyris, a seminal thinker in organizational theory, calls the Ladder of Inference "a common mental pathway of increasing abstraction, often leading to misguided beliefs." The ladder maps a human process that occurs in real time and usually out of consciousness. Understanding and making your thinking ladder explicit helps surface unspoken assumptions so they can be meaningfully discussed. The ladder helps you understand, for example, how people might draw very different conclusions from the same conversation. It also explains how people might have difficulty clarifying the basis for their decisions.

Rick Ross illustrated the ladder in Peter Senge et al., *The Fifth Discipline Fieldbook*.

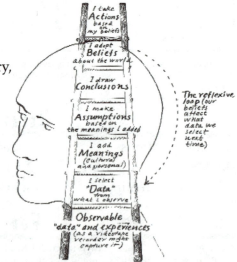

From *The Fifth Discipline Fieldbook*, by Peter M. Senge, Art Kleiner, Charlotte Roberts, Richard B. Ross, and Bryan J. Smith. Used with permission of Doubleday, a division of Random House, Inc.

In the example here, Lee is a Sr. VP for a large organization. Although busy, Lee still wants to congratulate Syd for attaining the best ratings on a recent customer service survey. Lee's assistant, also very rushed, calls Syd and says: "Lee wants to talk with you about sales. Can you come at 3 p.m. today?"

Read the left-hand column from bottom to top (from #1 to #6). Next, do the same with the right-hand column.

Syd's inferences before the meeting	Ladder step	Lee's inferences during the meeting
"I'd better get well-prepared and go in with all the sales data."	❻ **Take action**	"I'd better work this out so we don't lose Syd's sales leadership completely."
"I'll bet Lee is going to go through the roof over this one."	❺ **Draw conclusions**	"Syd wants to take medical leave. I can't lose my best sales leader!"
"Lee must be concerned about our low Canadian sales figures."	❹ **Make assumptions**	"The medical checkup must have gone badly. Syd must be looking for leave."
"Sales? They were good last month except for Canada."	❸ **Make sense**	"There's something wrong here. Syd has been having lots of health problems lately."
"Sales? I just got this month's report. Lee must be calling about that."	❷ **Select data**	"Syd should be happy, yet looks very distraught."
"The telephone call was very brief and much more curt than normal."	❶ **An experience**	Syd arrives, very nervous, toting many files.

HOW TO USE THIS LEADERSHIP TOOL

"We live in a world of self-generating beliefs which remain largely untested."
—Peter Senge et al., THE FIFTH DISCIPLINE FIELDBOOK

WEB WORKSHEET

Use the workspace provided to clarify and test your assumptions and beliefs. Sketch out a Ladder of Inference for a *miscommunication* you were involved with recently. Start with the bottom rung of the ladder, and work up to #6.

Briefly describe the miscommunication situation:

❻ Act on conclusions	Looking back, can you trace your ladder of inference? Where did you go offtrack?
❺ Draw conclusions based on your beliefs	On what basis did you draw your conclusions? What is the basis for your conclusions in general?
❹ Make assumptions	In hindsight, what assumptions did you make? Do you make these types of assumptions regularly? Which of your assumptions now seem unwarranted?
❸ Make sense and add meaning	Of the data you selected, how did you make sense of it? In hindsight, how did you add your own spin to this experience?
❷ Select data	Of all the data available, what did you select to focus on? On what basis did you select this data? In hindsight, what did you miss?
❶ The data (your experience)	What you saw, heard, and felt. In retrospect, what did you miss?

Use these questions to assess your patterns or habits and to make improvements in how you interact with others.

1. At what point along the Ladder of Inference did you make the greatest leap of faith (i.e., where your thinking now seems to have been the least accurate)?

2. At what point along the Ladder of Inference were you solid in your thinking (i.e., where your thinking was well-grounded and objective)?

3. If you decide to change your thinking about this person, relationship, or situation, where along the Ladder of Inference would be a good place to start?

4. What steps will you take to reexamine your assumptions, conclusions, and beliefs?

Related leadership tools

6.2 Assumption Analysis

8.1 Conversations

8.4 Dialogue and Discussion

8.5 Metacommunicating

8.6 Communication 101

8.7 Active Listening

13.6 Attribution Theory

14.7 Personal Preferences

15.2 Emotional Intelligence

For further assistance

Argyris, Chris. "Good Communication That Blocks Learning." *Harvard Business Review.* July-August 1994, 77–85.

Argyris, Chris. "Teaching Smart People How to Learn." *Harvard Business Review.* May-June 1991, 99–109.

Argyris, Chris, and Donald A. Schon. *Organizational Learning: A Theory of Action Perspective.* Addison-Wesley, 1978.

Argyris, Chris, and Donald A. Schon. *Theory in Practice: Increasing Professional Effectiveness.* Jossey-Bass, 1992.

Senge, Peter M., Richard Ross, Bryan Smith, Charlotte Roberts, and Art Kleiner. *The Fifth Discipline Fieldbook: Strategies and Tools for Building a Learning Organization.* Currency Doubleday, 1994.

Stone, Douglas, Bruce Patton, Sheila Heen, and Roger Fisher. *Difficult Conversations: How to Discuss What Matters Most.* Penguin USA, 2000.

15.5

HABITS: THE GOOD AND BAD NEWS
THAT LEADERS NEED TO KNOW

Inspired by Stephen Covey, Daniel Goleman, and Earnie Larson.

Your head tells you to check *Consumer Reports* when thinking of buying a new car. Your heart wants the Lexus, Corvette, or Land Rover. People fool themselves when they claim to act logically, based purely on reason and thinking. We are persuaded by reason, but we are moved to act by emotion. In our "business at the speed of light" world, most often our decisions and actions are habitual, based on feelings. Advertisers know this. They sell the sizzle and not the steak. They sell soft drinks with music that helps people feel young and alive. They advertise cars by implying power, status, or sex appeal. This tool will help you understand how people, leaders included, make decisions. Mechanisms for more conscious decision making are suggested, along with strategies for changing deeply ingrained habits of thinking and acting.

WHERE DO HABITS COME FROM?

Forgotten and buried deep within us is something that started as an emotional need long ago, perhaps even in childhood. That something might have been an idea, a way of behaving, or a necessary defense or self-protection mechanism. Whatever form it took, this something eventually became integrated with our *beliefs*—what we accept as true. Our beliefs become part of our core, part of who we are. This human *needs–beliefs* base is firmly established before *thinking*—our rationalization for action—enters the picture. Our thinking is then filtered through our *feelings* to produce decisions for action. The customary way in which we think (as influenced by our feelings) and then act is called a habit. Changing a habit involves a combination of thinking, feeling, and acting.

Your habits are unconsciously based on your emotions or feelings. Most of your behavior as a leader—how you decide things, how you work with others—is based upon habit. This may sound surprising, yet leadership actions must be based on habits. You couldn't possibly think through every situation, starting from first principles. Good habits form the basis of efficiency and effectiveness. As conditions change around us, how-

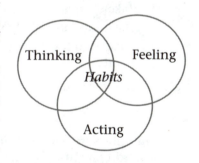

ever, some of our once-useful habits become limitations. For example, learning that you couldn't count on others may have been useful when you were working in a dysfunctional organization, but now that you're a leader in a highly functional and team-based organization, this habit has become a considerable limitation to your success as a leader.

CHANGING HABITS

To change a habit, first you need to surface and evaluate the habit. Thus, a prerequisite to changing a habit is to first recognize and own up to the dysfunctional habit. Since habits have a deeply ingrained emotional basis, they don't change easily, or with a vague "I should …" or "I shouldn't …" statement (e.g., New Year's resolutions). You have to declare war on bad habits! You will then need courage, discipline, and persistence to implement a) a good game plan, b) a few clear first steps, and c) consistent action.

While logic is involved, feelings dominate most of our decisions. For instance, why did you get married? Why did you take a certain job and reject another? To help you feel differently, you've got to think differently. Because it's difficult if not impossible to change a feeling directly, in order to change a habit, you need to insert and start from a new way of *thinking*. You must act on your new thinking in a conscious manner, rather than thinking in your habitual automatic way, based on your current feelings. For a while, this new way of thinking, and subsequently the new way of behaving based on your new thinking, will *feel* uncomfortable. Over time, as success and positive consequences from your new way of thinking and acting accumulate, your feelings will catch up and adjust. Now you have a new and improved habit, and the new way of working (thinking and acting) feels right. This is what is meant by the phrase, "Fake it till you make it."

How to use this leadership tool

"Habits are powerful factors in our lives. Because they are consistent, often unconscious patterns, they constantly, daily, express our character and produce our effectiveness … or ineffectiveness."
—Stephen Covey, *THE SEVEN HABITS OF HIGHLY EFFECTIVE PEOPLE*

It's common for leaders to prefer the familiar and comfortable habits, even though they know that these habits have significant limitations. In addition, there is no sure-fire way to change an ingrained habit. However, if motivational and contextual conditions are right, you have a fair chance of being successful at changing a habit. To change a habit, you need to:

1. Be significantly dissatisfied with the dysfunctional habit.
2. Have a vision of a better way of thinking and acting.
3. Take clear action steps to change the dysfunctional habit.
4. Have support to help you stick with it as you struggle to change the dysfunctional habit.
5. Be able to resist the pull back to the familiar and comfortable (although dysfunctional) habit.

These five conditions are summarized in the Personal Change Equation:

$$SD \times V \times FS \times SS > R$$

Multiply **S**ufficient **D**issatisfaction by a **V**ision for a better way, by **F**irst **S**teps in working toward changing the habit, by the **S**upport **S**ystem that will be helping you to make the change. For change to succeed and endure, the product must be greater than the **R**esistance that is keeping you stuck in the current habit.

WEB WORKSHEET

The Personal Change Equation will help you assess which habits you are happy with and want to keep; which habits you are unhappy with, but that aren't worth the struggle it would take to change; and which habits you are unhappy with and want to change. Changing habits is difficult work, and you will almost certainly need help with the process. Consider engaging a coach or counselor to ensure that you get ongoing feedback and support.

Feeling

Build on the positive: What are one or two habits that serve you well and that you want to continue?

Now face the music: What are one or two habits that you are dissatisfied with and want to change?

How can you create a sense of urgency to marshal your emotional resources behind changing a specific habit?

[☛ 5.1 Change Equation, 5.8 Human Transitions]

Thinking

What is your vision or image of the new habit? How would the new habit help you succeed?

[☛ 2.4 Visioning]
Write out your vision of the "new you" or your goal for the change.

[☛ 2.7 Goal Statements]
Share this vision or goal with a number of supporters, and ask for their help. (You may wish to engage someone as your change coach.)

[☛ 13.1 Coaching]

Acting

The stairway to heaven is a stairway, not an elevator. That is, often there is a daunting gap between the current situation (your current habit) and your vision of the desired state (your new way of working). This is where intermediate goals or mileposts can be useful. Write out the intermediate goals or first steps that will be necessary to successfully change the habit in question.

RELATED LEADERSHIP TOOLS

1.4 Leader Principles	5.1 Change Equation	9.4 Leader Impact
2.1 Systems Thinking	5.8 Human Transitions	9.10 Networking

FOR FURTHER ASSISTANCE

Covey, Stephen. *The Seven Habits of Highly Effective People: Powerful Lessons in Personal Change*. Simon & Schuster, 1989.

Goleman, Daniel. *Working with Emotional Intelligence*. Bantam Doubleday Dell Publishing, 2000.

Larson, Earnie. *Stage II Relationships: Love beyond Addiction*. Harper & Row, 1987.

15.6 MANAGING YOUR DEFENSIVE REACTIONS

Inspired by Robin Skynner and John Cleese.

Defense mechanisms protect people from anxiety, usually operate unconsciously, and always distort reality. Leaders, like everyone else, use defense mechanisms as strategies to reduce anxiety. Some defenses are healthy; others can severely limit a leader's potential for success by clouding judgment and interfering with the leader's ability to build and maintain strong working relationships.

Healthy defenses	Midrange defenses	Unhealthy defenses
Anticipation • Reducing the stress of some difficult challenge by anticipating what it will be like and thinking through strategies for dealing with it. *Suppression* • Being able to hold your fire while you wait for the right moment. Instead of pushing a frightening feeling out of awareness (repression), holding it in check and bearing the discomfort of feeling it. *Sublimation* • Finding other satisfying ways of expressing uncomfortable emotions and impulses. *Altruism* • Enjoying doing the types of things for others that you would enjoy having done for you. *Humor* • Using humor to deal with difficult situations or painful facts.	*Repression* • Pushing uncomfortable ideas and thoughts to the back of your mind and, for the most part, misleading yourself by assuming that they no longer exist. *Isolation* • Repressing thoughts but not the feelings (e.g., feeling anxious without knowing why). *Intellectualization* • Repressing the feeling but not the thought (e.g., imagining doing something violent to a coworker, but without feeling the horror that would result if this action were actually carried out). *Displacement* • Shuffling your thoughts and feelings (e.g., although you're angry at your boss, you avoid the risk associated with that, by being angry at your spouse). *Reaction Formation* • Avoiding feeling some feared emotion or impulse by emphasizing its opposite (e.g., adopting an uptight attitude to keep sexual impulses in check).	*Fantasy* • Living in a dream world where you imagine you are successful and popular, instead of making real efforts to make friends and succeed at a job. *Projection, Paranoia* • Blaming your limitations, incompetence, or ineptitude on other people. *Masochism, Hypochondria* • Trying to get what you want by manipulating others to give it to you, instead of taking responsibility for your own life. *Acting Out* • Giving in to your impulses without reflecting on their meaning or their consequences.

Note: A fourth group of very unhealthy defenses—psychotic—have not been included here. They are present but rare in the work environment.

HOW TO USE THIS LEADERSHIP TOOL

"The further down the scale of health you go, the greater the dislike people feel towards change of any sort, because it's much more painful for them to face their defects."
—Robin Skynner and John Cleese, *LIFE AND HOW TO SURVIVE IT*

Self-awareness is a critical aspect of leadership success, yet it's exceedingly difficult to look objectively at one's own defenses. After all, defenses, by their very nature, are usually outside of a leader's conscious awareness. One suggestion is to sit down with a coach or trusted colleague, someone who will be frank and completely honest with you, and use this tool to discuss which defenses you tend to use and when. Think of concrete situations or incidents in which you have used some of these defenses. In what way have these defenses been appropriate or limited your effectiveness? Think of and plan alternative behaviors that will serve you better in the future.

In the workspace provided here, circle the defenses that you use on the job, then plan a few action steps to improve your responses and to avoid, or at least minimize, your use of unhealthy defense mechanisms.

Healthy defenses	Midrange defenses	Unhealthy defenses
Anticipation *Suppression* *Sublimation* *Altruism* *Humor*	*Repression* *Isolation* *Intellectualization* *Displacement* *Reaction Formation*	*Fantasy* *Projection, Paranoia* *Masochism, Hypochondria* *Acting Out*

Steps you can take to make appropriate use of healthy defenses:

Steps you can take to minimize your use of midrange defenses and avoid using unhealthy defenses:

RELATED LEADERSHIP TOOLS

6.1 Logic Errors   12.7 Dealing with Conflict   13.6 Attribution Theory

8.7 Active Listening   13.1 Coaching   15.3 JoHari Window

FOR FURTHER ASSISTANCE

Skynner, A. C. Robin, and John Cleese. *Life and How to Survive It.* W. W. Norton & Co., 1996.

15.7

MANAGING THE STRESS ASSOCIATED
WITH BEING A LEADER

Contributed by Clem Blakeslee and inspired by Peter Hanson, David Irvine, Stephan Rechtschaffen, and Hans Selye.

"What you don't know won't hurt you" is a dangerous maxim, because stress is pervasive throughout today's knowledge-based, fast-paced organizations. Further, your stress and the stress experienced by others within your workgroup or team are related. Thus, you need to be sensitive to subtle stress cues within yourself, as well as from others within your organization. This tool focuses on personal stress and how to deal with it. A diagnostic checklist is provided to help you understand your personal stress and to assess stress levels within your workgroup. Suggestions are provided to help you reduce your level of stress. (Note: See ☞ 2.1 Systems Thinking to consider how systemic sources of stress can be reduced within your organization.)

CAN STRESS BE GOOD FOR YOU?

Hans Selye distinguishes among three kinds of stress.

Distress	Eustress	Too little stress
• Too much stress for a productive life	• The optimal amount of stress for a productive life	• Too little stress for a productive life

When leaders say they thrive on stress, or that some level of stress is necessary to challenge employees and to sustain a productive workforce, they're referring to *eustress*. It's important to acknowledge, however, that what leaders might think of as a positive stress, those around them might think of as *distress*.

A LEADER'S ROLE IN CREATING STRESS

Many leaders believe they must never display weakness, vulnerability, or personal inadequacies of any sort. This creates an unfortunate condition whereby leaders downplay or deny the pervasiveness, as well as the manifestations, of their own stress. And, since stress accumulates month by month and year by year, it may be possible to deny stress symptoms even long after there has been a considerable accumulation of physical, emotional, and relationship damage. Leaders need to struggle with these questions about their beliefs:

1. Is a leader a lesser person if he or she acknowledges the symptoms of stress?
2. If one learns to manage stress successfully, will that process impair performance or ambition?
3. Can work be challenging, yet free from stress?
4. Does willpower aggravate stress? If so, what is the alternative?
5. How much personal investment is required to manage stress successfully?

STRESS HAS BOTH FINANCIAL AND HUMAN COSTS

Stress generates enormous financial and human costs. Studies in the United States indicate that one-fifth of American professionals and managers are involved in the abuse of a wide range of prescription and illegal drugs. American per capita consumption of physician-prescribed mood-altering drugs averages 80 tablets per year. It's estimated that headaches and other forms of stress-related pain generate approximately $50 billion of business costs in terms of absenteeism and reduced productivity.

STRESS IS CONTAGIOUS

As a leader, you will regularly encounter people whose feelings are not especially pleasant, and who harbor continuing undercurrents of fear, anger, and hostility. As a result, you may experience levels of anxiety that are related to feelings you have unknowingly picked up from others. A *nonsolution* is tuning out or becoming less sensitive to the emotional undercurrents of others. This would simply deaden your awareness of what is going on around you. Rather, you need to stay alert to subtle cues from other people. You need to become even *more* sensitive, constantly monitoring your feelings and those of others in your organization. Then, whenever you start feeling stress, you can ask yourself whether your feeling is a signal that something needs attention. Simultaneously, you can contribute to other peoples' well-being by remaining alert and allowing them to pick up *your* feelings of calmness, emotional balance, patience, and optimism.

HOW TO USE THIS LEADERSHIP TOOL

"We think much more about the use of our money, which is renewable, than we do about the use of our time, which is irreplaceable."

—Stephan Rechtschaffen, *TIME SHIFTING*

WEB WORKSHEET

Here is a list of symptoms you are likely to encounter when you experience stress. As a first step in determining your level of stress, rate the degree to which you experience each of these symptoms. You might also use this instrument to assess stress levels within your workgroup or team. This could be used as a kick-off for a group discussion of stress.

Stress symptom	Rating 0 *(not at all)*, 5 *(very much)*
1. I am bothered by disturbances in my sleep.	
2. I frequently feel that my interpersonal relationships suffer from tension.	
3. I feel bothered by lapses in memory and concentration.	
4. I feel tense muscles or jitters in my body.	
5. I worry too much.	
6. I become immobilized.	
7. I can't make up my mind quickly enough.	
8. I perspire excessively.	

Stress symptom	Rating 0 *(not at all)*, 5 *(very much)*
9. I pace nervously.	
10. I imagine or dream terrifying scenes.	
11. My digestive system sometimes feels like a knotted cord.	
12. I grind my teeth at night.	
13. I am frequently angry or irritable.	
14. I frequently get digestive problems.	
15. I often feel fatigued for no apparent reason.	
16. I have frequent headaches for no known organic reason.	
17. I chronically suffer from cold hands and feet.	
18. My heart often beats very fast.	
19. I breathe in short, shallow breaths.	
20. I feel guilty when I take time out to relax.	
Add each rating to obtain a total score	

If you scored over 40, consider one or more of these ideas to reduce your own stress, or to reduce systems problems that are contributing to stress within your workgroup:

❑ Collectively attend a stress reduction workshop that focuses on individual stress-coping techniques.

❑ Analyze the stressors in the organizational system in which you work. Which contribute the most stress without contributing to productivity? How can these be reduced? [☛ 2.1 Systems Thinking]

❑ Make it okay to discuss stress levels and to use stress reduction methods at workgroup or team meetings. [☛ 10.8 Ground Rules]

❑ Make it okay to take time-outs at work for relaxation. [☛ 15.1 Balance]

❑ Celebrate successes. Often, workgroups or teams do not get enough recognition or positive feedback.

❑ Hold simple letting-go or venting meetings—simple, because you do not want the administration of these sessions to become a source of stress! [☛ 5.8 Human Transitions]

❑ As a leader, have one-on-one meetings with people who seem to be stressed out. If an individual's stress level is high, use the Employee Assistance Program or other resources to provide individuals with appropriate support. [☛ 13.1 Coaching]

Actions you will take to reduce stress (either your own, or stress within your workgroup or team):

RELATED LEADERSHIP TOOLS

4.7 Job Satisfaction	8.7 Active Listening	13.5 Time Management
8.6 Communication 101	12.7 Dealing with Conflict	15.1 Balance

FOR FURTHER ASSISTANCE

Hanson. Peter G., M.D. *The Joy of Stress.* Andrews McMeel Publishing, 1987.

Irvine, David. *Simple Living in a Complex World: Balancing Life's Achievements.* RedStone Ventures Inc, 1997.

Rechtschaffen, Stephan, M.D. *Time Shifting: Creating More Time to Enjoy Your Life.* Doubleday, 1997.

INDEX

Accountability agreements, 399-401
ACORN model for goal statement, 63
Actions of effective leaders, 8-10
Active listening, 251-253
Administrator of meeting, role of, 348
Adult learning principles, 438-440
Affection, 308-310
Affinity diagrams, 227-230
Agenda of meeting, 353-355
Aggressors, dealing with, 384-386
Aligning systems, 153-155
Alliances, 92
Appreciative inquiry, 166-168
Argyris, Chris, 462
Assumption analysis, 173-175
Assumptions, personal, understanding,
    462-466
    Ladder of Inference, 462-463
Attitude, importance of, 428-430
Attribution theory, 409-411

Balance in life, 451-454
Biases, personal, understanding, 462-466
    Ladder of Inference, 462-463
"Big fuzzies," 176-178
"Big picture" thinking, tools for, 39-67
    affinity diagrams, 227-230
    directional statements, 48-50
    measuring success, 65-67
    purpose, clarifying, 59-61
    7S model, 45-47
        hard and soft S's, 45
    systems thinking for managers, 40-44
    values and leadership, 55-58
    visioning and vision statements, 51-54
    writing goal statements, 62-64 (see also
        Writing)
Blanchard, Ken, 268

Board of directors of nonprofit organiza-
    tion, revitalizing, 129-131
Boards of play, leadership and, 18-20
Body Shop, value statement of, 56
Boston Consulting Group, 69
Bottleneck, 189
Brainstorming, 196-198
Brandenburger, Adam, 70
Breakthrough approach to change, 147-148
Built to Last, 59
Business process reengineering, 108-111
Business-unit strategy, fundamentals of,
    79-81

Career planning, Four Stages®model and,
    421-423
Caring for self, tools for, 450-475
    assumptions and biases, personal,
        understanding, 462-466
        Ladder of Inference, 462-463
    balance in life, 451-454
    defensive reactions, managing, 470-471
    habits, 467-469
        Personal Change Equation, 468-469
    JoHari Window, 459-461
    Leadership Emotional Quotient (LEQ),
        455-458
    stress factor, managing, 472-475
        distress, 472
        eustress, 472
Carver, John, 130
Chairperson of meeting, role of, 347, 350-
    352 (see also Meetings)
    opening remarks, 356-358
Champy, James, 109, 147
Change, tools for leading, 139-168 (see also
    Leading change)
Change equation, 140-141

Change window, 150-152
Character ethic, 15
Checklist for meeting, 342-346
Closure for group activity, 326-328
Coaching success of others, seven elements
    of, 391-394
    high performers, 395-398
    problem-based vs. high performers, 395-398
Commitment vs. compliance, 314-316
Commitment and teamwork, developing,
    308-310
Communication, tools for, 231-262
    active listening, 251-253
    conversations, powerful, 232-235
        negative communication cycle, 233-234
        positive communication cycle, 234-235
        understanding, four levels of, 232
    cross-cultural, 257-259
    80-20 rule, 231-232
    feelings, dealing effectively with, 248-250
    leader-to-employee communication,
        direct, 236-238
        with frontline employees, 236
    levels of, 242-244
    listening techniques, 254-256
    media relations for leaders, 260-262
    metacommunicating, 245-247
    organizational, leader's role in, 239-241
    Socratic method, 251
Competency, 415-417
Complex situations, sorting out, 176-178
    "big fuzzies," 176-177
Conflict, 249
    five levels for dealing with, 381-383
Confrontation, evaluating judiciously,
    378-380
Consensus, 326
Consultation, 326

Contingency leadership model, 267-270
Contingent actions, 219
Control, 274-275, 308-310
Conversations, powerful, 232-235
Corporate Cultures: The Rites and Rituals of Corporate Life, 117
Covey, Stephen, 1, 15-16, 56-57, 406-407, 450-451
Crainer, Stuart, 25
Creativity, leader's role in, 189-192
Critical thinking and innovation, tools for, 169-198
    assumption analysis, 173-175
    brainstorming, 196-198
        developmental versus evaluative thinking, 196-198
    complex situations, sorting out, 176-178
    creativity and innovation, leader's role in, 189-192
    force-field analysis, 183-185
    logic errors, recognizing, 170-172
        Occam's razor, 172
    mind mapping, 193-195
    optimizing thinking, 186-188
    verbal dealing with complexity, 179-182
        hourglass model, 179-180
        triage, 179-181
Cross-cultural communication, 257-259
Culture, 117-120
Customer service, 387-389

Deal, Terrence, 117
Debate, 242-244
Decision making, 215-218
    tools for, 199-230 (see also Problem solving)
Defensive reactions, managing, 470-471
Delivering on the Promise, 419
Dell, Michael, 117
Deming, W. Edwards, 225
Demographics, 136
Designing productive processes and organizations, 100-138
    business process reengineering, 108-111
    employee involvement, 112-116
    entrepreneurial thinking, 121-125
    hierarchy in organization, 105-107
    job satisfaction, 126-128
    nonprofit organization, revitalizing board of directors in, 129-131
    open-book leadership, 121-125
    organizational culture, 117-120
    organizations, productive, 101-104
    professional expertise, using, 132-134
    surveying employees, 135-138
    workgroups, involving in job design, 126-128
Developing Corporate Character, 117
Developmental versus evaluative thinking, 196-198
Dialogue, 242-244
Difficult people, dealing with, 384-386
Directional statements, 48-50
Directive, 326

Discussion, 242-244
Distress, 472
Disturbances in teams and workgroups, dealing with, 311-313
Documenting employee performance and behavior, 412-414
Double-loop learning, 431-433
Drucker, Peter, 76, 101, 103, 105, 133
    Theory of Business Specifications, 77

80-20 rule, 86, 231-232
Either-or mentality, dangers of, 212-214
Emotional competencies, 455-456
Empathy, 249
Employee involvement, 112-116
Employee job satisfaction, 126
Employee performance and behavior, documenting, 412-414
Entrepreneurial thinking, 121-125
Environmental scan, 76-78
Ethical behavior, 36-38
Eustress, 472
Evaluative versus developmental thinking, 196-198
Expertise delivery model, five-stage, 424-426

Feedback:
    do's and don'ts of, 372-374
    to employee, 412-413
    negative feedback, preparing yourself to give, 375-377
    skills, 248
Feelings, dealing effectively with, 248-250
The Fifth Discipline Fieldbook, 462-463
Force-Field analysis, 183-185
Ford Motor Company, vision statement of, 51
Foundational concepts, 1-38
    how effective leaders act, 8-10
    GAS model, 33-35
    integrity, 36-38
    leadership: the boards of play, 18-20
    leadership in twenty-first century, 2-4
    leadership and management, contrasting, 5-7
    leadership results equation, 21-24
    paradigms, 29-32
    principles to guide leadership techniques, 11-14
    recursive leadership, 25-28
    successful leaders, habits and practices of, 15-17, 21
Four Stages® model, 421-423
Friedman, Brian, 419
Frontline employees, communication with, 236

GAS model, 33-35
Gates, Bill, 2,3
General-Accurate-Simple (GAS) model, 34
Generative learning, 431
Gibbs, Nancy, 455
Goal statements, writing, 62-64 (see also Writing)
The Great Game of Business, 121-123

Ground rules for workgroups and teams, 320-322
Group leadership skills, assessing, 314-316
Groups, tools for leading, 291-334 (see also Teams)

Habits, 467-469
Hamel, Gary, 69
Hammer, Michael, 108-109, 147
Harvard process, 277
Hersey, Paul, 268
High-performers, coaching, 395-398
    and blinking, 396
Hourglass model to deal with complexity, 179-180
Human capital, people as, 418-420
Human Capital Accounting for the Knowledge Economy, 418-419
Human transitions through change, 160-162

Impact, increasing, 274-276
Inclusion, 308-310
Indecisives, dealing with, 385-386
Individual differences, capitalizing on, 447-449
Influencing others, tools for, 263-296
    impact, increasing, 274-276
        control, interest and influence, 274-275
    large projects, selling, 287-290
    leadership strategies for delegating work, 271-273
    leadership versatility, 264-266
    matching leadership style to situation, 267-270
        contingency/situational models, 267-270
        worksheet, 270
    power, 291-293
    presentations, making, 281-283
    principled negotiation, 277-280
        Harvard process, 277
    recommendations, gaining acceptance for, 284-286
    Selling Wheel, 284-286
    support networks, 294-296
Innovation, leader's role in, 189-192
    tools for, 169-198 (see also Critical thinking)
Integrity, 36-38
Interest, 274-275
International Organization for Standardization (ISO), 223
Intractable problems, dealing with, 212-214

Jaques, Eliot, 39, 105
Job competencies, 415-417
Job satisfaction, 126-128
JoHari Window, 459-461
Joint ventures, 92-95
Jung, Carl, 447
Juran, Joseph, 225

Kaizen, 74
Katzenbach, Joe, 299-300, 306

Kennedy, Allen, 117
Kepner, Charles, 208, 216, 220-221
Know-it-alls, dealing with, 385-386
Kotter, John, 117, 119, 142-143, 148
Kouzes, James, 55-56

Ladder of Inference, 462-463
Large projects, selling, 287-290
Leader as strategist, 69-72
Leader-to-employee communication,
    direct, 236-238 (see also
    Communication)
Leader's skills, assessing, 345
Leadership:
    and boards of play, 18-20
    GAS model, 33-35
    habits and practices, 15-17
    integrity, 36-38
    and management, contrasting, 5-7
        purpose, clarifying, 59-61
    paradigms, 29-32
    principles guiding techniques, 11-14
    recursive, 25-28
    requirements for effective, 8-10
    results equation, 21-24
    in twenty-first century, 2-4
    and values, 55-58
The Leadership Challenge, 55-56
Leadership Emotional Quotient (LEQ),
    455-458
Leadership versatility, 264-266
Leading Change, 117, 142-143, 148
Leading change, tools for, 139-168
    aligning systems, 153-155
    appreciative inquiry, 166-168
    change equation, 140-141
    change window, 150-152
    human transition through change,
        160-162
    major organizational change, 142-144
    readiness for change, assessing, 145-146
    resistance, surfacing and dealing with,
        163-165
        "two good-faith responses" tech-
        nique, 163-164
    small wins or breakthroughs? 147-149
    stakeholder groups, 156-159
Leading meetings, tools for, 335-361 (see
    also Meetings)
Leading others, tools for, 263-296 (see also
    Influencing)
Learning, tools for, 427-449
    adult learning principles, 438-440
    attitude, importance of, 428-430
    individual differences, capitalizing on,
        447-449
    learning styles, 444-446
    needs analysis, 434-437
    preferences, personal, 447-449
    single-loop and double-loop, 431-433
    teaching job, 441-443
Listening skills, 248
    techniques, 254-256
Logic errors, recognizing, 170-172

Logic of leadership, 25-28

Management and leadership, contrasting,
    5-7
    purpose, clarifying, 59-61
Management by objectives (MBO), 26,
    402-405
Marketing professional service group, 96-99
Matching leadership style to situation, 267-
    270 (see also Influencing)
Measuring success, 65-67
Media relations for leaders, 260-262
Meetings, leading, tools for, 335-361
    agenda, 353-355
    chairperson's role, 347, 350-352
        opening remarks, 356-358
    checklist, 342-346
    meeting roles, 347-349
    minutes, 359-361
    planning effective meetings and events:
        process cycle, 336-338
    purpose and function in workgroups and
        teams, 339-341
    skills of meeting leader, assessing, 345
Metacommunicating, 245-247
Mind mapping, 193-195
Mintzberg, Henry, 69-70, 291
Minutes of meeting, 359-361
Mission, definition, 129
Modeling behavior desired, 25-26
Moore, James, 70
Murphy, Shaun, 52, 62
Myers-Briggs indicator, 89

Needs analysis, 434-437
Negative communication cycle, 233-234
Negative feedback, preparing yourself to
    give, 375-377
Negativists, dealing with, 385-386
Negotiation, principled, 277-280
The New Rational Manager, 208, 216, 220-221
Nonprofit organization, revitalizing board
    of directors in, 129-131

Occam's razor, 172
Open-book leadership, 121-125
Optimizing thinking, 186-188
Organizational change, leading, 142-144
Organizational communication, leader's
    role in, 239-241
Organizational culture, 117-120

Paradigms, 29-32
    and change, 30
Participants in meeting, role of, 347
Participation of group, encouraging,
    317-319
People and transition through change,
    160-162
Performance, leading, tools for, 390-426
    accountability agreements, 399-401
    attribution theory, 409-411
    coaching and supporting success of
        others, 391-394

documenting employee performance
    and behavior, 412-414
Four Stages®model, 421-423
high-performers, coaching, 395-398
    and blinking, 396
    vs. problem-based, 395-398
human capital, people as, 418-420
job competencies, 415-417
management by objectives (MBO),
    402-405
professional expertise, 424-426
    expertise delivery model, five-stage,
        424-426
time management, 406-408
Urgency Addiction, 406-408
Performance, measuring and predicting,
    415-417
Perry, Lee, 69
Personal Change Equation, 468-469
Personality ethic, 15
Peters, Tom, 45-46
Polarities, dealing with, 212-214
Porter, Michael, 69
Positive communication cycle, 234-235
Posner, Barry, 55-56
Potential Problem Analysis, 219-222
    (see also Problem solving)
Power, 291-293
Prahalad, C.K., 69
Preferences, personal, 447-449
Presentations, making, 281-283
Preventive actions, 219
Principle Centered Leadership, 1
Principled negotiation, 277-280
Principles guiding leadership techniques,
    11-14
Priority setting in teams and workgroups,
    329-331
Probability, 219
Problem-based coaching, 395-398
Problem solving, tools for, 199-230
    affinity diagrams, 227-230
    decision making, 215-218
        worksheet, 218
    intractable problems, dealing with,
        212-214
    model, general, 204-206
    polarities, 212-214
    potential problem analysis, 219-222
        worksheet, 222
    reframing, 200-203
    systematic approach to finding cause,
        207-210
        worksheet, 211
    total quality leadership overview, 223-226
Process advisor of meeting, role of, 348
Process reengineering, 108-111
Professional expertise, using, 132-134,
    424-426
Professional services group, marketing,
    96-99
Public speaking, 281-283
Purpose, clarifying, 59-61

Quality, tools for ensuring, 199-230 (see also Problem solving)
  total quality leadership overview, 223-226

Rackham, Neil, 288-289
RAIR logic, 89-91
RASCI planning chart, 332-334
Readiness for change, assessing, 145-146
Recommendations, gaining acceptance for, 284-286
Recorder of meeting, role of, 348, 357
Recursive leadership, 25-28
Reengineering of business process, 108-111
Reframing, 200-203
Reich, Robert, 418
Relationships, leading, tools for, 362-389
  conflict, five levels for dealing with, 381-383
  confrontation, escalating judiciously, 378-380
  customer service, essentials of, 387-389
  difficult people, dealing with, 384-386
  feedback, do's and don'ts of, 372-374
  negative feedback, preparing yourself to give, 375-377
  triangulation, 369-371
  trust, building into working relationships, 366-368
    self-assessment of leader, 367-368
  working relationships, maintaining, 363-365
Resistance, surfacing and dealing with, 163-165
  "Two good-faith responses" technique, 163-164
Results-Based Leadership, 21
ROI, measuring, 434
Role versatility, 264-266

Scholtes, Peter, 40, 100, 154, 223
Self, caring for, 450-475 (see also Caring)
Self-awareness, 471
Selling Wheel, 284-286
Selye, Hans, 472
Senge, Peter, 39, 42, 105, 462-463
Seriousness, 219
7S model, 45-47 (see also Tools)
Sherman, Stafford, 117
Sigmoid curve, 73-75
Silence, role of, 251
Single-loop learning, 431-433
Situational leadership model, 267-270
Skills of effective leaders, 8-10
Skills of meeting leaders, assessing, 345
Small wins approach to change, 147-148
Smallwood, Norm, 21-22, 69
SMART model for goal statement, 63
Smith, Douglas, 299-300, 306

Socratic method, 251
Specialists, advice from, 132-134
Spencer, Lyle, 455
The SPIN® Selling Fieldbook, 288-289
SPIRO model for goal statement, 63
Stack, Jack, 121-123
Stakeholder groups, 156-159
Statistical Quality Control (SQC), 223
Sticklers, dealing with, 385-386
Stott, Randy, 69
Strategic alliances, 92-95
Strategic relationships, 86-88
  80-20 rule, 86
Strategic resourcing, 82-84
  model worksheet, 85
Strategic thinking, tools for, 68-99
  business-unit strategy, fundamentals of, 79-81
  joint ventures and strategic alliances, 92-95
  by leader as strategist, 69-72
  marketing professional services group, 96-99
  RAIR logic, 89-91
  sigmoid curve, 73-75
  strategic relationships, 86-88
    80-20 rule, 86
  strategic resourcing, 82-84
    model worksheet, 85
  SWOT, 76-78
Strategies for delegating work, 271-273
Stress factor, managing, 472-475
Success, measuring, 65-67
Success of others, supporting, 391-394
Successful leaders, habits and practices of, 15-17, 21
  character ethic, 15
  personality ethic, 15
Support networks, 294-296
Surveying employees, 135-138
SWOT, 76-78
Systems compatibility, building into change plans, 153-155
Systems thinking for managers, 40-44

Teaching job, 441-443
Team meetings: (see also Meetings)
  purpose and function, 339-341
Teams and groups, tools for leading, 291-334
  commitment and teamwork, developing, 308-310
  decisions and plans, helping group to make, 326-328
  disturbances, dealing with, 311-313
  ground rules, 320-322
  high-performing, 298-300
  leadership skills of group, assessing, 314-316

  participation, encouraging, 317-319
  priority setting, 329-331
  RASCI as planning tool, 332-334
  team competencies, 305-307
  team IQ, improving, 301-304
    questionnaire, 302-303
  visibility of information, 323-325
Thinking hats, 186-188
Thurow, Lester, 189
Tichy, Noel, 117
Time management, 406-408
Timekeeper of meeting, role of, 348
Toastmasters International Club, 281
Tracey, Michael, 70
Tregoe, Benjamin, 208, 216, 220-221
Triage, 179-181
Triangulation, 369-371
Trust, building into working relationships, 366-368
"Two good-faith responses" technique, 163-164

Ulrich, David, 21-22
The Ultimate Book of Business Gurus, 25
Unanimity, 326
Understanding, four levels of, 232
Urgency Addiction, 406

Values and leadership, 55-58
Verbal dealing with complexity, 179-182 (see also Critical thinking)
Visibility of information, importance of, 323-325
Visioning and vision statements, 51-54
Voting, 326

Walker, David M., 419
Waterman, Robert, 45-46
Weinburg, Stephen, 29
Weisbord, Marvin, 29, 127
Welch, Jack, 117
Why, people's desire to know, 59
Wiersma, Fred, 70
Wilkins, Alan, 117, 366
Win–win approach to negotiation, 277-280
The Wisdom of Teams, 299
Workgroups, involving in job design, 126-128
World Association of Girl Guides and Girl Scouts, value statement of, 56
Writing clear goal statements, 62-64
  ACORN model, 63
  SMART model, 63
  SPIRO model, 63

Zenger, Jack, 21-22

About the Authors

Murray Hiebert (Calgary, Canada: www.consultskills.com) has over twenty years experience as an international consultant. He also manages an internationally successful workshop for professional experts, *Consulting Skills for Professionals.*

Bruce Klatt (Calgary, Canada: www.murphyklatt.com) is a senior partner in Murphy Klatt Consulting, Inc. specializing in accountability and alignment, strategic alliancing and organizational effectiveness.